35-

Dante

Dante

Thomas G. Bergin

YALE UNIVERSITY

GREENWOOD PRESS, PUBLISHERS
WESTPORT, CONNECTICUT

Library of Congress Cataloging in Publication Data

Bergin, Thomas Goddard, 1904-
  Dante.

    Reprint of the ed. published by Houghton Mifflin,
  Boston, in series: Riverside studies in literature.
    Includes bibliographical references and index.
    1. Dante Alighieri, 1265-1321.
  [PQ4335.B4 1976]   851'.1   76-10974
  ISBN 0-8371-7973-4

Originally published in 1965 by Houghton Mifflin Company, Boston

Reprinted with the permission of Grossman Publishers

Reprinted in 1976 by Greenwood Press
A division of Congressional Information Service, Inc.
88 Post Road West, Westport, Connecticut 06881

Printed in the United States of America

10 9 8 7 6 5 4 3 2

To
Morris Bishop
and
Jack Adams

Preface

My aim in writing this book has been threefold: to present the essential facts of the life and times of Dante Alighieri, to summarize the content of his works, and to suggest, by reference and quotation, his significance for our own century. The chapter headings in themselves will suffice to indicate the plan of the book. I hope it will be useful as an introduction to Dante for those who know little about him and would like to know more. Professional "dantisti" will learn from the following pages little that is new to them, but they may find the method and approach not without interest. I think I may claim that my book contains more factual information — biographical and bibliographical — than can easily be found in any other single study of like compass, and I dare to hope that it may therefore have some value as a convenient work of reference.

As will be apparent from the notes, I am indebted to a great number of scholars who have gone before me — and indeed I am indebted to many more than I have had occasion to quote. My students over the years at Western Reserve, Albany, Cornell, and Yale have also taught me much. I should like to express special thanks to Thomas K. Swing for guidance in some delicate areas and to Miguel Marin, who prepared the map of Florence for me.

I am grateful to Appleton-Century-Crofts for permission to reprint a number of passages from my translation of the *Commedia* (Crofts Classics, 1955).

T. G. B.

New Haven
July 1964

Contents

1

Dante's Europe

DANTE's great work is concerned with matters not of this world; his subject is the afterlife, his pilgrimage takes him into realms which cannot be charted on physical maps, and his interests are in things eternal and not temporal. Yet for all that, he is very much of his century. His thought and his outlook were determined by the events and the theories of his day, and his own temperament made him more than a merely passive receiver of impressions. He played his part in the politics of his city, he had a critic's interest in the literature and philosophy of his time, and in all affairs of his generation he was an acute observer, with eyes ever "eager to see new things," as he says of himself. Mystic he may or may not have been; he was certainly no hermit. As Salvatore Quasimodo puts it: "In the contemplation of God Dante does not forget the world."[1] Our poet agrees with Charles Martel's assertion in the *Paradiso* that "it were worse for man if he were not a citizen" — that is, a man who accepts the need of human society — and elsewhere he remarks that he is by nature impressionable. Every aspect of contemporary politics, literature, and science aroused his interest, and not infrequently his partisanship. So that while the modern reader may justifiably seek in Dante's pages for eternal truth and esthetic beauties divorced from contingencies of time or place, yet fully to appreciate his

1

message, and even fully to understand his poetry, some knowledge of his century is essential.

The calendar is an arbitrary measurement of man's thought and activities. The thirteenth century, which was the time of Dante's spiritual formation, cannot be neatly set off from the twelfth or the fourteenth. Many of its major political and intellectual concerns — the role of the papacy, the rise of the communes, the emergence of the bourgeoisie, the elaboration of scholastic philosophy, the development of vernacular literatures — had their roots in an earlier century and were destined to persist into a later one. Yet the calendar is convenient, and, bearing in mind its limitations, we may still find that Dante's century had its own characteristics.

Politically it was a time that marked the high tide of the conflict between the pope and the emperor, and it was in this century that the empire was finally defeated, although the deeper conflict between the spiritual and the secular claims to political supremacy was by no means resolved. Likewise it was in this century that the city-states in Italy really succeeded in establishing their effective independence from feudal pretensions, which they had claimed from the time of Barbarossa's defeat and which they were to maintain, though with some change of character, until the end of the fifteenth century. The thirteenth century also witnessed the founding of two great religious orders, the Franciscan and the Dominican, and a religious renascence having its own peculiar character. By no means least among the particular attributes of this era is the emergence of Italian literature, which, thanks to the excellent foster-mothering of Provençal lyricists and learned doctors, grew from infancy to vigorous maturity (in the writings of Dante himself) in little more than fifty years.

If we begin with the political background we shall not only follow the interest of medieval chroniclers but also adapt ourselves to Dante's own point of view, for the *Commedia* is loaded with political observations and allusions, and the *De Monarchia* and many parts of the *Convivio* are wholly concerned with politics. We shall begin with the struggle between the Catholic Church and the empire (a matter of vital concern to Dante, the Guelph-born Ghibelline), fought out in the years preceding his birth by champions of deep convictions and strong personalities whose impress was still felt long after the issue was decided.

The issue was quite simply one of supremacy in temporal

power. No one contested the pope's spiritual pre-eminence, but how far this recognized authority should be allowed to dictate in purely temporal matters was a vexing question, ultimately resolved only by force. It could not be otherwise, since both parties laid claim to absolute power. The emperor, when he felt strong enough to maintain his position, laid claim to sovereignty over all Christendom. For example, Henry VI (1165–97), the son of Barbarossa and the father of Frederick II, regarded the kings of France, England, and Norway as his vassals, either directly or through the feudal system of dependent vassalage. At the time of his death he was clearly meditating an attack on the Eastern Empire as well as a crusade against the infidel in the Holy Land. But the popes in their more aggressive moments also claimed to be supreme arbiters ("the Pope may judge all and be judged by no man," proclaimed Innocent III), and they supported their claim by appeal not only to the theological supremacy of the spiritual over the temporal but also to the actual investiture with the temporal power which the Holy See (so they said) had had from Constantine. This celebrated "Donation," deplored by Dante, as we shall see, was, according to James Bryce, "a portentous fabrication" and at the same time "unimpeachable evidence of the thoughts and beliefs of the priesthood which framed it."[2] So it could come about, in the texture of feudal society, that the popes could regard the Kingdom of Sicily, for example — which meant all of southern Italy — as a legitimate fief. Given endemic doctrinaire intransigence on the one hand and much administrative confusion on the other, it is clear that even if there had been good will on both sides and an earnest desire to define the limits of the spiritual and the temporal pretensions, such a definition would have been impossible in a feudal world.

The struggle had gone on for many years before Dante's time. Points were scored on one side or the other; the pope crowned Charlemagne, and thus made the empire symbolically dependent on the papacy, but somewhat later (963) Otto I, a strong emperor, chose the pope. The spectacular humiliation of Henry IV in the snows of Canossa (1077) was a major triumph, heightened by its appeal to the imagination, of papal pretensions; yet it did not serve really to check Henry, much less to moderate the contumacy of succeeding emperors. In fact, in the last years of the twelfth century the emperors finally achieved a position of strategic superiority which, but for the hand of Fate, might well have reduced the papacy to an imperial appointment. In 1186 Henry VI married Constance, the last legitimate survivor of the Normans in Sicily. He came very close to implementing the absolute claims of the empire even though the Lombard cities which, with papal support and their own stubborn valor, had won their independence from Barbarossa, still preserved their freedom, and the Eastern Empire remained an obstacle to universal claims. Henry, to be sure, had plans for both and possessed the resources and the skill to make his plans effective, but, unhappily for imperial hopes, he died in 1197 at the early age of thirty-two, leaving his three-year-old son Frederick under the protection of a mother whose sole desire seems to have been to keep him out of involvement with the empire, and incidentally to rid her native kingdom of Germans.

The figure of Frederick II dominates the first half of the century in the political field much as the figure of St. Francis dominates it in the religious sphere. Indeed, Frederick, important enough in the chronicles of his day, transcends as does St. Francis the merely historical; even in his lifetime his person took on a dimension of legend and myth destined to assure for him in succeeding generations a position of superstitious reverence — or, as the case might be, horror. He was apparently a person of great physical attraction, of medium height but well formed, strong, and graceful, and excelling in the physical attributes associated with knighthood and warfare. The circumstances of his youth — he was fatherless at three and was left completely orphaned by the death of his mother a few years later — gave him in the eyes of the sympathetically disposed a touch of the pathetic, and his miraculous winning of the throne in spite of the misgivings of the pope and the opposition of the Welf emperor always appeared, even in his own eyes, to give him the stamp of the man of destiny. He never lost the belief in his own star, and the phrase *"Fortuna Augusti"* was frequently heard on the lips of his devoted followers. Legends gathered around him: it was said that his mother, before giving birth to him, had a vision that she was to bring forth a firebrand. (Dante tells a similar tale about the mother of St. Dominic, and Boccaccio, not to be outdone, ascribes a like premonition to Dante's own mother.) After his death men said that he had done ill to lodge in Castel Fiorentino, for prophecy had foretold that he would die *sub flore* (and indeed the emperor had taken care never to stay in the city of Florence itself).

It was prophesied of him that he would return again, even as it was of Arthur and of Barbarossa, and those who are attracted to him may, if they choose, think of him as still sleeping in the hills of Sicily, awaiting the day when the world will be ready to receive the emperor. His enemies had tales to match these: he was said by the Guelphs to be no son of the emperor at all, but a bastard begotten by a priest on the empress. The circumstances of his birth were indeed spectacular, for his mother, expecting her first child at the age of forty and well aware of the kind of tales that might be spread, arranged to be delivered in the public square of the town of Iesi; yet even such Spartan precautions could not avail to check the tongues of the ignorant or the malicious. Giovanni Villani, a hundred years later, speaks of Frederick as born of a nun (as the antichrist would be), and adds twelve years to the mother's age, thus establishing that Frederick's birth was "against spiritual laws and in a sense against natural laws,"[3] while the credulous Salimbene more unkindly describes the Empress as "aged and advanced in years" and strongly suggests that Frederick was really the son of a butcher whom the childless Constance had palmed off as her own.[4] The prophecies of the apocalyptic Joachim da Fiore were interpreted to fit Frederick in the role of antichrist; it was said of him (and Dante so believed) that he denied the immortality of the soul, that he preferred the society of Saracens to that of good Christians, that he kept a harem, that he lived in luxury and bathed daily. Tales were told of his inhuman cruelty (*Inferno* XXIII, 66). The troubadour poets and the nobles of the old school would hardly have been much concerned by these charges, for Frederick, whatever else one may say of him, had the virtues "of purse and sword," being generous and openhanded, as much perhaps out of policy as temperament, and unquestionably brave. Endowed with unusual intellectual powers and vast scientific curiosity, he seems to us today a kind of prefiguring of the typical Renaissance prince.

We shall not linger on the details of Frederick's reign. For three turbulent decades after his coronation by Honorius in 1220 (Innocent III had recognized his claim five years earlier) his alternating triumphs and frustrations were the central events in European history, and his personality lent to them also a kind of poetic color. He built up a strong government in southern Italy; he carried out a successful crusade and temporarily retrieved for the Christians the right of entry into Jerusalem. Characteristically this latter achievement came through negotiation rather than by force of arms, for Frederick was quite at home in dealing with Saracens. Characteristically for the times too — if somewhat paradoxically from our point of view — the successful crusader was excommunicate at the time. Frederick was indeed throughout his embattled career repeatedly excommunicated; only infrequent and uneasy truces interrupted the war *à outrance* between pope and emperor. The final ban was published by Innocent IV at a council in Lyons in 1245; since Frederick had frustrated an earlier convocation by the piratical kidnapping of several of the delegates, including a pair of cardinals, one can understand Innocent's feelings, but the papal proclamation, stripping the emperor of his titles and offering his throne to any prince of Europe willing to take up the struggle, boded ill for the future peace of Italy.

At the time no papal champion was willing to enter the lists, and Frederick continued to struggle on, optimistic to the end. Yet his last years were full of melancholy. His son Enzo was captured by the Bolognese and languished, a romantic and pathetic captive, for some twenty years before death released him. His son Henry died in 1242, and the hope of uniting the empire and the Kingdom of Sicily grew dim. Saddest of all, the emperor came to feel, as town and baron betrayed him, that there was no one he could trust. He suspected even Pier delle Vigne, his ambassador in many negotiations with the pope and the nobles, of conniving with papal agents; he had him blinded, and the hapless Pier dashed out his brains in humiliation and resentment. The emperor, still apparently vigorous, died suddenly of an attack of dysentery in the little town of Castel Fiorentino (*sub flore* indeed) outside Foggia in the year 1250. He was still excommunicate, but it is reported that he donned the habit of a Cistercian and received the last rites at the hands of the Bishop of Palermo. Although he had failed in his lifelong struggle with churchly authority, he had left his mark on the age, and certain institutions which he had almost casually established were to prove long enduring. He had encouraged the Teutonic Knights in the conquest of the eastern heathen and had in effect launched the modern state of Prussia; he had founded the University of Naples; and in the atmosphere of his court he had inspired the first poets of the Italian vernacular, the so-called "Sicilian school."

Frederick left behind him two sons. Conrad, the son of Isabella of Jerusalem, hoped to succeed him in the empire but died in 1254. Manfred, the emperor's illegitimate son by the beautiful Bianca Lancia, was eighteen at the time of his father's death and seems to have inherited a good deal of Frederick's charm and energy. The rising Guelphs of the north were checked at the battle of Montaperti (1260), and Manfred's marriage to Helena of Aragon gave him allies and promised him security on his throne. But the pope's invitation to one who should cast down the Hohenstaufen and make himself lord of the kingdom still stood, and was indeed repeated by Clement, who had succeeded Innocent IV. This time the call was answered by the French prince Charles of Anjou, brother of St. Louis, a man of ambition, energy, and, since his marriage to the heiress of Provence in 1246, substantial means. Encouraged by the pope, welcomed by the Guelph cities (including and perhaps especially Florence), Charles came into Italy and met Manfred's army at Benevento. Manfred's forces were defeated and he himself was slain (1266). The vengeance of the pope followed the defeated prince beyond the grave, for, as Manfred is made to tell us in *Purgatorio* III, 124–32, his bones were dug up after the hasty soldier's burial given him by Charles and buried in unconsecrated ground "with quenched tapers" across the Liri. An attempt to overthrow Charles made by Frederick's grandson Corradino, the last of the Hohenstaufen, came to disaster on the field of Tagliacozzo (1268); the young prince was taken prisoner and executed, a crime remembered by Dante in the *Purgatorio*. The Kingdom of Sicily was now definitely severed from the empire, and papal policy triumphed at least in that respect.

We can see now that the empire was dead in Italy from that day forth. Contemporary observers who did not have our perspective of the centuries could not be so sure. And indeed many Guelph cities, having cheered the arrival of Charles, were not entirely happy with the French intrusion into the peninsula (the popes themselves occasionally regretted it, for Charles was not always amenable, any more than Frederick had been) nor with the prospect of domination by the pope. For in effect the liberty of the cities had come about through playing off one great power against another. Thus in Dante's lifetime the coming of another emperor did not seem either unlikely or deplorable to many patriotic Guelphs or unreconstructed Ghibellines. The pope was happy to see the imperial crown go to "German Albert," whose position was such as to guarantee his permanence in Germany, but after Albert died in 1308, Henry of Luxembourg, emperor-elect— "wise, just, and gracious," in the words of Villani[5] — gave out his intention of coming to Italy to be crowned, and Dante was one of the many who welcomed him. He would bring, as the noble Frederick had brought before him, justice and harmony to an Italy which had relapsed into factionalism and feuding. Or so Dante thought. Henry's death at Buonconvento in 1313, leaving the country still unpacified and Florence still obdurate, was the last blow to Dante's hopes. Some day, he is sure, there will come the Righter of Wrongs and the pacifier of humble Italy, but though this great Dux, this heavenly hound, is foreordained and inevitable, the hour of his coming cannot be foretold, and Dante must have known — we can sense it from the tone of the *Paradiso* — that it would not be in his time.

The House of France and the papacy, which had combined to bring down the mighty Hohenstaufen, had not found ease in their new alliance. Charles and his liegeman the pope soon fell to squabbling, and the turbulent peerage of the kingdom, which had in the early days given Frederick so much trouble, was not to be lightly pacified by the invader. In 1282 an insult offered a Sicilian girl by a French soldier touched off the revolt known as the Sicilian Vespers. The arrogant and parsimonious French — for so they seemed to the Sicilians — were slain or driven from the island, which then turned to Peter of Aragon for protection. For all the fulminations of successive popes, the Aragonese made good their conquest. Charles died in 1285, leaving the kingdom, fairly well united, to his inept son. The troubles of the kingdom, no longer a principal focus of European attention, need not detain us further.

Victory at Benevento had not brought peace to the church. The pretensions of papacy and empire, as we have seen, were absolute, and neither could yield. But in the context of the times no ambitious medieval monarchy could compromise with papal claims in the temporal world any more than the emperor could. Emperors could be frustrated or defeated, but the secular principle was another matter. So the French monarchy which Clement had used to overthrow the emperor, when it found itself in the ascendant, had perforce to take the emperor's attitude of hostility towards the pope's intervention in the things of this world. The conflict was dramatized in the persons of Boniface VIII, a strong-minded autocrat as firm in the maintenance of his rights as any predecessor, and Philip IV, "the Fair," a more successful opponent of the papacy than the Swabian emperors.

Of the reasons for Dante's dislike of Boniface we shall have more to say later; it will be convenient here simply to trace the principal acts of his stormy pontificate. He assumed the purple in 1294 after the abdication of the simple Celestino (which many accused the new pope of bringing about). He is said to have been the first pope to wear the triple tiara, and he seems to have been a man whose arrogance (remarked upon by all contemporaries) was both personal and institutional. "I can't find anyone who can recall any pope of the past so delighting in vainglory," says the scandalized Jacopone da Todi.[6] Boniface attempted to launch another crusade; he proclaimed the Holy Year of 1300; he made a new collation of the Decretals. But he is principally remembered as the author of the bull *"Unam Sanctam,"* which, springing out of his quarrel with Philip of France, is an unqualified assertion of papal supremacy in the temporal sphere — "perhaps the high-water mark of papal claims, certainly their most incisive expression," as the *Shorter Cambridge Medieval History*[7] puts it. Philip's reaction was to dispatch a band of his followers to Anagni, where the pope was residing in the Gaetani palace; they seized the old man and mishandled him but, the city rallying to the papal side, were unable to hold him. He died, however, a month later, presumably from the psychological aftereffects of his rough treatment, "his imperious soul wounded in a vital part," in Gibbon's phrase.[8]

We may assume that many good Christians shared Dante's shock at this scandalous mistreatment of the pontiff; nevertheless it did the cause of Philip no harm. The next pope (who reigned less than a year) released the French kingdom from the excommunication laid on the nation by Boniface; his successor, Clement V (no favorite of our poet's either), was chosen by the French party, and it was he who, in 1309, removed the papal seat to Avignon to begin the long "Babylonian captivity" so much deplored by Dante, and in the long run so full of unhappy consequences for the church. As for Philip — "the evil of France," as Dante called him — it must be said that his was the triumph. In spite of his successive acts of wickedness, duly enumerated by Dante — the attack on Boniface, the carrying off of the church, the destruction of the Templars — his policy was victorious, and most historians give him a high place among the founders of the

French monarchy. He was killed in a hunting accident — "by a boarskin blow" as Dante says, perhaps with some undertone of contempt — in 1314, a year after Henry's death at Buonconvento. By now, as we have seen, the empire was dead and the church submissive; the future was to belong to the vigorous nationalism of which France was the symbol — and eventually, though that was far ahead, also to the middle-class capitalist democracy typified by Dante's own city, whose obstinacy he found so hard to accept.

Against the background of marches and countermarches of princes and emperors, great figures of spiritual and intellectual significance stood out, not only memorable for their own personalities but embodying the spirit of the century, on the one hand groping for reform and renovation of a decadent church, and on the other seeking new and firmer justification for the faith. The militant missionary vigor of the crusades had become somewhat enfeebled, perhaps as a result of the venal aspects of the fourth crusade, even though, as we have seen, both Frederick and Louis led armies against the pagans; and Dante on several occasions in the *Commedia* reproaches the pope for his indifference to the fate of the Holy Land. But the moral-religious ferment was, if anything, stronger than in the previous century, though it took new and sometimes unorthodox forms. The Albigensians, with their outspoken condemnation of the Church of Rome, their stress on austerity of morals, their heretical Manicheism, had become so strong in the south of France as to bring about the great crusade against them (1209–29), preached by the pope and carried to a successful conclusion by the combined efforts of the devout and well-disciplined northern barons and the vigorous efforts of St. Dominic. Other "protestant" sects also flourished: the Waldensians had established themselves in pockets of Piedmont and Lombardy, and as late as Dante's time the followers of Fra Dolcino had to be hunted down and extirpated in the Novara-Vercelli region (1307). But it was not among heretics only that the impulse toward spiritual renewal was strong. St. Francis' goal was — on a moral plane — the same as theirs, characterized by antimaterialism, a childlike and innocent faith in the brotherhood of man, and a kind of Christian pantheism; the Franciscan order was, however, recognized by the church in 1223, and became in the course of the thirteenth century a valuable ally of orthodoxy, as did the Dominican order (founded 1216), which was more intellectual in spirit and direction. Dante speaks for public opinion of his time in cantos XI and XII of the *Paradiso,* where, while deploring the state of corruption into which both brotherhoods seemed to have fallen in his day, he nevertheless exalts their founders and quite correctly gives them full credit for re-establishing the vigor of the church. Both of these great orders had intellectual-literary byproducts of enormous importance in the formation and direction of Dante's attitudes. On the fringes of these larger movements the religious obsession of the times took on somewhat irregular and exacerbated forms, as in the popular movement of the *flagellantes* in Tuscany and elsewhere in Italy, marked by a kind of evangelical fanaticism, not formalized enough to be heretical but deplored by pope and prince alike, or — at the other extreme — the cabalistic lucubrations of Joachim da Fiore, with his cryptic predictions of the age of the antichrist. Joachim died in 1202, but his prophecies lived long after him, interpreted and reinterpreted in the light of the political vicissitudes we have touched on. By 1300, the "ideal year" of the *Commedia,* many of these currents had spent their strength, at least in Italy, perhaps out of sheer weariness, perhaps under the influence of an embryonic humanism which in essence is Thomistic; Dante, however, had absorbed them all, and each of them will find its place in his poem.

If one were to try to characterize the thirteenth century in a few sentences, one could think of it as the age of St. Francis on the one hand and St. Thomas on the other. One could define it, in Italian terms, as the period of the empire fallen and the papacy embattled, with stress on the rise of the cities. One could call it the century of the faith reaffirmed, or quite possibly, if it suited one's thesis, see it as the century in which the Reformation is dimly adumbrated. We should hardly think of it as a century of much progress in such fields as science or exploration. Yet there was considerable activity in these areas, of which, no less than of the political and philosophical currents, Dante was well aware. If it is the century of St. Thomas, it is also the century of Roger Bacon (1214?–92?), who dared to dream of flying machines, horseless carriages, and the like, and whose concern with optics yielded not only memorable theoretical results but led to the invention of spectacles. The field of Bacon's primary concern, as well as his famous "experimental method," is represented in Dante's *Paradiso* when, in the second canto, he hears from

Beatrice the exposition of the "true cause" of the spots on the moon. For that matter, Dante's concern with light and his light imagery, such an important element for both its ornamental and its allegorical weight in the *Paradiso*, may have owed something to Bacon's scientific interest as well as to the neoplatonism of the day. This was the century too when the mathematical practices of the Arabs seeped into the western world. Slowly but inevitably during the course of the century Arabic numerals displaced the old Roman style, and Dante shows a consistent interest in theories of arithmetic. Medicine was taking its first steps to break the chains of Galen. Alchemy, for all its aura of magic, gave as a byproduct the techniques of distillation and some basic elements of methodology. The escapement clock is also an invention of this century, and there is an effective poetic reference to it in *Paradiso* X. As the historian Robert Lopez remarks in his summary of the science of the time: "One may contest the soundness of the basis of this or that medieval invention but it is undeniable that science is on the march."[9]

As we have mentioned Roger Bacon as symbolic of the scientific concern of the day, so too we may cite Marco Polo (1254–1324) as the most dramatic example of the exploratory interest of the age, which was considerable. Cartography made great advances during the century, and this scientific arm was put at the disposal of political, military, and proselytising movements. The crusades had already established contact between East and West; during Dante's lifetime various efforts were made to bring the Grand Khan into political alliance with Christian Europe, and missionaries were active among Mongols and Persians. When Dante speaks of "Tartar and Turkish" fabrics (*Inferno* XVIII), he indicates perhaps some of the commercial results of these political and ecclesiastical interests — not without their element of scientific curiosity as well, as readers of *Marco Millions* will attest. As for the other side of the world, various commentators have suggested that Dante's celebrated episode of the voyage of Ulysses may have been inspired less by poetic foreknowledge of Columbus than by the memory of the daring expedition of Ugolino and Vadino Vivaldi, who sailed west through the Strait of Gibraltar, never to be seen again, with the avowed intent of opening up trade with the Indies. Dante's day is not that of the industrial revolution nor of great explorations, but it is full of the stirrings of the vast restless European curiosity which would lead to man's conquest of the world, and our poet, "impressionable in all things," participated in the spirit of his times. Perhaps, *"natione florentinus"* and more *"moribus"* than he was willing to concede, he could hardly have done otherwise.

2

Dante's Florence

WHILE it is frequently said that feudalism never took root in Italy, or at least failed to flourish there, such statements must be taken with some reservations. The beginnings of feudalism, based on delegation of authority with reciprocal loyalty of vassal and lord, were apparent in the kingdom of the Lombards and later obtained in the Kingdom of Naples as elsewhere in the domain wrung from the empire by the barbarians. In Dante's century the cities, for all their *de facto* independence and their more or less effective self-government, nevertheless recognized their theoretical dependence on an overlord, and on occasions of need or expediency would commend themselves, just as fief-holders of more conventional nature did, to the pope, the emperor, or some deputy of either of these powers. In the thirteenth and fourteenth centuries the ancient Teutonic aristocracy in Italy, while shorn of its actual power, still retained a great deal of prestige and authority, as Dante's own writings testify. The concept of an independent city-state, owing allegiance to no one save its own citizens, would have been foreign to medieval political theory. The feudal idea, which remained very much alive in Italy until long after Dante's death, is woven into the *terza rima* of the *Commedia,* as well as eloquently defended in the *De Monarchia.*

It remains true, however, granted the persistence of the feudal concept, that, in contrast to such countries as England, France,

14

and Germany, Italy was scarcely amenable to the permanent exigencies of the categories of dependencies and fiefdoms that formed the standard pattern of the middle ages. One reason for this distinction was, no doubt, the presence and endurance of Rome. The memory of antiquity had survived in sufficient vigor to make the great *Urbs* difficult to fit into the feudal scheme. For Rome had senators, prefects, tribunes — titles whose very sound is alien to feudalism, and titles, it may be remarked, that other Italian cities imitated, to say nothing of their dimly remembered implications. Furthermore, Rome was, aside from its antiquity, something different. Its overlord was himself supreme, owing allegiance to none; he had, in fact, in the course of defending himself against successive invaders and making good his own peculiar claims, achieved a status at once above and in a sense outside the feudal system. His right was also unique in that it was not hereditary. Given this example and the memories of ancient glory, never entirely lost in the peninsula, it followed of necessity that feudalism of a barbarian, non-Latin stamp could never have existed in all its purity in Italy. Moreover, the Italian cities, although invaded and depopulated by the invasions, had never suffered extinction or metamorphosis to an extent comparable to that suffered in non-Italian lands of the empire, and they continued to preserve a certain sense of urban personality. In the later middle ages they began, through the accident of their locations on convenient harbors, navigable rivers, or important pilgrim routes, to acquire a wealth and a power based on commerce and industry, in contrast to the agricultural foundation of feudal strength. The crusades, greatly contributing to the growth of this wealth and power, accelerated a process already under way. The history of all the prosperous Italian city-states follows the same pattern, generally speaking, although with considerable individual variation; we shall concentrate on Florence, since it is the city of Dante's life and his hopes, as well as being in the main typical in the phases of its development from relative obscurity to emergence as a peninsular power in its own right.

According to the legend which was acceptable both to Dante and to Villani, Florence was founded in 70 B.C., when Catiline's followers, driven from Fiesole, made common cause with the Roman colony that had been established at the foot of the hill. "And note," says Villani, possibly echoing Dante, "that it is not to be wondered at that the Florentines are always at war and strife among themselves, being born and descended from two peoples so contrary and hostile and different in habits as were the noble Romans in their virtue and the rude Fiesolans fierce in war."[1] It cannot be claimed for classical Florence that she enjoyed any great importance in the Roman Empire, although Tacitus mentions her and there is an account of Stilicho's defense of the city against the Goths. Dante believed, although history does not support him, that the town was razed by Attila. Originally dedicated to Mars, the christianized Florence shifted allegiance to John the Baptist.

In the early middle ages, Florence formed part of the Duchy of Tuscany, defined, apparently, under the Lombards. The Carolingians called the region a "march." Villani tells us the tale of the rebuilding of the city by the great Charles. There is no historical basis for his account, but it would be a pity to omit it. According to him, the prominent survivors of the destroyed city

ordained to send to Rome ambassadors from the best among them to Charles the Emperor, and to Pope Leo, and to the Romans; and this was done, praying them to remember their daughter, the city of Florence (the which was ruined and destroyed by Goths and Vandals in despite of the Romans), to the end it might be rebuilt, and that it might please them to give a force of men-at-arms to ward off the men of Fiesole and their followers, the enemies of the Romans, who would not let the city of Florence be rebuilt. The which ambassadors were received with honour by the Emperor Charles, and by the Pope, and by the Romans, and their petition accepted graciously and willingly; and straightway the Emperor Charles the Great sent thither his forces of men-at-arms on foot and on horse in great numbers; and the Romans made a decree and command that, as their forefathers had built and peopled of old the city of Florence, so those of the best families in Rome, both of nobles and of people, should go thither to rebuild and to inhabit it; and this was done. With that host of the Emperor Charles the Great and of the Romans there came whatsoever master-craftsmen there were in Rome, the more speedily to build the walls of the city and to strengthen it, and after them there followed much people; and all they who dwelt in the country around Florence, and her exiled citizens in every place, hearing the tidings, gathered themselves to the host of the Romans and of the Emperor to rebuild the city; and when they were come where today is our city, they encamped among ancient remains and ruins in booths and in tents. The Fiesolans and their followers, seeing the host of the Emperor and of the Romans so great and powerful, did not venture to fight against them, but keeping within the fortress of their city of Fiesole and in their fortified places around, gave what hindrance they might to the said rebuilding. But their power was nothing against the strength of the Romans, and of the host of the Emperor, and of the assembled descendants of the Florentines; and thus they began to rebuild the city of Florence, not, however, of the size that it had been at the first, but of lesser extent, as hereafter shall be mentioned, to the end it might more speedily be walled and fortified, and there might be a defense like a rampart against the city of Fiesole; and this was the year of Christ 801, in the beginning of the month of April. And it is said that the ancients were of opinion that it would not be possible to rebuild it, if first there were not found, and drawn from the Arno, the marble image, dedicated by the first pagan builders by necromancy to Mars, the which had been in the river Arno from the destruction of Florence unto that time; and being found, it was placed on a pillar by the side of the said river, where now is the head of the Ponte Vecchio. This we do not affirm or believe, forasmuch as it seems to us the opinion of pagans and soothsayers, and not to be reasonable, but very foolish, that such a stone should have such effect; but it was commonly said by the ancients, that, if it was disturbed, the city must needs have great disturbances.[2]

As an imperial fief, the duchy, city included, came into the hands of the great Duchess Matilda (of Canossa fame), whom — the older commentators do not hesitate to affirm, however unesthetic the interpretation may appear to modern critics — Dante was later to meet in the earthly paradise. Matilda was a woman who greatly impressed her contemporaries; she was strong-minded and masculine in character, and even, it is said, led her troops into battle. She was the pope's stalwart ally in the wars of investiture with Henry IV, and on her death in 1115 she willed her march to the Catholic Church. By that time the Commune of Florence was well launched on an independent life of its own. Probably its location on the main pilgrim route to Rome had much to do with giving it an early start; Dante's haunting reference to the "pilgrims who go their pensive way" in chapter 41 of the *Vita Nuova* comes to mind in this connection, but of course the scene had been a familiar one in Florence for centuries.

The history of the twelfth and thirteenth centuries in Florence, as elsewhere, is that of the struggle of the rising banking and industrial classes against the feudal nobility, which tended to look to the emperor for support. It is also the story of the progressive adaptation of the administrative pattern of the commune to the growing strength of the former party, known as the *popolo*. For a time there were two cities in one, and the nobles had their *podestà* while the *popolo* had their "captain." As time passed, the nobles, by their very nature an irreconcilable element in a bourgeois city, were more and more deflated, losing first their authority and later even the right to serve, as nobles, in the government of the commune. Simultaneously during these centuries the city carried on long and eventually successful campaigns against the Alberti, the Conti Guidi, and other aristocratic feudatories of the Tuscan countryside. "In no other commune did the people win a victory as complete and enduring as in Florence," says the Italian historian Bernardino Barbadoro.[3] Since the nobles commonly depended on the emperor and were hence Ghibelline, it was inevitable that the *popolo* should be anti-imperial or Guelph.

The terms "Guelph" and "Ghibelline" go back to the rival German clans of Welf and Waibling. It is said that they were first employed in Italy at the time of the war between Barbarossa and the Lombard League at the end of the twelfth century. Villani's account of the introduction of the feud and its terminology into Florence is celebrated and may well be quoted here:

In the year of Christ 1215, M. Gherardo Orlandi being Podestà in Florence, one M. Bondelmonte dei Bondelmonti, a noble citizen of Florence, had promised to take to wife a maiden of the house of the Amidei, honourable and noble citizens; and afterwards as the said M. Bondelmonte, who was very charming and a good horseman, was riding through the city, a lady of the house of the Donati called to him, reproaching him as to the lady to whom he was betrothed, that she was not beautiful or worthy of him, and saying: "I have kept this my daughter for you"; whom she showed to him, and she was most beautiful; and immediately by the inspiration of the devil he was so taken by her, that he was betrothed and wedded to her, for which thing the kinsfolk of the first betrothed lady, being assembled together, and grieving over the shame which M. Bondelmonte had done to them, were filled with the accursed indignation, whereby the city of Florence was destroyed and divided. For many houses of the nobles swore together to bring shame upon the said M. Bondelmonte, in revenge for these wrongs. And being in council among themselves, after what fashion they should punish him, whether by beating or killing, Mosca de' Lamberti said the evil word: "Thing done has an end"; to wit, that he should be slain; and so it was done; for on the morning of Easter of the Resurrection the Amidei of San Stefano assembled in their house, and the said M. Bondelmonte coming from Oltrarno, nobly arrayed in new white apparel, and upon a white palfrey, arriving at the foot of the Ponte Vecchio on this side, just at the foot of the pillar where was the statue of Mars, the said M. Bondelmonte was dragged from his horse by Schiatto degli Uberti, and by Mosca de' Lamberti and Lambertuccio degli Amidei assaulted and smitten, and by Oderigo Fifanti his veins were opened and he was brought to his end; and there was with them one of the counts of Gangalandi. For the which thing the city rose in arms and tumult; and this death of M. Bondelmonte was the cause and beginning of the accursed parties of Guelphs and Ghibellines in Florence, albeit long before there were factions among the noble citizens and the said parties existed by reason of the strifes and questions between the Church and the Empire; but by reason of the death of the said M. Bondelmonte all the families of the nobles and the other citizens of Florence were divided, and some held with the Bondelmonti, who took the side of the Guelphs, and were its leaders, and some with the Uberti, who were the leaders of the Ghibellines, whence followed much evil and disaster to our city, as hereafter shall be told; and it is believed that it will never have an end, if God do not cut it short.[4]

It is interesting and somewhat ironic to note that at the actual time of the picturesque incident the emperor was a Welf, indeed the only one of that clan to win the title. The subsequent election of Frederick II of course gave to "Ghibelline" and "imperial" the same political meaning, a synonymity which the terms were thenceforth to preserve, while "Guelph" carried the implication of the papal or at least the anti-imperial faction. It must not be assumed that the individual members of each major party were always ideologically consistent, as we should say today. A man or a town might be Guelph not necessarily from conviction of the justice of the pope's cause but rather out of hereditary loyalty or particular interest, because friends and allies were Guelph, or, perhaps more often, because foes were Ghibelline. One would expect the cities to be Guelph, but in Lombardy, precisely because Milan was Guelph, Cremona and Pavia were staunchly Ghibelline. Again, because Florence was Guelph and an enemy, Pisa and Siena were consistently Ghibelline. On the other hand, one would expect the ancient nobility to take the imperial part, but there were Guelph noble families, the Este's for example, and to balance them there were Ghibelline clerics, such as the celebrated Ottaviano degli Ubaldini, "the Cardinal" of *Inferno* X. By way of further complication of this checkered pattern of loyalties, the allegiance of either family or city could shift with the fortunes of war.

Like every other city and region of Italy, Florence reacted, though in her own way, to the successive stages of the long struggle between the Hohenstaufen and the papacy. The great factions that developed out of the Bondelmonti episode were precariously balanced in power and prestige: the Ghibellines, in the main, with the weight of tradition and social pre-eminence in their favor, the Guelphs supported by the growing wealth of what was called *il popolo grasso* (the word "people" is somewhat misleading, since it referred to the rich and independent commoners and by no means included what we now call the proletariat). As the city slowly fought her way to a primacy attained by force over the other communes of Tuscany, the factions within the walls continued to wrangle. The implication of many Ghibelline families in the Patarine heresy gave the Guelphs the upper hand for a while (1244–45), and it is significant that even Dante, Ghibelline sympathizer though he is, mentions mainly members of that party among his heretics of canto X. But the entrance into the city of Frederick of Antioch, the emperor's son, with his well-armed German knights, turned the tide, and in 1249 the Guelphs were expelled en masse, setting a precedent for exile of the vanquished that the Ghibellines were later to rue bitterly. In the imperial collapse that followed the death of Frederick, the Guelphs were able to come back and, in their turn, expel their foes. The victory of the pro-imperial coalition, supported by Manfred at Montaperti, brought the Ghibellines into power again, and such was their thirst for vengeance that, as Dante tells us in *Inferno* X, but for the intervention of Farinata degli Uberti, Florence might have been razed to the ground even as years before Barbarossa had razed Milan. It had become, however, increasingly clear that the city, left to its own bent and freed of external pressure, could never be Ghibelline, and the defeat and death of Manfred at Benevento brought the Guelphs home once more, this time for good, as Dante tauntingly reminds the venerable Farinata.

Meanwhile the city government had been modified to give increased power to the *popolo*. The ancient *buoni uomini*, originally aristocrats who had assisted the regional overlords in the dispensing of justice, were assisted by a Council of a Hundred, drawn from the ranks of the *popolo*. Even so, tension continued

lifetime. Other buildings familiar to him and still standing were the ancient Badia and the Bargello, or Palazzo del podestà. The great churches of Santa Maria Novella and Santa Croce, begun in his century, were in use well before his exile, but the enlargements and embellishments of later generations have completely altered their appearance; Dante would hardly recognize either edifice in its modern dress. Yet if all the steeples and towers built since 1265 had been there for our hypothetical tourist to admire, he probably could not have seen them, for the chief architectural feature of Dante's Florence was the multiplicity of private family towers. The rise of the popular party — and the various factional vendettas — gradually reduced them both in number and height. Even so, Robert Davidsohn estimates their number at about 250 in the middle years of the century.[6] The much smaller town of San Gimignano, which has preserved a number of these private fortresses, gives us some faint notion of the bristling appearance of the typical medieval city.

Dante's Florence was much smaller than the city of today. Villani estimates a population of "90,000 mouths," not counting members of the religious orders;[7] his figure is probably low, but it could hardly have been anything like the present-day number of some 400,000. Still it must be remembered that in the compact Europe of the thirteenth century, with America (and for all practical purposes the Orient) as yet undiscovered, and with such modern capitals as Berlin, Vienna, and Madrid still in the early stages of growth, Florence, whatever the demographic estimate may be, would rank higher on the list of great population centers than she does today. Her prestige too was greater than sheer census figures would imply; her autonomy, however precarious, was genuine, she was a nation as well as a city, and her wealth was more than keeping pace with the steadily increasing population.

Dante's life corresponded with a time of expansion; during the thirteenth century the town was straining at its old bonds and indeed repeatedly breaking through. The original Roman walls had included a rather small area, a square whose northern side ran along what is now the Via de' Cerretani and the northern flank of the Duomo, and whose eastern rampart ran along the Via del Proconsolo. The southern limit is less easy to designate in contemporary terms; its center was marked by what is now known as the Porta Santa Maria, and running west it joined the

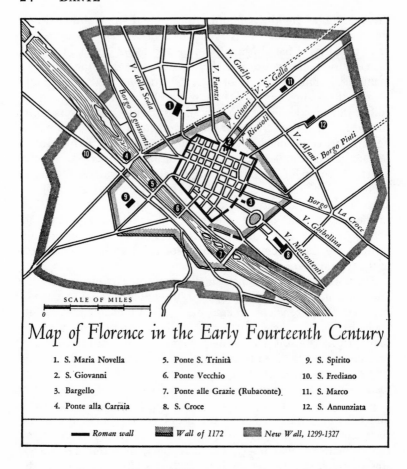

Map of Florence in the Early Fourteenth Century

1. S. Maria Novella	5. Ponte S. Trinità	9. S. Spirito
2. S. Giovanni	6. Ponte Vecchio	10. S. Frediano
3. Bargello	7. Ponte alle Grazie (Rubaconte)	11. S. Marco
4. Ponte alla Carraia	8. S. Croce	12. S. Annunziata

━━ Roman wall   ▨ Wall of 1172   ▨ New Wall, 1299-1327

fourth side of the square at the southern end of what is now Via Tornabuoni; the present street follows the line of the western wall, which joined the northern one a little to the west of where nowadays Via dei Cerretani runs into Via Panzani.

These boundaries served the city for a long time, although a great deal of building went on immediately outside them. In the eighth decade of the twelfth century new walls were built, considerably enlarging the city, as will be seen from the map, and enclosing the *"cerchia antica"* so nostalgically recalled by Cacciaguida in *Paradiso* XV. As time went on, more and more gates had to be made for the convenience of dwellers in the suburbs, and in the last years of Dante's residence the outer circle was begun, not to be completed until 1327. These were no doubt the hated walls built, in part at least, to resist the emperor, so giving Dante a political as well as a sentimental reason for deploring them. For clearly Cacciaguida's remarks may be taken as expressing our poet's own feelings at the increasing expansion of the town and the concomitant inclusion of "foreigners." It should be added that many lived outside the walls; Davidsohn, alluding to Brunetto Latini's description of the fortified castles on the surrounding hills, comments that as capitalism triumphed over feudalism many of these gaunt fortresses became charming villas, and many others were built to stand with them, meant for the pleasant diversions of *villeggiatura*. This change must have been going on rapidly in Dante's lifetime.

It is hard for a man of the twentieth century to sense the texture of life in a medieval town. Florence was, thanks to the prosperity and initiative of its citizens, in many ways ahead of its time. Streets were paved and drainage was well provided for, but since all transportation was by horseback, and goods and supplies were borne through the streets on mules and donkeys, the condition of the streets was all but indescribable; and the lack of even elementary sanitary facilities made certain areas of the town unapproachable. (Such conditions may partly explain the recurrent plagues to which medieval society was subject.) If we add to the unesthetic visual and olfactory elements the spectacle of many blind and deformed beggars and many more mutilated under the harsh penal codes of medieval society (which somehow never succeeded in reducing the number of prostitutes, pimps, pickpockets, and plain thugs), we shall have to concede that our much-abused twentieth century is not without its compensations. (Nor was Dante blind to these unhappy aspects of his time: in *Inferno* XVIII the reference to privies is hard for some readers to stomach; his view of the envious recalls the huddles of beggars around the church doors; he speaks in *Purgatorio* XXVII of bodies he has seen burnt; and his reference in *Inferno* XIX to the penalty dealt out to certain kinds of criminals is horrifying in its casualness.) We may add, for a better understanding of our poet's milieu, that most people were cold all winter long, the only system of heating available to most citizens being the venerable and ineffectual brazier; and the class we now euphemistically describe as underprivileged was permanently unwashed.

Yet all things are relative, and relatively the Florence of Dante and his fellow poets was a comfortable as well as an exciting place to live. Dante himself speaks (though of course with disapproval) of the larger houses being built in his time; in contrast to many of the buildings of an earlier generation they were of stone, and so cleaner and safer than the older wooden dwellings. There were public baths and hospitals. In matters of dress and food the upper classes at least had nothing to complain of. If the peasantry and the poor lived largely on bread, greens, and olive oil (as indeed many still do), and if — refrigeration being nonexistent — salt pork was the staple winter diet for all, yet we get from many of the minor poets and later from Boccaccio evidence of many fine banquets of fowl, roast meat, fish, and rare delicacies (roast peacock, for example) among the upper and articulate classes. Folgore da San Gimignano, Dante's contemporary, speaks on this subject in a sonnet:

> Siena in July! The court is cool.
> The flasks are filled with Trebbiano wine
> Or with sweet Vaian, chill and plentiful.
> In gay brigade, from morn to night we dine
> On aspic jellies that, incarnadine,
> Garnish fat grouse or partridge, good to taste;
> On capon or on kid, piquant and fine
> As sauce is when with garlic it is laced;
> On these we live as jocund as we may,
> Nor ever venture forth into the heat,
> But loll within, silk-clad, having grown wise,
> Where only joy and ease have rule and sway,
> And heap our table up with drink and meat.
> With wives away, no need t' economize.[8]

Repeated sumptuary laws throughout the century testify to the growing luxury of women's dress and jewelry and their cult of personal adornment in the matter of cosmetics, coiffures, and the like. It was necessary, too, to make laws limiting the display of pomp at public occasions such as funerals. There was a good deal of gaiety and conspicuous expense: parties, feasts, weddings, and banquets. In short, to paraphrase Davidsohn, capitalism was working.

The nourishment of this healthy community was drawn from commerce, based firmly on the wool trade. Villani counts more than two hundred *botteghe* of the wool guild, giving employment to 30,000 and turning out cloth to the value of 1,200,000 gold florins, not counting the eighty factories of the Calimala (a technique for preparing foreign wools) and eighty banks;[9] we should add that the Florentine banking families, of which the Bardi and the Peruzzi were perhaps the best-known, had already replaced the Jews and the religious orders as the international experts in this field. The florin, whose evil influence on the clergy Dante deplores in the *Paradiso,* was the soundest and most respected coin in Europe.

The city's concerns were by no means exclusively materialistic, even though they may have seemed so to an austere and somewhat embittered exile. Elementary education was available to children, girls as well as boys. Villani speaks of from eight hundred to a thousand children learning to read and another thousand to twelve hundred learning the abacus and arithmetic.[10] We need look no further than the *Vita Nuova* for evidence of a lively cultivation of poetry among the brighter spirits. Art too flourished: this is the century of Cimabue and Giotto, both of whom worked in Florence and were well-known to Dante, as the reference in *Purgatorio* XI will attest. The episode of Dante's drawing an angel mentioned in the *Vita Nuova* testifies to a kind of amateur interest in the arts, and we may reasonably assume that Dante was not the only one of his generation to engage in such avocations. How large this class was that concerned itself with intellectual and artistic matters is impossible to say. It was no doubt an élite, but so it always has been, and in Dante's time it was at least large enough and active enough to give character and personality to the city.

We have already noticed some of the buildings begun in Dante's time, and it would be easy to add to the list. Villani assures us that buildings were going up continuously, churches and monasteries as well as numerous private dwellings, inside and outside the walls.[10] Perhaps we may be pardoned the reflection that the architectonic quality of Dante's work may owe something to the interest in masses, proportions, and perspectives which must have been aroused in any observant youth in late thirteenth-century Florence. Taken all in all there could hardly have been in our poet's day a happier or livelier city in which to grow up and to pursue a career and cultivation of the arts. Even in exile Dante knew this; he never realized that it was so precisely because of the "new people and quick profits" which he held to be so dangerous. He is on firmer ground when he speaks more generally in *Inferno* VI of the endemic *"superbia, invidia e avarizia"*; such scourges of humanity are by no means limited to Florence or even to the thirteenth century, but translated into political factionalism and intransigence under the pressures and circumstances of the time they did indeed have their unhappy consequences for our poet. But his city was also rather more their victim than their embodiment.

We may, in leaving this summary of Dante's social and cultural milieu, recall a paradox of his times, both sides of which set the middle ages apart from our modern world. It has been said often and rightly that in cultural matters medieval Europe was united as it never has been since. Through all Christendom, which was all the western world, one faith, one corpus of philosophical concepts, and one truly international language, Latin, maintained a cohesiveness later to be undermined by the Reformation, nationalism, and to some degree, discovery and exploration. Any educated man from Edinburgh to Hungary could have read Dante's *De Monarchia,* understood its terms of reference, and found relevance in its substance. Yet, at the same time, on the level of day-by-day living, to move as much as fifty miles from one's own city would signify a kind of alienation unknown to a modern man. One would have met with different legal codes, different weights and measures, differences in dress and manners and speech. The scholar would have felt at home anywhere; the man would be certain to encounter not only indifference and misunderstanding but more often than not hostility. A recent writer, not without his own experience of exile, puts it very graphically: "No modern exile can measure the anguish of the medieval expatriate. The medieval city, loud and fierce as a bee-hive, had developed in the narrow interplay of its actions and passions a system of psychic self-sufficiency which approaches the completeness of an animal instinct. The bee-hive, for all its cruelty, is the only possibility of life to the single bee; so was a medieval society like the Italian commune to its children. Expulsion was a curse. Exile was agony."[11] The human aspects of this paradox are obvious in a glance at the Dantesque canon. The discussions on government, language, and style in letters, "the question of earth and water," these are written for the integrated world of scholarship. The *Commedia,* rich though it be in philosophical learning, is not primarily for scholars; it is written by a banished Florentine, eager to have contact with his fellow citizens, yearning, as he overtly tells us, for an invitation to return. The bread of angels is the same everywhere, the bread of Verona or Ravenna tastes of salt.

❧ 3 ❧

Dante's Life

INTO such a world as we have described, and at a delicate time in the history of "the great city on the Arno," Dante Alighieri was born. We have Boccaccio's testimony in his biography of the poet that the coming of "this singular glory of Italy" was marked by unusual portents: his mother,

when pregnant, and not far removed from the time when she should be delivered, saw in a dream of what wondrous kind the fruit of her womb should be; albeit it was not then understood of her nor of any other, though now, because of the event that has come to pass, it is most manifest to all.

The gentle lady thought in her dream that she was under a most lofty laurel tree, on a green meadow, by the side of a most clear spring, and there she felt herself delivered of a son, who in shortest space, feeding only on the berries which fell from the laurel tree, and the waters of the clear spring, her thought grew up into a shepherd, and strove with all his power to have of the leaves of that tree whose fruit had nourished him; and as he struggled thereto, her thought she saw him fall, and when he rose again, she saw he was no longer a man, but had become a peacock. At the which thing, so great amazement laid hold of her that her sleep broke; and in no long space the due time came for her labor, and she delivered of a son, whom by common consent with his father, they called by name Dante [the Giver]; and rightly so, because, as will be seen in the sequel, the issue was most perfectly consonant with this name. This was that

30

Dante of whom is the present discourse. This was that Dante granted by the special grace of God to our age. This was that Dante who was first to open the way for the return of the Muses, banished from Italy. 'Twas he that revealed the glory of the Florentine idiom. 'Twas he that brought under the rule of due numbers every beauty of the vernacular speech. 'Twas he who may be truly said to have brought back dead poesy to life. The which things, when duly considered, will show that he could not rightly have borne any other name but Dante.[1]

That Dante was born in Florence and in the year 1265 we know from his own words as well as from Boccaccio's account; our poet tells us furthermore that he was born under the zodiacal sign of Gemini — that is, between May 21 and June 21.[2] At the time of his birth Florence was a Ghibelline city, for the defeat of Manfred did not occur until some months later. As for his ancestry, Dante tells us in *Inferno* XV that his family was of the seed of the Romans who colonized the original city; in the *Paradiso* — for not even there does his pride of family desert him — he has his ancestor Cacciaguida set forth the illustrious connection of the Alighieri line, relating it to the Elisei and the Frangipani, both families of high social importance in the middle ages. Of his mother's family he says nothing; it has been suggested that she came from the clan of the Abati.

However distinguished his origins, Alighiero, the father of the poet, seems to have been a figure of little importance. He was apparently allowed to remain in Florence when the prominent members of the Guelph faction (which was his) were in exile. It is not known for certain what his profession was; apparently he lived on the income from some small holdings and may have been a moneylender. It is not necessary, however, to believe that he was a usurer. In Dante's childhood his mother died and his father remarried. Whether the sister so touchingly referred to in the *Vita Nuova* was of the same mother or a half-sister is uncertain. If his full sister, then she was the only other child of the marriage; Dante had, however, three half-brothers. His father died shortly before Dante reached his eighteenth year, after affiancing the boy to Gemma Donati, cousin of the Forese of the *Purgatorio* and the Piccarda of the *Paradiso*.[3]

It is perhaps a matter to be remarked here that Dante, in some ways the most personal of poets, filling the pages of his work with references to friends, enemies, and prominent contemporaries, never mentions his father or his mother. Sentimentalists, anxious to have the poet conform in all respects to the matriarchal ideal, have made much of the phrase of Virgil in *Inferno* VIII, 45: "Blessed she who bore you." It will seem to the unprejudiced reader a somewhat general statement, however, hardly adequate to justify the presentation of Dante as a lively exponent of the mother cult. It may be added here that some have found it equally remarkable that the *Commedia* contains no reference to Gemma. If we follow Boccaccio's highly colored account of the difficulties of married life for a poet and philosopher, and his strong suggestion that Dante was happy to see the last of his wife when he went into exile, we shall need to ask no more about the matter. On the other hand, there is nothing to prevent us from believing that the poignant if rather unspecific reference in *Paradiso* XVII to the loss of everything "most dearly loved" may include Gemma and the children. Indeed we may if we wish, and some modern critics do so wish, believe that in his last years in Ravenna Gemma joined him and comforted his twilight days. There is unhappily no evidence for such an attractive theory. And in any case the fact remains that there is no allusion to Gemma in any of Dante's works.

But to return to the poet's youth. Boccaccio tells us that the young Dante studied the arts of poetry, painting, and music. The *Vita Nuova* certainly gives evidence of considerable study of the poets, particularly the Provençal, the contemporary Italian, and certain of the classics, and the chapter in which Dante speaks of painting an angel would seem to indicate some familiarity with the pictorial art. And the presence of such figures as Belacqua, the maker of musical instruments, and Casella, the singer, in the *Purgatorio* (somewhat more than their presence indeed, for Dante's presentation of them is affectionate and intimate) may well justify the claim for his musical interests. Similarly, his open statement of his indebtedness to Brunetto Latini would point to his instruction under this great master. Whether that instruction was formal in the sense that the venerable scholar actually tutored Dante is debatable and to most seems unlikely, but certainly he must have given counsel and guidance in abundance, otherwise the allusion would be meaningless. We may therefore accept Boccaccio's statement, but it is impossible to supplement it with details as to what schools Dante frequented, what specific subjects he studied, or what particular years were dedicated to the pursuit of learning. It is likely that Siro Chimenz is right in suggesting that Dante's education was largely self-directed.

We know that in 1287, or shortly before, Dante was in Bologna, and it would be pleasant to think that he attended the university then; this is indeed quite possible. What is certain is that by the age of eighteen he felt himself sufficiently a scholar and a poet — and in the context of the times the terms were interchangeable — to submit a sonnet to such a recognized authority as Guido Cavalcanti, who received the attention with such appreciation as to enable Dante to speak of him as his "first friend."

To think of Dante as nothing but a scholar or apprentice poet during the years of adolescence and youth would, however, be erroneous. Leonardo Bruni, another early biographer of our poet, affirms that in spite of his scholarly interests Dante "did not shut himself up at ease, nor sever himself from the world, but living and moving about amongst other young men of his age, he approved himself gracious and skilful and valiant in every youthful exercise."[4] The *Vita Nuova* hints at a lively social life, as it was understood in those days, marked by frequent contacts with friends and equally frequent flirtations with various young ladies of Florence. Further evidence to this effect is supplied by some of the *Rime*. We know that Dante took part in the battle of Campaldino, fighting among the nobles in the first rank, and was present at the siege of Caprona. All of this would demonstrate a normal and healthy participation in the life of his generation and the affairs of the town — a supposition which is of course strengthened by his later concern with politics and his prominent role in the government of the commune.

But the most important part of Dante's youth — at least as he made it seem in later years and certainly too for its effect on his verse — was his relationship with Beatrice, so tenuous as hardly to be described as a relationship at all, yet so lasting in its effect as to dominate all his remaining years. He first met Beatrice, he tells us in the *Vita Nuova,* at the age of nine. Boccaccio's highly colored description of that meeting, whether *vero* or simply *ben trovato,* is worth citing:

In that season wherein the sweetness of heaven reclothes the earth with its adornments, making her all to smile with diversity of flowers mingled amongst green leaves, it was the custom both of men and women in our city, each in his district, to hold festival, gathering together in their several companies; wherefore it chanced that Folco Portinari, amongst the rest, a man in those days much honoured of the citizens, had gathered his neighbours round about, to feast them in his house on the first day of May. Now amongst them was that Alighieri already spoken of; and thither (even as little lads are wont to go about with their fathers, especially to places of festivity) Dante, whose ninth year was not yet ended, had accompanied him. And here, mingling with the others of his age — for in the festal house were many of them, boys and girls — the first tables being served, he abandoned himself with the rest to children's sports, so far as the compass of his small years would extend. There was amongst the throng of young ones a little daughter of the aforesaid Folco, whose name was Bice (though he himself always called her by the original of the name, to wit, Beatrice), whose age was some eight years; right gracious after her childish fashion, and full gentle and winning in her ways, and of manners and speech far more sedate and modest than her small age required; and besides this the features of her face full delicate, most excellently disposed, and replete not only with beauty but with such purity and winsomeness, that she was held of many to be a kind of little angel. She then, such as I am painting her, or may be far more beauteous yet, appeared before the eyes of our Dante, at this festival, not I suppose for the first time, but for the first time with power to enamor him; and he, child as he still was, received her fair visage into his heart with such affection, that, from that day forth, never, so long as he lived, was he severed therefrom.[5]

Austere critics have long debated whether a child of nine is sufficiently mature to suffer the powerful emotional impact of which Dante gives such eloquent report in the *Vita Nuova.* Yet any man who has children or who still remembers his own childhood must readily concede that attraction between little boys and girls is by no means uncommon. T. S. Eliot, after consulting an expert, believes that nine may even be a little too old for such an experience.[6] In this case the death of Beatrice must have very naturally heightened the emotion with which Dante looks back to their first meeting. He met her again, he tells us, nine years later, and at this time was privileged to receive her salute. The subsequent developments in their relationship, culminating in the death of Beatrice (1290), are described in detail in the *Vita Nuova.* We may anticipate briefly here some aspects of the Beatrice question by saying at once that, although Dante does not ever clearly identify her, most critics, including Michele Barbi,[7] have accepted Boccaccio's declaration that she was the daughter of Folco Portinari and was married in 1288(?) to Simon de Bardi, although Ernst Curtius,[8] among others, disagrees. Her marriage would have been no bar to Dante's devotion to her. In fact, it would have been in harmony with the Provençal tradition of courtly love which at first he followed, and would of course have been simply irrelevant in the later stage of his devotion, when the woman had all but vanished in the symbol.

There is no reason to doubt that the death of his Beatrice was a crucial event in Dante's life. Whether it would of itself have turned his attention to meditation and study and the preparation of the great work of his life may be open to question. It may well be that his exile was of more decisive importance, but the *Vita Nuova,* composed after Beatrice's death and before the exile, certainly reveals a maturity of purpose — even if the last chapter with its overt statement of dedication be a later addition, as some suspect — and a sensitive personality that has been disciplined by tragedy.

Boccaccio says that Dante's marriage was urged on him by friends and relations to distract him from his grief at the loss of Beatrice. Yet we are not really sure of the date of his marriage to Gemma; if the Giovanni Alighieri destined to be exiled with his father was in fact his eldest son and eight years old at the time of the poet's banishment, it seems clear that Dante must have been married some time before 1294.[9] He had two other sons by Gemma, Pietro and Jacopo, and a daughter, Antonia, called Bice, who seems to have kept her father company in the last years of his life at Ravenna. Political life, Boccaccio tells us, was another distraction, and after the death of Beatrice Dante threw himself into it with such intensity as to become in a short time one of the leading figures in the absorbing and dangerous business of communal government. We have seen that in 1293 nobles as such were excluded from any share in the administration of the commonwealth; Dante therefore in 1295 had himself inscribed as a member of the guild of apothecaries, one of the major guilds of the city, and thenceforth began to assume a role of some importance in the political life of Florence. Distraction it may have been, but from the zeal with which he dedicated himself to civic affairs as well as from the persistent interest in political matters amply evident in the pages of the *Commedia,* we may conclude that it was a passion as genuine as his cult of the Muses and his devotion to Beatrice. One may legitimately suspect that had Dante been more fortunate in his political career he might have found it more rewarding than the arts; it is beyond doubt that had it not been for the failure of his political life we should never have had the *Commedia*. Yet it should be noted that, in spite of political and domestic preoccupations, the period between Beatrice's death and the poet's exile, according to the *Convivio*, was the time when he dedicated himself most intensely to philosophical studies, frequenting, as he tells us, the schools wherein philosophy was expounded — possibly those of the Dominicans in Santa Maria Novella or those of the Franciscans in Santa Croce. If Dante ever was a Franciscan — and some critics have seen a hint of such a possibility in the reference to the cord in *Inferno* XVIII — it must have been during this decade.

It was certainly at some time in this same decade that Dante lost the rightful path and fell into the dark wood of sin from which it was necessary for Beatrice to send Virgil to extricate him. We know from Beatrice's diatribe — there is, alas, no other word for it — on the summit of the Mount of Purgatory that the poet's wayward period occurred after her death; we may assume that Dante had become aware of the error of his ways and set his feet on the path of atonement somewhere around the ideal date of the vision, 1300. But what precisely was his sin? Some scholars, notably Barbi,[10] have seen in it nothing more than a preoccupation with earthly affairs to the exclusion of higher things, but Beatrice's words seem to imply something graver. One very persuasive theory is that the study of philosophy had sapped or threatened to sap the foundations of his faith. Something of the sort can be read into the *Convivio*, which for all its protestations of orthodoxy has a kind of pagan or at least freethinking savor. And this theory would be reinforced by Beatrice's references to "your school." Nor can it be denied categorically that Dante, shortly after the death of Beatrice, in his despair may have turned to a life of dissipation and sensual enjoyment. Beatrice's reference to a *"pargoletta"* ("chit of a girl"), taken literally, would indicate one or more unworthy love affairs. Boccaccio says that Dante, even in later years, was ravaged by the vice of lust, and his indulgent treatment of the sensual sinners, both in the *Inferno* and the *Purgatorio*, indicates a good deal of sympathy for that weakness. Furthermore, if the scurrilous *tenso* with Forese Donati is of this time (which seems likely although it cannot be dated, for it is clearly later than the death of Dante's father), a period the length of which is unknown, of loose language and presumably somewhat relaxed conduct is indicated. We know that during these years Dante fell into debt, for we have documentary evidence of his borrowing on three separate occasions.[11] I am inclined to think that both the theories of philosophical aberration and of loose living have some truth in them. If we assume that at some point in his studies Dante's faith in revelation had been shaken, such a crisis might well have been followed or accompanied by a yielding to the abiding temptations of the flesh. Vincenzo Pernicone postulates a "real experience" of "moral, intellectual and religious" aberration.[12] Such crises are common enough in youth, and it may be argued psychologically that the idealistic tension which attended his adoration of Beatrice and which is almost painfully evident in the *Vita Nuova* must have brought a reaction in its train. We cannot be sure of the kind of sin Dante fell into or precisely what years were given over to it, but we know that to him it seemed a period of grave spiritual peril and that it occurred sometime in the decade of the nineties.

Although the nature of his inner crisis is obscure, certain moments in his public life during this time can be dated. Just as Dante began to plan an active part in the political scene, the differences within the White party began to deepen. There had been rivalry ever since Campaldino, and it had centered primarily around the families of the Cerchi and the Donati. Both Vieri de' Cerchi and Corso Donati (the latter described by Compagni as "more cruel than Catalina"[13]) had become, through their own ambitions and the prominence of their respective clans, rivals for leadership in the city. As we have noted in Chapter 2, the Cancellieri feud was brought from Pistoia to Florence in 1296, and the Donati espousing the Blacks, the Cerchi took up the cause of the Whites. Dante, so far as we can tell from his actions and from the chronicles of the time, was strictly neutral during his active political life and was attached to neither faction. Events were to change his attitude, however, and even do away with his Guelphism, but at the outset he seems to have been among the few impartial and truly civic-minded citizens of the *"città partita."*

The chronicles tell us that from November, 1295, to April, 1296, he was a member of the special council of the *capitano del popolo*. In December, 1296, he participated in the *Consiglio de Savi*, whose task it was to set up the conditions for the election of the priors; and from May to September of the same year he was one of the Council of a Hundred, whose responsibilities were primarily fiscal. In 1297 he was a member either of the council of the *capitano del popolo* or that of the *podestà,* we are not certain which. In 1300 he was sent to San Gimignano with the purpose of strengthening Florence's federation of allies, and in the same year he was elected (for the two months from June 13 to August 15) one of the six priors. It was during Dante's incumbency, unfortunately, that the rivalry between the Whites and the Blacks, fomented by the partisan intervention of Boniface VIII, came to a head. Boniface had been seeking for some time to take advantage of the dissensions among the Florentines to bring the city under his control. In 1296 he had willingly heeded the plea of the nobles to take steps to prevent the possible recall of Gian della Bella, still understandably cherished by the people, and had gone so far as to threaten the city with excommunication if any such amnesty was offered the banished liberal. He had sent Cardinal Aquasparta to Florence in the following year to seek support in his crusade (as he called it) against the Colonna family. He had requested Albert of Habsburg on his election to the imperial throne to renounce his rights in Tuscany in favor of the church, and, on Albert's refusal, he had declined to recognize him as emperor and had arrogated to the papal authority all rights over Tuscany. In April, 1300, a plot by three Florentine bankers to turn the city over to the pope had been unmasked. The plotters were condemned during Dante's absence in San Gimignano, but it fell to his lot to be one of the priors to ratify their sentence, against the furious protests of the embattled pontiff. Concurrently the pope had again sent Cardinal Acquasparta to the town, ostensibly with the purpose of making peace between the Cerchi and the Donati. An outbreak of factional violence on St. John's Day caused the *Signoria* to send into exile certain leaders of both parties. Dante concurred in this action, even though among the banished was Guido Cavalcanti, his "first friend" — surely ample proof of the high impartiality which has been mentioned above. The *Signoria* persisting in its refusal to give Acquasparta the assurances he sought, the frustrated cardinal, following the orders of the pope, left Florence the following September after excommunicating the city and its magistrates. By this time Dante was out of office. He may have been a member of the group sent in November to Rome to ask for the raising of the interdict; at any rate he visited Rome, according to *Inferno* XVII, and it seems probable that he would have been chosen for the mission.

It is believed that Dante took part in the council of March 15, 1301, and spoke against the proposition to subsidize the projected reconquest of Sicily by Charles II of Naples. It is certain that he took part in the council of the following month, where in the discussion of the selection of the new administration he suggested that men of experience who were not prejudiced in favor of the papal claims should be chosen. He was a member of the Council of a Hundred from April 1 to September 30, and during that time was in charge of the widening and improvement of the Via San Procolo, where he owned some property. In June, 1301, he spoke before the council of the *capitano del popolo* and the Council of a Hundred, against the pope's request to lengthen by two months the services of Florentine troops whom he had hired to assist him in his campaign against the Aldobrandeschi. Dante's advice was not heeded, but we may assume that his speech did not go unnoticed in Rome.

It was during late summer of 1301 that the approach of Charles of Valois began to be a matter of concern to patriotic Florentines. This prince had been invited into Italy by the pope to aid his Angevin kin in the long-planned reconquest of Sicily, but Boniface had in mind other uses for his ally. In September, Charles being already in Anagni, the pope formally designated him "peacemaker" of Florence, and again, in two speeches in that same month, Dante called attention to the danger and urged immediate measures of defense. As Charles drew closer to the walls of Florence, the alarmed inhabitants, fearing that armed resistance might be their only alternative, sent an embassy of three citizens to the pope at Anagni. Dante was one of the three and possibly the head of the mission. This is the occasion of which Boccaccio tells that Dante, being chosen and fully aware of the delicate condition in which he was leaving the city, exclaimed: "If I go, who is left? And if I stay, who goes?" The embassy reached Rome towards the end of October; the pope, remaining at Anagni, assured him that his intentions looked only toward their peace, and sent two of the mission back to Florence, keeping Dante with him.

Meanwhile the *Signoria,* having received from Charles written and sealed guarantees that he would do nothing against the honor of the city or offensive to the municipal laws, allowed him to enter. As might have been foreseen, Corso Donati and the Blacks returned with him, bringing their creature Cante da Gubbio as *podestà*. Under his protection the *Parte Nera* began to take effective control of the city, paying off old scores as it did so. A new law was passed, enabling the *podestà* to review the actions of preceding magistrates. One of their victims was Dante; on January 27, 1302, following his prudent refusal to return and defend himself in person, he was accused of various misdemeanors, including barratry, extortion, and opposition to the pope, Charles of Valois, and the Whites. Dino Compagni specifically mentions him, stating that he was "ambassador at Rome" at the time.[14] He was tried and sentenced to two years of exile and permanent exclusion from public office. It should be said that no scholar has ever found any ground for taking seriously any of these charges. On Dante's persistent refusal to appear and accept his sentence, he was condemned along with fourteen other priors on March 10, 1302, to be burned to death should he ever fall into the hands of the commune.

The effect of this sentence was to make Dante a White; he had for all his basic impartiality no other choice. And with the Whites and the older exiles, the Ghibellines, he made common cause in the first years of his banishment. In 1302 he took part in a general council of White exiles, and in 1303 we find him in Forlì in the company of Scarpetta Ordelaffi, who was in charge of the White forces. It may be that at this time he first made his way to Verona to seek further aid from Bartolommeo della Scala. In both these years ineffectual attempts were made by the Whites to fight their way back to their home; in 1304 a ray of hope shone upon them when Cardinal Niccolò da Prato, sent to Florence by the new pope, made a sincere effort to secure the return of the exiles under peaceful conditions. One of Dante's letters reflects this hope and sets forth the conciliatory attitude of the offended exiles. The Blacks would have none of it, however, and on taking up arms again the luckless exiles suffered a crushing defeat on July 20, 1304, at La Lastra. But even before that unhappy day, Dante, disgusted by the ineptitude of his associates and perhaps not entirely at home in their partisan atmosphere, had left them "to make a party for himself," as he says in *Paradiso* XVII. The parting does not seem to have been a pleasant one, for Dante tells us, putting the words in the mouth of Brunetto Latini (*Inferno* XV, 70–72), that both Blacks and Whites thirsted for his death.

Scholars have found it impossible to plot save in a very fragmentary fashion the course of Dante's wanderings during the years of his exile. We may guess, from the reference to the "first refuge" in *Paradiso* XVII, that he spent some time at the court of the Scaligeri in Verona, either immediately after his sentence or after parting company with the Whites. It is thought that after that he accepted the protection of Gherardo da Cammino (the "good Gherardo" of *Purgatorio* XVI, 138) at Treviso, and maybe proceeded thence to Padua and Bologna. It is known that at some time in 1306 he was in Lunigiana, the guest of the Malaspina, for they designated him as their representative in the negotiations for peace with the Bishop of Luni which was ratified in October of that year. The laudatory reference in *Purgatorio* VIII to the pre-eminence of that house in affairs "of the purse and the sword" is testimony of the warm reception that Dante must have received from the family. Between 1306 and 1308 the poet seems to have been in Lucca, well received, we may argue from the reference in *Purgatorio* XXIV, 37, by a noble lady known to us only as "Gentucca." During this year he may have made his reputed journey to Paris. Barbi does not seem inclined to accept it, nor does Siro Chimenz in his authoritative summary of Dante's life, but both Boccaccio and Giovanni Villani mention it as a fact,[15] and Boccaccio also describes Dante's meeting at Lerici — presumably en route to Paris — with a Friar Ilario who received an annotated copy of the *Inferno* with instructions to present it in homage to Uguccione della Faggiuola. This meeting never took place, although *Purgatorio* III, 49 does indicate that Dante was at Lerici at some time.

According to Leonardo Bruni, it was during this early period of his restless peregrinations that Dante strove in every way by good conduct and good works to win permission to return to Florence; "to this end," adds Bruni, "he bent every effort and wrote several times not only to individual citizens in the city government but to the people as a whole, among others a very long letter beginning '*Popule mee, quid feci tibi?*' "[16] Although the letter has been lost, the close of the *Canzone on Justice* seems to contain something of the wistful and humble tone in which it may have been written. Most critics believe that it was during this period that Dante began the composition of the *Convivio* and the *De Vulgari Eloquentia;* no doubt these titles must be numbered among the "good works" mentioned above. Perhaps both were put aside for the same reason: the new hopes aroused in the poet's breast by the election of Henry VII as emperor, and the happy prospect of the restoration of law and order (and incidentally Ghibelline authority) in Italy.

In truth the prospect was promising. In 1310 Pope Clement V wrote from Avignon to the cities of Italy, inviting them all to welcome the new emperor as the great bringer of peace of which the pensinsula stood in such dire need. There is evidence that Dante and many of his contemporaries took the pope's words at face value and looked forward to a period of happy harmony between the princes of the church and state, that ideal accord of which Dante speaks in the *De Monarchia*, and which the middle ages forever longed for and never achieved. To Dante it must have seemed that his dream of return was nearing fulfillment, and, eager to speed the emperor on his way and re-establish justice in Florence, the exile put aside his early humility and became an articulate Ghibelline, an aggressive partisan of the emperor against his own fellow citizens. In October, 1310, as the emperor was about to enter Italy, Dante wrote a letter to the lords and peoples of Italy urging them to welcome their savior — the word indeed is not too strong, for Dante reports that on paying his homage to the emperor, to whose wandering court he at once betook himself, he heard within his heart the words *"Ecce agnus Dei qui tollit peccata mundi."*

The lamb soon had need of a lion's heart, for Henry's troubles began as soon as he reached Lombardy. In Milan he had to deal with the rebellion of the Torrigiani, and once that had been put down the cities of Cremona and Brescia rose against him. Behind them, giving them aid, stood Florence; the *Signoria* sent money to the rebels, appealed to Robert of Naples to intervene, and called on the pope likewise to check the imperial march. Such an attitude seemed to Dante downright impious, and in a letter of March 31, 1311, he excoriated his fellow citizens for their obduracy and their folly, predicting their downfall and extermination. In another, a few weeks later (April 17), he begged the emperor to raise the siege of Brescia and proceed forthwith to attack Florence, as the very root of the rebellion. Dante's fury, understandable enough, turned out to be a serious political mistake. The Florentines, alarmed and anxious to close ranks, offered in September, 1311, a general amnesty to the White exiles, but specifically excluded Dante. The emperor did in fact move to the assault of Florence in 1313 but had to turn away frustrated. Dante does not seem to have been present at the time of the siege, and so may be cleared at least of the charge of actually engaging in hostilities against his fellow citizens. His position had been made all too clear, however, and we can hardly blame the resentful Florentines for the hardening of their resolution to forbid his return.

The emperor's defeat at the gates of Florence was the beginning of the end of imperial hopes. Clement V (perhaps under French pressure, perhaps merely following a line of policy he had always intended to pursue) turned against Henry. His ally, Robert of Anjou, declared the imperial seat vacant and asserted that its privileges had now reverted to the church. Possibly if the emperor had lived he could have reversed the tide of ill fortune, but unhappily for the Ghibelline cause and Dante's hopes, the harassed monarch did not long survive his coronation. His coming and his probably sincere intention of giving Italy just and impartial government had fortified Dante's latent Ghibellinism, which in his later years became so intense that, according to Boccaccio, he would fly into a rage if he heard anyone speak ill of the Ghibelline party. It seems likely that Dante composed the *De Monarchia* at this time. This perfect statement of the Ghibelline position was written, as Ernst Kantorowicz, the biographer of Frederick II, indicates,[17] some fifty years too late, because, in the words of William A. Bowsky, Henry's foray "definitively discredited the medieval imperial solution to Italy's problems."[18]

We may easily imagine the depth of Dante's despair at the death of the emperor. It signified the hopelessness of any realization of his political theories and on the personal side the end of any possible hope of his return to his "fair sheepfold wherein he had slept as a lamb." But his spirit was unbroken, and a year after the emperor's death, on the occasion of the conclave which had assembled to elect a successor to Clement V, Dante addressed a letter to the Italian cardinals urging the election of a pope who would bring the papal seat back to Rome. In May, 1315, the Commune of Florence, in danger from the army of Uguccione della Faggiuola, stood ready to permit Dante's return, but on conditions which seemed humiliating to him. He wrote indignantly to a Florentine friend that this was not the way to return, but that if conditions not prejudicial to his honor and fame could be set he would accept them. By now, clearly, he had resigned himself to exile and had found in his own conscience and in his own work (for these were certainly the years of intense labor on the *Commedia,* whether or not it was begun at this time) consolation for his outcast state. It was well for him that it was so, because in November, 1315, after his rejection of the conditions proposed to him, on his persistent refusal to acknowledge any guilt on his part, he was again sentenced to death. At this time he was probably again under the protection of the youthful Can Grande della Scala at the court of the Scaligeri in Verona, where he presumably remained for some years, receiving the generous treatment that he speaks of in *Paradiso* XVII.

It is not certain when the poet left Verona to take up his final residence at the court of Guido da Polenta in Ravenna. This wealthy and generous kinsman of Francesca da Rimini seems to have made Dante's last refuge comfortable and consoling; the poet was joined by his two sons, Jacopo and Pietro, and his daughter, Antonia, who at his death entered a nunnery, taking the name Sister Beatrice. He was apparently well established in Guido's court when Giovanni del Virgilio invited him to Bologna to receive the laurel crown. Some scholars find evidence for believing that in Ravenna Dante gave public lectures, but this is not entirely certain. In 1319 he visited Mantua to hear a learned discussion on the question of the relative altitude of water and land on the earth's surface. A year later in Verona, in the presence of the clergy, he stated his own convictions on the matter. He was sent in the summer of 1321 by Guido Novello on a mission to Venice, and apparently he fell ill on his return and died the night of September 13, having just finished the final cantos of the *Paradiso.* The fact that at the time of his death these cantos had not yet been circulated is the kernel of truth underlying the poetic legend recounted by Boccaccio of the return of the poet's spirit to point out to his son the hiding place of the precious manuscripts. The poet was, as Villani tells us, buried with honors, and in the costume of the Franciscan order, in a little chapel near St. Francis' Church (at that time San Piero Maggiore).

❧ 4 ❧

Dante's Reading

DANTE is the most scholarly of poets, and many authorities have remarked that the *Commedia* is a synthesis of medieval learning. He was both an eager student and a disciple of the earlier schools of Romance vernaculars. The strongest and most easily detectible current that flows in his early work is the lyric stream whose fountainhead is the love cult of Provence, modified by Italian influences in the generation immediately preceding his own.

Provençal poetry begins with the eleven poems of William of Poitou (1071–1127). In William's work there emerges a concept of sexual love previously unknown in literature. The poet's attitude toward his lady is characterized by reverence, timidity, and awe, with occasional flashes of hope of successful courtship. The lady is almost unattainable, and the poet's worship of her is a source of torment and melancholy pride. "The True Lover desired not to conquer but to serve and to adore . . . he looked to his lady not for satisfaction but for blessedness."[1] In short, with the troubadours, romantic love is born. C. S. Lewis believed that the development of the concept of love that William and his followers celebrate represents one of the few changes in human sentiment on record; he reminds us too that this new attitude is still very much with us.[2] Indeed, the endurance of William's innovation suggests that it was not so much an invention as a discovery: Salvatore Battaglia says of him that he "translated one

45

of the human truths underlying every form of culture."[3] But the novelty of William and his successors lay not only in their theme; their verses too were from the beginning technically very complicated constructions, with meticulous metrical arrangements and severe rhyme patterns. They were regularly set to music and sung either by the poet himself or by a jongleur in his employ.

For both manner and matter, various origins have been suggested, liturgical, oriental (i.e., Saracen), heretical (Averrhoistic or Catharic). The worship of the lady suggests a kind of literary mariolatry; but the love celebrated, for all its refinement, was adulterous, and most of the old troubadours recanted before death. Certain metrical arrangements seem to spring from Moorish sources, but a good case can be made for the liturgical origins. Happily we are not so much concerned here with the sources of Provençal poetry as we are with what Dante found in it, and its considerable effect on his work.

It is not too much to say that Dante's Beatrice is clearly outlined in the lady of the troubadours. William of Poitou writes of his beloved:

> In her is all nobility
> And worth and valor, birth and fame
> And worldly joys themselves proclaim
> Liege vassals of her sovereignty;
> A man might strive a century
> Nor fairly favor of her claim.

> Let her but smile, the sick arise
> And madmen have their wits restored;
> Her frown is a death-dealing sword,
> A glance from her envirtued eyes
> May cast a king down from the skies
> Or from a churl creat a lord.

> Fairer than all the queens of old,
> Her peer has ne'er been seen nor sung
> In any new or ancient tongue;
> Keep her I will to have and hold,
> Through her my spirit is consoled
> And blood and flesh kept ever young.

Let her consent my wooing seal
And humbly will I homage pay
And gladly serve her night and day;
From prying eyes I will conceal
Our love, and with a grateful zeal
Her every wish I will obey.[4]

The unquestioning devotion, the jealous secrecy, the identification of the lady not only with virtue but with a kind of supernatural aura, are all present in full measure in the *Vita Nuova* and in many of Dante's other early verses, and all are constants of the Provençal *canso* or love poem. Peire Vidal, for example, speaks of his beloved in a manner strikingly suggestive of the Dante of the *Vita Nuova*:

Bona domna, Deu cug vezer,
Quan lo vostre gen cors remir.[5]

Fair lady, I think I see God/when I look at your
fair person.

And, among the hundreds of other passages that could be cited, are these lines from William of Montanhagol, one of the last of the troubadours, who proclaims, in language almost as idealistic as Dante's own:

Ben devon li amador
De bon cor servir Amor,
Quar amors non es peccatz,
Anz es vertutz que·ls malvatz
Fai bos, e·lh bo·n son melhor,
E met om' en via
De ben far tot dia;
E d'amor mou castitatz,
Quar qui·n amor ben s'enten
No pot far que pueis mal renh.[6]

Truly should lovers/with willing heart serve Love,/ for love is not sin,/rather it is virtue which makes the wicked/good, and the good are made better by it,/and it sets a man on the path/of doing good every day;/and from love springs chastity,/whence whoever devotes himself to love/cannot so do that he lives an evil life thereafter.

A reading of the *Vita Nuova* shows how deeply these attitudes are a part of it.

But the *canso* was not the only genre of the Provençal lyricists. Next in importance was the *sirventes,* which was, in substance, a nonamorous lyric, and usually satirical. It could have an immediate political objective, or it might contain more general social-philosophical commentary, usually on the decay of the times and the superiority of the past over the present. Guiraut de Bornelh and Bertran de Born, both of whom Dante admired, wrote verses of this nature, and Bertran in fact is celebrated for his battle songs (all with political purpose) and to a lesser degree for a more philosophical sort of poem. In the *sirventes "Be·m platz lo gais temps de pascor"* he writes of the glories of warfare as follows:

> I am happy when the skirmishers put to flight travellers with all their possessions, and I'm glad when I see pressing close on them a great body of armed men; and I rejoice in my heart when I see strongholds under siege and the ramparts broken and crumbling and the host on the bank which is protected all around by ditches and palisades bristling with sturdy stakes. . . . Maces and swords, gaycolored helmets, shields and all shall we see shattered and pierced once the press is joined, and we shall watch liegemen deal out strokes all as one man, whence the steeds of the slain and the wounded will wander riderless; aye, and once he has entered the melee no man of baronage will give thought to aught save splitting heads and limbs; better death than life to no purpose. I tell you neither food nor drink nor sleep has such savor for me as the moment when I hear the cry "Charge" on either side and hear likewise in the shadows the whinnying of riderless horses, aye and thereto the cry "Help, help" — and when I see the great and the small lie stricken in the green of the fosses and the dead asprawl on the ground, with pennoned shafts sunk in their flanks. My lords, I charge you, pawn castles and towns and cities ere you renounce the joys of warfare.[7]

Elsewhere Bertran sings (following a familiar theme of the middle ages and one frequently taken up by Dante):

Kingdoms there are but no longer true kings, counties but no counts nor barons; aye and marches still but no marquises: rich castles and fair dwellings still stand, but empty of true chatelains; wealth too is more abundant than ever, and there are banquets aplenty, but scanty is the fare — the fault of the avaricious rich.[8]

Subgenres of the *sirventes* were the *planh,* or lament, and the crusade song. Bertran's moving *planh* on the death of the Young King seems to have lingered in Dante's memory, because there is some trace of its gloomy hyperbolic overture in *Inferno* XXVIII, and the *planh* of Sordello for his lord Blacatz probably contributed to the portrait of Sordello and the depiction of the ensuing gallery of princes in *Purgatorio* VI and VII. Sordello's theme is that the heart of Blacatz was so full of valor that now that he is dead certain living sovereigns would be well advised to eat of it, since it may supply them with the virtue they lack. It is a mixture of the *planh* and the *sirventes* and, aside from its direct influence on Dante, is an example of the elaboration of genres characteristic of the end of the Provençal period.

Other traditional modes of composition were the *tenso,* a debate in rhyme, sometimes ending in an exchange of insults; the *alba* or dawn song; the *enueg* and the *plazer,* versified catalogues of things the writer found respectively repugnant and pleasant; and the *pastorela,* a dialogue, usually between an amorously inclined troubadour and a more or less reluctant shepherdess. It would not be hard to find echoes of many of these genres in the *Commedia.* But after the great or classical period of Bernart de Ventadorn and Guiraut de Bornelh, the verse of the troubadours tends to extremes and elaboration, both thematically and formally. The anticlerical satire in Peire Cardenal, for instance, is quite virulent; at the other end of the spectrum, religious verse (such as some of the poems of Folquet de Marselha) begins to loom large in the bulk of lyric production, and after the Albigensian war it dominates the literature. In addition to the adulteration of genres exemplified by Sordello's *planh-sirventes* we find such new creations as Aimeric de Peguilhan's *flabel* or nonsense verse, Guiraut Riquier's *serena* or twilight poem to correspond to the *alba,* and Peire Cardenal's metrical vehicle for satire, the *estribot.*

The private nature of the troubadours' vision and the excessive elaboration of their metrical arrangements tend to make their verses difficult to understand. Such great poets as Bernart de Ventadorn and Bertran de Born strive to make their meaning clear, but many of the Provençal poets, beginning with the pioneer Marcabru, deliberately cultivate an obscure style, in which a tortured grammar and an exotic vocabulary are employed to express (or disguise) concepts that are or at least are meant to be personal or unique. This hermeticism, which the poets themselves called the *trobar clus* (obscure style), was largely a manifestation of intellectual snobbery. Raimbaut d'Aurenga openly states that he would not care to have his songs appreciated by the simple-minded.[9] The most celebrated exponent of this school is Arnaut Daniel (fl. 1180–1200), who fascinated Dante. He is the inventor of the straitjacketed *sestina,* a master of odd and unusual verse forms, a coiner of fantastic images ("I am that Arnaut who harvests the wind, hunts the hare with the ox, and swims against the current"[10]), and a persistent collector of rare rhymes and rarer words. His patterns are all original, and many of them are antitraditional. His favorite theme is the essentially desperate solitude of love — not an especially novel theme in itself, but stressed with particular insistence. The following stanzas (translated by Ezra Pound) will give some idea of his verse.

> Sweet cries and cracks and lays and chants inflected
> By auzels who, in their Latin belikes,
> Chirm each to each, even as you and I
> Pipe toward those girls on whom our thoughts attract;
> Are but more cause that I, whose overweening
> Search is toward the Noblest, set in cluster
> Lines where no word pulls wry, no rhyme breaks
>   gauges.
>
> No culs de sacs nor false ways me deflected
> When first I pierced her fort within its dykes —
> Hers, for whom my hungry insistency
> Passes the gnaw whereby was Vivien wracked;
> Day-long I stretch, all times, like a bird preening,
> And yawn for her, who hath o'er others thrust her
> As high as true joy is o'er ire and rages.[11]

What Dante found appealing in Arnaut is clearly what charmed Ezra Pound six centuries later: the cult of the word and the obsession with technique. Dante felt a true affinity with Arnaut in these matters; he echoes something of his tone in certain of his lyrics, he imitates his *sestina* (and does him one better, producing a *sestina farcie*), and high on the last terrace of purgatory he has a fellow Italian poet hail Arnaut as the *"miglior fabbro del parlar materno"* (the "best wordsmith of the mother tongue"), presumably meaning the Romance languages in general.

Provençal literature had a short life. William of Poitou was born in 1071, and the last authentic troubadour, Guiraut Riquier, was a contemporary of Dante. Actually the virtue had gone out of the tradition before Dante was born. The social milieu which had nurtured the lyric was destroyed by the Albigensian crusade, but probably it was doomed anyway by its narrowness and rigidity. It had no popular base in the sense that the *chanson de geste* may be said to have had, and it had no true philosophical depth. It was, as Erich Auerbach puts it in his *Dante,* "inseparably bound to . . . the unique moment, to a particular and therefore short-lived society."[12] But before it died its message was carried widely abroad, to the *trouvères* of northern France, to the Minnesingers of Germany, to Spain, and most of all — and most importantly of all for the history of letters — to Italy.

It was carried there in two ways. A number of troubadours, such as Peire Vidal, Gaucelm Faidit, and Raimbaut de Vaqueiras, came in person to the courts of northern Italy, notably to Monferrato. Their example infected Italian intellectuals, and such poets as Lanfranc Cigala, Bonifazio Calvi, and Sordello, all Italians, wrote gracefully and effectively in the *langue d'oc.* Of more lasting importance is the fact that the courtiers of Frederick II, whose court, as Francesco Flora says, anticipated the renaissance,[13] were encouraged to take up the art themselves and in their own tongue. One may note as an item of historical-literary curiosity that the first Italian lyric verse recorded may well be the vernacular *ripostes* that Raimbaut de Vaqueiras puts in the mouth of his imaginary interlocutor in his fictitious *tenso* with a Genoese woman. But the versifiers of Frederick's entourage — the Sicilian school (so called, though many of the poets were not Sicilian) — are the true founders of the Italian lyric. Among them one may mention Rinaldo d'Aquino, Jacopo da Lentino (the inventor of the sonnet), and Pier delle Vigne, whom we have mentioned before as Frederick's secretary and who is so touchingly portrayed by Dante in the circle of the suicides. The

Sicilians were not especially original in their subject matter. It is still love, conceived of with an aristocratic refinement in which are perceptible the echoes of the feudal customs of the courts of Provence. Their verse, though not lacking in charm, is essentially derivative and hence somewhat arid. Their virtues, aside from serving as transmitters of a still vital poetic tradition, lie in their use of their own language and in the cultivation of a style studiously purified and disciplined for poetic expression. E. H. Wilkins says, "Their chief claim to fame is metrical; their *canzoni* set the pattern for the main Italian lyric form and one of them invented the sonnet."[14]

As the destruction of the Provençal socio-political complex had swept away the troubadour poets, so the death of Frederick signified the end of the Sicilian school. Wilkins more accurately describes it as "Frederician," for under the emperor's hand the school began and with his death it ended. But the seed had been planted and the flower was destined to bloom. The rising Guelph burghers took up where the Ghibelline courtiers left off. The next great name is that of Guittone d'Arezzo (1225–94). In his prolific verse there is much repetition of Provençal-Sicilian themes, a great deal of somewhat heavy moralizing (Guittone became a friar in middle age), and one memorable *sirventes* on the defeat of the Florentine Guelphs at Montaperti. To reread Guittone objectively today is to have, I think, considerable respect for the integrity of his inspiration and even for his craftsmanship. Dante seems to have been blind to his virtues, however. He always speaks of him disparagingly and seems to think of his own verse as something not only different from but positively opposed to Guittone's. A certain feeling of rivalry may have been at the root of Dante's disparagement, since Guittone must have loomed large in the poetic world of a young man attempting to win his spurs as a poet in 1285. Probably, like all young poets, Dante felt obliged to draw a line between his own work and that of an established predecessor. Or perhaps out of admiration for Guido Guinizelli he wished to stress the latter's excellence by contrasting him with Guittone.

Guido Guinizelli (ca. 1235–76), revered by Dante as a "father" (*Purgatorio* XXVI), did make an original contribution to the lyric tradition we have been following (though we may note that Guido had thought of Guittone as *his* "father"). Guido's originality lies in a further refinement of the troubadours' lady, reinforcing her identification with *gentilezza*, explicitly exalting her to a quasi-celestial height, and protecting her new status with the kind of intellectual subtlety that we might expect of a Bolognese jurist, as Guido was. Perhaps, looked at closely, what he has to say is not so very different from the run of troubadour poems, but it has both a philosophical gravity and a sophistication of expression that make its impact on Dante easy to understand. His most important poem (in a literal version) is as follows:

> Love seeks his shelter in the gentle heart
> even as bird in greenery of the wood:
> Nature made not the gentle heart before love
> nor love before the gentle heart;
> Straightway the sun came into being
> the light began to shine
> but not before the sun.
> So love takes his place in gentleness
> as fittingly
> as brightness in the glowing of the fire.
>
> Love's fire in the gentle heart obtains
> even as the virtue in a precious stone;
> no strength descends on it from any star
> before the sun gives it nobility;
> but once the sun, in virtue of his power,
> has drawn from it the baser element,
> the star then gives it worth.
> Even so the heart, which is by nature made
> pure, clean, and gentle,
> is by a lady moved as by a star.
>
> Love stands within the gentle heart
> for that same cause that makes the candle flame
> shine at its flickering tip, all bright and joyous,
> else there it would not stay, so proud it is.
> But wicked nature acts
> toward love, as water with its chill
> upon the burning fire.
> Love in a gentle heart takes residence
> in its congenial place,
> even as the diamond in lode of iron.
>
> The sun beats down daylong upon the mud,
> which base remains, nor does the sun lose heat.

"Gentle I am by blood," the proud man says:
Him liken I to mud and true worth to the sun.
For no one should believe
that gentleness past property of heart
pertains to rank inherited,
unless by virtue too the heart be gentle.
The water takes the ray
but heaven retains the splendor and the star.

God the Creator on Heaven's Intelligence
shines more brightly than the sun on mortal eyes:
she comprehends her Maker through the veil,
and moves to heed Him, turning heaven's sphere,
and so straightway achieves
blessed fulfilment of the righteous God.
So should fair Woman give
the truth which is resplendent in her eyes,
of her own gentle inclination,
to one who ne'er will seek to disobey her.

Lady, God will charge my soul
standing before Him: "How could you presume?
You passed through heaven, coming up to Me,
Having made Me an image of vain love;
to Me all praise is due
and to the Queen of all the worthy realm
through whom all error fails."
Then may I say to Him: "She had an angel's sem-
    blance,
as being of Your kingdom.
So if I loved her, be it not my fault."[15]

From Guinizelli our path leads directly to the second Guido,
who, in Dante's phrase, took from the first "the glory of our
tongue," whom Dante called his "first friend" (though he was to
deal harshly with him later under the stress of political pressure),
and to whom he dedicated his first book. Guido Cavalcanti's
fifty-odd compositions cover a great range. His most famous
canzone, "Donna mi prega," suggesting the darker side of love,
seems to have had relatively little influence on Dante, who probably admired his friend's verses more for their technical perfection
and polish than for their content. It seems quite possible that
the nature of Dante's admiration for Cavalcanti may even have
been more personal than professional, since Guido was well born,

well educated, elegant, and as important in the political as in the cultural life of his city. He was ten years older than Dante, and could hardly have failed to exert a strong fascination on his young admirer, but Dante in his maturity seems to have had reservations. He assigns Guido's father to the circle of the heretics in hell and, while he does allow the implication to pass that Guido is his intellectual equal, he hints that there is some element of perception (or perhaps orthodoxy) wanting in him. Commentators are not yet agreed as to the meaning of *Inferno* X, 63, but it is clear that Guido lacks some qualification to share Dante's journey and vision. This fault was not apparent, however, to the young poet of the *Vita Nuova*.

Many other poets were at work in the second half of the thirteenth century: Bonagiunta da Lucca (later to be met in purgatory), characteristic of the older generation; the outspoken Dante da Maiano; the more-than-outspoken Cecco Angiolieri of Siena; and the sybaritic Folgore da San Gimignano, chief among Dante's contemporaries. More intimately associated with him in later years was Cino da Pistoia, himself an exile like Dante, although a Black. When Dante has Bonagiunta refer to the practitioners of "the sweet new style" (*Purgatorio* XXIV, 58), it is not quite clear how many poets he wants to include in that group with him, but certainly Cavalcanti and Cino are among them. It is clear also that, whatever else may be meant by that elusive term, it signifies precisely what we find in the *Vita Nuova* — an intellectualized refinement of the Provençal theme of lady-worship, with meticulous attention to grace in expression.

The subjective lyric of the troubadours, with its subsequent development, was not the only literary current of the middle ages, nor indeed the only one known to Dante. It would have sufficed for the *Vita Nuova* perhaps, but the *Commedia* is fed by many other streams. For example, Dante shows considerable knowledge of Old French; his reference to the *Chanson de Roland* is quite specific (*Inferno* XXXI, 16–18), and his allusion to William of Orange in the *Paradiso* suggests familiarity with the later *chansons de geste*. The *De Vulgari Eloquentia* will give us further proof of his reading in other Old French writers, some of them, like Thibaut de Champagne, practitioners of the imported art of the troubadours. And we cannot forget that Francesca was reading of Lancelot when passion betrayed her.

It seems certain too that Dante was familiar with the *Roman de la Rose,* the great erotic-satiric poem of the thirteenth century, which was enormously popular throughout Europe, and which, in C. H. Grandgent's phrase, made allegory "king of poetry."[16] The *Fiore,* which some have attributed to Dante, paraphrases the *Roman de la Rose,* and it may be said that the mystic white rose of the *Paradiso* is a kind of answer or companion piece to the red rose of the lover. Barbara Seward has said of this celestial flower that it "embraces Mary, Paradise, grace and Divine Love, and at the same time reconciles these spiritual concepts with the hitherto opposing concept of terrestrial courtly love."[17]

Two other kinds of literature began to flourish in Italy in Dante's century: a didactic school of verse and the religious lyric, simple in expression, spontaneous, and endowed with a certain linguistic innocence, which must have been well-known to Dante. The greatest poet in the religious tradition was Jacopone da Todi (1236–1306), a passionate and enraptured Franciscan. As a poet he is the only man of his century to be compared with Dante for intensity of inspiration and purely technical skill. Although in language and form his verses have a rough-hewn quality, a closer study reveals the hand of a very self-conscious artist. It is odd that he did not find his way into the *Commedia.* Although now and again Dante's language shows traces of the popular vigor found in Jacopone's verses — in such lines, for example, as "Better for you had ye been sheep or goats" (*Inferno* XXXII, 15) and "Let them scratch wherever is the itch" (*Paradiso* XVII, 129) — he makes no direct allusion to the school. Perhaps he was aware of an intellectual gulf between them. Somewhat similar in diction, though very different in content since its message was grossly erotic, was the unique *Rosa fresca aulentissima* of Ciullo D'Alcamo, a southern Italian who, however, had little to do with the genteel lucubrations of the refined poets at Frederick's court.

As for the didactic school, Guittone d'Arezzo belongs to it to some extent, as does Dante's compatriot, Francesco da Barberino (1264–1348), author of the *Reggimento e costumi di donna,* containing prescriptions for the proper behavior of women, and the allegorical *Documenta amoris.* Ristoro d'Arezzo's *Book on the Composition of the World* (1282), full of astronomical lore, seems to have been of some use to our poet. Two members of the school were Dante's predecessors in the exploration of the other world, although there is no evidence that either of them influenced him. The Milanese Bonvesin da Riva wrote *The Book of the*

Three Writings, wherein the black scripture speaks of mortal life and the pains of hell, the red describes the Passion, and the gold dilates on the joys of paradise. A Franciscan friar, Giacomino da Verona, produced *The Heavenly Jerusalem* and *The Infernal Babylon.* Apparently, ideas about the nature of the other world were in the air. Another didactic work is the anonymous *Intelligenza,* of encyclopedic intent, allegorical and undisciplined but full of happy descriptive passages.

The most important of the didactic writers, so far as Dante was concerned, was Brunetto Latini (1220–95), whose life is almost a prefiguring of Dante's. He was also a Guelph and a man of scholarly and poetic interests who became involved in politics and was obliged to suffer exile. Happier than Dante in his end, he was able to return to Florence after the defeat of Manfred, and there he lived out a long and honored life among his fellow citizens. His *Trésors,* written in French, is a vast, encyclopedic study of all human knowledge, arranged in various categories; his *Tesoretto,* also informational, is an allegory of the poet's experience in this life. It contains, particularly in its opening lines, some motifs that look both backward to the *Roman de la Rose* and forward to the *Commedia.* For instance, after learning of the outcome of Montaperti (which would make him an exile), Brunetto says:

> Assuredly my heart was rent with great sorrow/
> thinking on the great honor/and mighty power/that
> Florence used to have/in the eyes of the whole world./
> So I, in such travail/brooding, head downcast/lost
> the main highway/and followed a side path/into a
> strange wood./Then, coming to myself again/I turned
> and gave heed under the mountain/and beheld a
> great number of strange animals/I cannot rightly say
> which. . . .[18]

To a modern the *Tesoretto* is dry reading: its short lines have a soporific effect, and the author is a little too eager to impress us with the variety and strangeness of his experience. But we may imagine that Dante found it fascinating. He may also have been familiar with other didactic literature besides the Italian. He probably knew the Provençal *Ensenhamen* of his beloved Sordello, whose most recent editor, Marco Boni, suggests that the *Ensenhamen* as well as the lament for Blacatz may have won Sordello his privileged position on the Mount of Purgatory.[19]

The middle ages were of course rich in Latin literature. Curtius contends that Dante was well versed in it but chose to suppress his knowledge of it, and he goes so far as to say that the poet "conceals his sources as he does his education. . . ."[20] I think that Curtius is writing polemically here. Such an unqualified statement will hardly stand against Dante's openly expressed indebtedness to Cicero and Boethius in the *Convivio* and to Virgil, Brunetto Latini, and Guido Guinizelli in the *Commedia,* to mention a few examples. But it is true, as Curtius states, that Dante never mentions Cicero's *Somnium Scipionis* (even though it is back of the Cacciaguida episode, central to the prophetic side of the *Commedia*), nor the *Commentary* on Virgil of Bernard Silvestris, nor the *Anticlaudianus* of Alan de Lille. Many scholars, however, are not as sure as Curtius is that Dante knew the last-named work.

Miguel Asín's work on the Islamic *Mohammed's Journey,* which resembles in many details Dante's design of the afterworld, suggests other sources of the *Commedia* about which the poet himself gives us no clue. Asín argues that the works of the Spanish Mohammedan mystic and poet Ibn Arabi, particularly his *Futuhat,* may have been the source from which Dante drew the general idea of the *Commedia,* and he mentions Brunetto Latini (who had lived in Spain) as a likely transmitter of such material to Dante.[21] It is possible that the legendary substance of Ibn Arabi and other Islamic poets had simply become current in Europe as a result of the crusades or trade with the East, or that what Curtius calls "the obvious points of contact" between Alan and Dante were not as direct as he assumes.

On the subject of sources of Dante's journey and vision, G. A. Scartazzini long ago warned us: "The form of a journey through the realms of the next world was suggested to him by the age in which he lived; the literature of that age is so full of visions of the future state, of descriptions in prose and poetry of the torments and the bliss of eternity, that it were childish to ask which of these visions and legends Dante may have known and used."[22] It remains true that there is a lacuna in Dante's acknowledgment of medieval Latin authors; even as in his history of the empire he skips from Titus to Charlemagne, so too his Latin authorities (literary as distinguished from purely philosophical or theological) seem to end with Boethius.

Dante's reading in classical Latin literature was voracious. Henry Osborn Taylor says that "he studied all the classic Latin authors available."[23] Edward H. Moore's exhaustive survey[24] lists them all, giving chapter and verse, where possible, for Dante's specific cases of indebtedness. In the preface to his volume, Moore speaks of his "amazement at the variety and extent of Dante's learning and studies." Of the classical poets Virgil looms largest and unquestionably had the greatest influence on him. Dante's statement in *Inferno* I that to Virgil he owes the style that has (already) brought him honor (he may have had in mind the *canzoni* of the *Convivio* cycle) is interesting as an indication of his early study of the poet. Virgil's remark in *Inferno* XX that Dante knew his *Aeneid* "tutta quanta" (i.e. "every bit of it") is overt testimony of what would be reasonably apparent to any reader of the *Commedia,* which has its essential genesis (at least in one sense of the word) in the sixth book of the Latin epic. Dante compares his own journey to the underworld with that of Aeneas (*Inferno II,* 32) and uses Virgil as one of the key symbols of his work. In the conventional interpretation of the allegory, Virgil is Human Reason ("because he is the singer of Universal Empire, not merely because he had had experience in Hell," as J. H. Whitfield shrewdly observes[25]), the counterpart to Beatrice, who is Revelation. For Dante he is, of course, a good many other things besides. It is not too much to see in him the "father image" so dear to the moderns, and certainly he becomes in political terms the personification of the empire, with all the reverent sanctions with which Dante surrounded that concept. He is also (considered purely as a writer) more than a poet: he is a veritable "sea of all wisdom" (*Inferno* VIII, 7), a prophet, and perhaps (as indeed the middle ages held him to be) a magician. "Leader, lord, and master" he is called — and we know how carefully Dante measures his words. He is also the "sun that heals all troubled vision." In truth, however much we may appreciate the theological propriety of his disappearance at Beatrice's advent, we share Dante's emotional distress. We might be troubled for other reasons too, for the *Commedia* is a different kind of poem without him.

Next to Virgil in Dante's esteem, if we may judge by the prominence of his role in the "sacro poema," is Statius, the epic poet of the Silver Age. Moore expresses his surprise at Dante's "enthusiastic, and as it appears to us, somewhat extravagant admiration of a poet whose prolix and often inflated style is the very antipodes of his own." (But Arnaut Daniel is a similar case; and

it must be said that Statius was well thought of in Dante's time.)
Moore cites nineteen quotations from Statius, all from the *Thebaid*
and the *Achilleid*, for the *Sylvae* were then unknown. Dante assigned Statius a high place in his work, making him a convert to
Christianity as a result of his reading of Virgil's "prophetic" fourth
eclogue. Dante and Virgil meet him in the *Purgatorio* at the
moment when his soul is released from its penance and he is
preparing to mount to heaven. He accompanies Dante the rest
of the way right through the terrestrial paradise. His allegorical
role, Moore suggests, is a kind of intermediate one between Virgil
(Reason) and Beatrice (Revelation), something "such as Human
Reason, generally enlightened by Christianity." Grandgent, following this interpretation, makes the interesting observation in
his edition of the *Commedia* that "in view of Dante's extraordinary
love of symmetry" we might have expected to find three guides for
three journeys, and ventures the surmise that in Dante's original
conception Statius may have been assigned an even more important role.[26]

Moore remarks very perceptively that the poets mentioned in
chapter 25 of the *Vita Nuova* as authorities for poetic practice
are precisely the same as the group that comes forth to meet the
pilgrim in the fourth canto of the *Inferno*.[27] Homer is present
merely as a quotation in the *Vita Nuova*, and Virgil is Dante's
companion, rather than simply one of the group in limbo, but in
both cases the same five great names are represented — Homer,
Virgil, Horace, Ovid, and Lucan.

Perhaps we may here digress briefly to cite other cases of
Dante's grouping of poets: the little procession of Virgil, Statius,
and himself through the upper terraces of the Mount of Purgatory is augmented by Bonagiunta da Lucca, and (very provoca-
tively, it seems to me, though unobtrusively) in canto XXVI,
where Dante seems to be recording his lineage, for a few golden
moments pagan Virgil, Christian but classical Statius, Provençal
Arnaut Daniel, and Bolognese Guinizelli stand with Dante on
the highest terrace of embattled humanity, on the threshold of
revelation.

But to return to the group in limbo. Of Homer, "sovereign
poet," Dante could have had no direct knowledge, though Scartazzini was willing to admit that he may have known the Greek alpha-
bet and the meanings of a few words[28] — more than some scholars
would concede. He knew a few quotations from Homer and Aris-

totle, he knew the "matter of Troy" from the current medieval romances, and he accepted Homer's sovereignty on authority. Horace, *"satiro,"* comes next, and Moore reminds us that "satirist" here really means "moralist," since Dante knew only the *Ars Poetica* (the middle ages in general had scant use for the Horace of the *Odes* and *Epodes* that we esteem so highly; the satires, known as "sermons," were more highly regarded, but Dante seems not to have known them). Ovid, the third in the group, was the most widely read Latin poet of the middle ages; he is, according to Moore, Dante's main authority for mythological matters. Apparently he knew only the *Metamorphoses,* and in this connection the passage in *Inferno* XXV where he challenges his Latin confrere on his own ground (translating a few of his lines in the process) is interesting. Lucan, last of the welcoming committee, seems to have been for Dante more historian than poet, and Moore mentions that Villani too thinks of both Virgil and Lucan as historians. From the *Pharsalia* Dante picked up many items of historical nature which served him well in the *Commedia,* and Lucan was perhaps responsible for our poet's high opinion of Cato. We may note in passing that he is another poet whose style, like that of Arnaut Daniel, might be called *"baroque avant la lettre."*

Dante's favorite prose historians are Livy and Orosius, yet there is considerable uncertainty as to how much of Livy he had actually read. Moore points out that all the documentable references are to the first books, and other allusions suggest that Dante may simply have assumed that "Livy" was a kind of general authority for early Roman history. From Orosius he derived many ideas basic to some of his theories: the argument, for instance, that Christ chose to be born under Augustus and so sanctioned the imperial government of Rome, and the belief that Titus was God's chosen instrument for avenging the Crucifixion. Furthermore, he seems to have taken many of his geographical ideas from Orosius (who in turn was indebted to Strabo). Charles Till Davis stresses an even more significant contribution: it was Orosius who first explicitly said that *populus christianus* and *populus romanus* could be interchangeable.[29] It is no wonder that Dante rewarded him with a place in heaven (though refraining from mentioning his name).

In the *Convivio* Dante tells us of his discovery of Cicero and Boethius, and indeed both loom large in his works. His admiration for the former was not quite as extravagant as Petrarch's was to be, because Dante saw a different Cicero. He shows no knowledge of the *Orations,* for instance. The works of Cicero which are for him most meaningful are the *De Senectute,* the *De Amicitia,* the *De Finibus,* and above all the *De Officiis,* which he found very useful in his moral design for the *Inferno.* It is of the *De Amicitia* that he speaks in the *Convivio;* of the *Somnium Scipionis,* which Curtius considers so important for the *Commedia,* Moore cites only one echo, although he too conjectures that Dante must have known the work.

Boethius is one of the Latin authors most quoted by Dante: Moore lists thirty-nine specific quotations (most of them in the "readily identifiable" category), and we know from the statement of the poet in the *Convivio* in what great esteem he held the *Consolation of Philosophy.* In view of the high reputation for wisdom and sanctity enjoyed by Boethius in the middle ages, it is not hard to understand Dante's admiration. The wrongful sentence passed upon him by the emperor probably gave the exiled Dante a feeling of kinship, and it has been suggested that Francesca's reference to "your teacher" (*"dottore"*) in *Inferno* V may indicate Boethius, whose Latin she seems to echo in the famous passage *"Nessun maggior dolore."*

Moore's work also brings out with convincing statistical clarity the extent to which Dante had immersed himself in the Bible (quoted or referred to more than five hundred times) and in Aristotle (more than three hundred times, half again as numerous as the quotations from Virgil). The figures for the Bible, though impressive, are perhaps not as significant as those for Aristotle, which are clear evidence of Dante's philosophical (and, one might say, rationalistic) bent. Dante was in fact very well read in the theologians and philosophers (the terms were almost interchangeable in his day) and the mystics, both those of the early years of the church and his near-contemporaries. First of all we must cite St. Thomas Aquinas (1227–74), the "Angelic Doctor" of the Dominican order, and nowadays the Catholic philosopher par excellence, but in his own time regarded as something of a revolutionary (indeed on certain occasions some of his pronouncements were held to be heretical). His great works are the *Summa Theologiae* and the *Summa Contra Gentiles.* The intention of his work was to bring the philosophical or rational truths which the Averrhoists had derived from Aristotle into harmony with Christian dogma. In the course of this effort he reexamined all phases of doctrine and created a coherent philosophy whose influence is still strong and vital in our day.

There has been in recent years considerable discussion of the extent and genuineness of Dante's Thomism. It was possible for Scartazzini to "affirm indeed that Aquinas had no more faithful disciple,"[30] and for Paget Toynbee to say that Dante was deeply indebted to the *Summa Theologiae* and that its influence is perceptible throughout his writings.[31] But in more recent years Dante's Thomism has been questioned. Étienne Gilson, focusing on the implications of the *De Monarchia* and Dante's political theory in general, finds him to be neither a true disciple of St. Thomas nor an Averrhoist.[32] (On Gilson's book Curtius remarks, almost gleefully, that it "finally rids us of the mistaken idea that Dante was a Thomist."[33])

It has been pointed out by various authorities that in the ultimate Christian relationship of the soul to God, Dante gives the will priority over the intellect — an "Augustinian," as against a "Thomistic," concept. Some, such as T. K. Swing,[34] have argued that Dante's supplements to his master's thought are such as to justify our thinking of him as a philosopher in his own right. One may grant all these points readily enough, but they call for some proper distinction. As a theologian and philosopher Dante was not faithful in every detail to St. Thomas. As a human being and an intellectual of the late middle ages he probably felt himself attracted to both the rational and the mystically contemplative, as indeed most Christians still do. But when we consider the cultural impact of Thomism, with its effort to bring the classical ethical system into harmony with revealed truth, its respect for reason, its willingness to give this poor mortal world of ours its due, its all but revolutionary "freedom" in the interpretation of traditional authority, we can see at once that it is of the essence of the *Commedia*. Henry Osborn Taylor puts it very well: "Dante is akin to both these men [Bonaventure and Thomas], but when he thinks, more frequently he thinks like Thomas, and the intellectual realization of life is dominant with him."[35] Without the mystical element we should have had a very different *Commedia;* without Thomas we should have had none at all, as Zingarelli observed many years ago. And even Gilson concedes, with many caveats, that "Dante's attitude to philosophy actually presupposes the existence of Thomism."[36]

For the work of St. Thomas the way had been prepared by his

master, Albertus Magnus, who was born in 1193, joined the Dominican order in 1223, taught at Paris and Cologne, and not only made the works of Aristotle available for the first time to his contemporaries but carried out his task of interpretation with a combination of respect and discrimination which is of the essence of Thomism. Albertus was also, with all reservations made for the limitations of his time, a scientist, with acute curiosity about the world around him. St. Thomas became his pupil in 1245 and maintained an intimate and cordial relation with him as long and as faithfully as his own career permitted. Taylor suggests that the association of these great scholars was similar to that of Plato and Aristotle, and goes on to say: "Thomas, dying, left Albert to defend the system that was to be called 'Thomist,' after him who constructed and finished it to its very turrent points, rather than 'Albertist,' after him who prepared the materials."[37] Dante shows great familiarity with Albert's works, particularly in the *Commedia*, and, as is his wont, indicates his indebtedness by placing him in the heaven of the sun, where his great pupil, properly and poetically, presents him to the pilgrim.

Thomas' "ring," it may be convenient to note here, includes other authorities to whom Dante felt indebted either for information or direction: aside from Orosius there are Gratian, who composed an important textbook on canon law; Peter Lombard, author of a theological manual known as the *Sententiae;* Solomon; Dionysius the Areopagite, the putative author of *The Celestial Hierarchy,* from which Dante got much of his information about angels; Boethius; Isidore of Seville, compiler of the widely read *Etymologies;* the Venerable Bede; Richard of St. Victor, author of *On Contemplation;* and Siger de Brabant, whose doctrines had been combated by St. Thomas and later pronounced heretical. One would have expected to find Richard and Dionysius in the other ring (of St. Bonaventure and the antirationalists), and the inclusion of Siger has baffled most commentators. Gilson suggests that he may represent "the doctrine of the mutual independence of philosophy and theology,"[38] with which our poet (no true Thomist in this regard) had some sympathy.

If Thomas and Albert are the principal rational philosophers on whom our poet drew, the mystics are no less well represented. We may follow Dante in first mentioning St. Bonaventure (1221–74), the great Franciscan leader who is as it were Dante's co-host in the fourth sphere. Dante was familiar with his work *Itinera-*

rium mentis in Deum, and his role in the *Paradiso* is certainly as
much that of a representative of the extrarational or mystical
approach to illumination as it is that of the symbolic Franciscan.
The "Franciscan" ring presented by Bonaventure, and paralleling
Thomas' group, consists of two humble followers of St. Francis,
Hugh of St. Victor (much admired by Bonaventure) and Peter
Comestor, author of an analogical commentary on the Bible;
"Peter the Spaniard," i.e., Pope John XXI, the only contemporary
pope whom Dante puts in paradise, a logician; Donatus the gram-
marian; Rabanus Maurus, a biblical commentator; and two
prophets, Nathan and Joachim da Fiore. The last named is a
matching figure to Siger: the historical Bonaventure had condemned his doctrines even as St. Thomas had condemned those
of Siger, and the church had declared some of his works heretical.
But, as we have noted, his apocalyptic prophecies haunted Dante's
century. He was thought to have predicted the founding of the
Franciscan and Dominican order, the coming of the antichrist,
and eventually a new age of the Holy Spirit, to which Dante's own
oracular predictions of the Hound and the Dux seem to point.

Two other great authorities who might seem in some sense to
belong to the tradition of Bonaventure should have special mention. One is St. Bernard, founder of the Abbey of Clairvaux,
preacher of the second crusade (1147), and celebrated for his
mysticism and his devotion to the Virgin. Dante gives him a high
place in the *Commedia,* making him the last of his guides, and so
in a way ranking him above Beatrice; allegorically he would seem
to symbolize the mystic, intuitive perception of truth. St. Augustine, too, is a case apart, and may even be considered the fountainhead of the school represented by Bonaventure. Antonio Lubin
showed that the *Commedia* can be so read as to reproduce the
successive stages in the mystic ascent as laid down by Augustine.[39]
There are Augustinian elements easily perceptible in the *Convivio*
and the *De Monarchia,* and one can detect the Augustinian presence in the *Purgatorio* and the *Paradiso.* Yet for all that, he does
not have a great role in the *Commedia:* he appears only once,
somewhat mechanically assigned to a seat in the celestial amphi-
theater, a high place, to be sure, but in the context suggesting
that he is there more as a representative of the order than as a
Father of the Church. Dante has no interview with him as he has
with Benedict and Bernard and Peter Damian, nor is his life
recited with the detail expended on St. Francis and St. Dominic.

As especially useful to Dante on the purely informational side we may note the *Magnae Derivationes* of Uguccione da Pisa and the *Elements of Astronomy* of Alfraganus. He may have read Plato's *Timaeus,* and of course he was well informed about many classical figures to whose work he had no direct access, as his catalogues in the *Inferno* and the *Purgatorio* as well as other references attest. It is indeed sometimes hard to say whether Dante's acquaintance with an author is direct, through a *florilegium* (anthology), or through hearsay from another source. In considering his individual works we shall look more closely into specific sources. It is not always possible, either, to state when Dante read or studied any given author. It is, I think, worth pointing out that the writers quoted in the *Vita Nuova* are predominantly poets, along with one reference to Ptolemy, one to Aristotle's *Metaphysics,* and, of course, scriptural echoes. The mixture of prose and poetry suggests Boethius, but Dante first mentions him in the *Convivio.* Many of the mystics and theologians appear for the first time in the *Paradiso.* Dante's education began with poetry.

✽ 5 ✽

The *Vita Nuova*

THE *Vita Nuova* is a highly original work in concept, style, and substance. Nothing remotely like it had appeared in medieval letters, and it is not too much to say that it has remained unique through succeeding ages. It may be regarded, for those who are addicted to categories, as a fusion of the secular lyric tradition with the conventions and interests of scholastic philosophy. It may be seen as a renascence of the autobiographical impulse, dormant in European literature since St. Augustine. It is certainly one of the earliest examples since the classics of a coherent and carefully planned "book" in the modern sense of the word, where the reader feels from the beginning that the author has a definite story to tell, where the sense of an end — in the double significance of conclusion and purpose — looms large in the author's consciousness, and where the consideration for form and proportion is not merely perceptible but indeed forced on the reader's attention.

The work is also highly characteristic of Dante, in that while the narrative line is simple enough, the implications of allegory, the carefully planned ambiguities, and some quite strategic reticences open the way to a great variety of interpretations. Before considering the puzzles and obscurities with which Dante has so obligingly given a foothold to the more enterprising commentators, let us survey the contents of the little book.

67

"In that part of the book of my memory," Dante says in chapter 1, "before which little could be read, is found a rubric which saith: *Incipit Vita Nuova.* Beneath which rubric I find written the words which it is my purpose to copy in this little book, and if not all, at least their substance."

After this brief introduction he proceeds in chapter 2 to his first meeting and immediate falling in love with Beatrice, when they were both nine years old. At the sight of her his "vital spirit dwelling in the most secret chamber of the heart" trembled and said: *"Ecce Deus fortior me, qui veniens dominabitur mihi"* ("Behold a God stronger than I, who, coming, will master me"); "the animal spirit dwelling in the high chamber whither all the spirits of sense carry their perceptions" said, addressing especially the spirits of sight: *"Apparuit jam beatitudo vestra"* ("Your beatitude has now appeared"); and the "natural spirit, which dwells in that part where our nourishment is absorbed," began to weep, saying: *"Heu miser! quia frequenter impeditus ero deinceps"* ("Woe is me, for henceforth I shall often be disturbed"). From this time on he looked for Beatrice frequently.

The next chapter is devoted to the meeting between the two which occurred nine years later, at the ninth hour of the day, and a dream which this meeting inspires. At their meeting, Beatrice, walking between two somewhat older women, is dressed in "purest white," and for the first time in their acquaintance she speaks to him.

In his dream a flame-colored cloud appears before him "wherein I discerned the figure of a Lord of fearful aspect," who is, of course, Love. Love had a joyous air, and though he spoke at length, Dante understood only the phrase *"Ego dominus tuus"* ("I am your Lord"). Love carried a sleeping figure, whom Dante recognized as Beatrice, and in his hand he held Dante's heart, in flames. Love awakened the lady and bade her eat of the heart. She obeyed, though fearfully, Love's joy turned to tears, and he ascended heavenward with the lady.

Dante's emotion breaks his sleep, and awakening he notes that the vision has appeared at "the first of the last nine hours of the night." He decides to write a sonnet in which he will ask the poets of the time for their interpretation of the dream. He inserts at this point the sonnet *"A ciascun' alma presa e gentil cuore"* ("To every captive soul and gentle heart"), which reproduces the substance of his vision; it is followed by a paragraph indicating its divisions and the content of each division. He remarks that many poets answered his sonnet, including Guido Cavalcanti, whom he calls "first among his friends." This exchange was the beginning of their friendship. The true meaning of the dream, Dante concludes, was not then seen by any but is now clear to all.

In chapter 4 Dante describes his lovesickness. The forebodings of the "natural spirits" ("Woe is me, for henceforth I shall often be disturbed") appear to be justified, because, from thinking too much about Beatrice, he grows frail enough to disturb his friends, to whom he admits that he is in love, but not with whom.

Chapter 5 describes an occurrence common in Italy even today: Dante is looking at Beatrice in church ("where the words of the Queen of Glory are being heard"), and another lady, assuming that his glance is meant for her, looks back at him. Her belief is shared by other observers of the incident, and Dante makes her "the screen of the truth" for some years. He says that he wrote poems for her which will not be included in the *Vita Nuova* except as they also refer to Beatrice. (Some of these are doubtless included among the *Rime;* see the following chapter.) Dante recalls that at this time he composed a *sirventese,* mentioning the names of sixty of the most beautiful ladies of the city, and that Beatrice's name would fit in only if placed ninth in the list.

In chapter 7 the screen lady is obliged to leave the city, and Dante is dismayed at losing the protection she has afforded him. Since people might guess the truth if he does not seem to be moved by her departure, he says he "uttered some lamentation" in a sonnet, wherein Beatrice is the occasion of certain words. The sonnet *"O voi che per la via d'amor passate"* ("O ye who pass by on love's way"), followed by an analytical exposition, is included at this point, and Dante calls attention to the fact that the first words are from Jeremiah: *"O vos omnes qui transitis per viam."*

Shortly after this (chapter 8), another young woman of the city, who has been a companion of Beatrice, dies, and Dante shares in the general grief. He composes two sonnets for her: *"Piangete amanti, poi che piange amore"* ("Weep, ye lovers, for Love weeps") and *"Morte villana di pietà nemica"* ("Churlish death, foe of pity"), which he inserts here, adding the customary analysis.

Not long afterward (chapter 9) Dante leaves the city, unhappy since he is away from Beatrice, and as he grieves he fancies that Love appears, dressed as a pilgrim. Dante imagines that Love tells him that he has come from the screen lady, who will never return, and that he will give "the heart I made thee for her" to another screen lady, whose name he tells Dante. Bidding Dante to report their conversation, but in such a way as not to reveal the true state of affairs, Love vanishes. The next day Dante composes the sonnet *"Cavalcando l'altro ier' per un cammino"* ("Riding the other day along the road"), which tells of the meeting. The usual analysis follows.

On his return (chapter 10) Dante seeks out his second "screen," and his devotion to her becomes so conspicuous that Beatrice will not speak to him.

Chapter 11 is devoted to the effect of Beatrice's salutation upon him. He says that by the mere hope of her wondrous salute, a flame of charity would possess him which made him forgive any who had offended him. At her approach a spirit of love destroyed all the senses but sight, so that anyone wishing to know Love could do so merely by observing the tremor in his eyes. His body, under the absolute domination of Love, would move like an inanimate thing. Clearly, then, he concludes, his beatitude — which often surpassed his capacity to receive it — resided in the salute of Beatrice.

He cries himself to sleep in chapter 12, because Beatrice will not speak to him, and dreams that Love, in the semblance of a pensive youth dressed in white, says to him: *"Fili mi, tempus est ut praetermittantur simulata nostra"* ("My son, it is time to put aside our pretenses"). As the poet looks at him, Love weeps, and, being asked the reason, replies: *"Ego tanquam centrum circuli, cui simili modo se habent circumferentie partes; tu autem non sic"* ("I am as the center of a circle, distant equally from all parts of the circumference; but thou art not so"). Asking for an explanation of this obscure sentence, Dante receives the answer, "Ask no more than may be for thy good." Love then tells him that Beatrice no longer greets him because she has heard that the second screen lady has suffered some annoyance on his account. Love counsels Dante to write a poem to Beatrice, avowing his long devotion to her and appealing to Love himself as witness. He cautions him not to address the lady directly, nor to send the poem to her without Love's escort. He also says that the poem is to be "adorned with sweet music." Herewith he vanishes, and Dante wakes, to note that the vision had occurred at the ninth hour of the day. Before leaving his chamber the poet writes the poem *"Ballata, i' voi che tu ritrovi Amore"* ("Ballade, I would have you seek out love"), which is set down here and followed by an analytical division.

After the dream, in chapter 13, Dante finds himself tormented by conflicting thoughts, of which four seem more troublesome than the others: "the lordship of Love is good since it draws the mind of his followers from all evil things"; "the lordship of Love is not good since the more faithful his servant is, the greater suffering Love asks of him"; "the name of Love is so sweet that his actions must in most things be sweet too, for 'names are the consequences of things' "; and that Beatrice is not as other ladies, with a heart to be lightly moved. He brings these reflections together in the sonnet *"Tutti li miei pensier parlan d'amore"* ("All my thoughts speak of love"), which he then analyzes.

Chapter 14 tells of a wedding party. In the midst of the festivities Dante is overcome by a strange tremor. He sees all his senses destroyed but sight, which is replaced by Love. The other guests are amazed, and, talking with Beatrice, begin to make sport of the poet. A friend leads him away, and asks him what troubles him. Dante, his senses restored, replies: "I had my feet in that region of life beyond which one cannot go with intent to return." He goes home to his "chamber of tears," reflecting that if his lady knew his state she would have compassion on him instead of mocking him. He puts this thought into the sonnet *"Con l'altre donne mia vista gabbate"* ("With the other ladies you deride my aspect"), without the usual analysis, stating that the divisions are clear enough. He adds, however, a rather cryptic remark about the "dubious words" in the prose preceding the sonnet, meaning such concepts as "Love slaying his senses." Those who are not Love's vassals, says Dante, could not understand such language while those who are have no need of explanation.

Chapter 15 consists of a sonnet, *"Ciò che m'incontra nella mente more"* ("What happens to me vanishes from mind"), and an analysis of it. The sonnet is occasioned by the paradox of the poet's love: how can he wish so much to see her, when seeing her reduces him to such a sorry state? A "humble thought," according to the sonnet, answers that the recollection of her beauty is strong enough to destroy the memory of its effect.

Other reflections on his condition follow in chapter 16: how he would often grieve at Love's treatment, how Love overcame him so as to leave him no thought other than of his lady, how when he went out to look at her, the sight of her would inevitably complete the destruction wrought upon him by love. These thoughts are set forth in the sonnet *"Spesse fiate vegnonmi a la mente"* ("Many times there come to my mind"), followed by a division.

The next three chapters mark an epoch in Dante's thought, at least in this book: the transition from the conventional tradition of courtly love to a mystical, apocalyptical atmosphere, previously unknown in the secular lyric. Dante indicates the change by saying that after writing the sonnets in the previous chapters he intended to say no more, but now he finds that he must continue, taking up "new and nobler matter." He explains it in the context of courtly love, by describing a meeting with a group of ladies who know the secret of his love for Beatrice, one of whom asks him to explain the nature of his strange love, which does not permit him to look upon his beloved. He tells her that the goal of his love was once his lady's salutation, but since she no longer greets him, Love has placed his blessedness in what cannot fail him: words that praise Beatrice. The lady points out that such has not been the tenor of his verse up to now, and Dante leaves in some confusion.

He resolves that henceforth the praise of Beatrice will be the only burden of his song, but the loftiness of the theme causes him to remain silent for some time. Inspiration in the form of a first line finally comes to him as he strolls beside a stream. He returns to the city, and having "pondered for some days," begins the composition of a *canzone*, the first poem dealing with the "new and nobler matter." It marks the turning point in the work, and a new phase in his spiritual and poetic development. It begins *"Donne ch'avete intelletto d'amore"* and should be read in full:

> Ladies, ye who understand love,
> I would speak with you of my lady,
> not that I think to exhaust her praises,
> but rather to relieve my mind in speech of her.
> I say that, as I think upon her worth,
> love makes itself so sweetly felt within me,
> that, if I did not then lose courage,
> I would, in speaking, cause folk to fall in love.
> I wish not to speak so loftily

that I should become cowardly through fear;
but rather I will treat of her gentle state
lightly in relation to her,
with you alone, ladies and damsels, versed in love,
for it is not a matter to speak of with others.

An angel, calling out within God's mind,
says, "Sire, in the world there can be seen
a miracle in act, which issues forth
from a soul whose splendor reaches up to here."
Heaven, which has no other lack
save having her, requests her of its Lord,
and every saint asks grace of this favor.
Pity alone defends our side;
so God speaks, having my lady in mind:
"My beloved, suffer now in peace
that your hope may remain as long as pleases Me,
there where there is one who is destined to lose her
and who will say in hell: "O ill-born,
I have seen the hope of the blest."

My lady is desired in highest heaven;
now I would have you know of her virtue:
I say, whoever wishes to seem a gentle woman,
let her go with my Lady, for when she passes by,
into base hearts Love casts a chill,
so that their every thought freezes and perishes;
and whoever would endure to stand and see her
would become a noble thing or else die.
And when she finds anyone who is worthy
to behold her, he experiences her virtue,
for what she gives him falls out to his welfare
and makes him so humble that he forgets any offense.
Further, God has conceded her yet greater grace:
none who has spoken with her can come to a bad end.

Love says of her, "A mortal thing,
how can it be so fair and so pure?"
Then he looks upon her and within himself he swears
that God must mean to make of her something new.
Color as of pearls she has, in such form
as is fitting for a woman, not beyond measure;
she is the fullness of good that nature can create;
beauty is proved by her example.

From her eyes, whichever way she turns them,
come spirits afire with love,
which wound the eyes of whoever looks upon her
and so penetrate that each one reaches the heart;
you may see love depicted on her face
whereon no one may look with fixed gaze.

Canzone, I know you will go your way speaking
with many ladies, when I have sent you forth.
Now I admonish you, since I have raised you
as a young and simple daughter of love,
that wherever you go, you say in entreaty:
"Show me where I must go, for I am sent
to her with whose praises I am adorned."
And if you would not waste your time
do not stay where there are churlish folk;
strive, if you can, to be open
only with ladies or with a courtly man,
for they will send you on with expeditiousness.
You will find Love with my Lady herself;
commend me to him as is your duty.

This ode is followed by a very long analysis in which Dante observes that the nature of the poem calls for more subtle division and apologizes for not making his analysis even more detailed.

The ode becomes so well-known that a friend asks Dante for a definition of love. He supplies it in the following sonnet, *"Amore e 'l cor gentil son una cosa."* No prose summary of its contents is appended, but the divisions are indicated. (chapter 20)

Love and the gentle heart are the one thing,
as the sage puts down in his verse;
and so one dares to be without the other
as a rational soul without reason.
Nature makes them when she is love-inclined,
Love for the lord and the heart for his dwelling,
wherein sleeping he reposes
sometimes for a short while, sometimes longer.
Beauty then appears in a virtuous woman
so pleasing to the eyes that within the heart
desire of the pleasing thing is born,
and lasts so long therein
that it awakens the spirit of Love.
And like effect a worthy man has on a woman.

Chapter 21 consists of a digression on how his lady's glance could awaken love even where it did not exist potentially, and a sonnet on the subject, *"Ne li occhi porta la mia donna Amore"* ("My lady bears love in her eyes"), followed by the usual division.

Shortly after this, Beatrice's father dies, and chapter 22 deals partly with events that occur at his funeral. Dante hears Beatrice described as appearing so wretched that anyone looking at her must die of pity, and himself described as one who had looked at her. These comments inspire two sonnets cast in the form of a conversation: *"Voi che portate la sembianza umile"* ("Ye who have the appearance of humility") and *"Se' tu colui c'hai trattato sovente"* ("Art thou he who has so often treated").

Chapter 23 contains an account of a dream that Dante has a short time after the funeral. He falls ill, and on the ninth day of his illness thoughts of Beatrice and of the fragility of his own life occur to him at the same time. They make him realize that Beatrice, like her father, must die, and at this point his dream or delirium occurs.

Faces of "disheveled women" prophesy his death, and other "terrible faces" cry out that he is already dead. The sun dims, and stars that look as though they were weeping appear; birds fall dead, and the earth shakes. A friend tells him that Beatrice is dead, and he describes weeping real tears in his delirium.

He sees angels carry a white cloudlet to heaven with them. He looks at Beatrice's body while it is being covered with a white veil, noticing the humbleness of her face, as though she were "looking upon the fount of peace." He calls on Death, who must now himself be gentle because he dwells in such a gentle person. He returns to his room and weeping says: "O soul most beauteous, how blessed is he who beholds thee."

These words are audible, and his sister, who is watching at his bedside, thinks that he is lamenting because of his illness. She weeps, and the other ladies in the room dismiss her and awaken Dante. He wakes saying, "O Beatrice, blessed be thou," but not clearly enough to be understood by the ladies. He tells them of his dream but not of Beatrice's part in it, and when he recovers from his illness he puts the episode into the *canzone* *"Donna pietosa e di novella etate"* ("Compassionate lady of tender years").

In chapter 24 Love tells Dante to bless the day he captured him, and Dante sees Giovanna, Guido Cavalcanti's beloved, called

Primavera (Spring) because of her beauty, approaching him, followed by Beatrice. As they pass, Love tells Dante that Giovanna's nickname was designed for this occasion and that it is a pun on *prima verrà* ("she will come first"), because she precedes Beatrice in this fantasy. Love reminds Dante that "Giovanna" is the feminine of "Giovanni" (John), the name of the forerunner of Christ, and he adds that Beatrice should be called "Love" too "for the great likeness that she bears me." The chapter concludes with the sonnet that Dante makes out of this episode, *"Io mi sentii svegliare dentro a lo core"* ("I felt awakening within my heart"), which he addresses to Guido Cavalcanti.

He then digresses to justify the personification of love, since it is not a substance but an accident.* This "excursus, which does not fit into the framework and is not very convincingly motivated," according to E. R. Curtius,[1] is highly significant for what it tells us of Dante's poetic preparation, his sense of artistic mission, and the seriousness with which he looked upon his work. Dante states that rhyming verse in the vernacular is suited only to love poems, since the first poet to write in the vernacular did so because his lady did not understand Latin. Dante puts the beginning of vernacular verse about a hundred and fifty years before his time (he was wrong by about fifty years) and contends that the first Italian versifiers were famous because they were innovators, not because they were good poets. Returning to the main point, he says that since the modern rhymers are the equivalents of the classic poets, they too should have the poetic privilege of using rhetorical figures and colors. He cites examples of personification from Virgil, Lucan, Horace, and Ovid. The Latin poets, however, always used their privileges with reason; hence the moderns who use rhyme should, in employing such figures, have in their mind some sense of what they are saying so that when the figure or color is stripped from their words some real meaning will remain. But that there are some who rhyme stupidly both Dante and his "first friend" know. (chapter 25).

In chapter 26 he resumes his narrative with a description of Beatrice's progress. "Clad in humility she would go her way admired, and many would speak of her as an angel and some as a miracle of God." So that others might know of her ennobling effect, Dante wrote the sonnet *"Tanto gentile e tanto onesta pare"* ("So gentle and so modest seems my lady"). Noting that it

---

* A philosophical term meaning an attribute which is not part of the essence of a thing.

needs no "division," he adds a sequel showing how honoring Bea-trice honors other ladies as well, together with a complete analysis of the poem. In chapter 27 Dante describes beginning another poem, "*Si lungamente m'ha tenuto amore*" ("So long a time has love held me"), which he breaks off on hearing of Beatrice's death. He quotes Isaiah at the beginning of chapter 28: "How doth the city sit solitary that was full of people! How is she be-come a widow, she that was great among the nations." He says that he will not treat fully of Beatrice's death for three reasons: first, it was not a part of the purpose of the book as set forth in the introduction; second, he would be inadequate to handle the subject; and third, it would not be appropriate to do so since he would be obliged to praise himself. He will, however, say some-thing of the relationship of the number 9 to Beatrice.

By the Arabian calendar, he continues in chapter 29, her death occurred in the first hour of the ninth day of the month, by the Syrian calendar in the ninth month of the year, and by the Julian calendar in the year when "the perfect number" was completed nine times in the century of her birth (1290). It seems probable that Dante says that 9 was "friendly" to her to indicate that the nine moving heavens* were in the most perfect accord at the time of her birth. More subtle reasoning, he adds, would show that Beatrice *was* a 9, for 3 is the square root and sole factor of 9, as the Trinity is the sole factor (maker) of miracles. Hence 9 accompanied her to show that she was a miracle whose root was in the wondrous Trinity alone. A subtler person, he concludes, might find an even subtler significance; this, however, is what he is pleased to see.

Chapter 30 only mentions a letter that Dante has written to the city government after Beatrice's death. All he tells us of it is that it begins with the passage from Isaiah quoted in chapter 29. The letter itself is not included because it is in Latin, and he and the friend to whom the *Vita Nuova* is dedicated have agreed that the book shall employ only the vernacular.

In the next chapters Dante describes trying to relieve his sor-row at Beatrice's death by writing the *canzone* "*Li occhi dolenti per pietà del core*" ("My grieving eyes for pity of my heart"), which is printed after the usual divisions, "in order that it might appear more widowed." After he finishes the poem, Folco Portinari, Beatrice's brother and his best friend after Guido Caval-

* See page 103 for an explanation of Ptolemaic cosmology.

canti, asks him to write something for a lady recently dead, not mentioning Beatrice. Dante understands what Portinari means, and writes the sonnet *"Venite a intender li sospiri miei"* ("Come listen to my sighs"), in which he expresses his own feelings while seeming to speak for his friend. Once finished, however, it seems inadequate, and so before giving it to his friend he writes two stanzas of a *canzone*, one in his friend's name, the other in his own, though at first glance both would seem composed by one person. This poem, *"Quantunque volte, lasso! mi rimembra"* ("How many things, alas, I do recall"), comes at the end of chapter 33.

Chapter 34 is merely a framework for a sonnet, *"Era venuta ne la mente mia"* ("Into my mind had come"), and its accompanying analysis. What happens in the chapter is that on the first anniversary of Beatrice's death Dante is thinking of her and drawing a picture of an angel, when he notices that there are people with him. He apologizes for not noticing them, saying, "Someone was with me just now." When they leave he writes the sonnet to them.

The next five chapters describe Dante almost falling in love with another woman, and finally contenting himself with thoughts of Beatrice. He sees the other woman looking pityingly at him from a window, and her compassion moves him to tears and inspires the sonnet *"Videro li occhi miei quanta pietate"* ("My eyes beheld so much compassion"). As he continues to see her, her paleness reminds him of Beatrice, and this makes him weep. The sonnet *"Color d'amore e di pietà sembianti"* ("Color of love and signs of pity") describes how he looks for her because of the relief his tears afford him. Again the analysis is omitted as unnecessary.

His self-pity begins to turn to love, and in the sonnet *"L'amaro lagrimar de voi faceste"* ("The bitter tears you shed") he upbraids his eyes for being disloyal to Beatrice. Next he begins to think that Love has sent the new lady to bring him peace, but this seems to disparage his love for Beatrice. He expresses the conflict between his memory and his sight in the sonnet *"Gentil pensiero, che parla di voi"* ("Gentle thought, that speaks of you"), which is a dialogue between his soul (reason) and his heart (appetite).

The conflict resolves itself when Dante has a vision of Beatrice as she was at nine, when they first met. He recalls his years of devotion, and returns to thoughts of Beatrice. He expresses the resolution and his sorrow in the sonnet *"Lasso! per forza di molti sospiri"* ("Alas! because of many sighs").

Soon after this (chapter 40), Dante sees a group of pilgrims on their way to Rome. He feels that if he can detain them and tell them of the grief of the city (being foreigners they probably know nothing about it) he can make them weep, and on this theme he writes the sonnet: *"Deh peregrini che pensosi andate"* ("Say, pilgrims who go sadly on your way"). Here again he omits the formal division, and instead discusses the sense of the word "pilgrim" and its distinction from "palmers" and *"romei"* (pilgrims going to Rome).

When two noble ladies ask him for some of his rhymes, he sends three sonnets, including the one which concludes the *Vita Nuova*. This sonnet should be read in Dante's own words:

> Beyond the sphere of widest gyre
> passes the sigh that goes forth from my heart;
> a new intelligence, which Love
> weeping puts into it, draws it ever upwards.
> When it has come where it desires to be,
> it sees a lady, who receives honor
> and light to such degree that for her splendor
> the pilgrim spirit looks upon her.
> It sees her in such state that when it tells me of it
> I cannot understand, so softly does it murmur
> to the grieving heart which makes it speak.
> I do know that it speaks of that gentle one
> because it often recalls Beatrice,
> so that I understand it well, my ladies dear.

A final paragraph hints at a great work in preparation which we would like to think is the *Commedia*. (chapters 41–42)

As is apparent from the summary, the *Vita Nuova* is a work *sui generis*. It is worthy of study for its own special qualities as well as for the light it sheds on the young Dante and for its relation to the *Commedia*.

That Dante, a youth of the lesser nobility, the leisure class in thirteenth-century Florence, should at an early age turn to verse-making is hardly unusual, and, as he tells us in chapter 25, rhyming in the vulgar tongue was nothing new. As far as the early poems in the book are concerned, the attitude toward the beloved is purely traditional, as old, basically, as William of Poitou, although refined by intervening generations of Provençal and Italian poets. Even the grafting of scholastic concepts on to this courtly plant was common practice among Dante's immediate predecessors. So, like many others whose names have come down to us and many more of whom we have no record, our poet made love rhymes to ladies whom his fancy adorned with the virtues appropriate to the cult, and he cast his verses in the lyric-intellectual idioms of the day.

That there was more than one lady in Dante's youthful shrine seems clear from his own artifices. Minimized, subordinated, metamorphosed as they are, yet the screen ladies, the lady who dies, even some of the sixty of the lost *sirventese* must have served at some time or other as the object of Dante's adolescent devotion. Beatrice, we may assume, is the last in the series (this does not necessarily mean that the poet's tale of a childhood meeting is to be rejected), and she captures his sensitive imagination at a time when a certain maturity makes it less inclined to wander. At the height of her ascendancy, at a time when she is the only woman in his life, Beatrice has the good fortune to die. Henceforth she will be unchallenged, and the poet will confirm his allegiance by making it, as it were, retroactive. Wishing to immortalize her and the devotion which he has now persuaded himself has been constant since his infancy, he conceives the notion of selecting from his youthful verses some which may not be unworthy of her and which, whatever their original inspiration, seem to deal with her or with events associated with her in his *via amoris*, making a memorial volume of his love. Since he is a young intellectual as well as a young poet, the prose accompaniment affords him the opportunity of giving to his rhymes a consistency which of themselves they would not have, and allows him to display his erudition.

To a modern reader the action of the *Vita Nuova* may seem unexciting; Francesco De Sanctis indeed found it *qua* story "not very interesting, mixed as it is with artificial and cold pretences."[2] Yet the form the little book takes is new in western literature, and the treatment the poet accords himself (the truly central figure of the drama) no less than his lady is original and arresting. The idea of putting verses together in a chronological order, with a story to tell — and his own story too — is something new and daring. To be sure, Dante could have found the mixture of poetry and prose commentary of a narrative nature in a number of noteworthy predecessors. The most famous example of a medieval work of this nature is *Aucassin and Nicolette;* it seems, however, an unlikely source, and we do not know that Dante ever read it. We do know that he read the *Consolation of Philosophy* of Boethius, for he tells us so in the *Convivio* — and he read it in the period immediately following the death of Beatrice. We know too that he was familiar with the Provençal poets whose works were commonly read in *chansonniers,* in which the productions of individual authors would be preceded by the appropriate *vida* in prose and interspersed occasionally with prose *razo* explaining the circumstances of composition of a certain poem and invariably preceding the poem thus illustrated. Alfredo Schiaffini calls attention to Dante's use of *ragione,* the italianized form of the word *razo,* in exactly the sense of prose explaining the occasion of a poem;[3] years ago, Pio Rajna suggested Dante's specific indebtedness to a manuscript of Bertran de Born's poems.[4] On the other hand, the *Vita Nuova* is closer to the *Consolation of Philosophy* in its nature and level, and, like it, is written in the first person. Perhaps both of these models had their influences; Dante may well have found the usage of the *chansonniers* appropriate to his purpose. He speaks of a "rubric" in his opening lines, as if to give the whole *Vita Nuova* the character of a chronicle set forth in a manuscript, a point elaborated at some length by Charles Singleton in his *Essay on the Vita Nuova.* At the same time he may have been reassured by the example of Boethius that such a mixture of styles would not be unseemly in a work where lofty and quasi-philosophical matters were to be discussed and visions described. So there were predecessors for the form no less than for the content; yet for both form and content the traditions were surpassed and given new significance. The *razos* of the *chansonniers* are without plan or purpose, and the expositions of Boethius are a very different thing from the vigorous narrative of the *Vita Nuova.*

The analytical divisions of the lyrics are clearly derived from the methods of the schoolmen, notably in their application to the interpretation of Holy Writ. It is apparent that Dante added these pretentious and usually quite unnecessary commentaries to give to his verse something of the dignity of solemn writing. They reinforce, here and there, the atmosphere of the apocalyptic and the arcane that imbues some of the lyrics, yet the young poet is not quite easy in his mind about this scholarly device. The artist eventually gets the better of the scholar, and Dante, realizing that the lyric impact is dulled by such pedantic footnotes, dispenses with them. Yet perhaps one would not wish them away: the unique combination of the courtly lyric, the confessional narrative, and the scholarly commentary not only gives the book its rare flavor but is symbolic of the interests and passions that dominated Dante's life.

Perhaps the most impressive aspect of the book for a reader somewhat familiar with medieval literature is the highly personal and almost realistic color that Dante gives to an accepted and stylized convention. Unfortunately, scholarly emphasis on his allegorical passages and on the more abstruse aspects of his work has made it all too easy to overlook his passion for realism and naturalism. For many years lovers had adored their ladies with the same idealistic devotion and with many of the same phrases as Dante uses, but the ladies in the poems had remained lay figures, however hot-blooded they may have been in real life. The Lover wooed the Lady; each adopted the proper attitudes and spoke the prescribed lines, as if they had all studied the *Art of Courtly Love* — as in fact many had. But in the *Vita Nuova* we find, as Auerbach puts it, "a creative logic, a gift of organization which enabled [the poet] to weave the equivocal abstractions of the *stil nuovo* into a unified whole."[5] Dante gives his lady a name, and apparently her true name; he speaks of her father, her friends, her brother; he even tells us the exact year of her death. He refers to his own comings and goings; he speaks of his sister and of his "first friend." To be sure, partly no doubt because he is a man of his times and cannot completely break with tradition, and even more for other reasons which we shall soon consider, he does not tell us that the town is Florence and that Beatrice is a Portinari and his "first friend" Guido Cavalcanti, but nonetheless he gives to the figures of his tale if not a name at least authentic reality — and Florence too is a figure and not an unimportant one. "Il y a toute la petite Florence de ce temps là, des scènes de la ville et des scènes de campagne . . . ," as Gillet comments in his *Dante*.[6] We may cite as examples of naturalistic detail the description of the first contact with the screen lady in church and the scene of Beatrice's "mockery" of the poet, nor should we fail to note that some of Dante's most convincing realistic descriptions are of events that take place in his visions. Some descriptions may of course be found in the Old French romances or the Provençal *Flamenca*, but in the lyric-subjective school they are as new as the use of prose itself.

The author's self-confidence and awareness of his skills and his goal are striking too; an unusual sense of purpose and direction is evident in the construction of the work. From the beginning Dante knows what he is about and has a conviction of the seriousness of his mission. He places himself confidently among the new rhymers, whom he does not hesitate to put on a level with the classic poets. He establishes a line of succession from Virgil and Ovid to himself and his contemporaries. It is part of his purpose to establish the dignity of the vernacular as a vehicle for lofty verse. The common tongue is as yet restricted in its subject matter, but as the true heir of the Latin muse it has a right to the adornments which the classical poets had used, and characteristically Dante makes this point first by example and then by specific argument. Springing from this linguistic assurance and esthetic self-confidence is the determination to compose a work with unity and impact in his own linguistic and spiritual idiom. So clearly and visibly does Dante know his own mind that the reader sometimes has an impression of cold-blooded calculation on the part of Dante the author, however much Dante the character may give himself over to sentimental and apparently undisciplined indulgence. It cannot escape us that the visions, the rebuffs, the premonitions, dark, dismaying, and apocalyptic as they are, are strategically arranged, trimmed down to due proportions, and consciously planned to set off the sonnets and *canzoni*, which are themselves so well ordered as to lend themselves to scholarly analysis. Dante, in all his romantic perturbation and adolescent embarrassment, even in his profound and sincere grief, never loses his grip on the *fren dell' arte*.

But the effect of this discipline and of his realistic details is not to spoil the otherworldly, dreamlike character of the tender and delicate story. It is made apparent that these things happened to and within the poet at a certain time and place. Yet the narrator's experience has wider and deeper implications, and the story is not all in the events of history, nor is it Dante's story alone. Hence the solemn apparatus of the divisions, the cryptic statements of Love, who is fond of using oracular Latin, the skillfully aroused suspicion that these individual experiences hide a universal parable which we could read if we could find the key. This is the reason, artistically at least, why Dante, with all his fondness for concrete detail, stops short of names and places. *"Nomina sunt consequentia rerum"* and should be handled with care. If there are supernatural or metaphysical or universal implications in the story,

if the autobiography is also a myth, then for the interpretation of
the hidden significance we must look to Beatrice. This is why for
centuries critics have concentrated their attention on Beatrice.
The reader coming fresh to the story will inevitably fall to wondering about her, and certainly Dante, who clothed her in a veil
of mystery, would not have had it otherwise.

Leaving aside for the moment the historical Beatrice and the
Beatrice we are to see at later stages of the poet's progress, what
do we know of the Beatrice of the *Vita Nuova?* Apparently she
was a real person: Dante sees her, others see her, she has friends,
she goes to church, she smiles, she weeps, she is capable of being
moved to displeasure, she dies. We even know her age. She has
a brother and a father. We know what colors she wore on certain
occasions, but we are not told whether she herself was short or
tall, blonde or brunette. And were her eyes, whose effect on
Dante was so catastrophic, blue, brown, or green? Her complexion
is *color di perle,* and that is all we know of her appearance. It
is not certain in fact that we know her name: we know only that
"People called her Beatrice, not knowing what they were calling
her"; that is, presumably they called her that not realizing that
her name fitted her function, which was to bring beatitude. But,
further to cloud the issue, the syntax of the original is ambiguous,
perhaps deliberately so, according to C. H. Grandgent.[7] Karl
Vossler says that "even the answer to the question whether his
Beatrice was actually the daughter of Folco Portinari and became
the wife of Simon de' Bardi will depend on the temperament of
the inquirer."[8]

In contrast to the obscurity which surrounds the factual Beatrice, we learn a number of things about her essence which Dante's
insistence puts beyond the realm of doubt. Her glance has a supernatural virtue, ennobling yet almost terrifying, not only for Dante,
but for all with whom she comes in contact, and she is the enemy
of all things unpleasant. The events of her life — at least so far
as they are associated with Dante — are related to the wheeling
of the heavens and have a cabalistic significance to which the
number 9 is the key. The conclusion is inescapable that she is
herself a miracle, a creation of the heavens made under the perfect disposition of natural forces or perhaps transcending them.
But can we further define this miracle? Is she "in her degree, an
image of nobility, of virtue, of the Redeemed Life, and in some
sense of almighty God himself," as Charles Williams[9] suggests?

Is she "an analogy and a metaphor of Christ," as Singleton concludes[10] (an interpretation to which Dante's pun on "Giovanna"
and *"prima verrà"* lends weight)? Is she already in the *Vita Nuova*
what she will be in the *Commedia*, a symbol of theology, learning
illuminated by grace, perhaps even the Christian faith? Perhaps
we may leave the last word to De Sanctis, who says that the Beatrice of the *Vita Nuova*

is more like a dream, a phantom, a heavenly ideal, than a definite
reality that produces its own effect. . . . And for the very reason that
Beatrice has such a faint reality and personality, she lives chiefly in
Dante's imagination, coexisting and mixing with the ideal of the
troubadours, the philosophers, and the Christian, a mixture made in
perfectly good faith, undoubtedly grotesque but not false nor conventional.[11]

Nicolette Grey describes the work as "a supreme example of
the particular seen with almost intolerable brightness, so that the
mind which sees feels itself in an unknown world."[12] It is as
though a supernatural light focused on the poet and his immediate
surroundings, leaving the rest of the world in a mysterious and
suggestive darkness. The meaning of Beatrice is the key to the
parable. It is to be stressed that she brings her beatitude to all,
exercises her magic effect on all. Apparently it is merely Dante's
good fortune that he can see the miraculous nature of his beloved
better than his fellow citizens can. We must infer something like
this from the rather cryptic remark in chapter 28 that to speak
properly of her virtue would entail some praise of himself. It is
his privilege to understand the supernatural significance of his
lady so far as is humanly possible; perhaps simply his privilege to
write what others might have written of her had it been given to
them as it was to him to record the impression she made upon
mankind. In fact, it is hard to see how Dante can fail to be a
symbol of universal significance if Beatrice is one. So the ambiguities are brought into play lest the story, personal enough in so
many details, appear limited and circumscribed also. The suggestion of other meanings of almost oracular significance is carefully built up by these same ambiguities, cunningly disposed and
dramatically emphasized. The very title of the work is susceptible
of various interpretations. Does it mean the "Life of Youth" and
imply that this is the story of Dante's young manhood, viewed in
its most significant light? It is a reasonable definition and seems

to be supported by Beatrice's use of the phrase in *Purgatorio* XXXII, where she says of Dante that "he was such in his new life. . . ." But it might well mean the "New Life" that was born when Beatrice appeared to him, the rebirth that she brought about in him. Nor must it be forgotten that in Italian the word *nuovo* has the connotation of "strange," "unusual." If we are to accept Beatrice as the figure of Christ, it is not difficult to see in the "New Life" a purely Christian significance. A passage suggestive of implications beyond the facts of the tale is the apocalyptic vision in chapter 23, with the poem that follows, and the celebrated "*Donne ch'avete intelletto d'amore*" may certainly be interpreted in universal terms.

An allied feature which should not be overlooked is the rather formal arrangement of the poems, which seems to hint at some cabalistic pattern as yet undeciphered by the critics. "The apotheosis of woman is accomplished in symmetrical chapters symbolically numbered," says Vossler.[13] McKenzie[14] and others have noted that the poems are arranged as follows: ten short poems of which nine are sonnets — *Canzone* I — four short poems, all sonnets — *Canzone* II — four short poems, three sonnets and one quasi-sonnet — *Canzone* III — ten short poems, all sonnets. There may be in this clearly designed pattern nothing more than a kind of architectonic caprice not much to be wondered at in a poet who was later to build his more complicated structure on threes, sevens, and tens. Still, it may have its own meaning, and the pattern, once perceived, challenges our curiosity and adds its own contribution to the atmosphere of mystery.

We may in conclusion remark the significance of the *Vita Nuova* as it reveals the esthetic and psychological personality of its author, and as it presages the character of his later works, particularly the *Commedia,* to which it is in fact, thematically and otherwise, an introduction.

This first book tells us a great deal about the man who wrote it. It is made out of his experience, which includes his reading, his passion, and his aspirations. It shows us a mind at once receptive and original. In its pages Dante, with the docility of the good disciple, follows an old and established tradition, makes use of recognized authorities, and expresses himself in an idiom familiar to all his contemporaries. At the same time he gives to his work a significance that is personal and original, and a structure that is novel and highly efficient for his purpose. Already he reveals the keen eye for detail and the economy of expression which we shall admire in their full maturity in the *Commedia;* already, as in the *Commedia,* he finds in his own experience universal and transcendental meanings. We may take note too of the nature and scope of his scholarly and technical preparation. He has written poems since the age of eighteen at least. He has established himself in literary circles. He knows something of his Provençal and Italian predecessors in the lyric tradition. He has considerable knowledge of the classics. He knows scripture well enough at least to quote it to his purpose, and clearly he has learned the method of the schoolmen. His passion, idealistic enough to begin with, has by the end of the story been refined beyond all earthly desires. His verse is graceful and simple in structure; surpassing that of all his contemporaries and predecessors in clarity and polish, it bears the stamp of an assured poetic personality. His prose is smooth and expressive, and any archaic effect it may have upon us is derived largely from certain obsolete words and forms. If these were replaced by their modern equivalents we should more readily appreciate his lean and forceful syntax and his apt choice of word and phrase. Finally, let it be remembered that Dante never wrote anything without a clear-cut purpose, and one cannot fail to be impressed by his skill in accomplishing the task he has set himself in the *Vita Nuova.* The certainties and the obscurities are so artfully blended as to give to his narrative both conviction and mystery. The episodes are skillfully arranged and the line of the story moves, yet a dreamy air of reverie seems to surround the action. He finds room to indicate his attitude toward the vulgar tongue and the uses of poetry, and even to instruct us on the kinds of pilgrim that roam the world and the true significance of the number 9 (for he never writes anything without a strong didactic intent). Even the analyses, faintly disturbing to the modern reader, serve their purpose. In the contemporary context they unquestionably added an element of elevation and ennoblement. Had Dante rewritten the book he might have abandoned them somewhat sooner, but one cannot think easily of any other excisions or changes that he might have made or indeed that one would dare to suggest. The *Vita Nuova* is a carefully planned, homogeneous creation, which says, implies, or suggests exactly what the author meant it to say, imply, or suggest. Pegasus is firmly ridden and the young rider has easy control of "the bridle of art."

❧ 6 ❧

The *Rime*

THE collection of lyrics known as the *Canzoniere* or, considering their nature, more accurately as the *Rime* ("Rhymes") is made up of disparate items, covering many years of the poet's activity and reflecting in a fragmentary way various impulses of his muse. Dante himself never arranged or collected them. They are simply scattered lyrics for which he could not find room in the *Vita Nuova,* or whose projected niche in the *Convivio* was never completed, along with others, topical or occasional, which are difficult to characterize in relation to any work of the poet or to assign to any period of his life. They have come down to us in various manuscripts and editions which are full of inconsistencies, and have been prepared by scholars only in quite recent times.

Modern editors definitely attribute to Dante fifty-four short poems (not including those in the *Vita Nuova* and *Convivio*), and are doubtful about an additional twenty-six. A few of them may have been written before the *Vita Nuova,* and probably no more than a small number after the *Convivio,* but dating them accurately is an insoluble problem.

It will be convenient to follow in our discussion the arrangement of these verses that Michele Barbi has made in his edition.[1] One group is made up of poems composed in the *Vita Nuova* period, clearly reflecting the lyric attitudes of that work. This section comprises twenty-five poems: seventeen sonnets, one double sonnet, four short poems, and three *canzoni*. With few exceptions these compositions are more interesting historically than esthetically. Among them are some of the earliest exercises of the young Dante that have come down to us. The crudeness of their composition and their purely conventional inspiration reveal greater immaturity than does the opening sonnet of the *Vita Nuova*, which was composed, according to Dante's own testimony, in his eighteenth year. Good examples of this youthful period are the sonnets exchanged by our Dante and Dante da Maiano, wherein Alighieri maintains that the greatest grief in life is unrequited love — a traditional, not to say hackneyed, motif, in sharp contrast to the subtle idealizations of the *Vita Nuova*. The very first sonnet in Barbi's edition is an answer to a request from this same Dante da Maiano to explain the significance of a mysterious dream, a device our Dante was later to adopt to bring himself into contact with other poets of his generation. In fact, the major interest of these apprentice rhymes lies in the evidence they afford us of such contacts. There are not only exchanges with Dante da Maiano and Guido Orlandi (although unfortunately we have only Guido's answer to Dante's original communication) but messages as well to Lippo Pasci de' Bardi and Meuzzo da Siena, and the celebrated sonnet to Guido Cavalcanti which we shall discuss presently. Their effect is to reveal to us a Dante by no means hermetical, but in rapport with his fellow versifiers and eager to share his amatory lucubrations with them. Two of the poems seem clearly dedicated to Beatrice, and two others just as clearly seem to celebrate other ladies. The sonnet *"Sonar bracchetti, e cacciatori aizzare"* ("Baying of scent-hounds and hunters' urgent cries"), with its lively description of the hunt (so lively that it is hard to imagine the young gallant turning away from it to lover-like meditation, as he would have us believe), gives us a glimpse of the Florentine youth who took his part in the sports and pastimes of the day. It shows, as Gianfranco Contini has noted,[2] some affinity with the mundane sonnets of Folgore da San Gimignano.

These rhymes are interesting for the light they shed on the sources of Dante's inspiration. Some of them can hardly be distinguished from similar compositions by Dante's Tuscan and Sicilian predecessors. Others, notably the *canzone "Lo doloroso amor"* ("My dolorous love"), show something of the dark and tortured melancholy of Cavalcanti, while such a sonnet as *"De gli occhi de la mia donna"* ("From my lady's eyes") is in the idiom of the *Vita Nuova,* and one can only wonder why the poet did not make room for it there. This sonnet is one of the few lyrics in this first group that can be read today for its own sake. Another is the sonnet to Cavalcanti, *"Guido, i' vorrei che tu e Lapo ed io"* ("Guido, I would that Lapo, you, and I"), justly famous for its graceful objectivization of a mood of romantic escape. It has in form, expression, and intonation all the grace that characterizes the verses of the *Vita Nuova.* We should hardly expect to find it there, however, for the lady whom Dante would take with him in his magic bark, as Guido would be accompanied by Giovanna and Lapo Gianni by Lagia, is not Beatrice. Perhaps this little jewel is the only surviving offering to the first screen lady, to whom Dante's devotion may have been greater than he would have had us believe. Like reasons explain the exclusion from the *Vita Nuova* of the smaller poems *"Per una ghirlandetta"* ("For a little garland"), whose haunting and simple refrain seems to anticipate the refinement of Poliziano, and *"Deh, Violetta, che in ombra d'amore"* ("Ah, Violetta, under Love's shadow"), playful and surely persuasive to Violetta, who as yet has not been identified with Beatrice. Inevitably the attempt has been made to reduce these two ladies to mere allegories; if they had been that and nothing more, perhaps they would have found their way into the *Vita Nuova.*

From these early lyrics a picture emerges of the adolescent Dante, still an apprentice in love as in poetry, experimental, ardent, no doubt fickle, determined to make himself known to his contemporaries and feeling his way, with very little lost time, to his own style and manner, finding his idiom as well as his true love after a few years of experiment with both techniques and ladies. If Beatrice were not already overloaded with allegorical meanings, we could see her as the personification of the poet's achievement in his art.

These first fruits are followed in Barbi's edition by a poetic exchange in six sonnets of a very different nature: the famous *tenso* between Dante and Forese Donati. It disturbs readers who like to think of Dante as removed from the weaknesses of common mortals, and there has been some effort by delicate-minded critics to dismiss it as apocryphal.[3] Modern criticism, however, accepts it as genuine, and the dialogue between Dante and Forese in the *Purgatorio* supports its authenticity — unless even worse things are hinted at in that melancholy conversation.

In the first sonnet Dante accuses Forese of neglecting his wife, who lies forever cold and sniveling in bed. Forese counters by accusing Dante's dead father of usury. Dante then charges Forese with gluttony and thievery. Forese alludes to Dante's poverty, charging him with mendicancy and suggesting resources available to beggars, both professional and amateur. Dante repeats his accusations of thievery and gluttony and adds that Forese is probably a bastard. Forese says that Dante has no such luck, since it is obvious that he is the same kind of coward as his father, who left unavenged an affront to a relative that would normally call for a vendetta. This ends the *tenso*.

These unprepossessing invectives have a double historical interest. Forese's hints imply something disreputable in the career of the elder Alighieri, and Dante's failure to rebut the charges, when added to the circumstance that nowhere in his work does he mention his father, seems to confirm the accusation. F. Torraca suggested that the elder Alighieri might have died an excommunicated heretic, but Barbi and Contini reject the hypothesis. There is no evidence of poverty or mendicancy in Dante's immediate family, but he was repeatedly compelled to borrow money, and Forese's words may be an exaggerated allusion to Dante's straitened circumstances. The greatest historical interest lies not in these references, however, but in the portrait of a Dante who could take delight in such an exchange of compliments as the *tenso* provides. In a sense the verses, though deplorable, are helpful in deepening our understanding of a many-sided personality. If the true portrait calls for "warts and all," here are the warts. These sonnets show how Dante might have had something more to blush for in the presence of Beatrice than merely philosophical aberration.

These little compositions inevitably bring up their own puzzles for scholars. One would like to be able to date them with precision, but that is very difficult to do. Clearly, since it is the ghost of Dante's father with whom Forese affects to converse in his first sonnet, they must have been written between the death of the elder Alighieri (1287) and the death of Forese himself (1296). This is closer than we can come to dating some other works of Dante, including the *Commedia*. Still, one would like very much to know if the composition of the debate preceded or followed the death of Beatrice. It is impossible to say, although a certain facility in composition indicates a more experienced hand than the one which penned the earlier sonnets of the *Vita Nuova*. Further, if the period of loose living and scurrilous company which the rhymes attest comes after the death of Beatrice, it would, as noted, afford a very convincing explanation of his shame at confronting her in the earthly paradise. Most modern critics assign the sonnets to a period later than 1290, although some feel that they must have been written during an earlier period of youthful waywardness (of which we have no other evidence), since it is hard to think of them as the products of the young idealist of the *Vita Nuova*. It is also possible that the *tenso* was not a serious exchange of invective, but a joke.[4] Both kinds are common in the Provençal tradition, as are false *tensoni* written by one person. Even if the verses were a joke, their contribution to a better understanding of the young Dante is still great. Many a truth is spoken in jest, and even to play with coarseness is to display one's familiarity with it. Virgil's reproach to Dante as the latter follows eagerly the exchange of diatribes between Adam of Brescia and Sinon in *Inferno* XXX is further evidence that Dante knew of this weakness in himself.

Barbi's group of "allegorical and doctrinal rhymes" includes a ballade, two sonnets, and a *canzone*. The ballade is on the conventional theme of the cruel lady and sounds like the later *Vita Nuova*. The *canzone*, "*Poscia ch' amor del tutto m'ha lasciato*" ("Since love has quite abandoned me"), celebrates the man of true courtliness, and was probably meant to find a place in the *Convivio*. It defines "*leggiadria*" ("courtliness") as dependent on virtuous deeds; as poetry it is hardly remarkable.

The next group, "Other rhymes of love and correspondence," includes six sonnets, two ballades, and two *canzoni,* and is noteworthy for three love poems dedicated to the "*pargoletta*" which have a truly lyric grace and freshness. Commentators have speculated about the "*pargoletta*," identifying her with Pietra (of whom more later), with the lady of the window (of the *Vita Nuova*), and with Gentucca of *Purgatorio* XXIV.[5] Apparently, the only definite attribute she has is not being Beatrice, since Beatrice herself refers to a "*pargoletta*" when in *Purgatorio* XXXI she reproaches Dante for his fickleness, and "*parlogetta*" means "young girl," not a term used for Beatrice. Because I believe Dante used words carefully and remembered his own vocabulary, I am inclined to agree with the view that Beatrice in her reproaches has the same girl in mind, and that she may well have been a special object of Dante's devotion at some time in the years between the death of Beatrice and the poet's exile. The *canzoni* of this group, *"Amor che movi tua vertù dal cielo"* ("Love that bringest thy virtue from the heavens") and *"Io sento sì d'amor la gran possanza"* ("I so feel the mighty power of love"), were probably also written for the *"pargoletta."* Both are Guinizellian and the second is noteworthy for its envoi, in which Dante addresses his work to "the three least wicked men of our city" (in *Inferno* VI he speaks of only two), urging two of them to preserve the third, who may be Guido Cavalcanti, from wickedness and folly.

The sonnets, replies to other poets or merely exercises, are not particularly interesting except for one to Cino da Pistoia, apparently written in exile, in which Dante laments, in tones which seem to anticipate Giacomo Leopardi, the lack of congenial spirits in the crude and barbarous surroundings which have all but suffocated his muse, and *"Due donne in cime alla mente mia"* ("Two ladies in the summit of my mind"), in which the poet, against the laws of love, defends his devotion to two ladies (who turn out to be beauty and virtue) at the same time.

Another figure from Dante's shadowy gallery of love emerges, tantalizingly veiled, in the next division of the *Rime,* consisting of four poems dedicated to the Lady Pietra. These works have their own craggy individuality within the *canzoniere.* In form they are wilfully bizarre: one, *"Al poco giorno e al gran cerchio d'ombra"* ("To the scant day and the great wheel of shade"), is a *sestina* (a tortuous pattern invented by Arnaut Daniel); of another, *"Amor, tu vedi ben che questa donna"* ("Love, thou well seest that this woman"), Dante says, with a rather ingenuous complacency, that nothing of like nature has ever been attempted before, though it seems to bear some affinity to a *canso* of Peire Vidal.[6] The two *canzoni* are conventional in structure, but one of them openly proclaims the author's desire to seek for harsh rhymes, and the other is couched in very artificial language. All of them speak of the harshness and obduracy of the Lady Pietra ("stone"). The two principal critical problems to which these poems have given rise may be simply stated: (1) Are they merely exercises in virtuosity, springing from Dante's reading of Arnaut Daniel and consequent desire to imitate the master of the *trobar clus,* or are they verses written with serious intent and real passion to the Lady Pietra? (2) If the latter, who is the Lady Pietra, and if a symbol, then of what? For Contini the answer is easy; he brushes aside all suggested identifications and finds the lady simply a device to bind together Dante's most technistic lyrics, "in which the lexical energy and unique nature of the rhythms . . . are transformed into the theme of the harsh woman. . . ."[7] For Flora too the adjective "stony" has an artistic (rather than a personal) sense.[8] Yet the passionate language of one of the *canzoni*, "*Così nel mio parlar voglio esser aspro*" ("Thus in my speech I would be harsh"), seems to give evidence of something more than stylistic experimentation. We might add too that the statement in the *Vita Nuova* to the effect that any poem should have a substance of meaning under its allegorical vestment would justify, generally speaking, the hypothesis that all of Dante's verses are built around a core of reality and that the stony girl too may have been of flesh and blood. For Salvatore Quasimodo, who studies these poems with the intuition of a poet rather than the calculation of a scholar, the *Petrose* have a "motion of truth and in the sphere of the contingent," and he alludes pointedly to Boccaccio's comment on Dante's abiding sin of lust.[9] As to the identity of Pietra, the most acceptable theory would make of her a girl of the countryside, otherwise unknown, although in the past various other suggestions have been made — that she is the "*pargoletta*," or a lady of the Scrovegni, or even Dante's sister-in-law.

Because the *Petrose* do have a special quality not found elsewhere in Dante's verse (except perhaps for some lines of the *Commedia*), the following version of a stanza of the above-mentioned *canzone* may be of interest.

> If I could lay hands on those gentle tresses
> which are become a lash and scourge for me,
> seizing on them before tierce
> I'd cling through vespers and through evening chimes.
> I'd show no pity nor be courteous
> but would act rather as a bear at play;
> and if love scourge me now on their account
> I'd well revenge myself a thousandfold.
> Yet more: into those eyes whence leap
> the sparks that fire my heart, consumed within me,
> I would look deep and hard
> in vengeance of the flight she forces on me
> and then I would give her peace with love.

The last division, "Various rhymes composed during exile," contains three *canzoni* and five sonnets. Two of the *canzoni* are clearly of the group ideally forming a part of the *Convivio*. The first, *"Tre donne intorno al cor mi son venute"* ("Three ladies have gathered round my heart"), is known as the *Canzone on Justice*. In it Dante, finding that three noble ladies, Justice, Natural Law, and Human Law, are banished by human society, finds his own exile easier to bear; "the exile that has been given me, I hold it an honor," he proclaims. Yet in the *commiato* he sends his *canzone* not only to "hawk" with the Whites but also to hunt with the black hounds, suggesting to the latter that "to pardon is a fair victory of war," and he even makes the — for Dante — astounding concession that he may have been somewhat at fault: "Whence if I was at fault/yet the sun has caused many moons to come and go since the fault was spent,/if guilt dies so that one repent."[10] Clearly, then, the poem, more remarkable for these personal revelations than for poetic beauty (although De Sanctis thought it the most beautiful allegorical poem ever written), must have been composed in the early years of exile when hope of honorable return had not been completely extinguished. The second *canzone*, *"Doglia mi reca ne lo core ardire"* ("Grief brings daring into my heart"), known as the *Canzone of Liberality* and planned originally as the last ode of the *Convivio*, castigates the vice of avarice in tone and even idiom suggestive of the treatment of this sin in the *Commedia* as well as in the *Convivio*. The third *canzone*, *"Amor, da che convien pur ch'io mi doglia"* ("Love, since it is my lot to grieve"), is written in praise of a *"montanina"* (identifiable with Pietra?) who is consistently cruel to the entreaties of the poet; it concludes with an apostrophe to Florence, still without compassion for him, in which Dante states that even were this harshness of his native city to melt, yet the bond which binds him to his mountain love could not be broken. This is love indeed, but around the figure of the mountain charmer hovers the same veil of obscurity which envelops Pietra and other ladies of Dante's wooing. Of the more personal odes Auerbach has said that their "artful and meticulous composition is probably unequalled in the whole of literature."[11]

One of the sonnets is an invective against Pope Clement V,[12] its language recalling some of the bitter outbursts of the *Commedia;* its appeal to God's justice suggests that it was conceived at the same time as the *Canzone on Justice*. The two sonnets addressed to Cino da Pistoia are interesting for certain attitudes our poet assumes: in the first, *"Io sono stato con Amore insieme"* ("I have been in Love's company"), he sings of the power of love, stating with a kind of melancholy satisfaction that he has been under the rule of love since his ninth year; in the second, before proceeding to reproach Cino for his fickleness, Dante remarks that he had thought to have left behind love rhymes, his bark leaving the shore and faring forth on another course. Another sonnet tells of one Lady Lisetta who would storm the poet's heart only to find it held by love as by a chatelain on behalf of another lady, reminding us of the figure employed in the literal exposition of the first *canzone* of the *Convivio*.

A final group of "doubtful attribution" includes sixteen sonnets, a pair of *ballate*, a *descort* (which is a poem that treats of confused feelings), and a fable in the form of a Provençal *canso* with an artful rhyme scheme. Eight of the sonnets are addressed to other poets or "lieges of love," and deal with the conventional topics of amatory verse. One, dedicated to Sennuccio del Bene, is cast in playful rhymes, and one could wish it were safely attributable to Dante. Another sonnet would, if acceptable, fill out the cycle for Pietra; it tells of a Lady Pietra, now dead and buried, but with such tasteless and forced concepts and rhymes as to make its attribution to Dante very unlikely. The eight remaining sonnets treat of conventional subjects, in general resembling in tone the verses of the later *Vita Nuova*, and are of no special interest. Technically they are good enough to have come out of Dante's workshop, but their trademark is not, as it were, registered by a dependable manuscript tradition, and most of them are pretty certainly not Dante's. The same may be said of the *ballate* and the fable. The *descort*, if we could accept it as genuine, would give ample testimony of Dante's linguistic versatility: it is written in Latin, Italian, and Old French and tells, as a *descort* must, of the confusion created in the poet's heart by the mistreatment he has suffered at the hands of love. Unprepossessing as it is to the modern eye, it is the kind of composition that might have appealed to the strain of the *pedante virtuoso* which unquestionably existed in Dante.

7

The *Convivio* (I)

UNLIKE the *Vita Nuova,* the *Convivio* is, broadly speaking, not a work of art at all. In this respect the form in which it is cast is most revealing of the author's intention and the nature of the work. After a general introduction, the book consists of three *canzoni* or odes (there were to have been fourteen, but the work remained unfinished), each ode followed by a lengthy and highly detailed commentary. We saw how, in the interests surely of esthetic effect, Dante had in the *Vita Nuova* occasionally suppressed the divisions at the end of the sonnet; here it is as if, instead of doing away with those pedantic commentaries, he had enlarged them immeasurably. This would be sufficient clue to the fact that the book is, as we should say nowadays, critical, even scholarly, rather than creative. As usual, however, the clue is hardly necessary, since we have as well Dante's own statement of purpose — or rather purposes, for it is noteworthy that he is here serving again both the altruistic cause of knowledge and his own personal need for self-justification.

It is the latter need that is the immediate occasion of the work, begun after the author had gone into exile. Barbi, who dates the composition of the work between 1304 and 1307,[1] speaks of the *Convivio* as "seeming to be a continuation and development of the *Vita Nuova.*"[2] The stress is, however, on the seeming; Dante does indeed use the *Vita Nuova* as a point of departure, but in truth the story is not so much continued as revised, and the development takes a new turn. Temperamentally Dante was reluctant to admit any inconsistencies in his life; he had an almost obsessive drive for unity of pattern; superseded opinions or altered attitudes are never suppressed but always assimilated. His effort to assimilate the *Vita Nuova* with the *Convivio* is not entirely successful, but it is fascinating to observe.

Before making further remarks, let us look more closely at the contents of the work. The summary will be briefer, relatively, than that of the *Vita Nuova*, for the *Convivio* is full of details which, though here and there very illuminating and sometimes even amusing, are frequently irrelevant to the main topics.

Dante begins his introductory treatise by quoting "the Philosopher" to the effect that "all men by nature desire to know," since thus they find their natural perfection. This desire, however, is checked in many, either by some natural impediment, some moral fault, or some circumstance of life. Only a blessed few sit at the table where the bread of angels is consumed. Dante does not claim that he is one of them; he merely sits at the feet of the more fortunate. He proposes to share with others the crumbs which have fallen from the banquet table. Excluding those ineligible either by physical disability or moral depravity, he summons those whose concerns with civil and family matter have kept them from the pursuit of knowledge and also those hitherto impeded by sloth. The "meat" of the banquet will be the fourteen odes, some of which have been previously rather obscured, lacking the "bread," which Dante now proposes to offer in the form of prose commentaries. And if the treatment of the present work is more "virile" than that of the *Vita Nuova,* no disparagement of the earlier book is intended; it is natural that the works should be different, since the *Vita Nuova* was composed "before entrance on the prime of manhood" and the *Convivio* when he had already "passed the same." (chapter 1)

Significant for all Dante's works, I believe, and not for the *Convivio* alone, is the concept he has of the public for which he writes; it is a public not of scholars, or mystics, but of intelligent and alert laymen, men of affairs, we should say, whose lives must be dedicated to practical matters but whose intellectual curiosity is strong. We may also note how at the end of this first chapter Dante anticipates the problem of the critics who, through the centuries, have found reconciliation of the *Vita Nuova* and the

Convivio a difficult if not impossible task. Clearly it was not an easy one for the author.

Dante begins the second chapter by asking the reader's pardon for speaking of himself and for speaking "too deeply." The former fault can be excused when the speaker must speak in his own defense (as Boethius was constrained to do), or when his speaking of himself may serve others (which was St. Augustine's intention in his *Confessions*). Happily both circumstances obtain in Dante's case. He must clear himself of the "infamy" which he has incurred because readers have seen in the odes only evidences of "passion," whereas in fact he was moved by "virtue." And the pleasure and subtle instruction which will be afforded the reader by Dante's examination of the allegories of the odes will indeed serve others. As for the obscurity, he regrets it, but finds it necessary in order to correct the impression of himself which prevails throughout Italy. For, ever since "it was the pleasure of the citizens of the most beautiful and famous daughter of Rome, Florence, to cast me forth from her most sweet bosom," Dante has been compelled to wander in exile through the peninsula; and so many have come to know him personally, and he has suffered from that great law of nature whereby familiarity breeds contempt. Hence he feels impelled to adopt a loftier (i.e., more obscure) style than he would otherwise use, "that it may seem a thing of greater authority." (chapters 2–4)

This passage not only enables us to date the composition of the work as later than the poet's banishment but will not fail to move the sensitive reader to a sympathy with the involuntary exile. And Florence is here still the "most beautiful daughter of Rome," not yet the avaricious and prideful city of the *Commedia*.

Dante proceeds next to explain the "substantial" blemish of his writing the commentary in the vernacular rather than in Latin. He chose the vernacular for a number of reasons. First, it would be against natural order if Latin, which is the nobler language, were to "serve" (for a commentary is a kind of servant to its text) the vernacular odes. He remarks, apropos of the nobility of Latin, that it is incorruptible, inasmuch as we see in the ancient writings of the Latin comedies and tragedies the same speech that we have today, whereas the vernacular undergoes continual change. But of this, Dante tells us, he will say more in a book he is preparing on the vulgar speech. Furthermore, a Latin commentary cannot serve the vernacular text as efficiently as the vernacular itself, for it cannot follow the turns of phrase, nor can it be a good servant to the vernacular, since it does not know its master's "friends," i.e., the readers of the vernacular. A Latin commentary would in fact explain the odes to many foreigners who could not understand the originals (which like all poetry are untranslatable) and would withhold explanation from many Italians who would be quite able to read the odes. Again, looking at the commentary as a gift (and the best gift is one perfectly suited to the recipient), a Latin version would have been imperfect because those who study Latin are rarely concerned for such things as beauty and virtue but have their minds fixed only on material gain; whereas among the nobler citizens of Italy whose affairs have kept them from being students of Latin there are many interested in just such things as Dante is going to discuss. Further, Dante offers the commentary to show what vernacular prose is capable of. Many disparage the Italian language, praising instead the *langue d'oc,* but they do so for the worst of reasons, some thoughtlessly accepting a tradition, others out of snobbishness, others because they blame the language for their own incompetence in writing, others out of jealousy of those who can use it, others finally moved by that strange twist of nature that sometimes makes us despise what is our own: poor reasons all. Dante confesses that his love of Italian is motivated by a number of things. It is after all his own language, "nearest to him" both "essentially" and "incidentally." It has also in full measure the most commendable distinguishing property of a language, which is "rightly to express a concept." In his case, as indeed for all Italians, it is the language to which he owes his existence both as a human being — for it was the language of his parents' courtship — and as a scholar — since it was his helper in learning Latin. Lastly, constant use of the language has caused him to love it. (chapters 5–13)

The first treatise of the *Convivio,* it seems to me, does little to substantiate Vossler's[3] feeling that the tearful period of the *Vita Nuova* was followed by the dry and austere scholasticism of the *Convivio.* The style, to be sure, is consciously stiff, yet perhaps nowhere in all his works does Dante speak in such a straightforward and open fashion of his feelings and his inspirations. Particularly appealing is his avowal of love for the Italian language. From this purely emotional attitude came the "scholarly" interest which led to the *De Vulgari Eloquentia,* already, it would seem, in preparation as he was writing the present treatise; the *Commedia* is of course the enduring monument to his mother tongue.

The next section begins with the ode *Voi che 'ntendendo*.

Ode I

Ye who by understanding move the third heaven,
hear the reasoning which is in my heart,
for I know not how to tell it to another, so rare it seems to me.
The heaven that follows your influence,
gentle creatures that ye are,
draws me into the state in which I find myself.
Whence discussion of the life I am undergoing
may, it seems, be worthily addressed to you:
So I beg you to hear of it from me.
I will tell you the new state of the heart,
how the sorry soul weeps within it,
and how a spirit speaks against her,
which comes down over the rays of your star.

Wont to be life of the grieving heart
is a sweet thought, that would go off,
full many a time, to the feet of our Lord,
where it would see a woman in glory,
of whom it would speak so sweetly to me
that the soul would say: I wish to go there.
Now there appears one who makes it flee
and overcomes me with such power
that the heart trembles therefore and gives outward sigh.
This (newcomer) makes me look upon a woman
and says: "Whoever would see salvation
let him gaze upon the eyes of this woman
if he fear not the anguish of sighs."

He finds such an opponent who destroys him,
the humble thought that was wont to speak to me
of an angel who is crowned in heaven.
The soul weeps, so grief-stricken it yet is,
and says: "O woe is me, now he takes flight,
this compassionate one who has consoled me."
Of my eyes this troubled one says:
"What an hour it was when such a woman saw them!
and why did they not believe me (warning) of her?
For I said, 'Surely in that woman's eyes

there must dwell one who slays my peers.'
Nor did it avail me that I was aware
that they should not look on such a one, whereof I am slain."

"Thou art not slain, but thou art in dismay,
our soul, that dost so lament,"
says a gentle little spirit of love;
"For that fair woman whom thou dost sense
has transformed thy life to such degree
that thou hast fear of her, so cowardly art thou become!
See how compassionate she is and humble,
wise and courteous in her greatness,
and henceforth think to call her mistress!
For if thou deceivest not thyself, thou'lt see
adornment of such lofty miracles
that thou shalt say, 'Love, true lord,
behold thy handmaiden; do as pleases thee.' "

Song, I think they will be rare,
those who will understand your subject well;
so hard and laboriously thou disclosest it.
Whence, if perchance it hap
that you come into the presence of persons
who may seem to you not well aware of it,
then I pray thee to take courage,
saying to them, beloved new song of mine,
"Remark at least how beautiful I am."

Comparing his book to a ship, and "adjusting the sail of reason
to the breeze of his desire," Dante begins the analysis of his ode.
He reminds us that writings should be expounded chiefly in four
senses. The first is the literal. The second is the allegorical, as
when Ovid speaks of Orpheus moving beasts and stones with his
music, signifying the power of eloquence over even the irrational.
Dante notes that theologians take this sense differently from
poets (presumably because they do not consider scriptures fiction),
but he will follow the sense of the poets. The third sense is the
moral, which has a didactic purpose; for example, Christ's taking
but three of his disciples with him on the occasion of the trans-
figuration signifies that "for the most secret things we should
have little company." And the fourth sense is the anagogical or
supersense, as when the scripture, by the things it signifies, signifies also certain eternal things. The prophet who says that

when the people of Israel came out of Egypt Judea was made
wholly free speaks literal truth and also signifies the spiritual
truth that when the soul turns from sin it is made holy and free.
In exposition the literal must always come first, since it would
be impossible to get at the "inside" of a thing without going
through the "outside," and also because it is impossible to proceed
to the "form" of anything without preparing the "subject" on which
the form is to be stamped, as, for example, we must first make
ready the wood before preparing to build a table. Aristotle tells
us too that our learning must proceed from that which we know
to that which we do not know so well. So Dante proposes to
expound the literal sense and then the allegorical, touching on the
other senses when it seems appropriate. (chapter 1)

The four senses, which are referred to again, and somewhat
more properly illustrated, in Dante's letter to Can Grande, were
well-known to medieval writing, particularly scriptural exegetists.
In the old rhyme: *"Littera gesta docet,/Quid credas allegoria,/
Moralis quid agas,/Quo tendas anagogia."* The Busnelli-Vandelli
edition of the *Convivio* refers the reader to the *Distinctiones* of
Garnier de Rochefort, where the four are very clearly defined.[4]
Passages exhibiting all four senses are somewhat rare in Dante's
own works — that is, in the narrative, as distinct from the multivalent image-symbol; in fact, for two odes of the *Convivio* only
two senses are expounded, and for Ode III only one.

This first ode, chapter 2 goes on, was born of the conflict between Dante's memory of Beatrice and the attraction of the lady
of the window who appeared to him two years after Beatrice's
death, as recorded in the *Vita Nuova*. It has three main divisions,
the invocation (stanza 1), the inner conflict of the spirits (stanzas
2–4), and the *tornata* (stanza 5) wherein the poet addresses
his own work.

Now, beginning with the literal sense, we must know whom
Dante addresses in the first line, and this leads to a discussion
of the order of the heavens. Aristotle had held that the revolving
heavens were eight in number (the moon, Mercury, Venus, the
sun, Mars, Jupiter, Saturn, and the heaven of the stars). Ptolemy
had postulated the ninth heaven or *primum mobile,* and Catholics
had affirmed the existence of the tenth, immovable and perfect.
The church, "which cannot err," assigns to the tenth heaven the
souls of the blessed, and there is some indication that Aristotle
does the same if we understand properly his *De Coelo.* So here

by the third heaven Dante means Venus, in which heaven the planet itself revolves on an epicycle, which is a circle having its center on a point in the larger circle of the revolving sphere. (chapter 3)

The "movers" of these heavens are "intelligences, commonly called angels"; Plato had called them "ideas," and the gentiles had made them gods and goddesses. Dante estimates that these intelligences must be very great in number. For since we on earth have the two beatitudes of the active and contemplative life, we must assume a like dualism in heaven. And since the spirits absorbed in guiding the world and the heavens cannot by their nature be free also to contemplate, we must postulate a class of the purely contemplative — greater in number than the others since theirs is the higher blessedness, for which God would naturally create a greater number. Though our senses cannot perceive these divine creatures, "yet some glow of their most lively essence shines in our intellect." (chapter 4)

This "division of labor" which Dante postulates for the heavenly intelligences has fascinating philosophical — or, better, theological — implications. Gilson has unerringly pounced on them:

. . . the two forms of beatitude are not merely distinct, they are mutually exclusive. Nowhere is the Dantesque breach of the classic relationship between the hierarchies of dignity and the hierarchies of authority more apparent than here, for Dante clearly affirms that the contemplative Intelligences are more divine and more beloved of God than the active Intelligences, but precisely because they are higher, they do not govern. It is typical of Dante to base the autonomy of an inferior order on its very inferiority in this way,

and he goes on to remark on the applicability of the principle to the thesis of the *De Monarchia,* concluding:

In contrast to that of St. Thomas Aquinas, Dante's universe is of such a kind that the hierarchy of dignities never gives rise to any jurisdictional hierarchy within it, but rather to their mutual independence.[5]

Is this heresy? Not quite, it would seem, but some glimmer of the Averrhoistic "double truth" shines through. The theme of "our two beatitudes" recurs in the *Convivio;* we shall find Gilson to our purpose again in chapter 17 of the fourth treatise.

The church teaches, Dante continues in chapter 5, that there are three hierarchies of angels, each subdivided into three orders and each with its particular object of contemplation. The first hierarchy and the lowest in the scale consists of angels, archangels, and thrones; the second of dominations, virtues, and principalities; and the highest of powers, cherubim and seraphim (all in ascending order). The highest hierarchy contemplates God the Father; the seraphim "without respect to aught save Himself," the cherubim with respect to his relationship to the Son; and the powers in his relationship to the Holy Ghost. The second hierarchy similarly contemplates the Son, and the lowest hierarchy the Holy Spirit. Out of all these orders, some (perhaps a tenth) were lost as soon as created, and human nature was created to replace them. On the rational assumption that the orders correspond to the moving heavens, we may assume that Venus is the charge of the thrones, who contemplate the Holy Ghost, and their association with the Heaven of Love would be appropriate. There must be at least as many of these "movers" as there are movements in the heaven itself. Of such there are four; that of the star on its epicycle, the revolution of the whole sphere in company with the sun, the movement of all the heavens following that of the stars (from west to east one degree a century), and the daily revolution under the influence of the *primum mobile*. To these "movers" who carry out their assigned task by understanding alone the ode is addressed.

The celestial orientation which Dante here offers us is very helpful to the understanding of the *Paradiso*. It is true that he changed his mind about the order of the hierarchies; it is probable that here he is following Brunetto Latini (*Trésor* I, i, 12) and ultimately Isidore of Seville. In the *Paradiso* he tells us that his authority is Dionysius.

Returning to the exposition of the ode, Dante reminds us that "hear" in line 2 does not imply that the movers of the third heaven hear sound but is an appeal for understanding by their intellects. The word "heart" should be understood simply as the "secret recess within" and not as any particular organ.

Dante proposes to speak to these "movers" of his state partly because it is strange and needs explanation, partly because their heaven is responsible for it. He promises them that the story will be unusual (since the most potent persuasion to render the hearer attentive is the promise to tell "new and great things"). The "spirit" of which he discourses is merely a constant thought of the new lady; the "soul" is the contrary thought which clings to the memory of Beatrice. The spirit comes on rays of the star, for it is through the rays that the virtues of the stars descend to us; Venus has great effect upon our souls even though it is distant 167 times "as far as it is to the center of the earth — which is 3250 miles." (This follows Alfraganus, of whom Dante makes great use in this work.⁶) (chapter 6)

Coming to the literal interpretation of the second part of the ode: it contains both sides of the inner conflict. Explaining that the life of a thing is the actualizing of its noblest part (a man who does not use reason is not alive as a man), Dante reveals that by the life of his heart he means his inner life, and so the meaning is that in thought he contemplated the realm of the blessed where he knows Beatrice dwells. The effect of such meditation was to arouse a longing for death. Against this came forth the thought of the new lady, hostile to the contemplation of Beatrice and seeming to conquer Dante's soul, a conquest revealed "without" by the change in his appearance. The power of this thought is shown by its effect in causing Dante to look upon the new lady. (chapter 7) Dante remarks here that these intelligences of love which might be expected to help him preserve the memory of Beatrice are in fact but following their nature when they endeavor to effect his love for a living being, since they cannot preserve their influence in objects not subject to them (i.e., souls separated from the body). In this connection Dante proposes to digress briefly on Beatrice (of whom he will say no more in this book) and immortality.

The most base and stupid belief, he declares, is that which denies immortality. For Aristotle, the Stoics, Cicero, and every gentile poet as well as all believers, whether Jews, Saracens, Tartars, or others who live according to any law, have constantly affirmed faith in immortality. So that if there were no immortality an incredible thing would be true, namely, that mankind, the most perfect of all natures here below (as Aristotle says), would have, by the numerous sacrifices many of its best spirits have made of this life in favor of the better one, revealed itself more stupid than the dumb beasts who have never made any such choices; hence, the most perfect creature would be the most imperfect, and nature would seem to have planted the hope of immortality in our minds to work against herself, as it were, an obvious impossibility. It would seem too that our dreams, which apparently put us in contact with immortal revelation, argue that we have our immortal part. Lastly and clinchingly, we have Christ's word for it. Dante concludes with a statement of his firm belief that his beloved Beatrice now "lives in glory." (chapter 8)

It is strange at first sight that Dante should reserve "the teaching of Christ," surely the only telling argument for a Christian, for his last "proof." It should suffice of itself. But this passage is significantly — if not uniquely — revealing of the overriding intent of the *Convivio,* which is to stress the importance of human reason. Intended, as seems clear, to demonstrate its support of revelation, the effect of Dante's argument is to set up a kind of double channel of authority. Beatrice, dismissed after this passage, will have good grounds for her attack on the penitent Dante on the summit of the Mount of Purgatory.

Returning to his analysis, Dante tells of the struggle between his soul and the new thought and how the soul accuses the eyes. (chapter 9) But beginning with the verse "Thou art not slain," the new thought reassures the soul, mentioning the virtues of the new lady, her tenderness, her humility; how she is "wise" (and what is more beautiful in woman than to be wise?), "courteous" (and courtesy does not mean merely liberality but signifies honor, and derives from the fact that of old — though not nowadays — courts were indeed the seat of virtues and fair manners). And he speaks of her "greatness," which is most appropriate when combined with the qualities just mentioned. For greatness is the light which brings out what is good — or bad — in a person. Better were it for many of the great, mad and foolish as they are, were they in low estate, as Solomon suggests. The spirit then orders the soul to accept the new lady as her own. (chapter 10)

Before explaining the meaning of the *tornata,* Dante discusses its origin and use. Originally it served the poets as a musical arrangement to which they could return when the ode had been sung. This is not Dante's use of it, as his metrical arrangements will show; he employs it when it is necessary to say something for the adornment of the ode apart from its own content. Dante remarks that the excellence of every composition lies in its meaning, and its beauty in its ornament; both give pleasure, though the excellence gives more. His esthetic theory, as here set forth, needs no elaboration, but should be noted; it dominates all his writing. Since the nature of his ode makes its excellence hard to perceive, he felt it advisable to point out its beauty. He follows rhetorical tradition in addressing his message not to the reader but to the ode itself. (chapter 11)

Taking up the allegorical exposition, Dante tells us that after the death of Beatrice he had sought consolation in the *De Consolatione Philosophiae,* a book "not known to many," and the *De Amicitia* of Cicero, both works seeming appropriate to his need of solace. These at first made hard reading, but with persistence he was able to enter into them. And like one who seeks silver and finds gold, so Dante, seeking only consolation, found in these books his pathway to philosophy, "the lady of those authors and those books." So he conceived of philosophy as a compassionate lady, and he began to go and seek her in the schools of the religious orders and the disputations of the philosophers. In some thirty months the love of philosophy had expelled every other thought. Moved by this realization, he wrote the ode, expressing it "under the figure of other things," for the true story would not have accorded well with vernacular verse, nor would his readers have understood him, or believed him even if they had. The lady, then, in the allegorical sense, is philosophy (chapter 12), and the third heaven is the heaven of rhetoric. For allegorically the heavens are sciences, since the sciences have certain similarities with the heavens, as follows:

The sciences revolve around their subjects even as the heavens revolve around their center; both are illuminators, the heavens of visible things, the sciences of intelligible things; and both bestow perfection on properly disposed things. The influence of the heavens on substantial generation is recognized by philosophers; the sciences are also the cause of the infusion into us of the second perfection, speculation. The correspondence indeed is very close; to the first seven heavens correspond the sciences of the trivium and the quadrivium, the eighth heaven (the starry sphere) corresponds to physics and metaphysics, the *primum mobile* to ethics, and the empyrean to theology. Dante outlines the specific correspondences of the moon to grammar, Mercury to dialectic, Venus to rhetoric. Venus, he says, is very bright to look upon and appears now at morn and now at eve; similarly rhetoric is the sweetest of sciences and appears at morn when the rhetorician addresses his hearers orally and at eve, that is from behind, when he discourses through writing. Likewise the sun may be compared to arithmetic, Mars to music, Jupiter to geometry, and Saturn to astrology for appropriate reasons. (chapter 13)

The properties of the starry heaven indicate correspondence with physics and metaphysics. It displays to us 1022 separate stars in addition to the Milky Way. The numbers 2 (II), 20 (XX) and *1000* (M) signify respectively simple movement, movement by alteration, and the movement of growth, the elements of physics. We can see the stars of the Milky Way only by their effects, which is the essence of the science of metaphysics. Similar correspondences will be seen in the movements of the heaven of the fixed stars. The crystalline heaven has a very obvious correspondence to ethics, for it is the heaven which "rules" all others and ethics regulates the other sciences. Dante speculates here (as he does later in *Paradiso* X in a more poetic passage) on the wondrous disposition of things brought about by the properly regulated circlings of the heavens, without which "there would be no generation here below, nor life of animal or plant . . . and the universe would have no order." The analogy between the empyrean, the heaven of perfect peace, and theology with its divine subject matter is also patent. (chapter 14)

So the "movers" of the heaven or science of rhetoric are the rhetoricians. The rays of her star are the writings of these rhetoricians, such as Boethius and Cicero, which inspired Dante to love of philosophy. The eyes of this lady are her demonstrations, the reference to the anguish of sighs signifies the difficulty of study. The allegory thus means that Dante, after some inevitable conflict, gave himself entirely to the new lady, the fairest and noblest daughter of the emperor of the universe, to whom Pythagoras gave the name of philosophy. (chapter 15)

The dismissal, however affectionate and devoted, of Beatrice, which the reader of the *Vita Nuova* will find harder to understand than does its author, calls for a word of comment. We had been taught to think of her as the moving force in the poet's life; here we see her vanquished and banished; she will reappear again only in the second canto of the *Commedia* (where there will be no more talk of Lady Philosophy). Volumes have been written on the successive Beatrices and their roles; we shall here simply indicate the outlines of the "problem," if such it be.

If we think of the *Convivio* by itself there is no problem. Dante says in effect that his love for Beatrice, celebrated in the *Vita Nuova*, was nothing to be ashamed of and he has no intention of repudiating it. Still it was essentially sense-motivated, and it was only natural for Dante, once adolescence was past, to move on from the life of the sensual (however refined) to the more mature activities of study and philosophical investigation, symbolized by Lady Philosophy. That is to say, in terms of the *Convivio*, an allegorical lady, philosophy, triumphs over a woman of flesh and blood — or rather over her memory — even though her soul now dwells in heaven and her memory in the poet's heart. This is logical enough and we could easily accept it, casting a tender glance back at the lost Eden of youthful passion while recognizing that our poet has more important things to tell us now — but the trouble is, it is a reversal of the situation in the *Vita Nuova*. To be sure, there too Beatrice was a woman of flesh and blood, but she was by no means only that. She was our poet's health, she was a perfection that heaven lacked and must call for; she was clearly a symbol even more than a living woman. On the other hand, the lady at the window, whose timing and role are very suggestive of the function of Lady Philosophy in the *Convivio*, apparently has no allegorical meaning at all. The roles are reversed. The *Convivio* is simply not in harmony with what goes before, as far as the characterization of Beatrice is concerned. Nor is it in harmony with what comes after. For in the *Commedia*, here is our idealized, allegorical Beatrice again, the same woman of the *Vita Nuova* (as is made clear in the meeting on the Mount of Purgatory), and beyond all doubt a symbol too, be it of revelation, of theology, or — for the moment — what you will.

Eager to preserve for the poet that appearance of consistency so dear to his own heart, some scholars have postulated a "first draft" of the *Vita Nuova* in which the lady at the window does indeed triumph; this would have been rewritten (in the form in which we now have it) when the revised (and one might say revived) Beatrice became essential to the *Commedia*. (The *Convivio*, says Gilson, somewhat overstating the case, had no more need of her than the *De Monarchia*.[7]) But that seems unlikely. The best solution for the reader is, I think, to follow the suggestion of Siro Chimenz:[8] accept the inconsistency, bearing sympathetically in mind the contingencies that made it necessary and also the medieval tendency, which Dante shared in full, to seek coherence even though in a fashion which may seem arbitrary and illogical to us.

Vossler sees in Dante's identification of heavens and sciences an evidence of "labored and tasteless" originality.[9] It should be noted first of all that the comparison is not really original. Busnelli reminds us that an authority as ancient as St. Gregory had affirmed that "*ornamenta coelorum sunt virtutes praedicantium,*" nor are other authorities lacking, from Alan de Lille's *Anticlaudianus to* Fra Remigio de' Girolami, a contemporary and possibly a teacher of Dante. Ristoro d'Arezzo has a like scale in his *Composizione del Mondo.*[10] It is true that no exact parallel to Dante's correspondences has been found. Zingarelli, who thought this "excogitation" was Dante's own contribution to celestial lore, states that it "pertains to a medieval method of research, that of the *moralisatio.*"[11] As to its "tastelessness," this must remain a matter of opinion. Father Kenelm Foster finds it "quaint but far from negligible."[12] We may regard the passage, I think, as another example of that striving to find unity and kinship in cosmic things which is characteristic of medieval aspiration. The detailed resemblances which Dante works out are to be sure a little forced. Yet perhaps some readers will not find them lacking in a certain kind of poetry.

The "meat" of the third tractate is the second *canzone* or ode, "*Amor che ne la mente mi ragiona,*" which Dante felt worthy to be heard on the shores of purgatory.

Ode II

Love that in my mind converses with me
of my lady, desirously,
often suggests to me concerning her such things
that over them my intellect goes astray.
His speech so sweetly sounds
that the soul that listens and hears it
says, "Alas for me, for I am not able
to say what I hear about my lady!"
And certainly I must first put aside,
if I wish to treat of what I hear of her,
things my intellect does not understand,
and of what is understood
a great deal too because I should not know how to express it.
Therefore, if my rhymes have some fault
when they take up the praise of her,
for that let the blame fall on the weak intellect
and our speech, which has not the power
to reproduce all that love says.

The sun, that circles all the world, sees never
so sweet a thing as in that hour
he shines in the region wherein dwells
the lady of whom Love makes me speak.
Every intellect from above looks upon her,
and such as here are drawn to love
find her still in their thoughts
when Love lets them feel of his peace.
Her being is so pleasing to Him who gives it to her
that He always infuses into her His virtue
beyond the demand of our nature.
Her pure soul
which receives this health from Him,
makes it manifest in what she bears with her:
for in her beauties things are seen
such that the eyes of those wherein she shines
send to the heart messengers, laden with longings,
which take on air and become sighs.

Into her descends the divine virtue
as it does into an angel that beholds it,
and any gentle lady who does not believe this
may go with her and observe her actions.
There where she speaks there comes down
a spirit from heaven, inspiring faith,
that the lofty worth she owns
surpasses what is proper to mankind.
The sweet gestures she displays to others
go calling on Love, in rivalry
with such a voice as he must hear.
Of her it may be said:
gentlehood in woman is what is found in her
and beauty is just so much as is like to her.
And it may be said that her aspect helps
(us) to accept what seems a miracle;
whence our faith is helped:
wherefore she was so ordained from eternity.

Things appear in her aspect
which show forth some of the pleasures of paradise:
I mean in her eyes and in her sweet smile,
for Love brings them there as to their proper place.
Such things surpass our intellect
as a ray of the sun overcomes our weak vision:
and since I may not look closely upon them

I must content myself with saying little of them.
Her beauty rains down little flames of fire,
animated by a gentle spirit
which is the creator of every good thought
and like thunder they shatter
the innate vices that make men base.
Whence whatever lady may hear her beauty
blamed for not seeming quiet and humble,
let her look upon her who is the example of humility.
This is she who humbles every perverse one;
she was the thought of Him who moved the universe.

Ode, it seems that you speak forth against
the speech of a sister that you have:
this woman whom you make so humble
she calls fierce and disdainful.
You know that the sky is always shining and clear
and, as concerns itself, is never troubled:
but our eyes for numerous reasons
now and again call the star clouded.
So when she [the other ode] calls her haughty
she is not considering her according to truth
but only according as she seemed to her;
for the soul feared —
aye and yet fears, that it seems to me a cruel thing
whenever I look where she may perceive me.
Excuse yourself thus, if you have need
and when you can, present yourself to her;
you will say, "My lady, if it please you
I shall speak of you everywhere."

Beginning the third treatise, Dante first recalls his increasing devotion to the lady and how many nights he remained awake, gazing at his love's dwelling. He was moved to speak of her partly as a way of doing honor to himself, for friend is like friend and where there is likeness praise and blame run in common (which should caution us in the selection of friends). And the good will he would show in celebrating his lady would serve to strengthen their friendship. He knew too that he would be charged with fickleness, and he hoped to escape some of the blame by telling of the irresistible quality of the new lady.

The ode is divided into three parts: the proem (stanza 1), the substance of the ode (stanzas 2–4), and the *tornata*. (chapter 1) The proem itself is subdivided into three parts: first the quality of the theme is mentioned, then Dante's inadequacy to treat of it (beginning "And certainly"), and in the third part he excuses himself for this insufficiency (beginning "Therefore, if my rhymes"). To begin with love then: love is "a spiritual union of the soul and the beloved thing." It is in the nature of the soul, which receives more of the divine nature than any other created form, to be united to God, and since the divine principles of nature are revealed in excellences of nature, the human soul tends to unite with them in spiritual fashion. This is what we call love, and the inner quality of the soul may be recognized by examining outwardly the things it loves. Love here then is the union of Dante's soul with the aforesaid gentle lady.

The mind wherein love discourses also calls for definition. Aristotle, in the second book of the *De Anima,* had spoken of the three main powers of the soul: life, sense, and reason; and these are so related that one is the foundation of another. The vegetative faculty (life) is the foundation for the sensitive life; this power may constitute a life in itself, as in plants. The sensitive faculty cannot exist without the vegetative, and it in turn is the foundation of the intellectual faculty. So among mortal things the rational is not found without the sensitive, but in animals, fish, etc., the sensitive is found without the rational. The soul which embraces all these faculties is the most perfect. The human soul, having reason, participates in the divine nature after the fashion of an angel, and man has been called the divine animal.

Most of what Dante says here, all soundly Thomistic, is to be found also in *Purgatorio* XXV, in the rather more poetic language of Statius.

In this most noble part of the soul various faculties exist, as Aristotle says in *Ethics* VI: the scientific, the ratiocinative, the inventive, the judicial, and others. To these faculties collectively the name "mind" is given. Only man has a mind, as Boethius plainly indicates; no brutes have it, and indeed there are many men who seem lacking in it. (chapter 2)

Now by where loves operates we may know what kind it is. For everything has a specific love; earth, for example, is forever attracted to the center, and fire always seeks to rise to the upper circumference. Minerals have a love for the place of their generation, plants have a more manifest love for places suitable to their composition, brute animals have not only a love for their place but also for one another. Men have their proper love for perfect and attractive things. Because man too has something of the nature of all these (lesser) things, he is in some way subject to what attracts them. His body, like weight, "loves to descend"; he loves the place of his generation (the fable of Antaeus signifies this); like plants he has love for certain foods, and he has the love of the beasts too, attracted by sensible appearance (and this is the love in man which most needs governance, because of its effect especially in the delight of taste and touch). And by the fifth and last nature, the truly human, which is also the rational and the angelic, man has a love for truth and virtue, whence springs the perfect friendship of which Aristotle speaks. So by the place of the discourse of the love which Dante speaks of, it is apparent that this is the love of truth and virtue, and not love for delight of sense. When he speaks of how love made his intellect lose its way, it is with reference to the difficulties his thoughts had in comprehending the things of this love. This is the first reason why Dante cannot utter all he would, the second being that even when the intellect perceives, the tongue cannot always follow. (chapter 3) Some might say that the avowal of these deficiencies in intellect and speech is not so much an excuse as an accusation, but an excuse it is, for the Philosopher in *Ethics* II states that a man should be praised or blamed only for that which lies in his own power. If Dante's material brought him to a level where fantasy must fail the intellect, it is not his fault if he does not understand; and if thought surpasses speech, as we know it does, this too is a limitation not of our making. It is the evidence of good will that one should consider in the matter of human deserts (chapter 4), which is another Thomistic affirmation, we may observe.

The second section of the ode consists of three parts: in the first the lady is commended in her entirety, in the second her soul is praised, and in the third her body. In the first line "world" refers not to the universe but to the earth. The nature of the earth and its relation to the sun have been much discussed; Pythagoras believed the world was a star circling the sun with another similar world, Antichthon, always opposite to it. Plato, in the *Timaeus*, held that the earth, slowly revolving, was at the center of the cosmos. Aristotle, however, showed that the earth remains fixed and the heavens revolve around it. Here Dante explains in detail the revolution of the sun around the earth, noting the variations of light and climate in the two hemispheres (chapter 5), and ending with an apostrophe of admiration to the "ineffable wisdom" which has ordained such things.

The Italian critic Angelitti, commenting on this chapter, calls it "the most admirable passage of scientific prose in Italian literature, not inferior to the finest pages of Galileo."[13] E. H. Moore, for whom it is "the most abstruse and difficult to be found in the works of Dante," and also a little unnecessary in the context, yet comments on "the extraordinarily clear conception and accurate knowledge which Dante possessed respecting the solar orbit."[14]

Now it is clear, Dante resumes, that if the sun circling the world sees nothing nobler than the lady praised, then she is the noblest thing it shines upon. With respect to the phrase "in that hour," we must note the two ways of dividing the day: one into twenty-four equal parts, the other into twelve equal hours of the period of daylight and twelve of the period of darkness. The latter, to which belong the church hours of prime, tierce, sext, and nones, are called temporal hours; the others are called equal hours. At the equinox they are identical. The words "Every intellect from above looks upon her" mean that the intelligences of heaven marvel at her; these intelligences, it should be remembered, have knowledge of things above them (their cause, which is God) and of things below them (their effects).

They must have knowledge too of the human form as far as it is regulated by intention in the divine mind. The motor intelligences, being special causes of it, have best knowledge of it. So Dante means here that his lady is made as the intentional example of the human essence which is in the divine mind, and made by the power existing in highest degree in those angelic minds which, with the heavens, fashion these things here below. The next line asserts that, with her power to give us perfect delight, she is as perfect as the human essence can be. The next line is to be taken as meaning that God Himself, for love of her perfection, infuses of His excellence in her beyond the limits of our natural due, which is possible to His love. And with the phrase "Her pure soul" Dante would signify that, since her bodily aspect is so wondrous, it is clear that her form (i.e., her soul) miraculously receives the gracious excellence of God. (chapter 6)

Passing to specific praise of his lady's soul, Dante affirms that, just as the sun's light, which falls alike on all things, is received diversely according to the body on which it falls, so too the excellence of God which "flows upon things" with one flowing is yet differently received according to the potential of the recipient, angels taking more of it than men, etc. And because in the order of the universe there is intellectual ascent by degrees from the lowest to the highest forms (we see some men so vile as to seem no better than beasts), there must be some among us very close to the angelic. Such natures Aristotle calls divine, and such Dante asserts his lady to be. The proof is in her speech and expression, and here it should be noted that man alone has rational speech and expression. So Dante advises ladies to learn from her example, and reminds us that she is helpful to all and to our faith (being herself miraculous, she will convince the skeptic who will believe only in the miracles he sees). And "from eternity" she was ordained in the mind of God in testimony of the faith to those living in these times. (chapter 7)

In praise of the bodily perfections of the lady, Dante remarks that man is the most marvelous and complicated of God's creations, containing as he does three natures. We have been warned by Ecclesiasticus not to be too curious about such miracles as mankind. So Dante will proceed with some timidity. He states that "things appear in her aspect" which reveal something of the pleasures of paradise. The first is the complete satisfaction accorded by gazing on her, so sweetly does her beauty feed the observer. The two places wherein this beauty chiefly appears (the eyes and the mouth) may be called the balcony of the soul. Indeed, the soul cannot be stirred by any of the emotions mentioned by the Philosopher in his *Rhetoric* (grace, jealousy, pity, envy, love, and shame) without its being revealed in the eyes, save through a great effort of the will. Some, like Oedipus, have even plucked out their eyes so as not to reveal their inward shame. The soul is revealed also in the mouth like color behind glass. What is laughter but a coruscation of the delight of the soul? The modest laughter of Dante's lady was never yet perceived save by the eye. The love that conveys these things to her there may be thought of as the special love of the soul for these places or as the universal love which ordains the soul to adorn these parts. Apologizing for saying so little of such beauties, Dante will next speak of their effects, as we must do with all things that overcome our intellects. He speaks of the "little flames of fire," i.e., the ardor of love and charity rained down; that is the right appetite, the source of good thoughts and destructive of the innate vices. For there are inborn vices, such as anger in the choleric man, and vices of habit, such as intemperance in wine. The latter can be overcome by acquiring the right habits; the former can be checked, as far as their persistence is concerned, by good habit, but the inborn impulse cannot be destroyed. A man who corrects a naturally bad disposition is more to be praised than one who does not have this handicap. These flamelets destroying the co-natural vices have the power to create a new nature in those who gaze upon the lady's beauty. (chapter 8)

Coming to the third part of the ode, Dante wishes to clear up an apparent contradiction between the character he assigns to his lady here and what he had said of her in the *ballata* "Voi che savete ragionar d'amore" — namely, that she was "fierce and disdainful." So he addresses his ode and by instructing "her" how to excuse "herself" he excuses "her." (The name of the figure, frequently employed, by which poets address inanimate things is prosopopoeia.) What needs excusing is the aforementioned difference between the ode and the *ballata*, and this contradiction can be justified through analogy. We know that heaven is always shining and clear, but it does not always seem so. Through sickness or exhaustion the eye may see things as discolored or blurred; so too the star may seem blurred. "And I experienced this," says Dante, "in that same year wherein this ode was born; for greatly taxing my sight in assiduity of reading, I so weakened the visual spirits that all the stars seemed to me to be shadowed by a kind of halo." Only by long repose and repeated bathing of his eyes was Dante able to restore his normal sight. (chapter 9)

Just what Dante's optical disturbance was has been the study of a number of modern eye-specialists, who, as might be expected in diagnosis ex post facto, have failed to agree. Readers of Dante may be justified in assuming that whatever his disability was, it turned his devotion to Santa Lucia, who rewarded it well by her (very appropriately) first "spotting" his plight in the "Dark Wood" and later bearing him up to the gate of purgatory.

So, he continues, the stars, though bright, may not always shine clearly for the eye of the beholder. And the *ballata* in question considered the semblance of the lady through a vision impaired by excessive longing. For it is well known that the more a soul is impassioned the more it departs from reason. Thus in his yearning Dante had found the august appearance of the lady proud and cruel; but in this ode he sees her without the distorting effect of passion, and hence the ode sees her as she is. Dante asks the ode to explain the discrepancy; the message is of course meant for the reader but is addressed to the ode itself, by the figure of indirect address which we may call "disguising." He charges the ode too to ask the lady's permission to speak of her, for even words of praise said of another without his consent may be indiscreet. Here ends the exposition of the literal sense. (chapter 10)

Turning to the allegorical meaning, Dante states that the lady of the ode is philosophy. The allegory will be easier to understand if we examine the significance of philosophy. At almost the beginning of Rome (750 B.C., according to Orosius), about the time of Numa Pompilius, lived a philosopher named Pythagoras. Before him seekers after knowledge were "sages," but Pythagoras would not accept the designation of "sage," claiming to be a mere seeker after wisdom. Hence the origin of the terms "philosopher" and "philosophy," meaning "lover of wisdom" and "the love of wisdom." Every man having the inborn human desire to know is in the wide sense a philosopher, but the term has been reserved to mean something more, just as "friend" has been reserved to mean something more than the common bond of humanity which in a broad sense makes friends of all men. Remembering what Aristotle says of friendship in his *Ethics,* we shall see that to be a philosopher a man must have love and zeal for wisdom. Philosophy for delight or profit is only incidental philosophy. Many who delight in composing odes and studying rhetoric and music but who follow the other sciences are not philosophers; nor do we call those men philosophers who love wisdom only for profit, as do "lawyers, physicians and almost all the members of the religious orders." So, as of friendship, the only perfect philosophy is generated by worthiness alone. The real philosopher loves every part of wisdom and wisdom every part of the philosopher so as to allow him to waste no thought on aught else. Philosophy has as its subject understanding, and as its form an almost divine love of the thing understood. Truth is the efficient cause of philosophy even as virtue is of friendship, and the goal of philosophy is that true bliss which comes through contemplation of the truth. And as sometimes under emotion the source or goal of an action or passion is called by the name of the action or passion (as when Virgil addresses Aeneas with the words "O light," and Statius makes Hypsipyle say to Archemoros, "Thou comfort of my estate," and as a father calls his child "my love"), so the sciences most closely contemplated by philosophy are often called by her name, i.e., the natural sciences, moral science, and metaphysical science, which is particularly called philosophy since it is a particular object of philosophy's contemplation. (chapter 11)

So in the allegorical sense the "Love that in my mind discourses with me" is the study devoted to philosophy. Now there are two kinds of study, one which brings a man to the habit of any given art or science and another that works in the habit when it has been acquired; it is the first kind that is meant here. The "sun" in stanza 2 is allegorically to be taken as God; for the sun, with its power to illuminate and quicken, is surely the best symbol we can find for God. The circling of the sun signifies the understanding of God, who sees no more noble thing than philosophy, which, being the loving exercise of wisdom, must exist supremely in God, who, contemplating philosophy, sees her thus in His own essence. "Oh most noble, excellent heart which is in harmony with the bride of heaven's emperor, bride, aye and sister, and most beloved daughter!" (chapter 12)

Having now considered her primary existence, we shall consider how she exists secondarily in created intelligence. The phrase "Every intellect from above" implies that intellects exiled from the supernal fatherland are excluded, for they are without love and so cannot philosophize. This means of course the infernal intelligences, who are those deprived of the blessedness of the intellect, a most bitter punishment. With the line "And such as are here drawn to love," Dante goes on to say how in a secondary sense she comes into the human intelligence, for in this world those who feel the peace of love perceive her. The phrase is restrictive, for a great proportion of mankind is dominated more by the senses than by reason, and those who live sensually cannot understand her. And of course, unlike the angelic intellect, that of man is not always "in act," and when our soul is not in the act of speculation it cannot be said to be in company with philosophy save, in the case of the happy minority, potentially. Such are indeed properly to be called philosophers, for men are called according to their habit; we call an eloquent man such even when he is not speaking. Yet in the case of philosophy the study necessary for the acquisition of any habit cannot bring us perfectly to win her, but such is her virtue that, perfect or otherwise, she always deserves the name of perfection. The soul of philosophy is love, manifested in the exercise of wisdom, which in turn brings content in temporal things and scorn for such things as others are slaves to. These others, when they feel the longing for perfection, fall to sighing, which is the meaning of the passage "the eyes of those wherein she shines. . . ." (chapter 13)

Moving from the general to the special praises of the lady (as in the case of the literal exposition): in the stanza beginning "Into her descends" Dante proposes to commend love, which, as said above, is a part of philosophy. And as a virtue descending and acting upon a thing draws the latter to itself (even as the sun reduces to light the things on which his ray falls, insofar as they have the faculty of receiving it), so God reduces this love to His own likeness as far as that may be possible. The quality of this new creation is set forth in the line "as it does into an angel that beholds it." We must know further how God stamps His power upon some things (on angelic intelligences directly, on others indirectly as reflected from those intelligences). Here too we must distinguish between "light" and "splendor" (following Avicenna). "Light" is light existing in its source, a "ray" is light existing in the medium between the source and the first body it meets, and "splendor" is light reflected. The statement that the divine virtue draws this love to it with no intermediary must be explained as follows: the divine love being eternal, its object must be likewise, and so this love makes us love, for wisdom whereupon it strikes is eternal, as is stated in the Proverbs of Solomon and in the beginning of the Gospel of St. John. And where the love of wisdom glows, all other loves are almost quenched, as the lives of the philosophers attest; some indeed, such as Socrates, sacrificed their lives for this wisdom. "Any gentle lady" means a soul noble in intellect, for the souls of others are not ladies but handmaidens; such noble souls are urged to look upon philosophy, for the ode affirms that the faculty of contemplating her was given us so that we might see the things that are revealed and long for those which she keeps concealed. As through her much is revealed that else would seem marvelous, so also she suggests that for a loftier intellect every miracle may have its reason, and consequently she reinforces our faith, the source of our hope and our charity, "by which three virtues we rise to philosophize in that heavenly Athens where Stoics, Peripatetics, and Epicureans, by the art of the eternal truth, harmoniously concur in one will." (chapter 14)

Now comes the commendation of wisdom, the other aspect of philosophy. The eyes of wisdom are her demonstrations, and her smile signifies her persuasions; from the contemplation of these two perfecting our reason comes the joy of blessedness which is the supreme good of paradise. As for the things "that surpass our intellect," that may surely be said of wisdom, for it leads to consideration of things such as God and eternity and first matter which we cannot understand except by negation. And if it be asked how wisdom can make a man blessed when she cannot reveal clearly certain things to him, the answer is that "human desire is measured in this life by that degree of knowledge which it is here possible to possess."

This statement has led some critics to wonder how closely Dante is following St. Thomas or indeed good Christian doctrine. But Busnelli and Vandelli have come to Dante's rescue, quoting from the *Summa Contra Gentiles* a passage where Aquinas makes it clear that perfect happiness *simpliciter* cannot be achieved in this life but leaves open the possibility of a happiness perfect *secundum quid*.[15] In fact, Dante follows his master very closely.

This is why the saints do not envy one another, for each one attains the goal of his desire, and his desire is commensurate with his kind of excellence. As Justinian will put it in the *Paradiso*: "in the measuring of our rewards/To our deserts lies part of our content. . . ." This longing for wisdom, then, bounded as it is by our intellectual potential, cannot be compared to the avarice of the miser, which, boundless, can never be satisfied. In the line "Her beauty rains down little flames of fire," the secondary felicity which proceeds from her beauty is intended. The beauty of philosophy is morality, resulting from the order of the moral virtues even as physical beauty results from the proportion and order of the members. The exhortation to ladies desirous of increasing their beauty to look upon that of this lady signifies that souls should try, by gazing upon wisdom, to rid themselves of such blemishes to their moral beauty as vanity or pride, for wisdom may make the vicious man upright and good. And, finally, wisdom is the mother of all origins, for she was with God (in the divine thought) when He gave beginning to the universe and specifically the generating revolutions of the heavens, as Solomon states in Proverbs; those that flee their friendship, says Dante, are "worse than dead." Let all recognize that they owe their existence to this divine wisdom, "and if you may not all come to look upon her

yourself, honor her in her friends, and follow their commandments, as proclaiming to you the will of this eternal empress."
Here ends the exposition of the "real" (allegorical) meaning. It
will be simple now to understand the *tornata*, for this wisdom had
indeed seemed "fierce and disdainful" as long as Dante could not
apprehend her persuasions nor perceive her demonstrations. The
fault was all his. The allegory is now entirely clear and "it is
time, in order to go further on, to conclude this treatise." (chapter 15)

✽ 8 ✽

The *Convivio* (II)

Ode III
"Le dolci rime d'amor ch'i' solia"

The sweet rhymes of love that I used
to seek out in my thoughts
I now must put aside; not that I do not hope
to return to them,
but because the scornful and fierce acts
that in my lady
have made their appearance have barred the way
of my accustomed speech.
And since this seems to me a time of waiting
I shall put down my sweet style
which I have maintained while treating of love
and I will speak of the virtue
whereby a man is truly noble,
in harsh and subtle rhyme,
refuting the false and base opinion
of those who hold that nobility's
source is riches.
And, beginning, I call upon that lord
who dwells in my lady's eyes
wherefore she becomes enamored of herself.

A certain man who once held empire judged that nobility,
according to his view,
was ancient possession of goods

with handsome manners;
and another there was of lighter wisdom
who recast that definition
and took from it the latter part —
for perhaps he had it not!
Following after him go all those
who affirm one is noble by virtue of a family
that has been for a long time wealthy;
and so long has endured
such a false opinion among us,
that we now call anyone
a nobleman if he can say: "I was
grandchild or son of such and such a man of worth,"
although himself he be of naught.
But most base will he appear — to one who looks upon the truth —
to whom the right road being shown, yet strays from it;
he is like to one who is dead yet walks the earth.

One who defines: "Man is a living trunk"
first of all does not say the truth
and, apart from the falsehood, does not complete the thought,
but perhaps he sees no further.
He who held empire was likewise
at fault in his definition,
for first he sets forth what is false and, on the other hand,
proceeds with defective thought;
for riches cannot — as folk believe —
either give or take away nobility,
because by their own nature they are base;
further, one who paints a figure
unless he himself can be it, cannot set it forth
nor is an upright tower
made to lean by a river which flows far away.
That (riches) are base and imperfect is clear
for however much be acquired
they cannot bring peace, but rather cause more care:
whence the soul that is upright and true
is not undone by their melting away.

Neither will they concede that a base man can become noble
nor that from a low-born father may descend
a family that can ever be called noble;
this is what they argue.
Wherefore their argument seems to attack itself
in that it affirms

that time is necessary to nobility,
defining it by reference thereto.
Further, it follows from what I have said above
that all of us are noble or all base,
or else there was no beginning to mankind:
this I do not concede
nor do they either, if they are Christians!
So that to healthy intellects
it is clear that their remarks are vain,
and so I refute them as false
and depart from them;
and now I wish to say, as I feel it,
what is nobility and from what it comes;
and I will tell the tokens that a noble man bears.

I say that every virtue in principle
comes from one root:
virtue, I mean, that makes man happy
in his action.
This is, as the *Ethics* says,
a selective habit
which dwells in the mean alone —
such words it sets down.
I say that nobility in its essence
implies always the good of its subject
as baseness implies always evil,
and such virtue
yields always good understanding of itself
so that in the same statement
the two agree for they are of one effect.
So it must be that one springs from the other
or else both from a third;
but if one has the value of the other
and something more, then more likely it will spring from
    the other.
And let what I have said here be presupposed.

There is nobility wherever there is virtue
but not virtue where it is,
just as heaven is wherever is the star
but not conversely.
And we in woman and in youth
see this soul-health,
insofar as they are considered susceptible of shame
which is different from virtue.

So, as from black comes perse, there will come
each virtue from that one,
or their generic kind, as I set down above.
Therefore let no man boast,
saying, "By inheritance I am with her,"
for almost gods are they
who have such grace, apart from all the guilty,
for God alone bestows it on that soul
which he sees within its person
dwell in perfection; so that to some
the seed of felicity, clearly,
has been sent by God into the well-disposed soul.

The soul which this goodness adorns
does not keep it hidden,
for from the beginning when it is wed to the body
it shows it forth and unto death.
Obedient, sweet, susceptible to shame
it is in the first age,
and adorns its person with beauty
with well-according parts;
in manhood (it is) temperate and brave,
full of love and courteous praise,
and finds its sole delight in loyal deeds,
and in its old age it is
prudent and just and renowned for liberality,
and it takes pleasure in itself
to hear and speak of other's excellence;
then in the fourth part of life
it is re-wed to God,
contemplating the end awaiting it
while it blesses the times past. . . .
Now see how many are the deceived!

O my against-the-erring-ones, go forth
and when thou art
in that place where our lady is,
do not conceal thy mission from her:
for surely thou mayst inform her:
"I go discoursing of thy friend."

Dante begins the fourth treatise by affirming that his love of
philosophy has naturally made him love all who follow the truth
and hate those who follow error; he feels impelled to make the
errant see their errors. Among the most dangerous errors is that

concerning human excellence, implanted in us by nature, which ought to be called nobility. This error has brought about false judgment with scorn of the good and exaltation of the wicked. And to avoid idleness when his lady had temporarily withdrawn her tender glances (when he was considering whether God understood the prime matter of the elements), he decided to attack this problem in an ode. For greater clarity, allegory has been put aside; and the ode will need exposition only as regards the literal meaning. The lady, however, is still philosophy. (chapter 1)

The question of God's "understanding" of matter afforded great scope for theological subtlety in Dante's time and seems to have been a favorite field of debate.[1] Wicksteed points out that Dante's statement here implies no unorthodoxy.[2]

The first stanza of the ode is the proem, itself subdivided into three sections. First Dante explains that he has temporarily abandoned the usual rhyming because of his lady's haughty looks, and now he has come to a time of waiting. "Time" is "the enumeration of celestial movement, which prepares things here below diversely to receive one form or another, as the seasons are variously disposed for receiving the seed." Similarly, the mind, linked with the body and hence with these natural changes, has various dispositions at various times. Words, the seed of actions, must be discreetly withheld or released according to the time or season. Solomon says, "There is a time to speak and a time to be silent." "For nearly all our troubles, if we rightly consider their source, proceed in a way from not knowing how to use time."

In the phrase "I will speak of the virtue," "virtue" means a power of nature or a goodness given by her. When Dante speaks of treating of it with "harsh and subtle rhyme," "rhyme" is to be taken in the broad sense of metrical rhyming composition: "harsh" since the words employed in the discussion of a weighty subject cannot be smooth, and "subtle" with reference to the meaning of the words and the nature of the subject. The proem states that the treatment of the truth is to precede the refutation of the false, while in the treatise the opposite sequence is followed. The purpose is the same in both, however — to emphasize the truth. It comes first in the proem to arouse the reader's expectation, and it follows the refutation of the false in the treatise so that it may appear more plainly. This latter is the method of Aristotle. The invocation of the lord is an appeal for the truth to assist Dante, for the truth is lord, and the mind when espoused to it is a lady

and otherwise a servant. The line "Wherefore she becomes enamored of herself" means that the philosophizing soul not only
contemplates the truth but contemplates its own contemplation
and the beauty thereof. (chapter 2)

The first part of the treatise deals with opinions of others, the
second with nobility's true nature; in the third part the ode is
addressed directly. There are also further subdivisions. This
elaborate structure is justified by the lofty subject, neglected by
others.

Dante will make the same claim of originality, but more affirma-
tively, for the *Paradiso:* "The sea I range was never coursed before,"
and will utter a like boast in the *De Monarchia*. Nor should it
greatly trouble us if Curtius lists such statements as rhetorical
commonplaces.[3]

The first part is divided into two smaller parts: in the first
the erroneous opinions are stated, and in the second refuted. The
first subdivision of this first part has two members, the first giving
"the emperor's" definition of nobility and the second the vulgar
interpretation of his definition. The phrase "A certain man who
once held empire" refers to Frederick II (the last effective emperor), who defined nobility as "ancient possession of goods with
handsome manners." The second qualification has been forgotten
or deliberately suppressed; it is now the common opinion that
anyone of a family that has long been rich is noble. This wrong
notion cannot be entirely overlooked, for "the Philosopher" says
that the opinion of the majority cannot be absolutely false, and,
further, we must respect the authority of the emperor. (chapter 3)

Enlarging on this statement, Dante argues that humanity, in
order to attain to happiness on this earth, must be organized as a
"single monarchy having one ruler" whose supreme authority will
keep the peace among lesser princes and who, having the world
at his command, will be beyond the temptation of greed.

Dante is satisfied that the supreme prince should be a Roman
emperor, since history clearly indicates that the triumph of Rome
was achieved by divine providence, as Virgil says. (chapter 4)
For it was proper that the Son of God should come to earth when
the earth was "best disposed" to receive Him, and this was at the
time of the perfection of the Roman Empire, under which universal peace prevailed. And Dante adds further proofs: David's
line and the city of Rome began at the same time; the growth of

the Roman power from the founding of the city to the empire shows divine guidance, since each of the seven kings had characteristics suited to his times; the heroes of the Roman Republic reveal divine inspiration in their lofty deeds, and as for Cato — "O most sacred bosom of Cato, who shall presume to speak of thee? Truly, none can speak of thee more worthily than by keeping silence" — even such a respectful silence as Jerome keeps with regard to St. Paul. Throughout all Roman history the hand of God is manifest, and calling Rome a holy city, Dante concludes: "I am of the firm opinion that the stones that are fixed in her walls are worthy of reverence, and the ground where she sits is worthy beyond the preaching or approval of men." (chapter 5)

Chapters 4 and 5 make up a kind of pocket *De Monarchia*, shorn of its polemics. Written presumably in 1307, before the coming of Henry VII, when Dante was, in the opinion of Passerin d'Entrèves, not directly concerned with politics,[4] it is hardly a first draft of that work. It is therefore significant as showing Dante's persistent preoccupation with Roman tradition; it proves — if proof were necessary — that the *De Monarchia* is not something whipped up for the occasion like a campaign biography. C. T. Davis remarks in *Dante and the Idea of Rome* that the reference to "the walls and stones of Rome . . . is especially interesting in view of the total absence in Dante of the cult of 'ruin worship,' that adoration of the tangible remains of the past which would later find in Petrarch so indefatigable an exponent . . . but historically."[5] Both Davis and Vossler note that much of Dante's material comes from St. Augustine, though he uses it for purposes quite different from those of his source.

Turning from imperial to philosophical authority, Dante defines "authority" as "the act of author," deriving the word from an obsolete Latin verb *aveio* in which all the vowels are bound together (this sense of "author" would apply to poets) and from a Greek word *autentin* meaning, according to Uguccione's *Derivationes,* "worthy of faith and obedience," the sense he has in mind. Such an authority must be Aristotle, the master who can best explain the purpose of man's life; Greek philosophy (the course of which Dante summarizes) had reached its highest perception in him.

So the authority of Aristotle (philosophical authority) still obtains and in this case is in accord with imperial authority. These two authorities should always agree, for the imperial without the philosophical is dangerous and the latter without the former is weak. And so it is written in the *Book of Wisdom:* "Love the light of wisdom, all ye who are before the peoples," which is a way of saying that these authorities should unite. "O wretched ye," exclaims Dante, "who at present rule, and, oh most wretched, ye who are ruled!" For no philosophical authority unites with their government, neither through their own study nor their counselors. He admonishes Charles II of Naples and Frederick II of Sicily and other rulers to follow good counselors. (chapter 6)

Dante speaks even more bitterly of the two kings in *De Vulgari Eloquentia.* In *Paradiso* VIII, however, he implies that Charles was at least not stingy, and in *Purgatorio* III he has Manfred describe Frederick as "the honor of Sicily."

The emperor's opinion then would seem to have the support of both authorities, but the vulgar interpretation of this opinion is erroneous, because the term "noble" is now wrongly applied to the son or grandson of any worthy man, without reference to his own worth. But even as a man who crossing a plain cannot follow the tracks of one who has gone before is less to be honored than one who has no tracks to guide him, so the unworthy descendant of noble ancestors is less noble than one born without such an inheritance. Such a man is, *qua* man, not even alive but dead since he is blind to reason, the attribute which makes a man more than a beast. The authorities here are Proverbs 5 and Aristotle's *De Anima.* (chapter 7)

Dante here digresses to explain that his arguments imply no irreverence toward philosopher or prince. Although Aristotle says "what the majority thinks cannot be absolutely false" while Dante attacks the vulgar notion of nobility, there is no real conflict: Aristotle is thinking of the inward or rational judgment of the majority, and would not deny that their "outer or sensuous" judgment can often be wrong (many would say, for example, that the sun is a foot in diameter). It is the sensuous judgment that Dante is attacking here: the vulgar, judging by appearances, think that ostentatious weddings and stupendous buildings are the cause of nobility, or are nobility itself. If they judged by reason, they would see that the opposite is true.

And as for his apparent contradiction of imperial authority, Dante is aware that he must here argue with great care, for "I who am speaking in the presence of so many adversaries cannot speak briefly. Let no one be surprised if my digression is lengthy." He then carefully explains that his opinion does not show irreverence to the emperor's authority, but rather unreverence, since in such matters the emperor's authority does not obtain. The imperial "art" covers such things as laws concerning matrimony, warfare, government, and in these we are subject to the emperor. Some matters are in nature's hands, such as coming of age; so too the definition of "nobility" is not a part of the emperor's art, and we are not bound to reverence his authority here. (chapters 8 and 9)

Refutation of false opinions begins with the line "One who defines. . . ." "Handsome manners" may stand; the refutation will be directed against the elements of time and wealth in the emperor's definition. The rejection of the emperor's inclusion of riches implies also a rejection of the vulgar opinion to the same effect. This section is again divided into two parts, the first asserting that the emperor was wrong and the second (beginning "for riches cannot") giving the reasons why. So in the phrase "Man is a living trunk," Dante asserts that first it is simply false in the use of the word "trunk" and, secondly, defective in the use of "living" instead of "rational." By the phrase "A certain man who once held empire" instead of "emperor," Dante would indicate that the question is not one for the imperial office. He adds that the emperor erred in laying down a false subject of nobility, ancient wealth, and then went on to a defective differentiating principle, gracious manners, which do not take in the whole formal principle but only a very small part thereof. And, although the text does not mention it, we may add, says Dante, that the emperor, though famous for his logic, erred in not drawing the definition of nobility from its effects rather than its sources, for it is itself a source, and so must be known from the things that spring from it. In the passage beginning "for riches cannot," the point is made that riches, being base in themselves, cannot give nobleness or take it away, since they have nothing to do with it: this baseness is demonstrated in the passage beginning "That (riches) are base." Here Aristotle's statement in *Metaphysics* VII is relevant: "When one thing is generated by another, it is generated by it in virtue of existing in its being." We also have his statement that everything which is destroyed is destroyed because of some preceding change, and everything which is affected must in some way be connected with that change. Wealth, being base, cannot produce nobility or take it away (see text beginning with "further, one who paints a figure"), for a painter cannot paint a figure which he does not already have himself "in intention."

The figure "Nor is an upright tower" indicates that riches have no more connection with nobility than a tower with a remote river. (chapter 10)

Dante goes on to demonstrate that riches are essentially base: their bestowal is without discrimination, their increase is dangerous, and their possession harmful. Wealth, he argues, whether lawfully or unlawfully come by, oftener goes to bad men than to the good, "and this is so obvious that it needs no proof." The good man, having better things to think of, either never attains wealth or, if he has it, cheerfully exchanges it for better things: who has forgotten Alexander, the good king of Castile, Saladin, the Marquis of Monferrato, the Count of Toulouse, Bertran de Born, or Galasso of Montefeltro — all exemplifying the virtue of liberality? (chapter 11)

Wealth is deceitful in that it promises satisfaction, but in fact its accumulation breeds only avarice, as Boethius, Solomon, Seneca, Cicero, Horace, Juvenal, "all the poets," and the Bible attest. In fact we have only to see for ourselves what kind of lives are led by those who pursue riches. Digressing, Dante denies that the pursuit of wisdom brings a like dissatisfaction, arguing that the successive desires are in fact satisfied as one learns all there is to know about a given branch of knowledge, but the same is not true of the greed for wealth, which is insatiable desire for more and more material things. Dante maintains that the longing for knowledge, whether in general or particular, can attain perfection; the thirst for riches cannot be slaked. He depicts the terrors familiar to the rich man which the poor man never knows, citing the case of Amyclas, in Lucan's *Pharsalia*. The rich are objects of hatred; sometimes even the son of a rich man will plot his father's death — there are many examples of this in Italy, says Dante, particularly between the Tiber and the Po. Boethius has rightly said that money is good only when transferred generously to others. The wise and upright man wants nothing to do with wealth save as it may be a necessity. (chapters 12 and 13)

Vossler remarks perceptively on chapter 13 that Dante, having abandoned a problem in metaphysical speculation (i.e., God's "understanding" of matter), in the course of his inquiry into the nature of nobility ran into another theoretical problem,

and what he had not been able to solve in metaphysics confronts him now once again, and most unexpectedly from the side of the theory of knowledge. . . . These two chapters contain the germ of a phenomenology of the spirit. Between the empirical incapacity ever to attain complete knowledge and the metaphysical possibility and necessity of a universally valid conclusion of knowledge, Dante has clearly seen the distinction.[6]

We can only add to this that the source of his passion, and perhaps the basis of his position, are deeply existential — not to say purely human. They are the reasonings of an impoverished exile and an ardent student as well as a philosopher.

The refutation of the argument for time as an element of nobility begins in the text with "Neither will they concede." First the fallacious reasoning of exponents of this view is exposed; then (beginning "Further, it follows") their main argument is refuted; and finally the exposition of the truth begins with "So that to healthy intellects." Concerning the refutation, it should first be remarked that such people hold that neither a churl nor his son can ever be noble. But following back through the generations on this principle there would never be a place where nobility could begin. And if they argue that such a change could take place when the base origins of a man had been forgotten, there are no less than four answers to that. First, it would imply that the greater the oblivion the greater the nobility, which is absurd. Second, it would imply that nobility and baseness exist only among men, but such distinctions we recognize in falcons, horses, pearls, and the like. And if one were to answer that in the case of other things nobility means the excellence of the thing but in the case of men it means that the memory of their low origins has been forgotten, then one would want to answer such stupidity "not with words but with a dagger." Thirdly, accepting the argument, the thing generated would often come before the thing generating, which is impossible. If Gherardo da Cammino had been the grandson of the lowest churl that ever drank of the Sile or the Cagnano, and if the grandfather was still remembered, who would dare call Gherardo base? If his nobleness had been perceived in him, as in fact it was, and his base ancestor was not forgotten, then nobility would have existed in him before its generating agent (forgetfulness of origin) had come into effect. Fourthly, under the argument, a man would be held noble when dead who was not noble when alive, which would be absurd. (chapter 14)

The ode now proceeds to a direct attack on the false opinion under discussion, beginning with "Further, it follows." If we accept the premise that a base-born man cannot become noble, nor a noble son be born from base stock, it would follow either that there is no nobility in the world or that the human race is not descended from one single man. If it is only a matter of inheritance, mankind is either all base or all noble, for it is all descended from Adam, and there is no distinction and no true nobility. Otherwise, we should have to assume two sources for humanity, which is counter to the teachings of Aristotle, to our faith, and to the ancient belief of the gentiles. Aristotle does not speak of a common ancestor, but he says there is one essence in all men. Plato maintains that all men depend on only one "idea." And Aristotle would laugh aloud if he heard people assume two origins for mankind as of horses and asses and say (apologies to Aristotle) that those who thought so might be considered the asses. Further, Solomon, speaking for our faith (which is to be preserved absolutely), calls all men sons of Adam, and Ovid in *Metamorphoses* I affirms that there was but one first man. So the ode says, "this I do not concede," and adds, "nor do they either, if they are Christians," for although other authorities concur, the Christian doctrine is of greater vigor.

With the verses "So that to healthy intellects . . ." Dante concludes that the error is refuted and the time has come to reveal the truth as he indicates in the verses, "and now I wish to say. . . ." The truth, he continues, will be plain to "healthy" intellects, for the intellect or the mind is subject to maladies, of which three are to be noted: "braggart natures" who assume they know everything, "abject natures" who assume that knowledge is beyond their reach, and the frivolous, who do not reason in orderly fashion. Cicero, St. Thomas Aquinas, and Solomon have denounced the first class; Aristotle calls the second incompetent and the third worthless. In addition there are those who are not sound because of real mental infirmity. It is to minds free of all these failings that Dante would point out the falseness of the definition discussed. (chapter 15)

As it is written in the *Book of Wisdom,* every true king supremely loves the truth, and therefore Dante says that every king shall rejoice because the false and pernicious opinion has been refuted. And beginning with "I say that every virtue in principle," Dante proposes to define nobility according to the truth. First he will show what nobility is and then show how one in whom it dwells may be recognized. The first argument has two divisions: in the first certain elements of nobility are investigated; in the second, beginning "There is nobility," the definition itself is sought.

Nobility really means the perfection of each thing in its proper nature. It may be used of things as well as of man. Solomon says, "Blessed the land whose king is noble," meaning perfect in mind and body, and "Woe unto thee, O land, whose king is a child," referring to a land whose king is not a perfect man, for a man may be a child not merely by reason of imperfection of age but for other defects, as Aristotle says. Many reject this definition of "noble," holding that it means "named and known by many" and comes from the verb *"nosco,"* "to know." This is clearly false; otherwise the best-known things would be the noblest: the obelisk of St. Peter's would be the noblest stone in the world, Asdente the cobbler of Parma the noblest of that city, and Alboino della Scala would be nobler than Guido da Castello of Reggio. In fact "noble" comes from *"non vile,"* ("not base"). Aristotle (*Physics* VII) says: "Everything is most perfect when it touches . . . its own proper virtue. . . ." We now know what nobility is; to learn where it is found, we must look to its effects, as Christ says, "By their fruits ye shall know them." We shall seek then these fruits, the moral and intellectual virtues of which nobility is the seed. (chapter 16)

The text, from "I say" to "a selective habit," gives Aristotle's definition of moral virtue. All virtues come from one principle, and "every virtue" means the moral virtues of which we speak, for these are entirely in our power. Aristotle lists eleven moral virtues: courage, temperance, liberality, munificence (which is the moderator of great expenditures), consciousness of greatness, proper pride, serenity, affability, frankness (which keeps us from undue boasting or self-depreciation), eutrapelia (which moderates us in sports), and finally justice, disposing us to love and righteous actions. Each of these virtues has two foes or vices, one in excess, the other in deficiency. The virtues indeed are the means between these opposed extremes and they all spring from one principle: the habit of right choice. All of them may be defined as "an elective habit consisting in the mean." Their practice leads to felicity, as Aristotle says. Some would call prudence a moral virtue, but Aristotle places it among the intellectual ones, though it is essential to the moral virtues.

In this life there are two attainable felicities, the good, the path of the active life, and the better, that of the contemplative, for Aristotle proves in *Ethics* X that the latter is the higher felicity. Christ says the same thing, according to Luke, in his words to Martha and Mary. And if anyone should ask Dante why he does not suggest proceeding to this greater felicity by the intellectual rather than the moral virtues, he would answer that the moral virtues are more common and better-known and so are easier to point out. (chapter 17)

Étienne Gilson in his *Dante the Philosopher* attempts to show wherein Dante differed from St. Thomas Aquinas in the interpretation of Aristotle:

What "superhumanizes" the contemplative life in Dante (as contrasted to Aristotle) is not the fact that the intellect which guides it is not our own; it is the fact that, even for the very precarious success that it may hope for in this life, our speculative intellect requires a divine Revelation, so that in the long run the success of this intellect, which is wholly ours, is not itself wholly ours. On the other hand . . . the practical department of the moral life enjoys complete self-sufficiency, since it consists in pursuing, by those purely natural and human means which are the moral virtues, that purely natural and human end which is happiness in this life in a society regulated by the most human of the virtues — justice.[7]

The *Convivio* proceeds to show that the eleven moral virtues proceed from nobility, as effect does from cause. This is supported by the philosophical proposition that when two things agree in any respect they are either both derived from a third thing or one is derived from the other as effect is from cause. The lines beginning "so that in the same statement" assert that nobility and moral virtue are alike in that both imply praise in the possessor, and the passage beginning "but if one be equivalent" makes the reasonable induction though not actual demonstration that one comes from the other rather than both from a third, for if there are in us both praiseworthy things and a principle whence praise of us might flow it is reasonable to make the inference. (chapter 18)

The passage beginning "There is nobility wherever there is virtue" contains two sections, the first proving something hitherto merely touched on and the second ("So, as from black . . .") reaching the conclusion and the definition we seek. The first point is that, if nobility has a larger scope than virtue, virtue will proceed from nobility instead of the reverse. It is obvious that there is nobility wherever there is virtue, "just as heaven is wherever is the star," as the ode says; but it does not follow that the reverse is true. Nobility is a heaven, and the stars shining in it are the intellectual and moral virtues and good dispositions and laudable emotions. Other stars may be thought of too, such as wit, beauty, and enduring health. "I dare to affirm that human nobleness considered under the aspect of its many fruits surpasses that of the angel, although the angelic be more divine in its unity." Such is the burden of the psalm "O Lord our God, how wonderful is Thy name," which says that man is but little less than the angels. We may well compare heaven to human nobility.

The ode, going on with "And we in woman," proves that nobility goes into areas where virtue does not. We see that "this soul-health" (i.e., nobility) exists where there is sensitiveness to shame as in women and youths, in whom it is a laudable emotion, though not, as Aristotle makes clear in *Ethics* IV, in old men nor scholars. (chapter 19)

We come now to the definition we have been seeking. The ode affirms that every virtue will proceed from nobleness, as perse derives from black. Perse is a mixture of purple and black, but black predominates; so virtue is made up of nobleness and passion, but nobleness predominates, so that virtue is called after it and is named goodness. The ode goes on to say that no one can think himself noble because of his stock unless these fruits are in him, and that those who have this grace are almost like gods. The gift can be given by God alone, with Whom there is no regard for worldly distinctions, as scripture tells us (Romans 2:2). It is not unreasonable to compare such beings with gods, for as there are men so base as to be bestial, so there must be and are men who are almost divine. Aristotle demonstrates this by reference to Homer. So let not any one of the Uberti of Florence or the Visconti of Milan claim nobility because of his lineage, for the divine seed falls not on the stock but on the individual; the man ennobles the race and not the reverse.

Beginning with the verse "for God alone . . . ," the ode says that God gives His grace to one disposed to receive it, for this right disposition is essential, as Aristotle says in *De Anima* II, and as Guido Guinizelli affirms in his ode *"Al cor gentil ripara sempre amore."* It may be that the soul will stand not well in the person because of defect of complexion or of season; such souls are like valleys facing the north, or caves beneath the earth. But the ode concludes that there are some to whom "the seed of felicity . . . has been sent by God," whence it is clear that human nobility is simply the soul that is perfectly disposed in every part. This definition will include all four causes: the material, for it says "into the well-disposed soul," which is the matter and subject of nobility; the formal, for it says it is the seed; the efficient, for it says "sent by God"; and the final, for it says "of felicity." (chapter 20)

We shall now consider how this nobility descends into us, first in the natural sense and then in the theological or spiritual sense. We are composed of both soul and body, but the seed of virtue pertains to the soul. There have been various theories about the difference in our souls: Avicenna and Algazel maintained that the soul in itself was either base or noble; Plato and others held that souls were base or noble according to the stars they were assumed to proceed from; Pythagoras believed that all souls — even those of animals — were alike in their nobility, the difference being only in the bodily forms. We may dismiss these and follow the opinion of Aristotle and the Peripatetics:

And therefore I say that when the human seed falls into . . . the matrix, it bears with it the virtue of the generative soul, and the virtue of the heaven, and the virtues of its elements, that is, its complexion; and it matures and disposes the material for the formative virtue given by the soul of the generator. The formative virtue prepares the organs for the celestial virtue which draws the soul from the potentiality of the seed into life. The moment it is produced it receives from the virtue of the mover of the heaven the possible intellect, which potentially brings in itself all the universal forms according as they exist in its Producer, but in a lesser degree in proportion as it is more removed from the first Intelligence.

(Cf. *Purgatorio* XXV, 37 ff.)

If his language is hard to understand it is not surprising, Dante says. It seems marvelous to him that argument can demonstrate and reason perceive such an operation; it is indeed a thing not to be expounded in any language "truly vernacular." He is moved to exclaim with the apostle, "O height of the wealth of the wisdom of God, how incomprehensible are thy judgments, and thy ways past finding out!" Because of variations in the complexion of the seed or the disposition of the sower or of the heavens for that particular effect, which varies greatly since the constellations are never still, the soul produced will be more or less pure, and on the degree of purity will depend the penetration of the possible intellectual virtue. When the purity is such as to free this virtue from every corporeal shadow, we shall have the seed of felicity of which we speak. Cicero says as much, speaking of the soul of Cato, in his *De Senectute.* Such a soul will have its own proper virtue and intellectual and divine virtue as well, as is written in *De Causis;* some say that if all the preceding virtues were to synchronize in their best dispositions for the production of a soul, the soul would almost be another incarnate God. And this is all that can be said from the point of view of natural science.

When God sees His creature ready to receive His benefactions, He bestows on it as much good as it is capable of receiving. Since these gifts come of love, they are called the gifts of the Holy Ghost, and according to Isaiah they number seven: wisdom, understanding, counsel, strength, knowledge, piety, and fear of the Lord. The first shoot which springs from this seed is mental appetite, which in Greek is *"hormen."* St. Augustine and Aristotle both insist on the need of the right habits that this seed may thrive and bear fruit. (chapter 21)

Moral philosophers have stated that a man desirous of bestowing benefactions on others should make them as useful as possible to the receiver. For this reason, Dante says, he would like to make his banquet in all its parts as useful as possible. Here it would seem that a discussion on human felicity would be most useful to those who do not know it, for, as both Aristotle and Cicero declare, one knowing not the goal can make little progress toward it. Leaving aside the opinions of Zeno and Epicurus, Dante passes on to Aristotle's opinion and takes up the concept of the *hormen,* or natural appetite of the mind. This natural appetite, rising from divine grace, at first appears similar to that which comes of nature, just as in their early growth one grain is like another. At first this natural appetite is shared even by animals, all of whom from their birth love themselves and fear things which are inimical to them. Presently these appetites begin to differ, and the one that leads us to our peace becomes distinguished from all others. First, it loves itself without discrimination. Then it begins to distinguish, following or shunning things as they are good or bad in themselves and according to their attraction for the different parts of its own nature, for it loves most the noblest of itself. The exercise of our mind constitutes our blessedness, to which no other delight is equal. "Mind" means the rational part, the will and the intellect, not the sensitive appetite, for no one doubts that the rational is more noble.

The exercise of our minds is twofold: practical and speculative. Both bring delight, but the contemplative yields the greater delight. The practical exercise of the mind consists in our virtuous activities, with prudence, temperance, courage, and justice. Speculative exercise does not call for our own activities but rather for considering the works of God and nature. Both exercises make up our blessedness, which is the sweetness of the above-mentioned seed. Sometimes the seed does not develop its sweetness for lack of proper cultivation, and conversely by careful cultivation some of the outgrowth of this seed may be made to flourish where it did not originally fall — this is a kind of grafting of one nature on another stock. So let no man be excused, for if he have not this seed from his natural root he may have it by engrafting. Would that there were as many who had engrafted it on themselves as there are those who have failed to cultivate what was their own!

The speculative, being the highest employment of the intellect, brings the greater bliss. The intellect cannot in this life have its perfect employment, which would be the contemplation of God, save as it contemplates Him in His effects. That His blessedness is to be sought above all is manifest in the Bible, where Mark tells of the three Marys seeking the Saviour at the tomb. They were told by one dressed in white that He was no longer there, but bidden to tell His disciples that He would go before them in Galilee. By the three Marys may be understood the three schools of the active life, the Epicureans, the Stoics, and the Peripatetics, for they go to the present world (the tomb), which is the repository of corruptible things, and cannot find the Saviour (blessedness). They find instead an angel (for so Matthew calls him), which is to say human nobility, which comes from God and, addressing our reason, tells all of us that it will be found in Galilee (speculation), telling the disciples and Peter (those who have gone astray) to seek it there. "Galilee" means "whiteness," and material whiteness has more light than any other color, just as speculation has more spiritual light than anything else here below. The Saviour "going before" signifies that God is always ahead of our contemplation, and "there you will see Him" is an assurance of the felicity which we have power to obtain. So the happiness we seek we find imperfectly in the virtuous active life and perfectly, in a way, in the intellectual life; these lead us toward the supreme blessedness which may not be had here. (chapter 22)

Dante's "original" allegory here seems to be an adaptation of a traditional theological version;[8] the odd meaning of "Galilee" goes back to Isidore of Seville.[9]

Dante next considers how we may recognize nobility in men. This part (beginning with "The soul which this goodness adorns") is divided into two sections, the first affirming how nobility illuminates the whole life of noble spirits, the second (beginning "Obedient, sweet") discussing its separate splendors. As to the first part, it should be noted that the divine seed we have mentioned flowers at once and alike in the vegetative, sensitive, and rational, developing and directing the appropriate virtues of each, until it returns to its most glorious Sower in heaven.

The second part, where the distinct signs are mentioned, has four subdivisions according as this seed works in the successive ages of adolescence, manhood, age, or decrepitude. These divisions are indicated in the ode. In general it should be noted that every effect, as effect, receives the likeness of its cause as far as it is possible to retain it. And since our lives and the lives of all earthly creatures are caused by heaven, but heaven does not show iteslf to these effects in a full circle but only in part thereof while its motion is above them, they must be likened to the image of an arch; following such a figure our life rises and descends. The "arch" of one man differs from that of another, but both the psalmist and Aristotle speak of a normal pattern. In the majority, the high point of the arch is probably between the thirtieth and the fortieth year. In those of perfect nature it would be thirty-five, Dante believes, recalling that Christ died at the end of his thirty-fourth year — at the sixth hour or apex of the day, he notes incidentally. It is not, however, especially with reference to this central point that scripture divides the arch, but rather according to the contrary qualities which compose us, by which four ages are marked: (1) adolescence, appropriate to the hot and moist, (2) manhood, appropriate to the hot and dry, (3) age, proper to the cold and dry, and (4) decrepitude, taken up by the cold and moist, as Albertus Magnus says in *Meteorics* IV.

These parts also occur in the year, with its four seasons, and in the day, whose four divisions are: (1) up to tierce, (2) up to nones, (3) up to vespers, and (4) from vespers onward. The gentiles gave the car of the sun four horses, with appropriate names, as Ovid writes. Further, as is said in chapter 6 of the third treatise, the church makes use of temporal hours, of which there are twelve in each day, and because the sixth hour, midday, is the most noble, she approximates her offices to it from either side. Hence the office of tierce is said at the close of that period (9:00 A.M.) and those of the third and fourth parts at their beginning (12:00 M. and 3:00 P.M.). (chapter 23)

Adolescence, according to all the sages, lasts up to the twenty-fifth year. Since in this period the soul is chiefly concerned with developing the body, the rational part cannot come to full discretion, and so there are certain things one of this age may not do without a guardian of full age. The second stage, manhood, the age of achievement, which may give perfection, is somewhat more difficult to define, but Dante says that in the majority this period lasts about twenty years, for if the apex is thirty-five and adolescence ends at twenty-five it would seem right that manhood should include ten years of descent from the apex to match the ten years of ascent. The period called age matches that of adolescence and, running twenty-five years from the end of manhood, ends at the seventieth year. But as adolescence does not begin with the beginning of life but some eight months after, and since nature is more eager to rise than to fall, the period of decrepitude, comparable to the pre-adolescent period, may run for approximately another ten years after the end of age. Plato, who we know had a most excellent nature, lived eighty-one years, according to Cicero. Dante holds that, if Christ had lived out the proper span of his years, he would have changed from mortal to eternal body in his eighty-first year.

The four ages may vary in length in different individuals, but the proportions will remain the same. In all these ages the nobleness of the ennobled soul manifests itself in varying ways suitable to the age. Passing over what Cicero, Virgil, and Egidius the Eremite have to say on the matter, and following only reason, Dante affirms that the first age is the gate through which we enter upon a good life, and here nature bestows on adolescence four appropriate gifts: obedience, sweetness, sensitiveness to shame, and grace of body. Dante stresses the importance of obedience at this stage, leaving the discussion of other appropriate virtues to the next chapter, since the present one is already too long. (chapter 24)

The sweetness appropriate to adolescence is also of importance

for, as Aristotle says in *Ethics* VIII, we cannot have perfect life
without friends, and the seeds of friendship are sown in this age.
Solomon speaks of the need for gracious speech and action at this
time. "Abasement" is almost necessary; by this term Dante means
"three emotions needful for the correct foundation" of life: wonder, "pudicity" (Wicksteed's word for *"pudore"*), and shame.
This is a period of life that has need to be reverent and restrained.
Wonder is the emotion one feels on seeing strange things; kings
have always surrounded themselves with objects designed to create
wonder, and the example of Adrastus is here cited.

"Pudicity," according to Dante, is a shying away of the mind
from foul things, as we see it in maidens and good women and
youths. Statius illustrates it when he describes the daughters of
Adrastus in the presence of the two strange men. What a fine
thing is this characteristic, says Dante. "Tully says in *De Officiis*
I, 'There is no foul act that is not foul to mention.' And a decent
and noble man never so speaks that his words would be improper
for a woman."

Shame is fear of disgrace for a fault committed. From this
springs repentance with its attendant remorse, which is in itself
a punishment of the fault. This is illustrated in the same passages
in the *Thebaid*, when Polynices hesitates to speak because of shame
for the faults he had committed.

In addition to the aforesaid qualities, the noble nature at this
age displays grace of body (the ode says "and adorns its person
with beauty"); this also is necessary for the excellence of our life,
since the soul must accomplish things through the body. The
right proportion of our members gives tne pleasure of harmony,
and good health gives them a color sweet to behold. (chapter 25)

Now, following the ode ("In manhood . . ."), we consider the
evidences of noble nature in the prime of life. At that stage the
five things necessary to perfection are temperance, bravery, love,
courtesy, and loyalty. These things are necessary for our perfection with respect to ourselves, which is the appropriate perfection
in manhood as perfection with respect to others is more appropriate in the next stage. For we must achieve perfection before
we communicate it. Here let us recall what we said of the inborn
appetite in chapter 22 above. This appetite must be guided by
reason, just as a horse, however noble he may be, needs a skilled
rider to guide him. Reason uses its rein when the appetite is in
pursuit, and this rein is called temperance; and it uses the spur

when appetite flees where it should not, and this spur is courage. (We shall find checks and goads in purgatory too.) Virgil shows Aeneas to have been under precisely such restraint at this stage of life: "And how great was that restraint, when having received from Dido such pleasure, as will be discussed below in the seventh treatise, he departed to follow an honorable path. . . ." Similarly, what a spurring was needed when Aeneas dared enter alone with the Sybil into hell!

It is necessary to be affectionate at this stage of life, loving one's elders out of gratitude for their guidance and one's juniors out of desire to pass on its benefits. *Aeneid* V illustrates this aspect of manhood, when Aeneas leaves the older Trojans to rest in Sicily, and when he instructs the young men, including his son, in the tournament.

Courtesy is of course becoming to all ages, but most to this one; the attentions that Aeneas pays to the corpse of the dead Misenus illustrate this courtesy.

Loyalty, which is action in accordance with law, is particularly fitted to the prime of life, for of the adolescent so much cannot be expected, and older men should heed the laws only as they are in accord with their own right judgment, which this stage of manhood is not yet prepared for. Aeneas exemplifies this virtue when, on the occasion of the games in Sicily, he loyally gives the victors the tokens of victory as they had been promised. (chapter 26)

Now, following the ode ("and in its old age . . ."), we turn to the graces that should adorn age. The noble soul at this season is prudent, just, liberal, and happy to hear and tell of the goodness of others (i.e., it is affable). Cicero says in *De Senectute* that there is a proper age for certain things in our life, and Aristotle reminds us that man is a civic animal and so required to be useful to others as well as himself. Of Cato we read that he considered himself as born not for himself but for his country and the world. So, after winning in manhood to our own proper perfection, we should in these later years win to the perfection which enlightens others, "and a man should open out like a rose that can no longer keep closed, and should diffuse the fragrance which has been generated within." The prudence appropriate to this age calls for good memory of past things, good knowledge of present things, and foresight for things to come. Aristotle says in *Ethics* VI that a man cannot be wise unless he be good, and therefore one who proceeds by tricks and deceits is not to be

called wise but astute. From true prudence comes good counsel to
lead both oneself and others to right goals. This is the gift for
which Solomon asked. A man of such prudence, when he sees
that his counsel is needed, does not wait until he is asked, but
offers it freely as the rose offers its perfume to the passerby. If
lawyers or doctors should here protest that they cannot be expected to give their advice free, Dante would reply that the
counsels which do not derive from their special training but from
their general good wit which was God-given should be given
freely. Professional advice may be sold, but it is proper also
occasionally to give it as tithes to the poor.

Justice is appropriate to this age that it may set an example to
others. The ancients, seeing that justice was best revealed to this
period of life, gave the control of their cities to the elders, as the
name "senate" indicates. "O my wretched, wretched country!
What pity for thee seizes me whenever I read or write of anything
touching civil government. But since justice will be dealt with
in the penultimate treatise of this volume, let it suffice for now
to have thus briefly alluded to it."

The generosity which should characterize this age, as both
Aristotle and Cicero tell us, must be practiced opportunely so
as not to harm either the giver or the receiver. This calls for
both prudence and justice. Here Dante reproaches the predatory
rich who use their ill-gotten gains for a show of generosity,
"snatching," as it were, "the cloth from the altar to cover the
robber," and he cites the *De Officiis* in support. Turning to
affability, he notes that Cicero has Cato remark on the enjoyment
of conversation at this age. All the graces befitting this period
of life are exemplified by Aeacus in *Metamorphoses* VII, his example being the more impressive as he was the ancestor of Ajax
and Achilles. (chapter 27)

Proceeding, as does the text ("then in the fourth part of
life . . ."), to the noble soul in its last age, Dante says that it
does two things: it returns to God as to a home port after a long
voyage, and it blesses the voyage made in that it has been good
and serene. Cicero in *De Senectute* speaks of death as our
"port." "And just as the good sailor, when he draws near to the
port, lowers his sails, entering softly and with gentle helm, so
ought we to lower the sails of our worldly activities and turn to
God with all our purpose and heart; so that we may come to that
port with all sweetness and with all peace." Even nature en-

courages this tranquillity, for natural death is not painful, but the soul leaves the body effortlessly as a ripe apple drops from the tree. Aristotle says that "death in old age has no sadness. . . . And as to him who returns from a long journey, ere he enter the gate of his city, its citizens come out to meet him; so come, and so should come, to meet the noble soul those citizens of the eternal life." And again Cicero says, in the person of the ancient Cato: "I am exalted in the utmost yearning to see your fathers whom I loved; and not only them but also those of whom I have heard mention." So the noble soul at this period awaits the end of life with longing. Alas for others:

O wretched and base, who with hoisted sails rush into this port, and where ye should find rest shatter yourselves in the full strength of the wind destroying yourselves in the very place to which you have made so long a voyage. Truly the knight Lancelot would not enter there with hoisted sails; nor would our most noble Latin, Guido of Montefeltro, for in their last years they put aside worldly pleasures and joined religious orders. Nor can the tie of marriage prevent us from turning to a religious life, for such is possible within marriage; we do not all have to put on the garment of St. Benedict or St. Augustine or St. Francis or St. Dominic. It is the religion of the heart that God seeks, as Paul tells the Romans: ". . . in spirit, not in letter, is circumcision."

The noble soul at this stage also blesses times past; this too may be compared to the reflections of the good merchant who returns safe to port congratulating himself upon the happy choice of his route.

The appropriateness of these things to the last period of life is figured by Lucan in *Pharsalia* II when he speaks of Marcia returning to Cato and imploring to be taken back. Marcia symbolizes the noble soul. And the truth of this figure is thus: Marcia was a virgin (signifying adolescence); then coming to Cato she symbolizes the stage of manhood, producing sons who signify the virtues fitting to that stage. Her departing from Cato to marry Hortensius signifies the departure of manhood and the coming of old age; the sons born to Hortensius signify the virtues appropriate to old age. Hortensius' dying signifies the end of old age, the widowhood of Marcia signifies decrepitude, and her returning to Cato signifies the return of the soul in decrepitude to God. "And what earthly man was more worthy than Cato to signify God? Truly none." All this is signified in Marcia's own words. And in conclusion she says that she wants to return to Cato, for she wishes to die as his wife and, further, she does not want it said of her that he dismissed her. So the noble soul wishes to depart this life as the spouse of God and wants to be reassured that God is not displeased with His creature. Wretched indeed are they who prefer to depart this life under the name of Hortensius rather than Cato, whose name may fittingly end our discussion of nobility. (chapter 28)

These chapters call from Casella the observation that "Dante the moralist, who will appoint himself judge of mankind in the *Commedia*, is already present in the *Convivio*."[10]

Now the text exclaims against those who have held false opinions. "Now see how many are the deceived," thinking themselves noble in merit of their lineage. And here two questions arise. "Sir Manfred da Vico," who now has the title of praetor and prefect, may say: "Whatever I be in myself, as a representative of an illustrious family I should be honored by the people." And again, he of San Nazzaro of Pavia or one of the Piscitelli of Naples may say: "If nobility were, as you define it, a divine seed placed in a soul, then, since a race or family does not have a soul, no family could be called noble, which would be against those who say that our families are the most noble in our cities."

The first objection Juvenal answers in his eighth satire, where he says among other things to an unworthy bearer of a great name: "Between you and a statue, made in memory of your ancestors, there is nothing to choose save that its head is made of marble and yours is alive." Yet here Dante would differ somewhat from his authority, pointing out that the marble may serve to remind later generations of the nobility of the man it represents, while the unworthy son or grandson on the contrary weakens the good opinion of his ancestry. So one bearing ill witness to the good should receive not honor but dishonor, as Cicero implies, saying that a worthy man's son should strive to bear good witness to his father. An unworthy scion of worthy stock should be shunned by all.

As to the second question, it is conceded that a family has no soul and yet it is called noble and in a sense rightly so. For every whole is composed of its parts; and some wholes there are (such as man) that have one simple essence together with their parts, and what is said to exist in the part is said to exist in the whole in the same sense. But there are other wholes which do not have a common essence with their parts, as for example a heap of grain which may be called white though the whiteness is that of the grains primarily and only secondarily of the heap. And it is in this secondary sense that a family can be called noble. As the white grains must preponderate to make a white heap, so the noble must preponderate to ennoble the family, and indeed, as you might remove the grains of wheat from a pile and substitute for them red millet till the heap changed color, so it would be quite possible for a family to change from noble to base if the members of the family degenerated. (chapter 29)

The *tornata,* composed as an adornment to the ode, begins "O my against-the-erring-ones." Here it should be known that a good workman on completing his work should beautify it as much as he can, and such is Dante's purpose, for, not claiming to be a good workman, he nevertheless aspires to be such. Now "Against-the-erring-ones" is a section of itself and is the title of the ode, even as Thomas Aquinas gave the name *Against the Gentiles* to a book which he made to the confusion of those who shun our faith. And the ode is charged to seek out our lady (which is to say philosophy), for, as our Lord says, pearls are not to be cast before swine, and Aesop tells us that a cock will sooner pick up a grain of corn than a pearl, so the ode must be directed to the right audience. Now this lady will be found where her chamber is; that is the soul wherein she dwells, and what kind of souls such are we have already seen. To such souls the ode is instructed to give its message, and such will be able to understand it. And when the text says, "I go discoursing of your friend," it is clear that nobility is intended, for nobility ever seeks philosophy, and philosophy looks only on nobility. "O what a great and beautiful ornament is this given her at the end of the ode, calling her the friend of her whose true source is in the most secret place of the divine mind." (chapter 30)

At this point the *Convivio* breaks off. Paul Renucci has very shrewdly pointed out that it ends with the orderly conclusion of a chapter, and adds that if it had not been for Dante's own mention of other treatises to come we might well have regarded the work as complete as it now stands.[11] Umberto Cosmo remarks that by the end of the fourth chapter the sentiments that had led to the composition of the work had been exhausted: the author had set forth his personal apologies, defended the vulgar tongue, and expounded his new political theory.[12] Dante does allude to chapters to come, however, and we are therefore sure that the *Convivio* did not fill out the design laid down for it. André Pézard, basing his arguments on the ignorance of the *Convivio* revealed by the early commentators and the untidy condition of the manuscripts, contends that the work as we have it may be — as the *De Vulgari Eloquentia* seems to be — a first draft, never "published" (i.e., circulated) by the author.[13] Critics have naturally discussed the possible reasons for Dante's abandonment of his grand design. Charles Singleton has suggested that Dante found the "allegory of the poets" no longer suited to his purpose and felt impelled to turn to the allegory of the theologians, which is found in the *Commedia*.[14] This is ingenious, but aside from the fact that it calls for some refinement in the definition of allegories it still leaves us wondering why Dante felt obliged to change. It may be that the explanation is a very simple one of personal taste and self-discovery. Dante is elsewhere the most orderly and symmetrical of composers: the *Vita Nuova* is cunningly and gracefully planned. But in the *Convivio,* carried away as the author is by his passion for erudition, the plan loses all sense of proportion, almost ceases to be a plan. Perhaps Dante contemplates with a terror akin to that of his readers the prospect of another dozen treatises, growing in geometric progression. Perhaps it was from the *selva oscura* of the *Convivio* that the Beatrice of a more graceful and harmonious work felt obliged to rescue her poet!

But there is another way of looking at it. The *De Vulgari Eloquentia* was written, it would seem, concurrently with the *Convivio,* perhaps in the intervals between the treatises. The *De Monarchia* is a special kind of work, tied to a particular purpose and, it may be, to a political contingency. The next "free" work that Dante undertakes after the *Convivio* is the *Commedia* itself. And if we compare the two works we may get a little closer to the reason why the first was abandoned.

The *Convivio* and the *Commedia* have much in common: both are encyclopedic in intent and suffused with the same emotional coloration, the desire to instruct, the strong ethical drive, the intrusion of personal experience and reflection. Like the *Convivio,* the Virgil-dominated first two *cantiche* of the *Commedia* owe as much to the classical tradition as to the Christian. Motifs, incidents, even characters — ranging from Asdente through Guido da Montefeltro and Gherardo da Cammino up to Virgil and Cato — reappear. Most important of all for the eternal fame of the poet and the enduring delight of his readers over the centuries, the *Commedia* is composed in the same language as that beaten out in the *Convivio;* Dante's mastery of the "robust and severe" (the apt adjectives are Casella's) vernacular gave him the confidence necessary to employ it also for his great poem.

Even so the differences are greater than the similarities. Banished from the last treatise of the *Convivio,* allegory comes back again in the *Commedia* to illuminate and embellish both narrative and doctrine. Prose is replaced by poetry. The language, even though under the fetters of rhyme and meter, is clearer, freed now of the compulsion to appear learned for learning's sake. And the whole *Commedia* points toward a mystical or at least extra-rational illumination. Lady Philosophy is gone forever, and even Virgil gives way at last to a reanimated Beatrice. Whether we think of the *Commedia* as begun shortly before the last line of the *Convivio* was penned or postulate an interval between the two works is immaterial. At some point the idea of the *Commedia* captured Dante's imagination and made it impossible for the poet to continue (or resume) the other work. Similarities and differences alike would make it impossible to ride two such horses at once. It became clear to Dante that what he had meant to say in 1304 — particularly in view of its new direction — could be better said in the language and form of the *Commedia.* Cosmo speaks of the "imperious necessity" to dedicate himself to the *Commedia* that Dante must have felt once the idea of the poem had come to him. Probing yet deeper for why this should have come about, the suspicion of some kind of personal crisis or "conversion" is bound to arise. Rocco Montano in a recent study suggests as much, assigning both the "conversion" (it is his term) and the composition of the *Commedia* to the insight born of the poet's disappointment at the failure of Henry VII's expedition.[15] Older scholars have argued along somewhat similar lines, and perhaps such a hypothesis is latent in Singleton's theory, although offered us in other terms. All in all, I am inclined to think that there must have been some kind of "conversion" or "return," although whether linked to a political disillusionment or to some undocumented personal incident or simply to a new development deep within the psyche of the poet I should not venture to guess. In any event, if continued work on the *Convivio* had entailed an unfinished *Commedia,* we can rejoice that Dante went no further with it. At the same time we cannot but be grateful for the four treatises where the raw material of the *Commedia* is displayed for us to see and examine and where, in the midst of much medieval lore — not all of it dull or outdated — there is visible an honest and attractive portrait of the artist himself.

✤ 9 ✤

De Vulgari Eloquentia

DANTE'S genius was both creative and critical. To a degree
unique among artists of his eminence, he combined the gifts of
poet and scholar — one might almost say, prophet and pedant.
Unquestionably a man of vision, conviction, and free poetic
fancy, he was also a technician, skilled in the tools of his trade,
and keenly interested in their nature and origin. This interest
finds expression in all of his works: the linguistic historian
emerges to discuss the uses of personification even in the poetic
landscape of the *Vita Nuova;* and in the early chapters of the
Convivio there is an emotional, yet rational, defense of the use of
Italian rather than Latin. In fact, he is always concerned with
words and the structure of language; even in heaven he cannot
refrain from asking Adam what the speech of the Garden of Eden
was.

This abiding interest, allied to his fundamental missionary impulse to share his knowledge, makes the *De Vulgari Eloquentia*
inevitable. Given time and opportunity, the scholar Dante was
bound sooner or later to set forth his views on language in general
and his own beloved Italian in particular. It is strange, in view
of these facts, that the authenticity of the *De Vulgari Eloquentia*
should have been doubted, as it was, for so many years.

But to say that the *De Vulgari Eloquentia* was predictable is
perhaps to obscure the equally valid and more demonstrable truth

153

that it was a very original work. To be sure, there had been Provençal and other tractates on technical matters of prosody: *Las razos de trobar,* for example, of which Aristide Marigo suspects our poet may have had some knowledge,[1] and the comments of Brunetto Latini, which were certainly known to him. There was available, too, a corpus of medieval works on rhetoric — to say nothing of classical authorities who will turn up in Book II of Dante's treatise. Yet it may be fairly said that no comparable study of language and "eloquence" had preceded Dante's work. Certainly no vernacular had been given the "scholarly" treatment implied in Dante's deliberate choice of Latin for his essay. His intention is clearly to give dignity to the subject of his discussion — his native tongue. We may fairly affirm that the approach, in part at least, is scientific, and the conclusions — in many cases, for again one must qualify — do not run counter to modern linguistic theory, which has seven hundred years of further investigation to draw on. Like the *De Monarchia* and to a certain extent the *Convivio,* the *De Vulgari Eloquentia* continues to attract readers nowadays not because of its intrinsic merits but because Dante wrote it, yet, as Saintsbury has observed, "the book would be of almost the highest interest if it were anonymous."[2]

Dante begins by pointing out the paradox that no one has written of the vernacular even though everyone speaks it. He proposes to fill this lacuna by appeal to the authority of others and his own intelligence. He defines the vernacular as "a speech we acquire without rule by imitating our nurses." The secondary speech, "grammar" (in practical terms Dante here means Latin), does call for learning of rules, and so relatively few learn it. The vernacular is nobler than "grammar" because it is most natural to us. (chapter 1) Speech, Dante affirms, was given to man alone in order that he might reveal his thoughts; the angels have intuitional knowledge, and animals do not have thoughts but only passions. (chapter 2) Man, gifted with reason which differs in individuals, needs more than the simple actions and passions of animals to make himself understood: speech is the "rational and sensible" means of communication for mankind (chapter 3) Adam must have been the first speaker (i.e., before Eve), since it is fitting that man should speak before woman, and his first word must have been one of joy (even as since the fall the first utterance of an infant is a cry of woe) and must have been the vocative "God." (chapter 4) And we may assume that man spoke at once, since being heard is more characteristic of man than hearing (which all animals share), and God, though He could read Adam's mind, wished him to speak that He might glory in the gift He had bestowed upon His creature. So the first word was spoken in paradise if man was created there, otherwise outside. (chapter 5)

These first five chapters may be viewed as composing the basic definitions of human speech. The deductive reasoning is characteristic of Dante's time, and such questions as whether Adam or Eve spoke first or just where the first word was uttered may well be viewed as "quaint" by the modern secular investigator. In these matters Dante is following standard authorities: St. Augustine, Aquinas, and their explicators. Yet one must admire the author's precise and economical treatment of such problems, still unsolved in the main, and particularly his definition of language itself, which is, so far as I can trace it, original with him.

The general axioms lead naturally — for a man of the middle ages — into the next question: what was the original language of mankind? And here follows a moving, highly personal comment, similar in its controlled nostalgia to that of the first chapters of the *Convivio*. Local pride, says Dante, would naturally incline a man to give linguistic primacy to his native vernacular. But Dante, now finding the world his native country even as the sea is to the fish, although he drank of the Arno while yet a child and loves Florence so dearly that for her sake he has suffered exile, yet is not to be moved by prejudice. So that, although for him personally there is no more attractive place in the world than Florence, yet objectively he concedes that there are many countries and cities nobler and more pleasing than Tuscany and Florence, and that many nations have a speech more agreeable and practical than the Italian vernacular. The first form of speech, God-created and granted to Adam, spoken by all men down to the time of the Tower of Babel and then remaining to the Hebrews "in order that our Redeemer might use the language of grace and not one of confusion," must have been Hebrew. (chapter 6) Dante here digresses briefly to recall the linguistic confusion occasioned by the construction of the impious tower: each category of workers was given a language of its own; the higher the type of work the more barbarous the language assigned. Only those who had disapproved of the enterprise retained their own tongue. (chapter 7)

These refinements on the simpler scriptural statement of the disparity of tongues are Dante's own; we may remark here that in the *Inferno* Nimrod is represented as being assigned a language so barbarous as to be comprehensible only to himself.

It is probable, Dante assumes, that the dispersion of the human race occurred at the same time as the confusion of tongues; as a result of migrations it came about that three principal linguistic divisions appeared in Europe: the Northern, the Southern, and the Greek speech of the East. The Northern tongue, spoken in the area from the Danube to England, is exemplified by the vernaculars of the Sclavonians, Hungarians, Teutons, Saxons, and English; the affirmation *iò*, found in almost all of them, reveals their common origin. To the east Greek prevailed, going even beyond the boundaries of Europe. The speech of the Southern area nowadays appears in a threefold form (again Dante classifies according to the word for "yes"): the Spaniards say *oc,* the French *oïl* and the Italians *sì.* Evidence of the common source may be seen in the similarity in these languages of the words for "God," "heaven," "love," "sea," "land," "live," "die," and the like. The *oc*-speakers live in the western part of southern Europe, "beginning with the Genoese boundary" (Dante here calls "Spanish" what we think of as Provençal, perhaps because the language of the troubadours was current beyond the Pyrenees; Castilian finds no place in his scheme); the *sì*-speakers live east of that line, in Italy and Sicily; and the *oïl*-speakers to their north. (chapter 8)

Concerning the subject of linguistic change, which no one has as yet investigated, Dante suggests that it is advisable to study the language we know and to assume that others develop analogously. That this threefold Southern tongue was originally one is apparent in the common vocabulary of "eloquent masters," Dante avers, quoting a line from Guiraut de Bornelh, another from Thibaut de Champagne, and a third from Guido Guinizelli, each containing the word *amor.* Yet there are differences between these vernaculars and variations within each vernacular. The Paduans have a different speech from that of the Pisans, the Veronese from the Milanese; within regional boundaries too there are differences — Neapolitan is not the same as Gaetan; and dialects vary even within cities. This is but another example of the instability of human things; language, like costume and fashion, changes with time. Dante believes that we differ more from our own countrymen of ancient times than we do from our contemporaries in other cities, however remote; he does not hesitate to affirm that if the ancient Pavians were to rise from the dead they would speak a language very different from modern Pavian. If then the speech of the same region varies with time, it is not surprising that distance should also create variation. It is because of this inherent instability of the vernacular that grammar was invented. "Grammar" Dante defines as a certain identity of language inalterable by time or distance and therefore necessary for the preservation of the records of the thoughts and deeds of those remote from us in time or place. (chapter 9)

One reads the conclusion of this discussion of linguistic change with a sense of disappointment. Up to a point our scholar had reasoned most persuasively — and let us not forget that he is, as he claims to be, a pioneer in these matters — on the subject of linguistic change. Further, he had grasped the relationship between current vernaculars and the *Ursprache* in each case. "He recognizes," says W. D. Elcock, "that linguistic investigation must be conducted not only on a geographical plane but also historically. . . The terms of reference of modern linguistic geography could scarcely be stated more aptly."[3] Yet the final link — that the Romance languages are children of his "grammar," instead of the latter being a superstructure erected upon them — this he misses. Otherwise one might claim for him that he had anticipated the basic principles of nineteenth-century Romance philology.

Which of the three forms of the Southern division should be preferred, Dante is reluctant to say. Italian may claim a certain pre-eminence from the fact that the inventors of grammar have taken the Italian word of affirmation (*sic* from *si*). The language of *oïl* may claim special excellence in translations or compositions in vernacular prose, such as the compilations of the exploits of the Trojans and the Romans, or the Arthurian legends. The language of *oc* may claim priority in poetry; Dante here cites Peire d'Alvernha as an example of the troubadour poets. Italian has two claims to pre-eminence: "the sweetest and most subtle poets of the vernacular" (i.e., of the Southern tongue as a whole) belong to its household, for example Cino da Pistoia "and his friend"; and it seems to rest more firmly on the grammar common to all (i.e., it is closer to Latin), a fact which Dante finds "a weighty argument."

He then passes on to a closer examination of the Italian vernacular. Following Lucan, he divides Italy into "right" and "left" (i.e., west and east), the line being the watershed of the Apennines; he enumerates the regions on each side, pointing out that each region has a different speech, which would give us a minimum of fourteen dialects. In fact, however, there are many more; for example the Florentines and the Sienese speak a different Tuscan. Indeed, the variations of the vulgar tongue may well number more than a thousand. (chapter 10)

Which of these can be defined as the illustrious Italian tongue? Let us clear out the brambles and tangled undergrowth, says Dante, and begin with the Romans, since they always think they should have precedence. Their dialect, he asserts, is rightly the first uprooted, for it is the ugliest of all — which is not surprising, since the Romans, with their depraved habits and manners, "stink more than all the rest." To show their linguistic depravity, Dante simply quotes a Roman phrase, not realizing that his only criterion is that it is not Tuscan. He follows the same system with other dialects, the Marchigiano, the Milanese, and the like, deeming it sufficient to cite a local phrase. He dismisses the Tuscan of the Casentino and Prato because of the "ugly irregularity" of their accent. His treatment of Sardinian is almost comical; one would think that he would admire it as being very close to "grammar," but he makes that very virtue count against it, stating that the Sardinians seem to have no vulgar speech of their own but imitate Latin "as monkeys do men." (chapter 11) Elcock comments that here "the poet-philologist had almost divined the truth" and wonders that his "linguistic insight" should so fail him.[4]

More serious consideration is given the dialects of greater literary prestige. Dante begins with the Sicilian, for Italian lyric poetry began with the Sicilian writers and in fact "we find that many have written serious poems" (*"graviter cecinisse"*) in that tongue. But the fame of Sicily survives only as a reproach to present-day princes, very different from their predecessors Frederick II and Manfred: "In truth those illustrious heroes, the Emperor Frederick and his well-born son Manfred, showing forth all the nobility and uprightness of their souls so long as Fortune permitted, followed human things, disdaining the bestial." Men of nobility or distinction strove to attach themselves to these monarchs; since their court was in Sicily, the adjective came to be applied to early Italian literature. But the modern princes, says Dante in a bitter apostrophe, citing specifically "the latest

Frederick," Charles II of Naples, John of Monferrato, and Azzo d'Este, summon to their courts not men of genius but "butchers, liars, and henchmen of avarice." Returning to his subject, Dante says that true Sicilian is not that of the poets but that of the people, and it is barred from pre-eminence because of its drawl (he quotes a line from the celebrated *Rosa fresca aulentissima* as conclusive proof); the language of the poets is a different matter (as in fact it is, since they did not write Sicilian at all and many were not Sicilians). The same distinction must be made for Apulian; the natives speak a dreadful language (*turpiter barbarizant*), yet some of them have written fine poetry (he cites a line from Giacomo da Lentino and another from Rinaldo d'Aquino) in a very polished language. (chapter 12)

The Tuscans would like to arrogate to themselves the claim to the illustrious vernacular which Dante is seeking, and not only the people but also certain famous men of the past, such as Guittone d'Arezzo, Bonagiunta da Lucca, and Brunetto Latini. But their language remained not "curial" but merely "municipal."

Marigo remarks with some surprise Dante's "severity" toward Guittone — whom he disparages elsewhere as well. In fact, Guittone had striven a generation earlier to establish the norms of an Italian literary language even as Dante does here. Evidently Guittone, having the same goal as Dante but using the wrong methods, had in the view of the poet actually hindered the cause.

Dante then disposes of the various non-Florentine Tuscan dialects by merely quoting a phrase containing a word "harsh" to his Florentine ear and sneering at it. He concedes, however, that certain poets of Tuscany — Guido Cavalcanti, Lapo Gianni, "another," and Cino da Pistoia (placed last because of the unworthiness of Pistoia) — "have recognized the excellence of the vulgar tongue," i.e., have written poetry in an elevated style. Yet by their very departure from the vernacular quoted, we can see that Tuscan cannot be the ideal vernacular we are looking for. (chapter 13)

We may here remark that nowhere else does Dante reveal so clearly the uncertainty of his criteria. His disparagement of his own Florentine has been regarded by some critics as motivated simply by an exile's spite, but more likely it merely reflects the confusion in Dante's mind, noted by D'Ovidio,[5] between language and style — a confusion that, as has been obvious, runs through the whole discussion of Italian dialects.

Our critic next crosses the Apennines and disposes of the dialect of the east. In Romagna he finds two types of speech, the first of which, "because of its softness," seems more like the speech of women than of men; they even use such terms of endearment as *oclo meo* and *corada mea*. (It is not clear whether here Dante is commenting on the pronunciation of these words or is, as seems more likely, simply confusing his terms and citing effeminate or affected speech mannerisms as phonetic deviations from his standard.) The other speech of Romagna, exemplified by that of the Brescians and Veronese, is on the contrary "hirsute and bristling" (*"hyrsutum et yspidum"*); all these speakers say *magara,* and furthermore syncopate participles and nouns in *tas*. The Trevisans, like the Brescians, say *nof* and *vif* for *nove* and *vivo*. And as for the Venetians, Dante demolishes their claim by quoting the sentence *"Per le plage de Dio non veras,"* a verse, it would seem, from a well-known Venetian poem. (chapter 14)

Here again we may comment on Dante's somewhat capricious subjectivity. For the sentence as it stands does not seem phonetically very objectionable; the two non-Tuscan words, *plage* and *veras,* are closer to "grammar" than their Tuscan equivalents, and this has elsewhere been accounted an honor. Clearly Dante is objecting to the bluntness of the language; or perhaps he didn't like the rest of the poem.

Dante is inclined to think that the Bolognese may be the best of all dialects; it has combined very successfully the softness (*"mollitiem"*) of the speech of such towns as Imola and the guttural quality (*"aliqualem garrulitatem"*) of the Lombard towns. But, in spite of its virtues, the fact that such great poets as Guido Guinizelli and a few others of Bolognese origin have chosen to depart from their dialect in their writings indicates that it can hardly be the illustrious vernacular we are seeking. In conclusion, Dante adds that the speech of such frontier towns as Trento and Torino can, in the nature of things, hardly be pure, and if their dialects were as beautiful as in fact they are repulsive (*"turpissimum"*) they could not be candidates for the illustrious vernacular. (chapter 15)

It cannot be said that Dante's standards are either scientific or objective as he reviews the dialects of the peninsula, and the reader may be permitted a little legitimate amusement as he follows this lively survey. It is clear that Dante is looking not so much for language as for literature; we have noted that he confuses style and speech. An equally serious defect lies in his Florentine prejudice, of which he is not at all aware. On the score of phonetics and grammar there is really nothing wrong with anything he quotes so disparagingly from other dialects — they simply do not satisfy a Tuscan ear. His two tentative exceptions, Sicilian and Bolognese, are only apparently such; as D'Ovidio pointed out, the verse of the Sicilian school had come to Dante through Tuscan scribes who had considerably modified the original, and the Bolognese were writing in a literary tongue deliberately modeled on the Tuscan.[6] His "impartial" disparagement of the Florentine simply reveals a double standard, or a shift in criterion wilfully employed to put his compatriots in their place, as though a disaffected Bostonian, having found all other English speech objectionable, should disparage his own language by citing a phrase picked up on a slum street. Schiaffini remarks that Dante uses two of the three ridiculed Florentine words in the *Commedia* — both, to be sure, in the *Inferno*.[7] Reading between the lines, it is clear that Tuscan is the only base that will really satisfy Dante, and further that he is not looking for language alone but for poetic diction.

Having sought vainly the panther that is being pursued through the woody hills and pastures of Italy, Dante proposes that a more rational method be attempted to capture her "who sends forth her perfume everywhere, while yet appearing nowhere." Arming himself again for the chase, he observes that for all things there is a standard by which others of the class are measured, as numbers by their relationship to unity, colors by white, etc.; in short, everything belonging to a kind may be measured by the simplest thing of that kind. As human beings we have the standard of virtue, as citizens we have the law, as Italians we have certain simple standards of manners, customs, and languages. The supreme standards by which our actions as Italians are measured are not peculiar to any one town, but are common to all Italy; among these is the vernacular, "whose fragrance is in every city but who dwells in none." It may be more perceptible in some towns than in others, even as God — the simplest of substances —is more perceptible in man than in beast, more in animals than in plants, etc. Hence Dante declares that "the illustrious, cardinal, courtly, and curial vernacular" of Italy is that which belongs to all the towns of Italy but not to any one of them; it is the standard by which all are measured. (chapter 16)

"Illustrious," we are told, means something which shines forth illuminating and being illuminated. Men are called illustrious who, illuminated by power, illuminate others by justice and charity, or who, having been excellently trained, give excellent training, like Seneca and Numa Pompilius. The vernacular of which Dante has been speaking has been exalted by training and power and in turn exalts its followers by honor and glory. As to exaltation by training, we can see how it has been purified from the rough elements of dialect to "the noble, clear, perfect, and refined" character it displays in the *canzoni* of Cino da Pistoia "and his friend." As to its exaltation by power, what is of greater power than that which can sway the hearts of men, even as this language has done and does? "How glorious it makes its familiar friends," says Dante, "we know who, for the sweetness of this glory, can cast even our exile behind our backs. Well may we call this language illustrious." (chapter 17)

We may well call the language "cardinal," too, for, as the door follows its hinge, so the whole family of dialects moves in accord with this vernacular which might be called the father of the family. It continually weeds out the thorny bushes and plants new shoots in the Italian wood; its "foresters" have merely to take away and bring in. "Courtly," next, it may be called in virtue of its common character, for it is the language that Italians would speak at court if they had a court. In other nations the frequenters of palaces always speak the illustrious vernacular; our illustrious language wanders about like a wayfarer and is welcomed in humble shelters, since we have no court. "Curial" is also a fitting term, for "curiality" is the justly balanced rule of things that have to be done. Because the appropriate scales are to be found only in courts of justice, it follows that "whatever in our actions has been well balanced is called 'curial.'" And if we have no imperial court of justice, as in Italy there is no court, yet the members of such a court are not wanting. Even as the members of the German court are united under the prince, so are the members of the court united by the "gracious light of Reason" (a statement, Zingarelli perceptively remarks, charged with both melancholy and pride[8]). (chapter 18)

This then, Dante says in concluding the first book of his treatise, is the Italian vernacular we have been seeking. For as there is a vernacular of Cremona but likewise one of Lombardy, and one could be found on the left side of Italy, so also there can be found one that belongs to all of Italy. And this has been used by the illustrious poets, Sicilians, Apulians, Tuscans, Romagnoli, and natives of both the Marches. It is of this language that he proposes to treat in the books to follow, with considerations of who should use it and to what purpose. He then intends to discuss the lower vernaculars, coming down to that of a single family. (chapter 19)

Those interested primarily in Dante's linguistic theories may feel some sense of disappointment at his failure to maintain his promise; had he finished the work we should have unquestionably learned much more about the spoken Italian of his time. But his second book takes a very different turn.

In the second book, Dante, again urging his "nimble pen" to useful work, affirms that the illustrious Italian vernacular is fit equally for works of prose and poetry. Since prose seems to depend on poetry, he will begin by discussing the use of the vernacular in meter.

It would seem at first sight that all writers of vernacular verse should use the illustrious language, since poets should certainly give their work all possible adornment. One might even say that inferior subjects and lesser writers could be improved by a loftier language. Yet this is false reasoning: in fact not even the highest poets should always assume the vernacular. Such a language deserves men of like quality, even as munificence calls for men of great resources and the purple requires men of noble character. For everything suited to us is so in respect to the genus or the species or the individual, as sensation, laughter, and war. But the language is not suited to our genus, else it would be suited to brutes, nor to our species, else it would be suited to all, and we can see at once that it would not be fitting to mountaineers and their rustic affairs; hence it is suited to us in respect of the individual. And since language is as necessary to our thoughts as a horse to a knight, even as the best horse is fitting for the best knight so the best language pertains to the best thoughts. These are found only in those who have knowledge and genius, and to such men only is the illustrious vernacular suited. It follows that not all should use this illustrious language; to be sure, all have an undeniable right to adorn their verse, but an ox with an embroidered harness or a pig wearing a belt is not adorned but disfigured. As for the mixing of inferior and better things, improvement in the former will come about when the blending is complete, as when we mix gold and silver together; but otherwise the inferior things appear worse, as when homely women mingle with beautiful women. And since the thought of poets is always an ingredient distinct from the words, unless it be worthy of the vernacular it will appear, if set forth therein, like an ugly woman in gold and silks. (chapter 1)

What kind of subject is worthy of the illustrious vernacular? Worthiness, Dante first explains, is an effect or end of deserts; a soldier who has fought well has attained worthiness of victory, one who has ruled well, worthiness of a kingdom; a liar, on the other hand, has achieved worthiness of shame and a robber worthiness of death. There are also comparative stages among the worthy, and likewise in their goals, and only the worthiest subjects are suited to our best vernacular. To determine what the worthiest subjects are, let us recall that, as man is endowed with a threefold life, vegetable, animal, and rational, he follows a threefold road, seeking, like a plant, the useful, like an animal, the pleasing, and as a rational man, what is right. In each of these three kinds of life there is an order of things, and only the greatest thing in each category should be treated of supremely in the greatest vernacular. With respect to what is useful, the greatest thing is safety, and surely with respect to what is pleasing, the greatest thing is love; with regard to what is right, virtue has the pre-eminence. Hence prowess in arms, the fire of love, and the direction of the will are the three appropriate subjects for the vernacular, and we shall see that the great writers of the vulgar tongue have written exclusively on these topics. Bertran de Born has written on arms, Arnaut Daniel on love, Guiraut de Bornelh on righteousness; Cino da Pistoia has written on love, and "his friend" on righteousness. Dante cites an example from each author, including one of his own. He confesses he has found no Italian who has written on the subject of arms. (chapter 2)

Dante reminds us that poets have used a number of forms: *canzoni, ballate,* sonnets and other "illegitimate and irregular" forms. He states that the *canzone* is the most excellent form, and so most fitted for lofty subjects. Now as to why the *canzone* is the most excellent, we should note first that everything we write in verse is in a general sense a *canzone,* and the preservation of the name for this particular form was deliberate and significant. Further, *canzoni* need no assistance; *ballate,* on the other hand, require the performers for whom they were written, and as it is conceded that *ballate* excel sonnets in nobility of form, it is apparent that *canzoni* must be the noblest of all. They also bring more honor to their composer than the other forms, and are the most carefully preserved of compositions; lastly, the whole of the art of poetry is embraced in *canzoni* alone. (chapter 3)

Leaving *ballate* and sonnets for his fourth book, on the "middle" vernacular, Dante takes up the technical aspects of the *canzone*. He recalls that he has called the writers of verse in vernacular "poets," and this is correct if we understand what poetry is, namely, "a work of fancy (*fictio*) set forth in verses in accordance with the art of rhetoric and music." These poets differ from the "regular" (i.e., Latin poets) in that the language of the latter was regulated by art, whereas the moderns write at random (*casu*). The more closely we follow the great poets the more correct our verse will be.

First of all we should follow Horace's advice and choose a subject suited to our strength. We should then consider whether our subject should be treated as tragedy, comedy, or elegy. If our subject calls for the tragic style, we must assume the illustrious vernacular and compose a *canzone*. If the comic style is fitting, we should choose the middle or the lower vernacular; of this, more in the fourth book. The lowly vernacular alone is appropriate to the elegiac style.

The tragic style we employ when the stateliness of the lines, the loftiness of the construction, and the excellence of the words accord with the weight of the subject. We have already seen that safety, love, and virtue are to be sung in this style.

Let anyone proposing to sing of such matters drink of Helicon and boldly begin his composition. But the caution and discernment needed can be acquired only by the effort of genius, practice in the art, and the habit of the sciences. It is of these that Virgil speaks in the sixth book of the *Aeneid* as beloved of God and sons of God (though said figuratively). Those who know nothing of art or science but trust in genius alone should recognize their folly; if they are but geese in their natural sluggishness, let them not think to imitate the eagle that soars to the stars. (chapter 4)

On this Vossler exclaims: "So far has Dante outrun his time! He composed with medieval profundity and medieval heaviness the first Renaissance 'art of poetry.' "[9] Chimenz, looking at it from another angle, finds the conclusion of the passage the "most vital and constructive" part of the work, revealing Dante's lofty concept of the true poet, not merely "gifted" but trained in the art.[10]

On the proper length of the line, Dante notes that no poet has yet used a line of more than eleven syllables or less than three; lines of five, seven, and eleven syllables are most common among the Italian poets. The eleven-syllable line seems the most stately of all because of its duration and its scope in regard to subject, construction, and words. The masters have begun their *canzoni* with this kind of line, as for instance Guiraut de Bornelh: *"Ara auzirets encabalitz cantars."* To be sure, says Dante, this looks like a line of ten syllables, but actually there is a vowel understood in the last consonantal group. The King of Navarre wrote *"De fine Amor si vient sen et bonté,"* where "if the accent and its cause be considered" the line will be seen to have eleven syllables. Other examples:

> *"Al cor gentil ripara sempre Amore."* (Guido Guinizelli)
> *"Amor che lungiamente m'ai menato."* (Guido delle Colonne)
> *"Per fino amore vo si letamente."* (Rinaldo d'Aquino)
> *"Non spero che già mai per mia salute."* (Cino da Pistoia)
> *"Amor che movi tua vertù da cielo."* ("his friend")

Dante remarks that the eleven-syllable line, if accompanied by the seven-syllable line (but not to excess), gains in loftiness. Next come in order of greatness the seven-syllable line, the one of five, and the one of three. The nine-syllable line, appearing to consist of three trisyllabic lines, has never been highly esteemed, nor are lines of an even number of syllables much used, because of their "harshness"; they retain the nature of their numbers, "which are subject to odd numbers as matter to form." Now, says Dante, we may take up the subject of construction and words and so, having prepared our sticks and ropes, we may proceed to bind up the faggot which is the *canzone.* (chapter 5)

On Dante's admiration for the eleven-syllable line (which without the unstressed ending characteristic of Italian would be a ten-syllable line, as he notes apropos of his Provençal quotations), we may further observe that he chose it for the *Commedia.* This choice was more original than it would seem to us who accept the long line as normal for narrative verse. Dante's master, Brunetto Latini, employed the seven-syllable line in couplets for his *Tesoretto,* and short lines had been used by Bonvesin da Riva and Sordello. The romances of Chrétien de Troyes and Marie de France and, more to the point, the *Roman de la Rose* were written in octosyllabic couplets. In choosing the longer line for his great narrative poem, Dante was making a decision based as much on his own taste as on any accepted tradition. As for the lines with an even number of syllables, Italian poets have largely followed Dante's advice and ignored them.

Dante passes on to a discussion of construction, which he defines as "a regulated arrangement of words," as "Aristotle philosophized in Alexander's time." Since we are here treating of the highest things, he continues, let it be remembered that the incongruous (i.e., erroneous) construction has no place in our *canzone*. Let the illiterate then abstain from the *canzone*, lest we laugh at them as at a blind man attempting distinction of colors. Yet not all congruous constructions have the required refinement. There is the insipid construction of the uncultivated, as "Peter loves Lady Bertha very much." There is that which has merely flavor and belongs to rigid scholars, as "I, greater in pity than all, am sorry for all those who, languishing in exile, only revisit their native land in their dreams." Again, there is the kind that has flavor and grace, characteristic of those who have had a shallow draft of rhetoric, as "Praiseworthy is the discretion of the Marquis of Este, and his well-disposed munificence makes him beloved of all." Lastly, there is the construction of illustrious writers, which has flavor, grace, and elevation, as "Having cast the greatest part of the flowers out of thy bosom, O Florence, the second Totila went vainly to Trinacria." This is the supreme degree of construction and represents what we are seeking. Of this exalted degree Dante cites examples from Guiraut de Bornelh, Folquet de Marselha, Arnaut Daniel, Aimeric de Belenoi, Aimeric de Pegulhan, the King of Navarre, Guido Guinizelli, Guido Cavalcanti, Cino da Pistoia, concluding with his own *"Amor che ne la mente mi ragiona."* Such numerous examples are necessary to make the point, says Dante. It would be useful, too, to survey the "regular" poets — Virgil, Ovid in his *Metamorphoses*, Statius, and Lucan — as well as the writers of the loftiest prose — Livy, Pliny, Frontinus, Orosius, and others. So let them who would praise Guittone d'Arezzo and his like for their plebeian words and constructions hold their peace. (chapter 6)

Dante's examples of varying styles have not unnaturally called for comment from his editors and critics. Saintsbury says of them that "they are hard to follow in detail, though the classes are clear enough, corresponding to (1) sheer prose, (2) efforts at style, (3) ornate prose without much distinction, (4) style achieved."[11] These distinctions are of course more perceptible in the original

Latin. Even so they have not entirely satisfied all critics. Auerbach, for instance, contends that "in writing this passage Dante was not thinking of Latin prose but of vernacular poetry in the lofty style, and that accordingly these sentences are presented not as models of Italian prose but rather as analogies by which to elucidate his ideas on style in Italian poetry."[12] What strikes the sympathetic reader is that, even in elucidating style, Dante is unable to overlook content; the first example is of course colorless and meant to be so, but the second clearly refers to Dante's exile and the fourth is a pointed and bitter summary of the intervention of Charles of Valois (the second Totila) in the affairs of Florence, resulting in the expulsion of the Whites ("the greatest part of the flowers") from the city. The third example may allude to the splendid reception and "loan" given to Charles by Azzo VIII of Este in the course of the same campaign; Ferrers Howell thinks it is ironical.[13] The catalogue of Provençal and Italian writers and the names of the classical authors cited are more than a scholarly reference; they are an open confession of Dante's indebtedness. We may remark too that, as in the *Vita Nuova,* he does not hesitate to put the distinguished "moderns" on the same level as the great "regular" poets of antiquity. "Personal sympathy," says Ferrers Howell rather charitably, explains the inclusion of Orosius.[14] Frontinus, first-century author of the *Strategematica,* is mentioned nowhere else in Dante's works and seems to have had little influence on him. The other names need no defense. For those interested in Dante's library this chapter is invaluable.

Taking up the subject of words appropriate to the *canzone,* Dante declares that there are indeed many sorts of words. Some are childish, some womanly, and some virile, and of the virile some are "sylvan" (*"sylvestria"*) and some "urban" (*"urbana"*); the urban includes "the combed-out and the sleek" (*"pexa et lubrica"*) and "the shaggy and the rumpled" (*"yrsuta et reborra"*). Dante calls the combed-out and the shaggy grand, while the sleek and the rumpled are superfluous and deceitful. Childish words, e.g., *mamma* and *babbo, mate* and *pate,* must be avoided because of their simplicity; womanly words, such as *dolciada* and *piacevole,* because of their softness; sylvan words, like *greggia* and *cetra,* because of their "roughness" (*"austeritatem"*); so too the sleek and the rumpled urban words, such as *femina* and *corpo.* This leaves only the combed-out and the shaggy. Dante defines combed-out words as those which have three — or as close to three as possible — syllables, without aspirate, without acute or circumflex accent, without z or x, without double liquids or a liquid directly following a mute; which having been, as it were, "planed" (*"dolata"*), leave the speaker with a certain sweetness: e.g., *amore, donna, disio, vertute, donare, letitia, salute, securitate, defesa.* As for the shaggy, there are two kinds: those which are necessary and those which are ornamental to the illustrious vernacular. Necessary are those which are unavoidable, as the monosyllables *si, no, me, te, se, a, i, o, u,* and the like. Ornamental Dante calls all polysyllables which, mixed with combed-out words, produce a "beautiful harmony of structure" (*"pulcram . . . armoniam compaginis"*), even though they may have some of the defects mentioned above in the definition of combed-out words; examples are *terra, honore, speranza, gravitate, alleviato, impossibilità, benaventuratissimo, inanimatissimamente, disaventurissimamente, sovramagnificentissimamente.* This last has eleven syllables and, although we could think of larger words such as *honorificabilitudinitate,* they would go beyond the ideal eleven-syllable line. As to how the shaggy words are to be harmonized with the combed-out, Dante promises to say more of that later; meanwhile readers of discernment will have had sufficient information on the nature of words. (chapter 7)

Marigo remarks on the "character of virile nobility" of the language here defined by Dante.[15] Without taking exception to this opinion one may also share Saintsbury's feeling that the classification is "more than a little obscure" in its principles[16] or at the least find it with D'Ovidio "curious."[17] In fact some words seem to be chosen — or excluded — for their meaning, some for their sound, and yet others because they have or have not been employed by poets who enjoy Dante's approval. Perhaps what we have here, as D'Ovidio suggests, is an a priori definition of the language of the *dolce stil nuovo,* a "language within a language."[18] The specific example of *"mamma e babbo"* gives us pause. For in *Inferno* XXXI Dante fearlessly uses this same "childish" pair and to excellent effect. Indeed it would not be hard to find in the *Commedia* many "childish" words (e.g., *"il pappo e'l dindi"* of *Purgatorio* XI), as well as those of the other categories here excluded. But what is precious about the chapter is the evidence it gives us of Dante's meticulous attention to his tools; that he found the limitations here set forth inappropriate to his great work is yet another clue to his approach to that work. It has been noted that such terms as "combed-out" and "shaggy" may have come naturally to a Florentine accustomed to terms used in the weaving of wool (the underlying figure is of course that of the word "clothing the thought"), though Marigo reminds us that the imagery had also been used by Matthew of Vendôme.[19]

Dante passes to a discussion of the *canzone* itself. According to the true meaning of the word, it is the action or passion of singing, just as *lectio* is the action or passion of reading. As the author's composition it is an action (this is the meaning exemplified in the first line of Virgil's *Aeneid*, "I sing of arms and the man . . ."); when uttered, however, it becomes a passion. And because it is someone's action before being someone's passion, it gets its name from its creator: we say "Peter's *canzone*," not meaning that Peter utters it, but rather that Peter composed it.

Dante notes too that it is the words which are called the *canzone;* the accompanying music is the melody. Indeed, the words even without the music are called a *canzone;* a *canzone* then may be defined as the completed action of one writing words to be set to music. In that sense, to be sure, *ballate* and sonnets are also *canzoni,* but Dante has in mind here the one supreme piece of composition of the vulgar tongue, which is the *canzone* par excellence. This is, specifically, the joining together in tragic style of several stanzas (without a *ripresa*) on one subject, as exemplified in his own *"Donne ch'avete intelletto d'amore"* of the *Vita Nuova.* If it were in the comic style, we should call it rather a *cantilena,* of which Dante says he will treat in the fourth book. (chapter 8)

A *canzone* is a series of stanzas, and the stanza (a term which has been invented solely for the *canzone*) is a "room" or receptacle for the whole art. It is not lawful for successive stanzas to call in any additional scrap of the art; they must clothe themselves solely with the art of the first stanza. The whole art of the *canzone* depends on three things: the divisions of the musical setting, the arrangement of the parts, and the number of lines and syllables. Of rhyme we shall say nothing, says Dante, for it is permissible for a new stanza to introduce new rhymes; this would not be the case if rhyme belonged to the art of the *canzone* as such. Anything relating to rhyme which is a proper part of the art will be treated under arrangement of the parts. Finally, then, our author declares that the stanza is a structure of lines and syllables limited by reference to a certain musical setting and harmonious arrangement. (chapter 9)

Dante reminds us that "the master of the wise" states in the beginning of the *Physics* that the perfect knowledge of things must include knowledge of their ultimate elements, and accordingly he proposes now to examine the things which define the defining terms of the *canzone*. He begins with the musical setting, and remarks that every stanza is set up for the reception of a certain "ode" (melody), but stanzas differ in the modes in which this is done. Sometimes the ode matches the stanza, without the repetition of any musical phrase and without any diesis, i,e., transition from one melody to another (vulgarly called *volta*). This is the kind of stanza Arnaut Daniel used almost exclusively, and Dante mentions as following Arnaut's example his own *canzone* beginning "*Al poco giorno e al gran cerchio d'ombra.*" There are other stanzas which contain diesis; this means that a repetition of one melody must be made before the diesis or after or both. If the repetition (one, rarely two) comes before the diesis, these elements are called "feet"; if after, the stanza is said to have "verses." If no repetition comes before the diesis, the first part is called the *fronte;* if none after, the stanza has a *sirma* or *coda*. This license, Dante begs the reader to note, has been granted by worthiness of authority, i.e., because of the pre-eminence of the *canzone* form. And now the musical setting has been made sufficiently clear. (chapter 10)

The arrangement of the parts of the stanza, says Dante, is the most important element in the art of the *canzone* in view of its central role in the divisions of the musical setting, the putting together of the lines, and the relation of the rhymes. Now the *fronte* with verses, the feet with the *coda,* and the feet with the verses may be differently arranged in the stanza. Sometimes the *fronte* may exceed the verses in syllables and lines (though Dante has never seen an example of this arrangement); sometimes it may exceed the verses in lines and be exceeded by them in syllables, as for example a five-line *fronte* of seven syllables to the line with verses of two hendecasyllables each. Again the verses may exceed the *fronte* in syllables and lines, as in Dante's *canzone* "*Traggemmi de la mente Amor la stiva,*" wherein the *fronte* is composed of four lines, three of eleven syllables and one of seven, an arrangement which would make it impossible to divide into feet, since these must match in lines and syllables, as must verses. And all that has been said of the *fronte* might be said of the verses. They might exceed the *fronte* in lines and be exceeded in syllables, as if, for example, each verse had three seven-syllable lines and the *fronte* were composed of five lines, two of eleven syllables and three of seven.

Sometimes, likewise, the feet exceed the *coda* in lines and syllables, as in Dante's *canzone "Amor che movi tua vertù dal cielo";* and sometimes the feet are exceeded by the *sirma* in both lines and syllables, as in Dante's *"Donna pietosa e di novella etate."* And what has been said of the *fronte* in relation to the verses may be said of the *sirma* in relation to the feet. When there are both feet and verses, the former may be greater or smaller in number than the latter, and may be of longer or shorter lines. Dante notes that his sense of the word "feet" is different from that of the regular (Latin) poets. He adds the final caution that feet must correspond in the number of lines and syllables, as must verses. (chapter 11)

He might here have added that his use of "verses" is also different from the classical and indeed medieval understanding of the term, as will be evident from the context above. Nor is "diesis" used in its normal meaning, though Dante found warrant for his sense of the word in the *Etymologies* of Isidore of Seville. His other technical terms were current in his time. As for the *canzoni* cited, *"Traggemi"* has not come down to us, and Marigo suspects that Dante may have found the form not to his taste;[20] *"Amor che movi"* was apparently meant to be the fourth ode of the *Convivio*[21] had that work been continued; and *"Donna pietosa"* is the second *canzone* of the *Vita Nuova.*

Coming now to the subject of the different kinds of lines and their relationship, Dante again affirms the pre-eminence of the lines singled out in chapter 5 and the superiority of the hendecasyllable for the tragic style. Some stanzas are made up of eleven-syllable lines alone, as for example *"Donna mi prega, perch'io voglio dire"* of Guido of Florence, Dante's own *"Donne ch'avete intelletto d'amore"* (from the *Vita Nuova*), and as a sample from the Spaniards who write in the *oc* vernacular, *"Nuls hom non pot complir adrechamen"* of Aimeric de Belenoi.

There is the kind of stanza where a single seven-syllable line is woven in; this obviously must be a stanza with a *fronte* or a *coda.* Similarly, there cannot be a stanza with an odd number of lines save it have a *coda* or *sirma.* Of course, more than one seven-syllable line may appear in a stanza, provided only, in the tragic style, that hendecasyllables predominate and that an eleven-syllable line begin the stanza. To be sure, some writers, Dante says, have begun with a seven-syllable line, and he quotes *"Di fermo sofferire"* and *"Donna, lo fermo core"* of Guido Ghisilieri and *"Lo meo lontano gire"* of Fabruzzo, both of Bologna, adding however that in their tragic style there is a faint sense of elegy.

The five-syllable line must be used much more sparingly, perhaps one per stanza or two at most in the foot. The three-syllable line has no place at all in the *canzone*, though a certain echoing of rhymes may make it appear to be used, as in the *canzone* of Guido of Florence cited above and Dante's own *"Poscia ch' Amor del tutto m'ha lasciato"* (text and translation in Temple edition), where it appears as a part of the hendecasyllable.

The relative position of eleven-syllable and shorter lines must of course be the same in each foot (or verse), since the melody must be followed. And now, says Dante, the reader has had sufficient instruction on line arrangements in the stanza. (chapter 12)

Our critic proposes to treat of rhyme in itself when he deals with poems in the middle vernacular. The relation of rhymes in the *canzone* may be properly discussed here. We may exclude from consideration the unrhymed stanza, often used by Arnaut Daniel, for example in *"Sim fos Amors de joi donar,"* and in Dante's own *"Al poco giorno"* (the *sestina* dedicated to Pietra). We may likewise exclude from comment the stanza whose lines have all the same rhyme. Of mixed rhymes we may observe the great liberty which poets have allowed themselves. Indeed, the arrangement of rhymes is the chief element in the charm of the stanza. Some poets do not make all their rhymes within the stanza but make rhymes between it and other stanzas: Gotto of Mantua, for example, always had in his stanza one line, called "the key," which rhymed only with a like line in other stanzas. Indeed, two or more unrhymed lines are permissible. Yet a line unrhymed within a stanza is, in practice, very rare. Some poets make the rhymes after the diesis different from those preceding it, others do not; a common device is to link the last line of the first part with the first line of the last part. Rhymes in the *fronte* or *coda* may be arranged as the poet desires, but it gives a happy effect if the last lines "fall with a rhyme into silence." The feet call for special care (since they must match); an unrhymed ending in one of the feet must find its echo in the other. If all the endings of one of the feet are rhymed, the other may either repeat the same rhymes or adopt new ones, providing always that the order of the first foot be followed; for example, if the first foot has three lines with the first and third rhyming, there must be rhyme between the first and third lines of the other foot. The verse too should almost always obey this law, though, because of the linking of the last line of the first part with the first line of the last part, this order may be upset. As for the things to be avoided in rhyme, they are: excessive repetition of the same rhyme (unless justified by some new experiment, even as young knights like to begin with some special deed, as Dante has attempted in the *canzone* "*Amor, tu vedi ben che questa donna*" — the famous creation evidently written to outdo Arnaut Daniel), useless equivocation, and roughness in rhyme, unless it be mixed with smoothness to a judicious degree. (chapter 13)

Chapter 14 was intended to treat of the number of lines and syllables in the stanza, but breaks off incomplete. This is to be regretted, of course, but, to quote Vernon Hall, "what we have is enough to enable us to appreciate [Dante's] originality." He goes on:

His *De vulgari eloquentia* largely disregarded the question of genres which so dominated classical criticism and concerned itself with language and style, the main interest of modern poets. It gave the highest place to the new subjects the Middle Ages had introduced into literature and praised above all forms the *canzone,* a lyric poem. And when today we think of poetry we, like Dante, think of the lyric before we think of the dramatic or narrative forms, tragedy and the epic. In several ways, then, Dante was the first modern critic.[22]

For Kenneth Burke, "the greatest attempt at a poetic of sound is Dante's *De vulgari eloquentia.*"[23]

The history of the *De Vulgari Eloquentia* is a fascinating one. Clearly, as Marigo, like earlier editors and commentators, suspects,[24] the work that has come down to us is merely an early draft. Evidence of this lies not only in the fact that the work breaks off and that references to discussions of other aspects of the study are never followed up, but also in the paucity of manuscripts. There are but three, and the third, which in Marigo's opinion is the oldest and most reliable,[25] came to light as recently as 1917. As for the date of composition, that too is a matter that cannot be definitively resolved. Both Villani and Boccaccio mention it, the latter assigning it to the poet's old age. Marigo dates the writing of the work between the spring of 1303 and the end of 1304,[26] and of course the allusion in the *Convivio* to the work in progress shows that Dante had at least a general notion of it at the time he was working on the *Convivio*.

The treatise was first published by Trissino in 1529 (from the Trivulziano manuscript), and not in the original but in Trissino's Italian; he had his own polemical axe to grind and sought in Dante's essay support for his side of the famous *"quistione della lingua."* Only in 1577 did Jacopo Corbinelli in Paris publish the original Latin, based on one manuscript. Pio Rajna, with two manuscripts and the resources of nineteenth-century scholarship at his disposal, brought out his edition in 1896. Marigo's edition is of 1937. Outside of Saintsbury, who gives the work enthusiastic and fairly lengthy treatment in his *History of Criticism,* and of course the valuable commentary of Ferrers Howell which accompanies his translation in the Temple Classics (1903), there has been very little attention given to the *De Vulgari Eloquentia* in English; in Italian, D'Ovidio's excellent study is still useful. On the genesis of the work we may remark, finally, that it springs from the sentiments, at once patriotic and personal, expressed so beautifully in the first treatise to the *Convivio.* "To praise the vulgar tongue was equivalent to praising his own work and thus restoring his dignity in the eyes of the many who had lost — or so Dante fancied — their esteem for him," is Cosmo's comment.[27] We may well agree too with Barbi that "Dante felt the necessity of art along with that of inspiration; art, for him, is study and knowledge and is acquired through assiduous devotion to great teachers."[28]

Various reasons have been adduced for Dante's breaking off his treatise with such abruptness. Curtius comments that he

keeps . . . making more and more severe demands . . . upon the poetic fledgling. They come close to being unrealizable. Must one really have read Orosius before one can write a *canzone* in the lofty style? Is the vernacular emancipated and urged to full development by Dante's treatise? Is it not rather intolerably shackled? And for what reason? The reason is the tension between Romania (i.e., the medieval culture of the Latin world) and Rome. Dante was unable to resolve it theoretically. This is presumably one of the reasons the treatise was never finished.[29]

In a sense Marigo agrees, suggesting that Dante put the work down not because of a chance interruption but in some uncertainty as to the direction he was going.[30] There is something, too, to be said for Chimenz's notion that Dante had possibly become bored with the treatise.[31] For in truth it had changed its character: the first book, for all its medievalism, was a work of humanism, attacking large, new, and exciting matters; the second, for all the delight it gives us in revealing Dante's obsession with the technique of his art and something of his critical scope, has become a rather dry manual. But Ferrers Howell, it seems to me, well deserves the last word. He says that although we cannot be sure when the *Commedia* was begun, it certainly does not fit the principles of poetic art laid down in the present treatise. "The *Comedy*," he goes on, "is in fact a repudiation of the doctrines of the *De Vulgari Eloquentia*. . . . Arms, love and righteousness are there [i.e., in the *Commedia*] treated of, but not in *canzoni*, not in the tragic style, and not in the illustrious vernacular as defined in the earlier treatise." He adds that by the standards of the treatise Dante would have had to classify his own greatest work among other "illegitimate and irregular forms of poetry," and concludes:

It is, indeed, not unreasonable to conjecture that the *De Vulgari Eloquentia* was interrupted by some temporary cause, and that its subsequent completion was abandoned by reason of the revolution in Dante's ideas as to the scope of poetry in the vulgar tongue wrought by his conception of the *Divine Comedy*.[32]

❧ 10 ❧

De Monarchia

DANTE was by nature a political animal. He played an active part in the government of Florence, and the circumstance of his unhappy exile must have intensified rather than diminished his interest in politics. Such interest was not foreign to the traditions of lyric poetry: the Provençal poets expressed themselves freely, though with a tone more emotional than scientific, on the virtues and defects of their leaders, and their *sirventes* was taken over by the Italians; the celebrated poem of Guittone d'Arezzo on the battle of Montaperti has political overtones, as do some of the *Rime*. Dante's readings of classical authors such as Livy, Orosius, and St. Augustine had led him into deeper and more general considerations of the proper government of human affairs as a necessary element in the search for felicity. Both from his experience as poet and citizen and from his scholarly studies came the desire to set down his thoughts on civil government. The originality of the *De Monarchia* lies as much in the order of its presentation as in its substance.

It is uncertain when the work was written. The most persuasive hypothesis, which Boccaccio put forth, associates it with the descent of Henry VII into Italy, either before or after his coronation in 1312. Gustavo Vinay, the most recent editor of the work, dates the book as of 1312–13,[1] but others have suggested that it might have been written some years later.[2] Whatever the time of composition, it is evident, as Michele Barbi says,[3] that the work was composed as a unit. To suggest that any substantial period of time intervenes between the writing of the sections would be to ignore the compact, coherent organization of the book, which testifies that it is the creation of a man not only dedicated to the task in hand but impassioned by his didactic zeal. Such zeal is apparent from the very first sentence, where Dante proclaims it the clear duty of every man whose learning enables him to do so to put his knowledge to the public use; he feels a particular need "to bear fruit for the public good and to expound truths unattempted by others." He admits, too, that he is undertaking this study in part for the glory that may accrue to him, even though he knows he has set himself a difficult task. He defines the empire that he has in mind as "a unique princedom over all men in time," and the basic questions he intends to examine are whether such an empire is needed, whether it is the rightful privilege of the Romans to rule over it, and whether its authority comes directly from God or depends on some intermediary authority.

Considering the first of these questions in Book I, Dante affirms that political affairs fall into the sphere of human action, i.e., into the area where action is possible and where the end affects the means, as when, for example, we cut wood one way if we are building a house and another way if we are building a ship. Defining the goal of the entire civilized human race will help us to see the kind of means needed to reach it. Now, as there is a purpose for which nature gives us a thumb, and another for which she intends the whole hand, and a further purpose for the arm, and yet a broader purpose for the whole man, so too there must be a goal for the man, and for the family, and for the city, etc., "and lastly, there is an ultimate end for which eternal God, by His art, which is nature, brings into being the collective human race." And we should note that it is for the attainment of this ultimate end that man is created. Man's specific and differentiating capacity is not merely being, or animation, or apprehension (these he shares with other creations), but "apprehension by the potential intellect." Citing Averrhoes for support, Dante states that since the same potential cannot be all actualized at one time by any man or group of men, a multiplicity of the human race must be assumed. So the speculative intellect may emerge in different individuals as the practical intellect engaged in "doing" (as in affairs of politics) or in "making" (as in the arts). Both are "handmaidens of speculation," the supreme activity for which the human race was created. To bring about conditions wherein the whole capacity of the potential intellect may be constantly actualized, a state of peace is necessary. An individual man needs tranquillity in order to grow in wisdom, and it must be the same for society as a whole, so that "universal peace" is the best of all things ordained for man's blessedness. This is why with the coming of Christ "Peace" was the cry of the angels, and "Peace be with you" was Christ's own salutation. (chapters 1–4)

These early chapters have had a strange and in some cases almost painful fascination for commentators on the work. Passerin d'Entrèves finds in them the one point where Dante appears to break away from any known tradition of political thought in the middle ages. Commenting on the originality of the concept of *humana civilitas*, d'Entrèves continues:

However, what is most striking in these chapters is to find the Aristotelian argument for the rational foundation of the State as the realization of human ends, extended to prove the necessity of the world-State if the end of the human race as a whole (the *genus humanum*) is to be attained. But Dante goes further. For if the extension of the Aristotelian argument from the city to the kingdom — from the *polis* to the *civitas vel regnum* — could appear to him, as it had to St. Thomas, so evident as not to require much comment, he seems now to be aware that its further extension requires a somewhat more detailed explanation. This explanation he provides by introducing the scholastic concept of the possible intellect, and by explaining that "the work proper to the human race, taken as a whole, is to keep the whole capacity of the potential intellect constantly actualized." This cannot be done without unified direction by a single authority,

and he points out the dangers springing from Dante's "Averrhoistic" flirtation:

If the end of the whole human race is more important than that of its components, does the part — the individual — thereby cease to be an end in itself? This conclusion would hardly be compatible with the Christian notion of the absolute value of human personality. Nor is this all. For if the whole human race is to be bound together not only for the attainment of peace, justice, and freedom, but for the realization of an end which is beyond the possibilities and indeed the very nature of the individual; if, in other words, the world-State is not only the condition and guarantee of the peaceful living together

of individuals, cities, and kingdoms, but the incarnation of a moral
end as well as of a legal principle — is this not going to make the
universal Empire dangerously akin to the universal Church, almost,
as Professor Gilson puts it so well, a secularized version of the Church,
"un décalque laïcisé de la notion de l'Église"?[4]

To show the necessity of a monarchy, Dante refers to Aristotle's
Politics, in which it is stated that when a number of things are set
up for a single purpose, one of them must guide or rule. Dante
says that the point can be established inductively also. The individual is ruled by his highest faculty, the intellectual; and the
family is ruled by the father. In like fashion, various political
units, from districts to kingdoms, need a chief; otherwise war
or anarchy ensues, and the unit falls. Therefore, if humanity is
to achieve its goal, the means toward it must be under the direction of one ruler. The same necessity can be established by considering the relation of the parts to the whole: the former exist
for the latter and not vice versa. Order and unity in the parts
exist only for the sake of the whole, and a like unity is necessary
if the whole is to be, as it should be, superior to the parts. Humanity, regarded as a component of creation, logically should
have its own prince, as its subdivisions have their special heads.*
There is also a theological argument: it is the duty of man, God's
creature, to imitate his Maker as closely as possible, and unity is
of course supremely realized in God. Finally, it may be argued
that since mankind is the child of the heavens (man is begotten
by man and the sun, said Aristotle), it should rightly imitate the
rule of the heavens, all of which follow the *primum mobile.*
(chapters 5–9)

To settle differences among princes, Dante continues, a superior
arbiter having authority to give judgment is necessary; this re-
quirement logically entails an emperor as supreme arbiter. Dante
supports this point by a quotation from Aristotle's *Metaphysics,*
which is in turn quoted from the *Iliad.* Further, the world is
best when justice is strongest; justice is indeed the Virgo of Virgil's
prophetic line *"Iam redit et Virgo, redeunt Saturnia regna."* Justice is an absolute, and the slightest admixture of greed renders
it imperfect. The application of justice also requires power.
Hence it is clear that justice is most potent when it exists in the
person of the least corrupted will and the greatest power. To

---

* This idea is put more poetically in *Purgatorio* VI and XVI.

establish the truth of this statement Dante, with reference to Aristotle's *Ethics,* remarks that avarice is the great enemy of justice, and if there be no reason for greed, then justice will be perfect. Lesser princes would naturally be susceptible to this sin, but an emperor, having no lands to envy, would not. Besides, a universal monarch would be the one most filled with charity, and so disposed to work for the good of mankind. The lovable thing is the more beloved the closer it is to the lover; men, collectively, are closer to the universal monarch than to lesser kings, who have only smaller groups of men under them, and so they are most loved by him — or, says Dante hopefully, "at least they ought to be." (In this connection it may be remarked that Dante is not, like Machiavelli, setting down the results of his observations, or if so, only infrequently and tangentially; he is throughout defining an ideal.) Furthermore, on the principle that a cause must love its effect, the most universal cause of man's happiness (the emperor) must love the good of mankind more than any other. As for the question of the emperor's power, it is clear in the meaning of the word "monarch." (chapters 10–11)

Freedom is essential to the best condition of humanity, but the principle of freedom is often obscure. To clarify it, Dante begins by stating that judgment is the link between apprehension and appetite. First something is apprehended, then judged, and then sought or shunned according to the judgment. If judgment moves the appetite, it is free, but when the reverse is true, as in the case of animals, it is not. Angels and souls free of the body cannot be said to lose their freedom of choice, which is God's greatest gift to man, giving us human happiness on this earth and divine felicity in heaven. Clearly, then, the human race is in its happiest state when it is free. It is most free under a monarchy, because only then does the human race exist for its own sake and not for some other purpose, and only a monarchy can correct perverted forms of government such as democracies, tyrannies, etc., which enslave mankind. Quoting Aristotle's dictum that under a right government a good man and a good citizen are interchangeable terms, Dante says that right government must assure freedom, for the citizens do not exist for the sake of the consuls, nor the nation for the king, but rather the reverse: the consuls and king are masters as regards the means, but servants as regards the end. The supreme monarch will be the servant of all, since his legislation must be conditioned by the end set before him. (chapter 12)

A further argument flows from the axiom that "nothing can act unless it is itself already what the thing acted upon is to become." Dante buttresses this by a reference to Aristotle, and digresses to point out the foolishness of those who would reform others by mere words rather than example. One who would dispose others best must himself be best disposed, and in matters of ruling this must be the supreme monarch. An agent is prepared for any operation with ease and perfection in proportion to the absence within it of any counteracting influences. (Those who have been taught nothing of philosophy come more easily to its use and understanding than those who have had misleading instruction, as Galen notes.) Since, as has been shown, the emperor has less occasion for greed than others, and greed is the corrupter of justice, the emperor must be more capable than any other of judgment and justice, the principal attributes of a good legislator or magistrate, as is shown by Psalm 71: "God, give thy judgment to the king and thy justice to the king's son." (chapter 13)

Vinay observes in his edition that at certain points in this chapter Dante seems to be thinking of his emperor as a creator as much as a lawgiver or arbiter.[5] If he is, the conception does not substantially affect what follows, since Dante does not pursue the notion of the agent seeking to create his own likeness but dwells only on the directive faculty of his emperor; still, the "sentimental attitude," as Vinay calls it, is worthy of notice, for without this reverence, almost as for something divine, that Dante feels for his emperor, the De Monarchia would never have been written.

On the principle that "the superfluous" is repugnant to God and nature, Dante declares that, if one monarch is sufficient to the task, more than one would be undesirable. This does not imply that the monarch should not delegate certain matters, nor does it mean that all laws should be the same for all regions. Some regulations might apply to the Scythians, living outside the seventh "climate," where the days and nights are of unequal length and the cold is intense; others to the Garamantes, of the "equinoctial climate," where day and night are of similar duration and the equatorial heat makes clothing burdensome.

For his "climates," which may be said to correspond roughly to our use of "zones," and his examples of the peoples living in the extreme regions (whose tribal names, one suspects, added a kind of exotic authority to his statement), Dante is indebted to Albertus Magnus (*De Natura Locorum*). And in the reference to the costume of the Garamantes, we can sense the kind of minor regulations Dante had in mind. Climate and local conditions may well determine the style of clothing and the "rules" perhaps of propriety in these matters. But, he continues, things common to mankind, "the principles of natural law," as Vinay defines Dante's meaning,[6] are included in the sphere of the monarch's rule. Even as the practical intellect receives the major proposition from the speculative, Dante continues, buttressing his argument by an appeal to scholastic logic, so should lesser princes receive the law from the emperor. He finds a scriptural example in Moses, who reserved to himself the "higher and more general" judgments, leaving the lesser to the tribal chieftains. So again Dante establishes that it is "better" for mankind to be ruled by one than by many. (chapter 14)

Trying another approach, Dante affirms that "being" and "oneness" and "goodness" are related in degree of priority according to Aristotle's fifth sense of *"prius";* "being" precedes "oneness" and "oneness" precedes "goodness," for that which is most existent is most "one" and what is most "one" is "best." Being "one" is the root of being "good," and consequently being many is the root of being evil. He adds that "to sin is nothing but abandoning the one to seek the many"; such, he concludes, was the sense of Psalm 4: "They are multiplied in the fruit of corn and wine and oil."

It follows then that concord, a uniform movement of various wills, must be "good." We might, were their action voluntary, call clods of earth concordant as they all tend to descend, or flames concordant as they tend to rise; so men are concordant when their separate wills move them to one end; this is indeed "formally present" in their wills even as gravity is "formally present" in the clods. For the virtue of volition is a potentiality, and the kind of good apprehended determines its form, which, though one in itself, is multiplied by the multiplicity of the recipient matter, just like such forms as "soul" and "number."

Clinching his point, Dante asserts that, as the human race depends — just as a town or a nation does — on concord for its "best disposition," and this calls for one dominating will, then clearly one prince is essential. (chapter 15)

Dante finds historical confirmation for his arguments in the circumstances of Christ's birth. The world was never so peaceful as it was at the time of the rule of Augustus, called by St. Paul "the fullness of time." This was the time awaited or produced by the Son of God for His incarnation, and it was a time of perfect monarchy. How sad that mankind, in its present condition, sick in wit and will, cannot accept, either through experience or divine persuasion, the truth which is contained in the sentence: "Behold how good and how pleasant it is for brethren to dwell together in unity." (chapter 16)

In Book II Dante comes to his second question, whether supremacy rightfully belongs to Rome. He confesses that at one time he failed to understand the reasons for the supremacy of Rome, attributing it merely to force of arms. When he learned that it was in fact the work of divine providence, he at first felt only scorn for all who still retained his own earlier misconception. However, natural love, "like the summer sun which scatters the morning mist and rising in splendor sends forth his beams," prefers to put aside derision and diffuse instruction. So he proposes in this second book to show that the Roman Empire existed by right, and thus dissipate the cloud of ignorance of usurping rulers and incidentally free mankind from their yoke. He will use both the light of human reason and the ray of divine authority in his exposition.

He reminds us of the similarity of art and nature in their operation; in both cases three aspects must be considered: the artisan, the tools, and the material. But God, the active principle of nature, cannot err, nor can His tools (the heavens, made by Him, through which He works) have any fault; so that any imperfection in terrestrial things must come from the imperfection of the material.* Right and the divine will are one; anything not in accord with the divine will cannot be right, and everything in harmony with it must be right. Under that principle, and bearing in mind Aristotle's statement that "Certainty is not to be sought to the same degree in every case, but according as the nature of the subject permits of it," Dante prepares to investigate the right of the Romans to rule, by the aid of manifest signs and the authority of the sages. Although God's will is invisible, it may be perceived in what it has brought about. Indeed, even human will is visible and perceptible to others only through signs. (chapters 1–2)

Wicksteed reminds us that for an understanding of Dante's point of view in what follows

* This doctrinal point is elaborated somewhat more poetically in *Paradiso* VII, 124–41, and VIII, 103–48.

we must keep constantly in mind the parallelism between the spiritual and temporal power, between the history of Palestine and the history of Rome, between their outcomes in the gospel and the system of Roman law respectively. The Roman empire existed for the elaboration and promulgation of Roman law, as the chosen people for the preparation of the gospel. Thus the proof that the Roman people were specially appointed by God for this purpose and were specifically protected by him in its execution, carries with it the permanent authority of Roman law, and of its appointed guardian, just as the miracles of the Old Testament are taken as giving divine authority to the gospel dispensation and to its ministers. Hence the logical hiatus between the proof of the mission of Rome to rule the world, and the obligation of the Italian cities to obey the nominee of the German electors, if it does not disappear, is at any rate notably reduced; and the slenderest links of legal fiction (as that the Roman people had deputed their right to the electors, and so forth) might bridge over the chasm even to such a powerful intellect as Dante's.[7]

The first justifications for the supremacy of the Romans, Dante begins, lies in their nobility, for it is proper that a noble people should be set above others. Men are ennobled by merit of virtue (the source of honor and preferment), either their own or their ancestors', nobility being, as Aristotle has said, "virtue and ancient wealth," and virtue, in the words of Juvenal, being the sole and only nobility of mind. Since the noble should properly be rewarded by preferment because of the nature of nobility, the most noble should have the highest pre-eminence. That the Romans were most noble is evident by the testimony of Virgil in the *Aeneid* that Aeneas was the father of the Roman people; Livy supports him in this statement. Aeneas was noble both by his own virtues and in merit of his progenitors and wives. For the personal nobility of Aeneas Dante offers Virgil's lines (*Aeneid* I, 544–45 and VI, 170). For his hereditary nobility Dante notes that Aeneas was descended from a royal line in Asia (*Aeneid* III, 1–2), Europe ennobled him since he was sprung from Dardanus, and Africa likewise since his most ancient ancestress was the daughter of Atlas (*Aeneid* VIII, 134–37).

And in like fashion was Aeneas ennobled by his marriages. His first wife was a daughter of Priam, a king in Asia; his second wife was Dido, an African queen; and his third wife was the European princess Lavinia, daughter of King Latinus of Italy, "the noblest region of Europe." So the father of the Roman people, and hence the people he fathered, must have been the noblest on earth, and his distinguished inheritance and consanguinity with every land are clear evidences of divine predestination. (chapter 3)

Some readers and even some editors have been a little troubled by Dante's definition of Dido as "wife," especially in view of the ambiguous sense of Virgil's line "She calls it marriage and hides her guilt under that word." And if she was in truth a wife, she seems rather harshly treated in the *Inferno*. However, there is no doubt of Dante's intention here.

God alone, says Dante, on the authority of St. Thomas, is capable of working miracles. Hence the presence of miracles in history is evidence of divine intervention. That such miracles occurred in the history of Rome is proved by the testimony of illustrious authors. Dante cites in evidence the miraculous shield fallen from heaven at the time of Numa Pompilius, the goose that aroused the garrison against the Gauls, and the passage of the Tiber by Cloelia, all of which are supported by such "authorities" as Lucan, Livy, and Virgil. (chapter 4)

Further, says Dante, to pursue the goal of the commonwealth is to pursue the goal of right. And, in his view, the Romans always had the good of the commonwealth in mind. He quotes Cicero as evidence of this point insofar as their orders (i.e., collective bodies: senate, armies, and the like) were concerned, and for examples of individual dedication to this goal he sets before us Cincinnatus, Fabricius, Camillus, Mucius Scaevola, the Decii, and climactically (and somewhat paradoxically) Cato of Utica. (For Dante's classic and medieval sources here see T. Silverstein, "On the Genesis of *De Monarchia* II, v," in *Speculum* XIII [1938].) These all give extreme evidence of their devotion to the commonwealth, which is to say "right" (and here it should be observed that Dante's word *"jus"* could also be translated "law"). Exercising considerable scholastic ingenuity, Dante proceeds to prove that since the end of the Romans was "right," it follows that their actions were rightful (*"de jure"*). By further arguments of the same sort he proves that nature must have ordained a certain people for universal domination; what has already been said proves that such were in fact the people of Rome, and this truth is reinforced by various statements in the *Aeneid*. All of which makes it clear that Romans won their empire by right. (chapters 5–6)

Embarking on another line of reasoning, Dante says that divine judgment in human affairs may be sometimes clear and sometimes hidden. Reason can understand certain judgments, as for example that it is fitting that a man should risk his life for his country (Aristotle's *Politics* affirms that a man is a part of his city); faith may grasp other judgments if reason cannot, such as the law requiring knowledge of Christ for salvation. The hidden judgments of God are more difficult to perceive. Simple revelation may make them clear, as in the case of God's "spontaneous act" in the judgment against Saul as revealed to Samuel, or in the deliverance of the Hebrews from Egypt, where God's will was revealed by signs. Sometimes revelation will come as a result of prayer, as for Solomon's prayer in II Chronicles. God's will may also be made evident through ordeals, either by lot or by contest. The substitution of Matthias for Judas in Acts 1:26 is an example of judgment by lottery. In the case of contests, there are two subdivisions, combat and competition, illustrated respectively by the examples of Hercules and Antaeus and of Atalanta and Hippomenes. In the first kind there should be no fouling (in spite of Virgil's toleration of Euryalus's victory). If we regard the supremacy of the world as a kind of prize disputed by various contestants, it is obvious that the Romans are the winners; other nations had contended for this prize but the Romans had won, as is evidenced by the testimonies of Virgil, Lucan, Boethius, and St. Luke, who says that "there went out an edict from Caesar Augustus that the universal world should be enrolled." Thus, divine judgment which prevails through contest clearly sanctioned the triumph of the Romans. Dante cautions the reader to note that trial by combat should be resorted to only when all other methods of reaching a verdict have failed, and that the combatants should enter the lists not in hate or love but only with zeal for justice. If all who gather at such combats with desire of justice in their hearts have God in their midst, how can injustice triumph? Even the gentiles realized this, as is evident in Pyrrhus' speech to the Roman legates. If it is feared that perhaps the champion of the right may be weaker than his opponent, we have but to consider the cases of David and Goliath and of Hercules and Aeneas. Clearly whatever is won by ordeal is rightfully won. And the Romans, at every crisis in their history, won victory through the ordeal of combat. Aeneas defeated Turnus to win the Trojans their foothold in Italy; the Horatii defeated the Curiatii to secure the supremacy of Rome over Alba; the wars with the Samnites, Greeks, and Carthaginians may be fairly regarded as ordeals by collective combat. With this

Dante concludes that part of his argument which is based on reason. (chapters 7–10)

This section makes fascinating, if hardly very convincing, reading for a twentieth-century reader, who may find the comments of St. Augustine more appropriate. For Augustine, in the *City of God* (III, 17–19), has some very anti-Roman comments to make on the "heroes" of the early republic, whom he saw as motivated purely by lust of glory. It seems as though Dante had very often fallen into the error he had feared: that of identifying right with might. It will be noted, however, that it is only Roman might that can so happily be equated with justice; of the "ordeal" won by Alaric, or of the collective victory of the barbarians, Dante has no justification to offer. The reason, as will be obvious from a perusal of even this skeleton résumé of Dante's arguments, lies in the kind of authorities that he turned to: the historical poets Virgil and Lucan and the poetic historian Livy. "Dante," writes Nancy Lenkeith, "is making the Romans a chosen people having in providential history a position and role analogous to that of the Jews."8 And the Roman poets are as so many prophets. This conviction of Dante's, suitable and indeed vital to his thesis, could have been arrived at only by a poet attracted by other poets. It is safe to guess that Dante's justification of the Romans may well have begun with his admiration for Virgil, and the foregoing chapters may be sympathetically read as a tribute not so much to Roman justice as to Roman poetry. Dante's arguments may fail to convince us, but his passionate involvement with his literary idols is still moving — and it lends its own aura of poetry to these somewhat irrational pages.

Turning to his demonstration by faith, Dante begins with scathing comment on the avaricious clergy, who plunder the church and have no heed for the rights of the poor or the emperor. He has such as these in mind when he propounds the theory that if the Roman Empire was not rightfully established, it must follow that God Himself sanctioned a wrong. For it was under the emperor that Christ chose to be born and registered as a member of the human race. And by implication, recognizing the legality of the census, He recognized also the justice inherent in the empire. Clearly, Christ could neither do anything unjust nor sanction an injustice. A like conclusion is reached by consideration of Christ's death, which was offered in atonement for the sin of all humanity in the person of Adam. But the punishment visited on mankind would not have been a true punishment if the judge had not been properly qualified.

Vinay remarks that while Dante's argument here is "new and paradoxical in form" it is not original in substance, and he cites a long passage of like tenor from Osnabruck's *De Prerogativa*.[9] We may say too that the basic theory is Thomistic.

So it was Herod, not truly realizing what he was doing, who sent Christ to Pilate for judgment; Herod was only a king, whereas Pilate was the representative of the empire. Patently it was a part of the divine intention that the empire, and the empire alone, should play this role. Dante concludes by deploring the Donation of Constantine, which enfeebled the empire and the twice-sanctioned authority of the Roman people. (chapters 11–12)

Dante now takes up in Book III the most dangerous of the three questions he has proposed, namely, whether the authority of the emperor derives directly from God or indirectly through the pope. He knows he may arouse indignation and hostility but, with the example of Daniel and the counsel of Paul in mind, he intends to enter into the ring and cast out the impious and the false. (chapter 1)

The basic principle of his reasoning in this book is simply that what is repugnant to nature is also inconsistent with the will of God, for clearly God must will the goal of nature; otherwise the heavens move in vain — a thought "not to be uttered." Dante remarks here that on this third question those who would argue with him do so not out of ignorance but out of partisan contentiousness; in this the third question differs from the first two, where his efforts were chiefly aimed at dispelling ignorance. We must here deal largely with those whose emotions fly ahead of their reason. Of the three classes of men who oppose Dante's argument it may be that the first group, including the pope (to whom, says Dante, we owe what is due Peter though not what is due Christ) and certain other sincere pastors and their sympathizers, may be moved by zeal for the church rather than by simple "insolence," but the members of the second group are moved solely by avarice, calling themselves sons of the church but being really sons of the Devil. The third group is made up of the so-called decretalists, ignorant of both theology and philosophy but attacking the empire on the basis of the decretals. Dante affirms that he too reveres the decretals, but it is nevertheless necessary to recognize that they are scriptures subsequent to the church, while there are other scriptures "before the church" (i.e., the Old and New Testaments) and scriptures "contemporaneous with the Church" (i.e., the decrees of the early councils and the writings of Augustine and others) which must be given more weight than the decretals. Christ specifically said in Matthew 15:3: "Why do you transgress the commandments of God for the sake of your tradition?" Clearly then it is not traditions (i.e., decretals) which give authority to the church, but rather the reverse. Those who rely solely on the traditions must be excluded from the debate. And by the same token should be excluded those of the second group, who parade "as white sheep, though covered with the feathers of crows," for their greed would prevent them from seeing even the first principles of truth. It is only with those misled by their zeal for the church that Dante will attempt to reason. (chapters 2–3)

Dante takes up the arguments of his opponents, drawn, he says, largely from analogies and scriptural references, though with some appeal to reason. First he attacks the argument of those who would quote the passage of Genesis which states that God made two great luminaries, one for day and one for night, by which they would understand the spiritual and the temporal powers. They say that as the light of the moon is not true light but only reflected from the sun, so is the temporal power not independent but as it were reflected and hence subordinate. Dante begins his refutation by pointing out that there are two ways of going astray in looking for "mystic" meaning: either by looking for it where it is not, or by misinterpretation. He quotes St. Augustine on both points: in the *City of God* it is stated that not everything which is told as having happened is to be assumed as significant, and in *Christian Doctrine* we may read that one who finds in the Bible something not in the intent of the writer may be compared to a man leaving the right road and reaching his destination by a circuitous way. Attacking the analogy proposed, Dante first points out the absurdity of the sequence, for it would imply that church and empire had been created before mankind, whom they were meant to serve. Nor would man have needed either if he had remained in his state of original innocence.* It would have been superfluous to produce remedies for man's sinful state when he was not only not sinful but not even existent, and no action of God can be super-

---

* Wicksteed points out that Virgil "crowns and mitres" Dante on their arrival in the earthly paradise on the summit of the Mount of Purgatory.

fluous. But, says Dante, there is a gentler way of disposing of this argument. For in fact, although the moon derives her light from the sun, she by no means derives either her existence or her operation from it. Here would be the proper analogy: the temporal power does indeed receive through the blessing of the pope the power of operating with greater virtue, but it does not owe to the spiritual power either its existence, its authority, or its basic efficiency. The logical error in the false analogy is in the identification of "light" with "authority"; they are in fact not the same thing. (chapter 4)

Another analogical argument set forth by the adherents of papal supremacy would compare Levi and Judah, the two sons of Jacob, to the papacy and the empire respectively; by this reasoning Levi the priest would be senior and hence superior to Judah. But this is syllogistically wrong in its assumption, for seniority is not authority, nor can it be argued that authority derives from seniority: there are many bishops younger than their priests. Another scriptural argument is based on Saul's deposition by Samuel, from which it is deduced that the vicar of God has authority to bestow or take away the temporal empire. But Samuel was not a vicar, but rather a special emissary, sent for a specific purpose. A vicar, though he has wider jurisdiction than a messenger, is not the same thing as a messenger; in fact God has done and will continue to do many things through His angels which His vicar, the successor of Peter, cannot do. Again it is argued, from the text of Matthew, that the gifts of frankincense and gold made to the child Jesus signify that He was to be lord of things spiritual and temporal, and the same must hold true of His vicar. But in fact, says Dante, a vicar is not the same thing as a sovereign. It is clear that with respect to the operations of nature, God's vicar is not the equivalent of his lord; clearly he cannot make earth go up or fire descend. In any case, although power may be delegated, the authority inherent in a supreme ruler is not truly his to delegate. He cannot confer the authority of his office even on himself; he may resign it or accept it, but he cannot make another his equal.

Yet another text often quoted is that wherein Christ says to Peter: "And whatsoever thou hast bound on earth shall be bound in heaven also, and whatsoever thou hast loosed on earth shall be loosed in heaven also." From this it is inferred that the successor of Peter has power over the laws of the temporal empire. Dante argues not against the legitimacy of the succession but against the scope of the authority. Clearly, "whatsoever" must be limited in meaning; the pope cannot dissolve the marriage bond and give a wife to a second husband while the first still lives, nor can he, says Dante, "absolve me when I am not penitent." So, Dante says, since "whatsoever" is clearly relative to something, we must look to the context. And since Christ has just said: "I will give them the keys of the kingdom of heaven," the "whatsoever" must apply only to things in that area. The successor of Peter may indeed loose and bind within the scope of the office committed to Peter, but this does not apply to the decrees of the empire. (chapters 5–8)

The passage in Luke in which Peter offers two swords to Christ is also adduced in defense of the papal supremacy; the meaning has been taken to be that Peter has the two swords of spiritual and temporal power, and hence his successors must likewise have them. Taken in context, it is clear that Christ was simply advising the apostles for their protection. He bade each of them to have a sword, and so Peter's answer has no allegorical significance; it is the simple answer that we would expect from the guileless and impetuous Peter, and no more. If there be an allegory in the two swords it is probably to be applied in the sense of the words and deeds of the disciples (this would be indicated by Matthew 10:34 and Acts 1:1). (chapter 9)

So much for the scriptural arguments on the other side. The adherents of papal supremacy also appeal to history, citing the Donation of Constantine. But Dante contends that the emperor had no right to make such a donation; for it is clearly "against the function conferred on the emperor to dismember the empire." And like the church the empire has its own foundation; it is counter to every human right should the empire destroy itself. Furthermore, the church had not the right to accept the donation. It was expressly charged (Matthew 10:9 ff.), "Possess not gold nor silver nor money in your girdles," etc., nor has Dante been able to find any subsequent retraction of that charge. Again, the historical fact that Charlemagne accepted the crown from Adrian[10] has been interpreted as indicating the church's right. As well argue, says Dante, that Otto's restoration of Leo VIII (now accounted an antipope) in 963–65 and his deposition of Benedict V in 965 prove that the emperor has a right to create the pope. "A usurpation of a right does not create a right."

Lastly, there is a so-called appeal to reason which calls for refutation. It is argued that the emperor and the pope are both men; there must be a scale among men, the pope obviously cannot be inferior, and so must be superior, and hence the empire must be dependent on the papacy. But, says Dante, the error in this reasoning is to confuse the "substance" man with the "accident" of office. Clearly among men there must be a best man, and the pope and emperor as men will be inferior to this man whoever he is. But emperor and pope are not men but offices. In order to find out who is superior between them one would have to be referred to some other kind of unity, either God Himself or some measure of authority (a kind of "accident" and not one of the measure of the "substance" man). The question of ranking them by their "manhood" does not arise. (chapters 10–12)

Dante now takes up the affirmative side of his case. The independence of the empire, he affirms, is established by the fact that before the church existed, Christ by His birth and death acknowledged the authority of the empire. Paul also recognized the authority of Caesar, as is indicated in Acts 25:10, 27:24, 28:19. Nor could Constantine have given what he did to the church had he not possessed true authority. And if the church claims the power to give authority to the Roman prince, we may ask whence comes this power. Surely not from natural law, for the church is not an effect of nature but of God; nor yet by divine law, since Dante has been able to find nothing in scripture that authorizes such a power; indeed, the scriptures would seem to exclude priests from temporal powers. Nor could the church have got such power from herself, since she never had it, nor did she get it from any emperor, as has been proved above. Nor can she claim the authority of all mankind, for most Europeans as well as all Asiatics and Africans would reject the thought. But Dante goes further and proves that it is not "formal" to the nature of the church to exercise temporal authority. For the form of the church is the life of Christ, as shown in His words and deeds. And Christ in the presence of Pilate specifically said: "My kingdom is not of this world," which is of course not to say that He is not lord of the kingdom — but not in the sense we are discussing here. And so — as previous evidence has shown — the power to authorize the temporal rule is against the nature of the church. (chapters 13–15)

Dante feels that it has been made sufficiently clear that the temporal authority is not dependent on the papacy, and it has been implied that it is in fact directly dependent on God. To prove that this implication is sound, Dante reasons as follows: Man is by nature made up of the corruptible and the incorruptible. There must therefore be a twofold end for man, one for each of his natures. In fact there are two such ends, one the blessedness of this life, figured by the earthly paradise, and the other the enjoyment of the divine vision given to our understanding by the celestial paradise. (Vinay points out the saving orthodoxy implicit in the wording[11] — although his own translation ignores the difference.)

For attaining these two ends there are two sets of means: philosophy with the moral and intellectual virtues is the means to one end, spiritual teachings and theological virtues are the means to the other. These ends are made plain to us, the one by reason and the other by the revelation of the Holy Spirit, yet greed would stand in our way of pursuing them if we did not have "bit and rein" to guide us. Like runaway horses, we need double guidance, that of the pope (to lead us to eternal life) and that of the emperor (to show our way to the felicity of this life). And it is the chief duty of the emperor to assure humanity the freedom and peace which is needful on the "threshing floor of mortal life." Since the dispositions of this world are subject to the revolutions of the heavens, it is proper that He who rules the motions of the heavens should have direct charge of choice and confirmation of the temporal ruler. And the imperial electors should be thought of as heralds of divine providence, even though sometimes the mists of greed prevent them from seeing the divine will aright. For they are but channels for the fountain of universal authority from which the imperial authority directly flows. (One wonders just how the electors got into Dante's historical view of the development of the empire! Augustus needed none, nor did Charlemagne, for that matter.)

Dante concludes that he has proved the case he set out to establish; he adds, however, that he does not argue that because the temporal authority is independent of the spiritual it must be co-equal. He grants willingly that Caesar owes to Peter the reverence which a firstborn son owes to a father; so may Caesar with greater power illuminate the world given into his charge by "Him alone who is ruler of all things spiritual and temporal." (chapter 16)

❊ 11 ❊

Letters and Lesser Works

Letters

ACCORDING to Boccaccio, Dante wrote many letters in Latin.[1]
This would seem only natural; as Scartazzini rather poetically
puts it:

He, brother, husband, and father; he, the friend of the famous men
of his age; he, poet, litterateur, and statesman, poor and compelled to
eat the bread that savors of salt, must, doubtless, have taken up his
pen at least once a month, perhaps once a week, perhaps even oftener,
to write, sometimes to his brother, sometimes to his wife, sometimes
to his children, sometimes to his relatives, sometimes to his friends,
and sometimes to other persons.[2]

In fact, however, very few have come down and not all the extant
letters attributed to him have been accepted as genuine. Those
now considered authentic are all written in Latin, and all are, in
a sense, public documents; we have no example of the intimate
sort imagined by Scartazzini.

Various editors have had their own ideas as to the number and
the order of the letters. I shall follow here the sequence in the
Temple Classics volume entitled *Latin Works of Dante,* as the
most convenient for the reader's reference.

The first one was written to the Bishop of Ostia, who as papal legate was attempting to establish peace between the Florentine factions (March 10 to June, 1304). After an apology for tardiness in answering, it expresses the writer's joy in the efforts of the legate, and professes that "the lawful point of our purpose, springing from the bowstring that we stretched, aimed, aims, and will aim at nothing but the tranquillity and liberty of the people of Florence." The letter promises that the group represented by the writer (presumably the exiled Whites) will abstain from warlike acts and put their faith in the legate's negotiations. Probably this epistle was written by Dante from Arezzo, perhaps while he was one of the "councilors" of the Whites (Bruni's *Life* assigns him that role). Although there have been some skeptics, most scholars, including Paget Toynbee, accept the letter as genuine.

The second letter is preceded by the statement "This epistle was written by Dante Alighieri to Oberto and Guido, Counts of Romena, after the death of the Count Alexander of Romena, their uncle, condoling with them on his demise." This is of course merely a copyist's note. It adequately summarizes the contents of the letter, in which Dante speaks highly of the munificence of Alessandro and deplores his own loss in the death of such a generous man, reminding the bereaved nephews that their uncle is enjoying his reward as "a chosen courtier in the eternal palace" and urging them to clothe themselves in his excellent character even as they take up the inheritance of his worldly goods. He apologizes for his absence from the funeral; this was occasioned by his poverty, a product of his exile. Since in *Inferno* XXX Dante speaks of this same Alessandro as an *anima trista*, the letter has puzzled its readers. Toynbee comments: "If Dante was the writer of the letter, we must suppose that he did not become acquainted with facts referred to in the *Commedia* until some time after Alessandro's death."[3]

Letter III is addressed to Moroello Malaspina, and describes in poetic language how Dante, while meditating "on things of heaven and earth" as he strolled by the streams of the Arno, was taken captive by a beautiful woman. It was, he says, like a lightning flash and followed too by thunder, in this case the voice of Love, "terrible and imperious." "Love," says Dante, "now reigns within me, and as to the nature of his rule you must enquire below, outside the boundary of these presents." Toynbee, arguing that the letter was written "from the Casentino, perhaps in 1308 but at any rate before 1310," places it after the following letter, which is the third in his edition.[4] The lady in question is thought to be the inspirer of the Ode *"Amor, da che convien pur ch'io mi doglia."*

The fourth letter, addressed "to the exile of Pistoia" "from one undeservedly exiled from Florence," is in effect a covering letter for a poem sent, it would seem, to Cino da Pistoia, with whom Dante was in correspondence at this time (1305–6?). Dante replies to Cino's query as to whether the mind can alter from passion to passion. He is grateful for Cino's question (though Cino could have answered for himself), since he sees in it an opportunity to enlarge his prestige. He refers to the poem ("in praise of Calliope"), where his answer is given. It is his opinion, expressed in the poem, that the intense love of one specific object may indeed perish and be replaced by another. This can be proved, he says, not only by experience but by reason, for the concupiscible faculty which is the seat of love is a power of the senses, and the power does not die with the death of one passion. For authority he cites Ovid's reference to the varying passions of the sun. He concludes by recommending to his "dearest brother" the reading of *Fortuitorum Remedia* (which Dante believed written by Seneca) as a proof against *"rhamnusia,"* i.e., retributive justice. Wicksteed suggests that the poem accompanying the letter may have been *"Io sono stato con amore insieme"*[5] (*Rime;* see p. 95).

The fifth letter is the first of a series dealing with the coming of Henry VII to Italy, and was probably written in the autumn of 1310. Speaking as a "humble Italian" in undeserved exile to the princes of Italy and the Roman Senate, Dante begins by announcing a new dawn and the return of justice to Italy. Henry VII is referred to as a second Moses and the bridegroom of Italy, and the bride is encouraged to dry her tears and look forward to release from the prison of the impious. Dante stresses his certainty that the emperor will be compassionate toward those who acknowledge their faults, but merciless towards men of presumption. He urges the Lombards to put aside their inherited barbarism and yield to the seed of the Trojans and Latins, if there are any left, and exhorts the "tribe of Scandinavia" to overcome the temptations of greed and submit to the emperor. He bids those who are now laboring under oppression to lift up their hearts, and counsels those who have, like him, suffered unjustly, to be merciful in their triumph. Thus all Italy will enjoy peace. He reminds all Italians — "ye who drink of his streams and navigate his seas; ye who tread the sands of his shores and the summits of his mountains" — that the emperor is in truth the temporal lord of all, that it is on his law that their property rights depend, and that the reign of the Roman prince was predestined by God and sanctioned by the church. This predestination will become clear to a student of Roman history from the Trojan war to the triumph of Octavian; in certain miraculous events the hand of God is evident — all of which is a summary of the arguments in Book II of *De Monarchia*. He reminds his readers of Christ's birth under Augustus, His command to render to Caesar that which is Caesar's, and His acknowledgment of the authority of Pilate. This king "ordained by the Lord for us" has also had the apostolic benediction of Clement, the successor of Peter.

The sixth, perhaps the most celebrated, as it is certainly the most passionate, of Dante's letters, may be properly studied in greater detail. It bears the superscription "Dante Alighieri, the Florentine, undeservedly exiled, to the infamous Florentines in the city," and is fiercely Ghibelline in argument. It begins with the statement that God's providence committed the government of human affairs to the Holy Roman Empire, so that the world might live in peace and fulfill its appointed temporal ends. Scripture and reason support this truth, and it becomes painfully evident when the imperial throne is vacant and the world turns from its course, the oarsmen of Peter's ship fall asleep, and wretched Italy "is tossed with such combat of wind and wave as the woeful Italians can scarce measure with their tears," a figure which is repeated in *Purgatorio*. Let those who have refused to see God's will in the imperial reign now turn pale, as judgment approaches. "You," says Dante, addressing his fellow citizens,

are particularly at fault; misled by your rapacity, you have refused your duty of submission and risen in rebellion. But the divine sanctions of the empire cannot forever be put aside; it is against God and nature to set yourselves up as a government separate from Rome. It would be as logical to set up a new church as a new civic order. In truth, you have lost not only wisdom but the very beginning thereof, which is the fear of the Lord. But if you are not frightened by your lawlessness or even by your ignorance, you must be terrified when you contemplate the ruin in store for you. How can your contemptible fortifications [*ridiculo cuiquam vallo*] hope to prevail against the arms of Rome, which have ever triumphed throughout the world, from the Atlas to the Caucasus?*

Dante foresees the destruction of the walls, the rebellion of the famished and terrified populace, the violation of the churches, and the exile of the great majority of Florentines; it will be like the fate of Saguntum save that in this case the struggle will not be for liberty but for slavery. Nor should the example of Parma (which had driven off Frederick II in 1248) be regarded as encouraging; in the long run the triumph of Parma worked to its own detriment. Recall rather, he bids his compatriots, the destruction of Milan and Spoleto by Frederick Barbarossa. "Vainest of the Tuscans," he cries out, "blinded by your own ignorance and lust, which enslave you to the law of sin and prevent you from obeying the true laws which are the image of natural justice; only in obedience to law is found true freedom."* He ends by assuring the "wretched descendants of Fiesole" that the vengeance of the divine and triumphant Henry is certain; it may already be too late for pardon. This letter is dated "the day before the Kalends of April, on the confines of Tuscany, under the source of the Arno, in the first year of the most auspicious progress to Italy of Henry the Caesar."

It is hardly surprising that the Florentines, after the death of the emperor, did not want to forgive their embittered compatriot. It is difficult to imagine what Dante had hoped to accomplish.

Letter VII is in like vein. It is headed: "To the most glorious and happy victor and sole master, Lord Henry, by divine Providence King of the Romans, ever august, his most devoted servants, Dante Alighieri, a Florentine undeservedly exiled, and all peace-loving Tuscans everywhere, a kiss on the ground before his feet."

Speaking for himself and all peace-loving Italians, Dante recalls that peace, the heritage of Christ, has been disrupted by the machinations of the adversary. Hope of a better world had come with the arrival of the emperor; many had recalled Virgil's eclogue celebrating the return of the Virgin. But now doubt has arisen because of the delay of the new sun, which, as the real sun once did at Joshua's behest, seems to have turned back

* Summarized quotation.

on his course. Yet hope and trust in the emperor still remain strong; Dante recalls his own act of fealty (which may have been performed on January 6, 1311, when Henry was crowned in Milan) and how at that time he had cried out within himself: "Behold the Lamb of God, which taketh away the sin of the world." But Dante and his friends cannot but wonder at the sluggishness of the imperial campaign, above all at the emperor's reluctance to attack Tuscany. For the empire is world-wide, as Virgil proclaims and as is evident in Luke 2:1, a passage which tells of Christ's acknowledgment of the law of Augustus. The Florentines are profiting by the emperor's delay — delay is always disadvantageous to the prepared party, as Curio said to Caesar. (Dante seems to show less sympathy with Curio's counsel in *Inferno* XXVIII.[6]) Besides, Henry should think of his heir, following the admonition given to the founder of the empire, Aeneas. "Your royal heir," says Dante, "is another Ascanius . . . who will rage like a lion against the followers of Turnus," i.e., Robert of Naples. Henry is also invited to recall the words of Samuel, ending "And the Lord sent thee on a journey, and said, "Go and utterly destroy the sinners, the Amalekites." (I Samuel 15:17–18) For a like purpose the emperor has been consecrated.

It is a mistake to spend so much time in Milan, dealing with the Lombard towns, Dante argues. They are like the heads of the hydra; if one falls, another will rise. The right action is to strike at the root of the evil. "Do you not know, most excellent of princes," Dante asks, "where this stinking vixen lies, safe from the hunters?" The waters of the Arno poison her lips and her name is Florence. Dante compares the city to Myrrha, incestuously involved with her father (the pope in Dante's allegory), and to Amata, the rash mother of Lavinia who had urged Turnus (here again, Robert of Naples) to fight against Aeneas. (The *Commedia* also memorializes Myrrha's impiety [*Inferno* XXX, 37–40] and Amata's intemperance [*Purgatorio* XVII, 35–39].) Unnatural, says Dante, is the city of Florence in rebelling against Rome her mother; she also corrupts her neighbors, and resists the commandments of God in spurning her legitimate king and trafficking with another; she is preparing her own punishment. Bowsky records that it was in this month of April that the Florentine chancellery began to refer regularly to Henry as King of the Germans.[7] Dante then bids the "new progeny of Jesse" to arise and overthrow this Goliath "with the sling of thy wisdom and the stone of thy strength." Only then will peace return. This letter was "Written in Tuscany, near the springs of the Arno, on the 16th of April, 1311, the first year of the descent into Italy of the divine and most fortunate Henry."

The eighth letter ("Dante Alighieri of Florence to the Italian Cardinals"), mentioned by Villani, must have been addressed to the cardinals in conclave at Carpentras in 1314. For a clearer understanding of the references in the letter, a brief historical summary may be useful. The feud between Boniface VIII and Philip the Fair, culminating in the tragic death of the former, had left a heritage of discord among the cardinals, some of whom adhered to the cause of Boniface and some to that of France (or, in Italian terms, the House of Colonna). The brief reign of Benedict XI (October, 1303–04), who did his best to make peace among the factions, was followed by the long and angry conclave of Perugia, which for almost a year wrangled and bargained to no effect. Finally the spokesmen of the Colonna-France faction (which included Napoleone Orsini) suggested an ingenious procedure. One party was to select three candidates from "across the mountains," presumably to insure their neutrality in the quarrels of Italian factions, and the other party was to choose one of the three, both ratifying the ultimate choice. The Bonifacians, headed by Francesco Gaetani, the pope's nephew, accepted, and put forward the names of three candidates, one of whom was Bernard de Goth, Archbishop of Bordeaux, a protégé and adherent of Boniface. The Cardinal da Prato, leader of the French faction, sensing that Bernard's avarice would in the long run triumph over his former loyalties, gave his approval, but first, taking advantage of the time accorded him for deliberation, he sent a secret message to the King of France, authorizing him to make certain conditions with Bernard. Villani gives an account of the meeting of king and archbishop at the monastery of St. Jean d'Angely and of the conditions to which the ambitious prelate was only too eager to subscribe.[8] All had to do with the reinstatement of the Colonna and the absolution of all the opponents of Boniface — in short, the justification and advancement of the House of France. There was also one unspecified condition "to be reserved till due time and place," which perhaps concerned the dissolution of the Templars. Bernard became pope in 1305 under the name of Clement V, and forthwith justified the cynical assessment of the Cardinal da Prato: not only did he meet all the French conditions, but by the creation of ten new cardinals, all French, and his decision to rule from Avignon, where he established his residence in 1309, he made the papacy subservient to the French monarchy. He died in 1314; a two-year interregnum ensued. The cardinals, this time French in majority, were convened at Carpentras, and it is to the Italian prelates at this meeting that Dante's letter is addressed. It is sad to report that the conclave broke up in violence, and only in 1316 at Lyons was the next pope proclaimed. He too was French and continued to maintain the papal seat in Avignon.

"How doth the city sit solitary that was full of people; how is she become a widow! she that was great among nations." With this quotation from the prophet Jeremiah, which he had used before in the *Vita Nuova*, Dante begins his epistle. Even as the avarice of the ruling Pharisees had brought destruction on Jerusalem and so evoked the lament of Jeremiah, so Dante mourns over Rome (to whom Christ had by word and deed granted the empire of the world and whom Peter and Paul had consecrated with their blood). Desolate Rome was as sad a sight to the good Christian as heresy itself. "The infidel mock us and attribute our downfall to their own plots; some astrologers have laid it to necessity, but in fact it is the misuse of your own choice," says Dante, addressing the cardinals. "You . . . have swerved from the right path like the unskilled Phaethon; you have brought your flock to the brink of the precipice." This is because the cardinals have taken the part of Alcimus and Demetrius. The reference is to I Maccabees 7, and these names of leaders opposed to Judas Maccabaeus are meant to signify Clement V and Philip the Fair, Wicksteed suggests.[9]

Perhaps, Dante says, he will be rebuked for following the example of Uzzah, who presumptuously put his hand forth to steady the ark, but he is one of the least of the sheep in Christ's flock, consumed only by zeal for the church. Ere now God's truth has been known to come from the mouths of babes and sucklings; and Aristotle himself says that the truth is to be preferred over all friendship. Nor is Dante like Uzzah, for the latter put forth his hand to the ark "but I only to the oxen who are refractory." Let Him who saved the storm-tossed ship come to the aid of the ark. "My comment," says Dante, "can provoke none to contention but may bring the blush of shame to your cheeks, since there is only one plaintive and private voice to mourn at the funeral of the church." He continues:

Small wonder, in truth. Everyone, even as ye, has taken Avarice to wife; what shameful sons the Bride of Christ must own, her daughters-in-law are neither Charity nor Justice but the daughters of the horse-leech; the Bishop of Luni is but one example of many. Gregory, Ambrose, Augustine, Dionysius, Damascenus and Bede have been cast aside in favor of the *Speculum juris* and the *Decretals* of Innocent II and the Bishop of Ostia.

In other words, proper theological studies are replaced by the perusual of works which will lead to wealth and benefices.

Dante reminds the prelates that many are murmuring the truths that he alone is uttering. He realizes he has become importunate but it is because they have provoked such reproaches, which might have been expected to come from heaven. "May shame beget repentance and the will to reform. Let the sight of Rome, now deprived of both luminaries, strengthen this resolution." Dante suggests that the Roman cardinals, even more than other Italians, should be moved by the "eclipse" of Rome which they have themselves helped to bring about. "Thou more than the others, Orsini," says Dante, remembering the part played by Napoleone Orsini in the election of Clement V. And "thou likewise, adherent of the other Trasteverine faction," i.e., Francesco Gaetani, of the Guelph-Orsini faction, inheritor it would seem of "the wrath of the deceased Pilate," Boniface. For though the infamous scar will remain, yet the wound may be healed "if ye who were responsible for this transgression" will but fight manfully and in union "for the Bride of Christ, for Her throne, which is Rome, for our Italy and for the community of all in pilgrimage on earth." So, from the area where the struggle has already begun "ye may hear the cry '*Gloria in Excelsis*,' and the example of the greedy Gascons lusting to usurp the glory of the Latins may remain an invidious example for the ages to come."

The ninth letter, to a Florentine friend, was for a long time regarded as apocryphal but has now come to be generally accepted as authentic. If it be truly Dante's own, it is worth quoting in full for the vibrant self-portrait that emerges from its impassioned phraseology. Modern critics date it as of May, 1315. I follow in general the text of C. S. Latham[10] with some modifications.

From your letter, which I received with due reverence and affection, I have learned with a grateful heart, and after diligent consideration, how dear to your soul is my return to my country; and you have thus placed me under so much the greater obligations, in that it happens very rarely to exiles to find friends. But I will answer its import; and if my answer is not such as perchance the pusillanimity of some might look for, I heartily pray that before judgment is passed it may be thoroughly submitted to the examination of your wisdom.

Behold then what in the letters of your nephew and mine, and also in those of many other friends, has been made known to me in regard to the ordinance but just now made at Florence relative to the pardon of the banished: that if I were willing to pay a certain amount of money and if I were willing to suffer the stigma of oblation, I should be pardoned and could return forthwith. In this, in very truth, there are two ridiculous and ill-considered things, O Father. Ill-considered that is by those who gave them expression, for your letter, more discreetly and advisedly conceived, contained nothing of the sort.

Is this then the gracious recall wherewith Dante Alighieri is summoned back to his country after an exile patiently endured for almost fifteen years? Did his innocence, manifest to any man, and his years of incessant study deserve this reward? Far be such senseless abasement of the heart from a man familiar with philosophy, that like a prisoner he suffer himself to be offered up after the manner of a certain Ciolo and other criminals. Far be it from a man who preaches justice, after having patiently endured injury, to pay money to those inflicting it, as though they were his benefactors.

This is not the way to return to my country, O my Father. If another shall be found by you, or by others, that does not derogate from the fame and honor of Dante, that will I take with no lagging steps. But if Florence is entered by no such path, then never will I enter Florence. What! Can I not everywhere look upon the face of the sun and the stars? Can I not meditate anywhere under the heavens upon the sweetest truths without first making myself inglorious, nay ignominious, to the people and state of Florence? Nor indeed will bread be lacking.

The last letter, the celebrated one to Can Grande, is the most interesting of all for readers of the *Commedia*. What better commentary could we hope for than that of the author himself, setting forth clearly his purpose and his method, and revealing the inner motivation, at least within certain limits, of the poet, and incidentally affording insight into the working of his mind? An essential document, certainly, and a proper beginning for any serious critical study of the work. But is the letter in fact Dante's?

Its authenticity has been questioned, primarily but not exclusively on the grounds that manuscript authority for it is late and suspect. Many scholars of an older generation considered it apocryphal, and more recently such Dantists as Porena, Pietrobuono, and Friedrich Schneider have expressed reservations. One critic, Mancini, has suggested that the first four paragraphs may be by Dante's hand and the rest an addition by a commentator. Yet many, most effectively Moore, have warmly defended its authenticity, and among the statements of other proponents of its genuineness we may profitably cite Barbi's dictum, which affirms that the letter "clearly reveals the mind and style of Dante," adding that "the revelation in fact is so clear that little more is to be desired; it ranges all the way from the title, where he designates himself a *florentinus natione, non moribus,* to the precise commentary on the first tercets of the *Paradiso.*"[11] Until it is proved otherwise, we may think of it as Dante's work. Toynbee suggests 1319, when Dante was living at Ravenna, as the most probable date. I shall summarize it in some detail:

Dante, in courtly phraseology, speaks of his generous reception at the hands of Can Grande, excuses his presumption in speaking of his patron as a friend, and ventures to offer as a token of gratitude the "sublime canticle" of the *Commedia,* called the *Paradiso,* which he hereafter dedicates to the Lord of Verona. The *Paradiso,* he says, cannot be understood without some reference to the *Commedia,* of which it is a part. Every doctrinal work must be considered with respect to six aspects: subject, agent, form, aim, title, and kind of philosophy. The *Paradiso* is distinct from the rest of the *Commedia* only as regards three aspects. Dante will speak first of these three and then of the others, and in the latter case he will consider them both in reference to the *Paradiso* and to the *Commedia* as a whole. (§§ 1–6)

The meaning of the work is not simple; there is one meaning derived from the letter and another derived from what the letter indicates. The first meaning is called literal; the second, allegorical or mystical. Dante illustrates his sense here by examining the lines from Exodus: "When Israel went out of Egypt, the house of Jacob from a people of strange language; Judah was his sanctuary and Israel his domain." Literally this refers simply to the historical exodus; the allegory signifies our redemption accomplished in Christ; the moral meaning signifies the conver-

sion of the soul from sin to a state of grace; the anagogical meaning refers to the departure of the soul from the slavery of this
corruption to the liberty of everlasting glory. All of the mystical
meanings are allegorical, since they differ from the historical
or literal meaning. (The reader may wish to compare the remarks
on the same subject in the second treatise of the *Convivio*.)
Literally, then, the work is a consideration of the state of souls
after death; allegorically "the subject is man, liable to the reward
or punishment of Justice, in accordance with the use he has
made of his free will." The work consists of three divisions,
divided into cantos, in turn divided into lines. The form or
method is poetic, figurative, descriptive, digressive, and tran-
sumptive (which Wicksteed defines as metaphorical), and it
proceeds by definition, division, proof, refutation, and display
of examples. (§§ 7–9)

The title of the work is: "Here beginneth the Comedy of
Dante Alighieri, a Florentine by birth, not by character."
"Comedy," Dante states, is derived from *comus* and *oda,* and
means a "rustic song." It differs from tragedy, which begins in
tranquillity and comes to a terrible end, and which derives its
name from *tragos* (goat) plus *oda*, signifying therefore "goat-
song," i.e., fetid like a goat (as Seneca's tragedies illustrate),
while comedy, though having some early adverse circumstances,
yet comes to a happy ending, as appears from Terence. And in
style of speech, tragedy is lofty and comedy humble, as Horace
remarks in his *Ars Poetica.* So the name "Comedy" fits the work
at hand: it begins in hell but ends with paradise; likewise its
speech is truly humble, for it is written in the vernacular, in
which even women communicate. (§ 10)

The subject of the entire work being the state of the souls
after death, the specific subject of the *Paradiso* is the state of
the souls of the blessed. Allegorically this part of the work has
for its subject man rewarded by justice according to his deserts.

Having now considered the things in which the part differs
from the whole, he passes to the other three, in which there is no
distinction. The "agent" of the whole and the part is the same,
i.e., Dante. The aim of the part, as of the whole, is to remove
those living in this life from a condition of misery and guide
them to a state of happiness. The kind of philosophy by which
he proceeds is moral philosophy or ethics, for the work was undertaken for practice and not speculation. (§§ 11–16)

Dante now enters on the interpretation of the literal, reminding us that this is in effect nothing but a revelation of the form of the work. The principal divisions of the *Paradiso* are two: a prologue and a principal part. The principal part begins with line 37 of canto I, "Rising to mortal men through diverse ports." What precedes is the prologue according to the terminology of Aristotle in his *Rhetoric*. This preamble is composed in a special manner by poets who have an invocation as well as an introduction; so with the present prologue: the first part is a statement of what is to be said, the second part, beginning "O good Apollo," is the invocation. In keeping with the advice of Cicero in *De Inventione,* the author, promising to speak of the things he saw in heaven, arouses in his hearers good will for the utility of the things seen in heaven, attention through their marvelous nature, and docility by their possibility. For utility is evident in the discussion of the joys of paradise, especially attractive to human desire; the marvelous is promised in the discussion of the nature of the kingdom of heaven; and the possibility is made apparent when he alludes to things which he was able to remember, for if he might, so might others. (§§ 17–19)

Dante continues with a meticulous line-by-line, word-by-word analysis, bristling with authorities, of the first canto through the invocation to Apollo. It is hardly necessary to follow him through this. He concludes by apologizing for failing to go on with his exposition; however, he is so hard pressed by domestic concerns that he must put aside "these and other matters useful to the public good." The poem, he says, will proceed from sphere to sphere, telling of the state of the blessed and disclosing how true blessedness consists in knowing the source of truth, as St. John says and likewise Boethius, who, in the third book of his *De Consolatione Philosophiae,* says: "To see Thee is our end." And since beyond God, the Source, there is nothing to be seen, the treatise will conclude in Him Who is blessed throughout all ages. (§§ 20–33)

Barbi remarks that this letter "has often proved a source of disappointment to Dante students,"[12] presumably because of its rather rigorous and at times arid scholasticism. If Barbi's observation had some validity for the scholars of his own and a somewhat earlier generation, I venture to say that it scarcely applies to contemporary critics. In fact, the letter studied in its own right is a splendid specimen of literary criticism within the framework of the times and traditions in which the *Commedia* was written. It would be unfair to expect it to be lyric and imaginative as well. Curtius has no hesitation in affirming that "the literary studies of the Latin Middle Ages are completed and crowned in Dante's Epistle 13. With this literary treatise too Dante stands in the scholarly tradition of the Latin Middle Ages."[13]

Questio de Aqua et Terra

The *Questio de Aqua et Terra* is an odd, pedantic little exercise, hardly calculated to charm twentieth-century readers. Indeed, its appeal was probably limited even in the author's time: Zingarelli was of the opinion that Dante never published it,[14] and the circumstances of its coming to light were such as to allow some room for doubt as to the real authorship. It was published in 1508 by G. B. Moncetti, who claimed that he had transcribed it from Dante's autograph manuscript, but the manuscript has never been found. There is therefore no external evidence to justify the attribution of the work to Dante. Largely thanks to the efforts of Moore,[15] recent scholarship has come to accept it as part of the canon, though the phraseology of Wicksteed is worthy of note; concluding his comments on the history of the work, he remarks:

"For my own part I have very little hesitation in accepting the treatise as belonging to Dante's age or near it; and the number of minute indications that appear to identify it as Dante's own work is so great that in spite of considerable difficulties I think we are justified in provisionally regarding it, with some confidence, as authentic."[16]

According to a statement affixed to the original manuscript, the *Questio* was in essence a thesis which Dante expounded before the clergy of Verona in 1320. The question at issue was whether water, being "nobler" than earth, stands higher than land on the earth's circumference. Dante maintains that such is not the case, and in twenty-four brief chapters proves his point to his own satisfaction and no doubt to that of anyone still interested in this typically medieval problem. As in the *De Monarchia*, Dante first refutes his opponents' arguments and then sets forth his own, leaving room for the refutation of rebuttals on the way. The design does indeed suggest that of the *De Monarchia* and to a certain extent that of the *Convivio*. A summary of the little work would hardly be profitable, but two things may be noted as characteristic of Dante's reasoning in these matters: the one as touching a particular notion of his own, the other as fundamental to his whole theory of reason and its limits. In explaining why the earth, protruding as it does in the northern or inhabited hemisphere, must and does rise higher than water, Dante ascribes the elevation to the influence of some stars or constellations of the starry heavens. This is an idea of his which also serves him well in his study of the spots on the moon, in the *Paradiso*. And, in the same passage, dealing with the operation of the heavens and the question that might be asked: why the northern hemisphere is raised up and the southern not, he answers that such was God's will and adds: "Let men desist, therefore, let them desist, from searching out things that are above them, and let them seek up to such point as they may, that they may draw themselves to immortal and divine things to their utmost power, and may abandon things too great for them."[17] This is indeed a passage worthy of study, and its burden is in harmony with the epistemology of the poet in his maturity, as certain passages of the *Commedia* make evident. The exercise of reason is not discouraged — far from it — but there are limits beyond which man has neither the power nor the right to move. This dry text contains, we may say, the essence of the moral so movingly illustrated in the mad voyage of Ulysses (*Inferno* XXVI) and expressly stated in Virgil's admonition: "Be satisfied, O human folk, with the *because*."

Eclogues

The Latin odes addressed to Giovanni del Virgilio form a small but appealing item in the canon of Dante's minor works. The exchange took place during Dante's sojourn in Ravenna, only a few years before his death. Giovanni del Virgilio, a professor of Latin in the University of Bologna, where, as we have noted, Dante probably studied, addressed to him an epistle in Latin hexameters. The burden of his verse was to reproach Dante for writing in Italian rather than Latin. It is true, he says, that Dante's subject is lofty (and apparently well known to del Virgilio, who speaks of the three regions of the poem: *"triplicis confinia sortis/ indita pro meritis animarum"*), but such subjects are wasted on the herd. Meanwhile, he complains, we "pale students" get nothing from the pen of the great poet. He reminds Dante that in the group of which he was sixth (*Inferno* IV) none of the others had written for the vulgar; all were writers of Latin verse. In language obscured by classical allusions he goes on to suggest various subjects for Dante: the death of Henry VII, the martial exploits of Moroello Malaspina, Can Grande, and the like. He further promises that any such work will be rewarded; he himself will be happy to see that Dante receives the laurel crown in the University of Bologna. Dante replies in an eclogue, speaking in a sort of pastoral code, as it were, not too difficult to read. He and Meliboeus, he says (Meliboeus being his friend Ser Dino Perini of Florence), were tending their goats (possibly giving instruction in rhetoric or poetry — we have Boccaccio's word that Dante spent his last years in such teaching) when the letter arrived. Coaxed by his friend, who Dante jokingly suggests is unworthy to hear the import of del Virgilio's message since he is concerned only with the vernacular, Dante finally discloses the substance of the communication. Meliboeus urges him to accept the offer, but Dante implies that he would prefer to wait to be crowned in Florence, undertaking meanwhile to send to his correspondent "ten measures" milked from his one cherished ewe (*"ovis gratissima"*) — which is taken to signify ten cantos of the *Paradiso*. These may avail in winning over Mopsus to a more favorable view of the vernacular. Meanwhile he urges Meliboeus to give thought to his wanton goats (presumably his students).

Del Virgilio wrote an affectionate reply, hailing Dante as a second Virgil and expressing the hope that he would indeed receive the laurel crown in Florence and at the hands of Phyllis (Gemma? — or, more likely, the city of Florence itself). But he also repeated his invitation to Dante to visit him in Bologna, assuring him that such a visit would be without danger. In the final poem, probably not written by Dante, del Virgilio's answer is reported as being brought back from Bologna and recited by Perini to Dante and a friend. Dante is urged not to accept the invitation, and after some debate he decides that in spite of his admiration for del Virgilio he would be wise not to risk the enmity of Polyphemus (perhaps the vicar of Robert of Sicily, perhaps a member of the Caccianemico family, one of whom Dante had singled out for unsavory mention in the *Inferno*). The writer of the ode concludes by saying that this conversation was reported to him by Iolas (Guido da Polenta, Dante's patron), who had himself overheard it.

The exchange is interesting not only for the information it gives us, or seems to give us, about the time of composition of the *Paradiso*, but also as suggestive of Dante's mood in his last years — tranquil, serene, and even disposed to be playful. One notes too the pathetic persistence of the hope to return to "the fair fold where as a lamb I slept" and there "on the font of my baptism to receive the crown." Perhaps it was at that time that these moving lines of the *Paradiso* were penned. With their obvious Virgilian inspiration, the charming verses of the eclogues stand in graceful contrast to the ragged medieval Latin prose of the *De Vulgari Eloquentia* and the *De Monarchia;* Casella finds in their "idyllic atmosphere" and "tender sentiments" an echo of certain episodes in the *Purgatorio*.[18]

Il Fiore

The odd and intriguing *Fiore* deserves some mention even though in the present state of Dante scholarship no critic of authority is inclined to attribute it to Dante: the most charitable recent phrase is that of Mattalia, who speaks of the attribution as "very dubious."[19] But *The Flower* is worth reading in its own right. It is an adaptation of the *Roman de la Rose,* telling in thinly veiled allegorical terms a realistic and at times cynical story of successful seduction. The lover in his search for the flower has various friends: Courtesy, Pity, and the more concrete and positivistic "Friend" and "Old Woman." The flower, in turn, is defended by such characters as Shame, Fear, and Foulmouth.

In the end Venus herself enters the combat, her traditional torch serving as a kind of flame thrower that breaks down all opposition. Although interrupted occasionally by long moralizing digression, the action develops with commendable tempo. It is a sequence of 232 sonnets. The language is Tuscan interlarded with frequent gallicisms. The attribution to Dante (defended in the past by such scholars as Mazzoni and, at first, Parodi) springs from the fact that the author is referred to as Durante (a form of Dante) and it is difficult to think of any other Dante gifted enough to have penned such a work. Certain lines too seem to echo a quatrain in one of Dante's sonnets. But in both language and tone the poem seems a very unlikely production to have come from the pen of the Dante we know (even though the thought of the *tenso* with Forese may give us pause). *Il Fiore* is preserved in only one manuscript (apparently of the late thirteenth century), originally published by Ferdinand Castets at Paris in 1881. It may be found in *Tutte le opere* (Florence, 1919), text edited by A. Della Torre, and in the *Opere* published by the Società dantesca italiana in 1922, where it appears as a separate volume *"in appendice,"* with introduction, notes, and vocabulary by E. G. Parodi.

Definitely apocryphal are the *Seven Penitential Psalms* and *Dante's Credo,* translations into *terza rima* from Latin texts. Passerini printed them in volume VII of his edition of the minor works (Florence, 1912) and they have been reprinted "simply as a literary curiosity" in the *Rime* of the Biblioteca universale (Rizzoli, Milan, 1952).

✻ 12 ✻

The *Commedia*: Narrative

THE *Commedia* may fairly claim to be the greatest poem of our tradition. T. S. Eliot says that after Shakespeare and Dante "there is no third,"[1] but no single work of Shakespeare can be compared to the *Commedia* in scope. Vico, the discoverer of the true Homer, applies to the *Commedia* the adjective "sublime," which he elsewhere reserves for the *Iliad* and the *Odyssey;* in the first draft of his *New Science* he remarks that Dante would have been more sublime if he had known nothing of scholastic philosophy or of Latin.[2] Some readers may be inclined to share that opinion as they labor through parts of the *Paradiso,* but in fact it is precisely the combination of these erudite elements with the "barbarous" purity of Dante's inspiration that gives the *Commedia* more depth than the Homeric poems. The nature of its greatness, the elements that have assured its immortality through varying cycles of taste, have been variously assessed by divers critics; so multifaceted is Dante, for all the straightforward simplicity of his story, that each reader may be said to have his own *Commedia.* It is documentable that each generation has its own. In what follows, the intent is not to offer any particular interpretation but rather to consider what the poet says and his manner of saying it.

A very useful principle to bear in mind in studying the *Commedia* is the rule of three. The work is divided into three *cantiche,* corresponding to the three realms of the afterlife; it is written

213

in *terza rima;* and there are numerous other examples of cabalistic or semiritualistic allusions to the pregnant number which had haunted Dante's mind ever since in the *Vita Nuova* he had made the happy discovery that Beatrice was a 3 × 3. We need not wonder unduly about the sources of Dante's triadomania. He had sanction in the doctrine of the Trinity itself; he had the prophetic example of the three kingdoms of Joachim da Fiore; we have seen that his contemporary Bonvesin da Riva had also written a *Book of the Three Scriptures.* Indeed, if his subject were to be the afterlife and its three realms, the number was forced upon our poet's consideration; given his love for symmetry and mysterious numerology, the ninety-nine cantos (*Inferno* I is of course a general prologue) and even *terza rima* followed naturally. Carducci was right too, I think, in seeing in the tertiary principle an element of discipline pervading the whole work.[3]

But one can push the rule of three still farther. In the study of the *Commedia* which lies before us we will find it useful to think of the work as in substance another trinity; with narrative, allegory, and doctrine as its component parts. To be sure, the first two are sometimes intertwined, but usually with no loss of individual identity, as I hope to make clear; and often when they are inseparable, one element is yet latent and the other predominant. Doctrine is tolerably easy to isolate from the other ingredients; again, one may say that the allegory is doctrinal too, but there are plenty of cases where no "veil" is cast over the instruction that the poet chooses to give us. I believe too that in a very rough and approximate — yet I think demonstrable and valid — way we may say that the three *cantiche* illustrate the progression of the three different kinds of substance: narrative predominates in the *Inferno,* unusual richness of allegory characterizes the *Purgatorio,* and in the *Paradiso* doctrine comes into its own.

I believe there is yet another embodiment of the rule of three, having to do not with substance but with the ordering of the material, operative in the maintaining of our interest and in the functional technique of the poem's dynamics. For Dante has given us three kinds of measure, almost three kinds of time, running concurrently and on different planes, yet cunningly crossing and converging to strengthen the fabric of the poem and enmesh the reader, who is captured without quite realizing how it has come about. To be precise, I think we may say that the cantos, the physical divisions in the narrative's landscape (i.e., circles in hell, terraces in purgatory, and spheres in paradise), and the subjects presented (a character, a topic, an argument) are three measures; their manipulation, unobtrusive but calculated, keeps the poem moving and gives it a kind of vitality of fibre, a persistent resilience, which is certainly its principal characteristic as a poem. E. H. Wilkins[4] has given us a kind of laboratory slide of this interaction without following out all the implications. I hope in the pages that follow to illustrate what I mean.

In approaching the study of the *Commedia* we may best begin with the narrative. In the course of outlining the story we shall inevitably discover the general design of the work and prepare ourselves for appreciation of the allegory and the doctrinal elements. Let us then, imitating our poet in his almost abrupt directness, consider the narrative. (The Roman numerals in parentheses are canto numbers for convenient reference.)

The *Inferno*

It is the evening of Maundy Thursday in the year 1300. Dante informs us that "in the middle of our life's road" he lost his way and found himself in a dark wood. He wandered in fear during the night, but the morning sun revealed to him a delectable mountain towards which he made his way. His ascent, however, was impeded by a succession of beasts. The leopard he might have dealt with, but the lion, coming up next, and climactically the she-wolf, most alarming of all, checked him, and he was about to turn back into the hopelessness of the wood when the soul of Virgil appeared beside him, sent to guide him in his hour of need. Virgil explained that the she-wolf makes it impossible to move directly toward the delectable mountain; this eternal enemy of humankind cannot be overcome, yet some day a hound will emerge which will be the salvation of Italy and drive the voracious animal back to hell. Meanwhile it is Dante's duty to undertake a long roundabout journey through hell and purgatory, and subsequently (but no longer under Virgil's direction, since the realm is forbidden him) to paradise (I). Dante's hesitation is overcome when Virgil tells him that his intervention was prompted by the interest of three ladies in heaven, the Virgin Mary, Santa Lucia, and Beatrice, who had descended to limbo to request Virgil's aid (II).

The poets then pass through the gate with its "harsh" inscription, on through the vestibule where the nameless "indifferent" are tormented, to the shores of Acheron. Here the lost souls wait their turn to be ferried across the river under the escort of the fiery-eyed Charon, who takes on Dante somewhat reluctantly. Dante faints from terror as a thunderclap is heard (III) and revives to find himself in limbo, where he is received by Homer, Horace, Ovid, and Lucan and is privileged to see the great souls of antiquity, whose only punishment is their unsatisfied desire for the divine vision (IV).

After limbo true hell may be said to begin. The poets pass successively through the circles of the incontinent: the storm-tossed lustful, where Dante swoons again on hearing the sad story of Francesca (V); the gluttonous, buried in mud, one of whom, Ciacco, gives him a gloomy prophecy (VI); the avaricious and prodigal, nameless and compelled forever to roll heavy stones about, in sordid and pointless striving (VII); and on to the muddy Styx, which contains the souls of the wrathful, one of whom, Filippo Argenti, tries to overturn the boat in which the poets ride, ferried by Phlegyas (VIII). On the inner shore stand the walls of Dis, thronged by demons so menacing that the poets must await the coming of a divine messenger to open the gate (IX).

Inside the dark city they find the burning tombs of the heretics, who include the great Ghibelline Farinata and Cavalcanti, the father of Guido (X). The land drops sharply as they come to the edge of a cliff, and the poets pause to accustom their olfactory senses to the mephitic odor of lower hell. Virgil takes advantage of the rest to expound the moral system of hell (XI).

We too may well rest here and, glancing back as Dante and his mentor look forward, comment on the nature of the poet's achievement up to this point. So rapid has been the pace that we have scarcely had time to absorb and thus admire as we should the skill, one might almost say the cunning, with which the poet has drawn us into his world, involved us in his personal concerns, and borne us along with him in his rapid descent. He wisely began *in medias res;* this is no mere deference to classical models, but psychologically shrewd. He wastes no time in preparation or presentation; he simply assumes that we will be interested, and the boldness of the assumption assures its success. He has given his narrative continuous motion; if the poets stop, it is only to carry on the drama of action by calling forth other accounts which are also full of incident and movement. He has arranged a series of climaxes; the mere passages from canto to canto might suffice, but he has varied the pattern with such strategic devices (always in context and functional in the main development) as the inscription on the gate, the challenges from Charon and Phlegyas, and the struggle with the Furies. Like Dante himself, we have been carried along, sometimes almost faster than we could wish; like the poet too we have, with the procession of sinners passing before us, become increasingly curious about the design behind it all. We have become aware that we are studying certain categories of sin, but the pattern is as yet not clear. Perhaps it should be said here that some critics have held that Dante had originally planned a more or less traditional treatment of the seven deadly sins (such as we shall find later in the *Purgatorio*) but at this point changed his design. If this be so, it is a magnificent piece of revision *in via;* if his thinking has taken on a new direction, it is certainly brought into harmony with the original design. But this is tangential; what would be unpardonable to overlook is the magnificent progress of the narrative which has carried us along so wholeheartedly. We are in fact at this point a little breathless, not so much willing as eager to sit at Virgil's feet and look at our chart.

Virgil's remarks on the tripartite scheme of hell (of which we shall say more in a later chapter) are extremely compact and I believe it is significant that this canto is one of the two shortest of the whole *Inferno* — indeed, of the *Commedia.* Virgil adds that his account is indeed meant to save time; now that Dante has a picture of the infernal plan in his mind, further explanation as they go down to the lower circles will be unnecessary. Throughout the *Inferno* the necessity of moving on at a fast rate is repeatedly stressed; it would seem that Virgil knows the schedule, as it were, and has the charge of bringing Dante to the Mount of Purgatory by Easter morning.

Resuming their descent, the poets pass through the successive circles of the violent. In the blood bath of Phlegethon, Dante sees the souls of murderers and robbers watched over by the centaurs (XII); in the strange forest of the self-destructive he hears the pathetic story of Pier delle Vigne (XIII); he observes with shocked horror the blasphemer Capaneus (XIV); an even more moving encounter is that with his old master Brunetto Latini punished by the rain of fire for his unnatural vice (XV). He

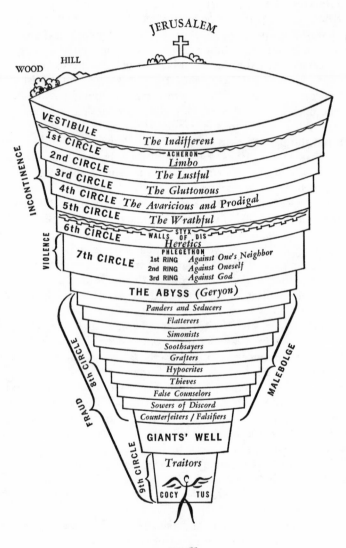

Hell

discusses the sad state of his city with three other great Florentines suffering similar torment (XVI). After a contemptuous glance at the usurers he is borne by Geryon deep down into the division assigned to the fraudulent, the cheaters of mankind (XVII).

This ultimate province of evil has the shape of a funnel, the lip of which is scoured by ten concentric indentations making a series of ditches, called *malebolge* — "dirty ditches," one might say. They are crossed by a series of bridges radiating from the center like spokes from a wheel, over which the poets may cross to observe the state of sinners below them. Successively they look down upon panders and seducers (scourged by demons), flatterers submerged in filth (XVIII), simonists buried upside down with flames licking their exposed heels (XIX), and soothsayers whose twisted necks make it impossible for them to look forward (XX). In the fifth ditch Dante is amused and frightened by the game played between the ferocious *Malebranche* (Bad claws) and the barrators dunked in the boiling pitch (XXI–XXII). The connecting bridges are broken over this trench, and he and Virgil are obliged to scramble over the ruins to escape into the *bolgia* of the hypocrites, oppressed by their gaily colored robes of lead (XXIII). The thieves of the seventh ditch horrify him as he sees human and serpentine figures intermingled in continuous metamorphosis (XXIV–XXV). Among the false counselors of the next division he finds, masked by consuming fire, the shade of Ulysses, who tells of his last voyage (XXVI), and Guido da Montefeltro, still resentful of the trick played on him by the pope (XXVII). The mutilated forms of the sowers of discord, which include Mohammed and Bertran de Born, at once horrify and fascinate him (XXVIII), and with the spectacle of various kinds of disease afflicting the souls of falsifiers (ranging from counterfeiters to plain liars) the grisly gallery of the *malebolge* is complete (XXIX–XXX).

Looking back over the passage of the *malebolge,* we may see, I think, how perfectly this section of the *Inferno* illustrates Dante's narrative strategy, which is based on subtle variation within a fixed pattern. The reader knows the shape of the *malebolge* before he crosses the first bridge; he knows that he will traverse a series of more or less similar ditches and that each will contain some specimen of fraud or cheat. The pattern, which gives him a kind of reassurance, is, however, saved from monotony by all kinds of variation. On the purely visual side some of the *bolge* are filled with liquid of one sort or another, some are dry; in some cases it is possible to see from the bridges what is going on in the depths, in others it is necessary to descend. Some are characterized by lively activity: the sport of the *Malebranche,* for example, or the swiftly shifting figures of thieves and snakes; in others a slow deliberate tempo underlines the eternal round of torment that is the doom of the damned — the panderers, for example, or the hypocrites. The broken bridge is an item of the unexpected, serving a purpose no less important to the narrative than to the didactic interest of the poet. And since the story is told in the first person, a wide range of emotional tone is achieved by the response of the narrator to the figures he meets in the successive ditches. Some he treats with disgust, others with respect, others with a kind of savage jocularity; from the comic and essentially plebeian "cops-and-robbers" game of the *Malebranche* to the high tragedy of the saga of Ulysses there is a complete spectrum of sentiment. Yet at the same time — here is evident the firmness of the pattern — not only are the ditches the same in contour but the dwellers in the *malebolge* are all linked by the moral bond of their condition. They are all damned, and, regardless of the subjective reaction of our narrator, the "story line" with its ethical and theological implications moves ever onward — which is to say downward.

The poets are lowered down through the spout of the funnel by the hands of Antaeus, one of the great giants who ring the brink (XXXI). They find themselves on a surface of the frozen Cocytus, hell's floor. Here, buried up to their necks in ice, their teeth chattering forever in the eternal cold, are the darkest betrayers: traitors to kin (*Caina*) and country (*Antenora*) — here Dante sees the Florentine traitor Bocca degli Abati, and hears the dreadful story of Ugolino — and to guests (*Tolomea*) (XXXII–XXXIII); climactically, blackest of all, the betrayers of benefactors (*Giudecca*). At hell's deep center the archetypal traitors to church and state, Judas and the conspirators Brutus and Cassius, are mangled in the three mouths of the great monster of infidelity and evil, Satan himself. Climbing down again through the crevice between the monster's flank and the ice, Virgil bears Dante past the center of the earth and into the southern hemisphere. A channel bored through the earth by a stream flowing from purgatory enables them to climb to the surface; in the dawn of Easter morning our pilgrims "emerge to see the stars again" (XXXIV).

Virgil's statement that "we have now seen all" is a fair assessment of the wealth of the literal narrative. The promise of the early cantos has been fulfilled: the pace has never slackened, has indeed accelerated; the story is crammed with action and variety. The poets have come through no less than twenty-one carefully identified areas. Dante has seen one hundred and twenty-eight sinners specifically mentioned by name (not counting the vast armies of the unnamed) and has had conversations with thirty-seven of them. He has met thirty monsters and five hybrid creatures. He has had two boat rides; he has ridden a centaur and a winged dragon. He has twice fainted. He has been exposed to excessive heat, bitter cold, strong winds, fearful sights, terrifying sounds, and foul odors. To this catalogue of physical trials must be added a complete stock of emotional and psychological experiences. He has felt compassion, pity, scorn, resentment, anger, vindictiveness, courage, and even, once in a while, a touch of amusement. And all these emotions are superimposed on the constants of terror, wonder, and lively curiosity. Nor do the pilgrim's own experiences exhaust the mine of the narrative. T. S. Eliot well says that the tale of Ulysses, regardless of its moral or symbolic interpretation, is a "well-told seaman's yarn";[5] we may add that Francesca's, by the same token, is a moving love story, Ugolino's is an unforgettable horror story; Pier delle Vigne and Guido da Montefeltro recount behind-the-scenes tales of intrigue in high places; from Farinata we get the "inside story" of a great decision, from Vanni Fucci a thief's detailed confession; Caccianemico, Bocca degli Abati, Bertran de Born, even in the compass of the few syllables allowed them, hint at other vicissitudes of humanity in action. This is the *cantica* of drama, "the realm of human passions," says Olschki[6] (including the poet's own, never more directly — Vico would say "sublimely" — expressed). It is also the *cantica* of personalities. There is a wide range of individuals in the depths of hell, much wider than we shall meet in the other two kingdoms. Many critics have urged the doctrinal significance of the stress on individualism in hell, making much of the notion that these self-centered souls cannot work together, lacking human charity one for another. Here, it is said, is the essence of damnation. Perhaps — though as a matter of fact the three Florentines whom Dante meets get on quite well together, and the grafters seem to have organized excellent team play. However doctrinal the reason may be, the effect is to make the *Inferno* the most fascinating of the three *cantiche* on first reading, precisely because it does focus on individual plights and passions. This is conceded even by those moderns, such as Eliot, who in general prefer the other realms. For Salvatore Quasimodo — perhaps more modern than Eliot — it is the living part of the *Commedia,* "the place of man in his contradictory nature."[7] It was the *Inferno* that stamped the popular image of Dante (the passerby did not say of him, "There goes the man who has been in purgatory"), that originally captured the imagination of the public, and that — via the romantics and their perhaps not entirely wholesome interest in Ugolino and Francesca — brought the whole *Commedia* back into European circulation after the restrictions of neoclassicism had somewhat obscured it. Franz Hettinger could say truly at the end of the last century that "even those who study the whole poem prefer the *Inferno* both to the *Purgatorio* and *Paradiso.*"[8] The implication of "even" are interesting; there are more editions of the *Inferno* alone than of either of the other *cantiche* (as a survey of Koch's catalogue will show), and the proportion is even greater in the area of translations.

All of which is testimony to the high fulfillment of the author's intent. He has an audience to instruct and educate and, he hopes, eventually to guide. But first he must hold its attention, and to secure attention there is nothing like a fast-moving narrative filled with exciting incidents and illuminated by memorable characterization. And, with the cunning of the professional storyteller, he concludes his first "chapter" on a high note of anticipation; with what impatient eagerness the reader looks forward to the new realm and its star-spangled sky!

The *Purgatorio*

After an introductory *terzina* rejoicing in the happier seas now open to "the little bark" of his genius, Dante resumes his narrative. His first nine cantos cover the Ante-Purgatory, a slope reaching steeply up from the shores of the ocean to the beginning of the mountain itself, inhabited by souls not yet ripe to begin their penance. The presiding genius of this outer region and possibly of all purgatory is Cato, eternal symbol of free will. He bids the poets prepare themselves for the ascent (I). A ship, angel-driven, bearing the souls of the recently departed, arrives, and among the passengers Dante recognizes his friend Casella, who graciously sings a song of Dante's composition, the first *canzone* of the *Convivio*. But Cato urges them on their way (II). Going up the steep hill they meet Manfred, whose last-minute repentance has wiped out his horrible sins, though having died excommunicate he is not allowed to enter purgatory at once (III); they then encounter Belacqua, who had indolently put off making his peace with God (IV). At the top of the slope they meet a large number of souls done to death by violence, among them Bonconte da Montefeltro, son of the Guido of *Inferno* XXVII, slain at Campaldino and saved by one truly repentant tear. Also of this group is the gentle Pia, who asks Dante, as they all do, to be remembered in his prayers (V). A little further on the pilgrims meet the shade of Sordello; his affectionate response on learning that Virgil is a fellow Mantuan moves Dante to a bitter invective against the present state of Italy, rent by civil war and dissension (VI). Sordello leads the poet to the valley of the princes, a fragrant and flower-strewn dell where many of the recently deceased contemporary rulers (including Charles of Anjou) prepare in prayer and meditation for nightfall. Sordello identifies the princes (VII), and Dante recognizes his friend Nino Visconti and exchanges compliments with Corrado Malaspina. After a symbolic repulse of the serpent by two protective angels, darkness comes on and Dante falls asleep (VIII).

In a way the pause here recalls the break in motion of canto XI of the *Inferno*. Again the course of the poets is arrested and the need for repose is stressed. But once more we may note the variation within the pattern. Virgil does not use the interval for his exposition of the design of the *Purgatorio;* that will come later. For in the *Purgatorio,* as we shall see, there are three "rests." There is also something reminiscent of limbo in the enumeration of prominent names; in the *Inferno* great classical figures, here Christian princes — an intellectual elite and a feudal aristocracy — and both groups pointed out with respectful and affectionate solicitude by a poet guide. From such parallels we may see how much the narrative gains in richness as the poet calls on the first chapter to reinforce the second, provoking the reader to compare, contrast, and so recall what has gone before.

In fact, one of the great fascinations of the *Commedia* is its life within itself, springing from the narrative and its pattern. Many critics have been all but obsessed by the correspondences and parallels, by the architectonic refinements of the poem. To develop this yet a little further while we linger here in the best of company with three poets of three great literatures: all of the ground we have so far covered in the *Purgatorio* matches, as it were, the vestibule of the *Inferno*. We are on the threshold of purgatory proper just as the indifferent were in the waiting room of hell. And some motifs reappear — in the minor, one might say. Cato plays a little the role for Virgil and Dante that Virgil himself had played for our solitary poet in the wood. (Yet there is a kind of echo of Charon too. Does not Cato's "honest plumage" make us think — if only to dismiss the thought at once — of the "woolly cheeks" of the infernal ferryman? Later, perhaps, we may conclude that a better parallel would be to think of him as foreshadowing the angel who bears the souls from Tibermouth to salvation.) Again, even as the poets in limbo come forth to greet Virgil as one of their own and graciously take Dante into their company, so here another poet salutes the imperial bard and again Dante is made one of the group. The recurrence of such motifs, half obscured, half underlined, serves as well to mark the contrast between the two realms. Here so far all is light; in hell the increasing darkness was an element of Dante's terror. In this connection it is interesting to compare the opening lines of *Inferno* II: *"Lo giorno se n'andava"* ("Day was departing"), and so on, with the *terzina* (fecund for Thomas Gray) with which *Purgatorio* VI opens: *"Era l'ora che volge il disio"* ("It was the hour that homeward turns the thought"). It is the same twilight mood in both, yet the context and the implications of the narrative lend to the first an air of uneasiness and terror, while the second, for all its melancholy, has no such effect. Another contrast: if the souls in *Purgatorio* II, as yet "unassigned," as it were, recall under that aspect at least the indifferent of *Inferno* III, yet the distinction is great and significant. There were many souls in the vestibule, but Dante recognized only one, and with none did he exchange words, bidden as he was merely to look and pass on. With what joy, however, he here greets Casella; and how gladly he would linger — even at the risk, though unknowingly, of some neglect of his duty. And hell's "waiting room" is not truly such; there the infernal doors will never open to the cowardly, while the souls in the Ante-Purgatory are secure in the knowledge that for them the ultimate ascent is only a matter of time.

Such correspondences, contrasts, and recurrences could be

multiplied almost indefinitely; the point to be made is that the disposition and manipulation of motifs add to the fascination of the story and keep the reader constantly alert and *engagé.* As we go forward we have new and rare spectacles on every terrace and at every turn, yet they are given added depth by the links that bind them to scenes, motifs, and characters already encountered. On the journey our pilgrims can put incidents and spectacles behind them and move on; but all that has gone before lingers in the memory and recurs in altered form or under different color in the experience of both the poet-pilgrim and his reader.

Dante dreams that he is borne aloft by an eagle; in fact it is Santa Lucia who carries him in his sleep up to the gate of purgatory itself. Virgil is still with him, and together, after admonition by the Guardian of the Gate, who marks Dante's forehead with seven P's, the poets enter (IX). Purgatory consists of seven terraces encircling a mountain and very similar in a characteristic formation. For each terrace there is a welcoming angel, and as each terrace is left behind an appropriate beatitude is uttered. As Dante comes in, he is in every case greeted by a series of "goads"; as he leaves, by a parallel sequence of "checks." The goads exemplify the virtue corrective of the sin being purged (e.g., humility on the terrace of pride), the checks examples of the evil consequences of the sin. Dante is consistently careful to mingle examples of the classical and Christian tradition, and in every case the goads begin with an example from the life of the Virgin. Sometimes these exhortations are seen (as the carvings on the terrace of the proud), sometimes heard (as on the second terrace of the envious), sometimes spoken by the sinners themselves (as by the slothful), but the order is always the same.

On the terrace of the proud, Dante sees the penitents plod along under heavy weights, their eyes forced to see the pictured examples of fallen pride on the floor. Significantly he too stoops down to talk with some of the sufferers, who speak of the vanity of earthly fame and achievement (X–XII). On the terrace of the envious, the eyelids of the penitents are sewn together; they wait, blind and patient, for their purgation to ripen. Here Dante meets the Sienese Sapia and the two noblemen of Romagna who deplore the degeneration of chivalry, brought about by materialism (XIII–XIV).

The same argument is continued by Mark the Lombard on

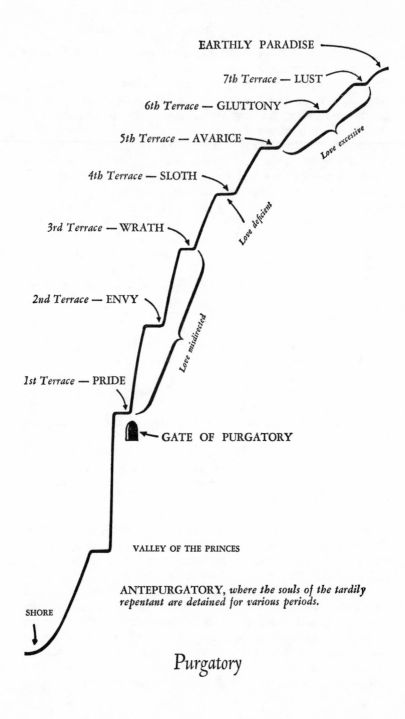

EARTHLY PARADISE

7th Terrace — LUST

6th Terrace — GLUTTONY

5th Terrace — AVARICE

Love excessive

4th Terrace — SLOTH

3rd Terrace — WRATH

Love deficient

2nd Terrace — ENVY

Love misdirected

1st Terrace — PRIDE

← GATE OF PURGATORY

VALLEY OF THE PRINCES

ANTEPURGATORY, *where the souls of the tardily repentant are detained for various periods.*

SHORE

Purgatory

the cornice of the wrathful, blinded by a continuous dark smoke; he tells Dante that it is for lack of imperial authority that Italians have become greedy and lawless. On this terrace the "goads" and "checks" come to Dante in a series of visions (XV–XVI). As the poets ascend to the terrace of the slothful, darkness falls, and again the pilgrims must stop to rest; Virgil seizes the opportunity to explain the scheme of Purgatory (XVII).

Once more, as the poets pause to consult their road map, the reader is well advised to follow their example and take stock of the scene around him, giving some thought to the changing landscape. We are halfway through the *Purgatorio,* or almost so, from the point of view of the pages our poet plans to dedicate to it; we stand on the central terrace. *Nel mezzo del cammin,* then, as far as the Mount of Purgatory is concerned, and we may now note with profit what characteristics have crept in, simply in terms of the literal tale, to differentiate it from the *Inferno* and so to enrich the narrative. Almost too obvious for mention, yet certainly too basic — for the literal as well as for the allegorical meaning — to pass without comment, we have had the continuous exhilaration of movement upward as against the disquieting sensation of continuous descent. Moreover, in the *Inferno* Dante is twice carried (almost against his will and in great terror) downward; but all the ascent of the *Purgatorio* is by his own effort save for the dream flight in the arms of Lucia, accompanied by an instinctive feeling of rapture. Much is made too of the fact that the purgatorial ascent is a daylight operation; here again, aside from the opportunity for development of the allegory and scope for pure ornament (references to shadows, hours of the day, and the like), the narrative itself has of necessity a different color from that of a subterranean pilgrimage in obscurity.

But there are other differences that we may not as yet have become aware of. Looking back now on the *Inferno,* we can better appreciate its characteristic of feverish action. Counting the physical divisions (whether moral categories or subdivisions), we can see at once that they far outnumber the physical divisions of the *Purgatorio.* At our halfway point through the *Inferno* we had already traversed the four circles of the incontinent and the three subdivisions of the violent. This meant for the travelers recurrent stimulation of the senses as well as equally frequent moments of doubt, terror, and exacerbated curiosity at the moment of transition — quite aside from the fact that the spectacles they encountered were likewise full of vigorous action and dominated by aggressive personalities. Fortunately, in the nature of the case, the *Purgatorio* cannot have the same kind of character. Yet the reassurance of the pattern is there: we have categories, we have physical divisions, we have continuous movement, we still have dramatic personalities that impress themselves on our memory by the poetry and indeed sometimes the vigor of their self-depiction. But gradually the nature of the narrative has altered. Its tempo is much gentler; with many fewer compartments to cover, the need for breathless rushing has gone by. The sights on the road do not change quite so often; none of the terraces is subdivided, and although there are different categories of the unready represented in the Ante-Purgatory, they do not offer substantially different appearances to the eye. There is increasing stress on groups working in harmony: the boatload of new arrivals, singing together — unlike the reluctant passengers of Charon; the excommunicates moving in the peaceful unanimity of a flock of sheep; the orderly procession of the proud. Here the characters mentioned by name are rather spokesmen for their comrades than independent individuals. The fearsome variation of infernal monsters has been replaced by a succession of angels, alike in their appearance and in their somewhat aloof benevolence. What has come into the story, gradually replacing the action or distraction of the *Inferno,* is the new current of reflection. What is said becomes, slowly but surely, not necessarily more important but more prominent and more memorable than what is seen by the pilgrims or done or suffered by the penitents. To cite but one example: the exploration, which takes on dialectical form, of the world's misguided pursuit of material goods runs through cantos XIV–XVI and leads naturally and logically to other themes of discussion; it is the analysis of this problem that dominates the movement of these cantos.

Another substantial difference — this has been remarked by many acute critics in recent years — is the development of the central figure, Dante the pilgrim. To be sure, one can easily overstate the difference. It is perfectly true that Dante began to "assert himself" as early as the second circle of the *Inferno,* where he took the initiative in calling forth Francesca's sad confession. He even went so far as to incur Virgil's passing displeasure by his fascination with the exchange of billingsgate in canto XXX. So far, at least, in the *Purgatorio* he has followed Virgil's lead with even more docility than he showed in some parts of the *Inferno.* It is not, then, that he has become more dominant or more wilful; rather, his character has deepened. Concerned no longer so much with sights and sounds as with their implications, he moves on — taking the reader with him — to a reflective-subjective level to which the *Inferno* gave slight scope. "The form of the drama of liberation . . . is also realized in the rhythm of the Pilgrim's inner life," says Francis Fergusson.[9] Happily for the narrative, there are external manifestations of this: our poet talks freely with Virgil, doesn't hesitate to "chip in" with his own comments on the position of the sun in the southern hemisphere, takes the lead in the conversations with Guido del Duca and Mark the Lombard, refuses to be content with Virgil's first answers on materialism, the soul, and the like, and imperceptibly moves to center stage. It is his world, of course; purgatory can harbor none but Christian souls, and our poet is on better than equal footing with his guide (to whom the journey is new, as the descent of hell was not). This is all as it should be from a doctrinal point of view. But it is also magnificent as a means of keeping our attention on the narrative. Pattern is always present, but monotony is never allowed to creep in; the shift in focus parallels the change of motion, of landscape, and of emphasis.

As Dante ponders Virgil's words, the slothful rush past, crying out their goads and checks as they go; they are the only penitents who do not rest at night. When they have passed, Dante falls asleep (XVIII) and has the second of his dreams. In this one, prophetic of the terraces above, a siren appears, at first hideous to view but becoming more seductive as Dante gazes on her. In his dream a lady calls Virgil, who reveals the foul nature of the enchantress; Dante wakes to find that Virgil is indeed calling him. Ascending to the next terrace, the poets find the avaricious lying prone on the earth, mingling the traditional self-admonitions with prayers. Among the victims of the "old she-wolf" of greed are Pope Adrian V and Hugh Capet, founder of the French dynasty, who excoriates his descendants for their rapacity, particularly Philip the Fair (XIX–XX).

A tremor of the earth, followed by a joyous shout, surprises the travelers as they leave the terrace. Statius, coming up behind them, explains that this occurs whenever a soul feels free to rise to heaven; in this case, after five hundred years on the terrace, it is he who has achieved this happy state. In identifying himself he expresses his debt to Virgil; great is his joy when he finds that he is in the company of his revered master (XXI). He discloses that his sin was not avarice but its very opposite. A line of Virgil's *Aeneid* had shown him the error of his ways; similarly Virgil's Fourth Eclogue had led him to become — though secretly — a Christian. Virgil tells him of the poets in limbo. On the sixth terrace the gluttonous are tormented by the sight of a tree bearing luscious fruit which they are not allowed to taste; the goads come from the branches (XXII). Here Dante meets Forese Donati, who speaks tenderly of his wife, unique among Florentine women in virtue (XXIII), and the poet Bonagiunta da Lucca, who draws from Dante a definition of the "sweet new style." A second tree, from which come the checks, stands before the entrance to the next ascent, through which the trio of poets climb to the next and last terrace (XXIV). Dante hears from Statius a detailed explanation of the creation of the human body and soul, and understands how the incorporeal shades of the dead may suffer physical delights or torments (XXV). Flames dart forth from the inner wall of the last ledge of all, and in these flames the lustful walk, divided into two files according as their sin was natural or perverse. They chant examples of chastity as they go. Among them is Guido Guinizelli; Dante tells him of his admiration, but Guido modestly gives place to Arnaut Daniel, "the best moulder of our mother tongue." Speaking in Provençal, Arnaut asks Dante's prayers and vanishes into the fire (XXVI).

Dante hesitates to go through the wall of fire, but coaxed by Virgil, who reminds him that Beatrice awaits on the other side, he finally consents; the flames do indeed burn, but do him no harm. Night falls as they reach the last stairway; here Dante has his final dream, in which he sees Leah and Rachel, figures of the active and contemplative life. He wakes with the dawn. The poets complete the ascent and Virgil invites Dante to go forth and view the beauties of the earthly paradise; he now needs no further guidance but wears his own crown and mitre (XXVII).

In terms of the narrative and its pattern, this is a climactic and beautiful moment. It is the "happy ending" — or, better still, the moment just before the happy ending when, assured that things will turn out right, we are yet left with some of the joy of anticipation. If we think of Dante's narrative as falling into the centuries-old pattern of the quest, then this is the moment when the Golden Fleece is in sight, when the suitors have been slain and the throne awaits the Hero, when the vision of the Grail has been promised and waits on one last vigil. And if we think of Dante's journey as a love-pilgrimage, which we are surely entitled to do, then this is the moment when the Sleeping Beauty lies before the Prince, ready to be awakened. With his usual evocative skill, the poet suggests the outlines of his design, neither too boldly stated nor too coyly concealed. As Virgil had announced the journey's beginning in *Inferno* I, he now announces the journey's end. There is, I have always thought, a subtle verbal signal here: announcing Dante's foreordained pilgrimage Virgil says in *Inferno* I, "Whence for your good, I think and *discern*"; and now, using the same verb form (the only two cases of it in the poem), he says, "Of myself I can *discern* no more." Full circle. And full circle in another sense: the journey began in a wood, and it ends in another — no longer *oscura* or *selvaggia,* but light (indeed with unearthly illumination) and full of beauty.

We may reasonably choose this point in the narrative for further consideration of some aspects of the pattern and its variation in the first two *cantiche.* For, in one sense at least, as Dante sets foot in the enchanted wood of the earthly paradise we have come to the end of the *Purgatorio.* We might be justified in considering the garden rather than simply the summit of the mountain as a kind of vestibule of paradise. Eliot, among others, has remarked that the final cantos of the *Purgatorio* "have the quality of the *Paradiso* and prepare us for it."[10] Sights and phenomena not of this world will be seen and sensed in it. Henceforth all the characters and figures that Dante is destined to meet are citizens of the third realm. There are of course good reasons, largely but not exclusively doctrinal, for keeping the last six cantos under the heading *Purgatorio,* but in one very real sense — which we may be tolerably sure was in the intention of the author — purgatory is behind us: Dante *climbs* no more.

I think too that we are justified in looking at the *Inferno-Purgatorio* as a unit within the larger framework, without neglecting at all their individual characteristics. Both hell and purgatory are, in Dante's concept, part of the physical world and part of our own earth; paradise is not physical at all, as we shall see.

Accepting this postulate, we may enjoy the working out of subtle and skilful variations within a pattern. The two *cantiche* have the same formal division (cantos of approximately equal length: the average in the *Inferno* is 138.8 lines and in the *Pur-*

gatorio 144) and the same interplay of thematic elements with physical divisions and subdivisions. Aside from similarities already noted, we may remark that both in hell and purgatory there are guardians and presiding geniuses over the various compartments; sinners or penitents serve on occasion as guides; certain "types" recur (popes, Provençal poets, Dante's teachers, political leaders), as do certain motifs (political invectives, prophecies, moral allegories). There is a like psychological recurrence: the picture of Dante and Virgil entering each new zone with curiosity, tempered by uneasiness or happy expectation as the case may be, is another constant. A similar cloth, and at first sight a not very different design. But look more closely and great and fascinating variations appear — the more fascinating precisely because they stand out against the familiar framework.

There is, though we have to look fairly close to see it, considerable difference in length between the space given to hell and that accorded to purgatory. If we agree that the account of hell proper begins with *Inferno* III, then from the time Dante enters it until he emerges to see the dawn stars of the mountain thirty-two cantos are consumed (and three days). The description of purgatory, proper, on the other hand, begins with *Purgatorio* X and, as we have noted, at the end of canto XXVII we have done with climbing — eighteen cantos as against thirty-two for hell. Yet there is another factor to balance this disparity. Counting the separate subdivisions of hell individually (without regard to "categories"), we arrive at a total of twenty-one. There are only seven terraces on the Mount of Purgatory. Hence in mathematical terms to each "item" on the infernal manifest approximately one and a half cantos; to each terrace more than two and a half. The effect is on the one hand to make the ascent of the mount much faster than the wearisome burrowing ever deeper into the earth, and at the same time to slow the pace within the terraces, as against that within the infernal compartments. Mathematically the pattern forces the one kind to be full of action (or compact description) and requires the other to be reflective.

Of necessity this means a difference both quantitative and qualitative in the two casts of characters. If only because there are more compartments to fill and hence a greater need of examples, the gallery of characters is much richer in the *Inferno*, more copious and more diversified. The range between Francesca and Ugolino, Ulysses and Gianni Schicchi, Ciacco and Brunetto

Latini is greater than anything to be found in the *Purgatorio.* This is not to say that purgatory lacks memorable and well-delineated characters: Cato, Manfred, Sordello, Pia — who could forget them? But they are fewer in number, and their common spiritual condition of patient humility gives them a certain likeness, in contrast to the rugged individualists of hell. So too the pilgrim looks upon them all with much the same feeling, made of participant sympathy and respect. For none can he feel the same horror that he feels for a Vanni Fucci or a Bocca degli Abati; for none can he feel quite the same depth of human pity (however doctrinally wrong) that he feels for a Francesca or a Brunetto. What he can feel — and could not in hell — is Christian kinship, from which springs inevitably free discussion. Dante can learn from the souls in purgatory in a sense that he could not learn from the damned, who have after all only one thing to teach him. It is for this reason — as well as because of the aspect of personal allegory, since Dante is doing his own penance before our eyes — that the focus of the story is gradually turning inward. We are increasingly less moved by the torture and more interested in the revelations of moral and philosophical truth as we go upward. T. K. Swing has well made the point that, broadly speaking, one remembers Dante in the *Inferno* as looking down on the sinners — from the bark of Phlegyas, from the dikes of Phlegethon, from the bridges of the *malebolge* — whereas in the *Purgatorio* he stands on the same footing — the floor of the same terrace — as those he interrogates.[11] Spectator — one might say in shorthand — in the *Inferno* (and the spectacles are memorable); participant in the *Purgatorio,* and, being participant, self-examining and self-searching. Vossler puts it strongly: "The living pilgrim, too, undergoes a sort of religious conversion."[12] The scaling of the Mount of Purgatory can be seen as an examination of conscience; this, to be sure, leads us into the allegory, but the inner process is clothed by action and response of the main character in an absorbing narrative. In both roles — penitent and *persona* — having attained the promised land, Dante is now prepared to stand alone before Beatrice.

Preceding his companions, Dante goes forward into the verdant and fragrant wood; across the crystalline Lethe he sees the maiden Matilda, who assures him that he is indeed in the earthly paradise and explains its nature to him (XXVIII). As she walks eastward along the riverbank, Dante follows on his side. A bright splendor fills the sky, and music is heard in the air; across the stream Dante sees the symbolic procession of the church (XXIX). On a gryphon-drawn chariot he recognizes Beatrice; he turns to Virgil to express his emotion, only to find that Virgil has vanished. Dante is moved to tears, but Beatrice, addressing him by name, sternly bids him to save grief for graver matters. Under her chiding Dante breaks down; Beatrice recalls his pursuit of false images of good after her death, her intervention with Virgil to guide him back to the right path (XXX), and asks Dante to confess the truth of what she says. He admits he has been misled by "things at hand." Beatrice accepts his confession and points out to him that after her departure no thing of earth, certainly no "slip of a girl" (*pargoletta*), should have distracted him. Raising his head under her charge, Dante faints with remorse; he reawakens to find himself being drawn across Lethe by Matilda. Under the guidance of Beatrice's four escorting nymphs Dante looks upon her eyes (wherein he sees the gryphon reflected), and she graciously smiles upon him (XXXI).

Recovering from his rapture, Dante walks beside the procession, which has taken up its march again. The gryphon ties the chariot to the tree of law, which breaks into foliage. The members of the procession break into song; Dante falls asleep. Awakening, he sees the chariot of the church undergo changes symbolic of its history from the early persecutions to the Babylonian captivity (XXXII). He learns from Beatrice that a leader will come to set the world aright; Dante is to bear her words to the world. It is now nearly noon, and Dante and Statius under the guidance of Matilda are washed in Eunoë, from which Dante returns "pure and prepared to mount up to the stars" (XXXIII).

We have found it useful to speak of *Inferno-Purgatorio* as set off against the *Paradiso,* and this is a perfectly legitimate division: both of the lower realms are set in our world and in time as against the nonspatial, extraterrestrial world of the *Paradiso,* and from this difference other distinctions follow. But we could also bracket purgatory and paradise against hell; the former are kingdoms of the saved and dominions of light as contrasted to the black world of the damned. This Janus-like quality is to be expected in the Middle Kingdom, which is the *cantica* of transition for the travelers and the chapter of liaison in the narrative. But if the *Purgatorio* will obligingly adapt itself to double classification, this does not mean that it is ill-defined or lacking in character. It has its own very special individuality.

For one thing it is the only transitory realm. It is not set beyond time, as is heaven; it cannot even boast that it will endure for eternity, as can hell. As an inhabited kingdom its days are numbered; it will cease to exist when the Last Judgment is heard. Its citizens too, individually and collectively, are but transient tenants, and this gives them a peculiar interest for both Dante and his readers. The penitents are comfortable within their lot, Bernard Stambler says,[13] but this is only a half truth; they are content not so much with where they are as with the fact that they are *in via*. Their condition of expectation and happy instability brings them very close to the world they have left behind: purgatory is nearer to Earth and its persistently hopeful mortality than either of the other realms, where the answers are in and the final assignments have been made. This is the one realm where Hegel's reference to the changeless destiny of the souls of the *Commedia* is at best a half truth. For change there must be, else purgation has no meaning.

The humanity of the *Purgatorio,* with its mingling of sunlight and shadow, its combination of suffering and hope, is in an esthetic sense reinforced and emphasized by its formalism; it is the most ritualistic of the *cantiche.* There is a fixed formula of ceremonial at the entrance into and departure from each terrace; the angels, the beatitudes, the goads and checks — these combine to give a sylized framework to the spiritual-pathetic contrast. Charles Williams has very rightly remarked that the *Purgatorio* is "full of the arts";[14] we have but to recall the bas-reliefs on the terrace of the proud, the music of the swinging gates and the harmony of the hymns, the pictorial images of Dante's hallucinations in the terrace of the wrathful, and of course the color of the final procession, as visually spectacular as it is dogmatically significant. Even within the sphere of literature alone it may be observed that certain genres are easily recognizable patterns in the great mosaic: Dante's outburst on his encounter with Sordello is a perfect *sirventes,* the meeting with Matilda is a true *pastorela,* and the Provençal verses of Arnaut are in themselves a display of linguistic virtuosity and a kind of penitent *canso* as well. Thus, even as in our own fragile world, the long road of trial and aspiration is marked by ritual and embellished by art. And lastly, to recall once more our rule of three, nowhere in the *Commedia* are narrative, allegory, and dogma more happily combined than in the last six cantos of the *Purgatorio*.

The *Paradiso*

The differences between heaven and the lesser realms of hell and purgatory are great and meaningful. To be sure, the reader, as he moves from the *Purgatorio* to the *Paradiso*, finds no sudden change. Indeed, a decided impression of continuity is felt: the verse is still *terza rima;* the division is still formally by cantos of about the same length as before (they average 144+ lines); there are the conventional topographical compartments (the great heavenly spheres in place of terraces or circles); and there is the same hero. But having said so much, one is immediately compelled to distinguish. For both the compartments and the central character are in one sense not in the least comparable to their counterparts in the first two *cantiche*. Very specifically Dante tells us that the celestial spheres he is to traverse have nothing to do with the real paradise. Beatrice, in the very first heaven, carefully explains to Dante that the moon-dwellers he has seen are not truly such at all; in fact "all make beautiful the primal gyre," and

> "Here they have shown themselves not that this sphere
> Is allotted them, but here to signify
> The sphere celestial of least high degree."

The great spheres are nothing but a device to make certain distinctions among the blessed clear to the eye of mortals. The true heaven is the empyrean beyond space and time wherein all the blessed have their home. Heaven is simply not there in a physical sense. Nor is Dante — or if he is, he is not at all sure of it. He does not know, and he says as much in *Paradiso* I, 73–75. In terms of his narrative both hell and purgatory are experiences, heaven is a vision and a memory. And, we may add, an imperfect memory. Dante had announced with some complacency in *Inferno* II that his "unerring mind" would faithfully reproduce the dreadful sights of hell. In the *Purgatorio* he accepted, apparently with some confidence in his ability to carry them out, the orders of Beatrice to write down what he saw and bear it all back to the living. But here he admits that in his celestial journey

> . . . such things I saw as one
> Who thence returns lacks wit and skill to tell,
> Because, as it draws near to its desire
> Our intellect so deeply penetrates
> That memory cannot follow after it.

Of course he had in the *Inferno* occasionally voiced his inability to reproduce all he saw; he had wished for "the harsh and rugged rhymes" appropriate to the description of hell's depth; he had understandably faltered in his attempt to describe for us Beatrice's smile at the summit of the Mount of Purgatory. But in the main he can remember, often in surprising detail, the sights and sounds of the earthly kingdoms. It must be said that he will remember much of heaven too, but he lays the stress on what he has forgotten. Another great difference, hidden under a semblance of fidelity to the pattern, is in the characters. For in paradise, Dante has many conversations and encounters with personages, but he never really sees a soul as he sees Francesca or Forese or Guinizzelli. In the heaven of the moon he can make out very faint images like those reflected in a clear stream; elsewhere the blessed are at best luminescent forms, and usually merely points of light. In the empyrean he sees human faces again, but these are the faces of eternity and not of our earth.

Doctrinal necessity has also deprived our poet of the most reliable prop to his narrative structure: the person of Virgil. To be sure, Beatrice takes his place, but with a distinction almost as damaging to the narrative as it is necessary to the doctrine. That the narrative, made up of some repetitive transitions and frequently quite predictable encounters, holds up at all is a tribute to the skill of the artist, and perhaps a little to the attraction of the pattern, which now fascinates us so much that we admire it for its own sake. I think it must be conceded that the narrative is subordinate in the *Paradiso;* it is overshadowed not so much by allegory as by doctrine, and its appeal is a result of the incredibly beautiful splendor of its ornament rather than its inherent virtue as a story. Yet narrative there is and we may at this point turn to it.

Announcing that his subject is to be none other than the glory of God and such experiences as he can remember from his ascent, Dante invokes the "good Apollo" (expressing incidentally a hope to win the laurel crown) and begins his account. It is a propitious time, very near the spring equinox, and the hour is noon.

Beatrice fixes her eyes on the sun, and Dante imitates her; hence he is "transhumanized" — an experience impossible to describe. The sun seems to flood the whole day, and quite unaware of movement Dante is borne through the sphere of fire and up toward the first heaven. This he has to learn from Beatrice, who also tells him that such an ascent is simply in keeping with law; it is the soul's natural tendency to rise, and only diversion through sin or error hinders it (I).

Cantos II, III, IV, and most of V are spent in the sphere of the moon (the heavenly divisions are much more spacious than those of the other realms). Dante begins the second canto with a warning that only those properly prepared should follow him on his journey, which to others might prove hazardous. In the sphere of the moon, which has the texture of a pearly cloud, Dante learns from Beatrice the cause and nature of the moon-spots and meets the soul of Piccarda Donati (Forese's sister). She appears to him, tenuous as a reflection seen in clear water, and tells him that she represents the inconstant, having, though against her will, broken her monastic vows. She explains that all the souls in heaven are content with their station, for "in His will is our peace." She points out the soul of Costanza, mother of Frederick II, whose fate had been similar to her own. Beatrice then explains to Dante that all the blessed dwell in the empyrean, but make themselves manifest to him in the successive heavens as an indication of their categories; she also takes up the question of the conditioned and the absolute will, respectively weak and strong in such cases as Piccarda, and discusses the significance of vows, suggesting that they should not be lightly taken.

Beatrice's enhanced beauty makes it clear that they have risen to the second heaven, that of Mercury, where, dimly outlined like fish in a pool, the souls come forth to meet the pilgrims. From Justinian (symbolizing the good rulers who had been so attentive to earthly honor as to detract somewhat from their concern for heavenly things) Dante hears the history of the Roman eagle from Aeneas to Charlemagne; Justinian warns the Guelphs not to attack it, and cautions the Ghibellines against using it as a partisan symbol. He points out to Dante the soul of Romeo of Provence, unjustly exiled after years of loyal service (VI). Referring to a phrase of Justinian, Beatrice explains how the Crucifixion could be at once pleasing to God, as necessary to mankind's salvation, and to the Jews for less worthy reasons; she speaks also of the primary and secondary creatures of God (VII).

In the bright heaven of Venus the souls appear as sparks against flame. The soul of Charles Martel, grandson of Charles of Anjou, makes itself known to Dante. He deplores the avarice of his brother Robert, which leads to a discussion of why sons do not inherit their fathers' quality; he suggests that society should consider the fitness of men for various vocations rather than their paternity. Dante speaks also with Cunizza da Romano, who predicts dire things for Romagna, and with the troubadour Folquet de Marselha, complacent in his achievement of blessedness through the path of profane love. He points out to Dante the soul of Rahab; her aid to Joshua stands in contrast to the neglect of the Holy Land by the present pope — in part, he avers, the fault of Florence and the avarice aroused by her florins; he concludes with a prediction of coming reformation (VIII–IX).

The tenth canto begins with a rather lengthy apostrophe to the reader. In a formal though not entirely functional sense it may be thought of as matching the exposition of *Inferno* XI and *Purgatorio* XVII; it is a pause in the narrative, and it occurs at the same stage in the development of the pattern, i.e., after the first division of the realm, properly considered — in the *Inferno,* we recall, Virgil's explanation comes after the account of the incontinent, and in the *Purgatorio* after the cases of love misdirected. (There is no exact heavenly parallel to these expositions; to be sure, Piccarda has stated the formal principle of the symbolic heavens, and St. Bernard will disclose the design of the empyrean.) This would lead us to assume that we have now left the first general category of heaven behind us. And although Dante does not say so, such is indeed the case. Piccarda, Justinian, and Charles Martel have all confessed to some slight imperfection which puts them (or obliges them to show themselves to Dante) in the lower tier, as it were. Folquet has also reminded Dante and the reader that the "point" of the Earth's shadow falls on Venus; it follows then that all of the lower planets must be more or less adumbrated by our world. It would be irreverent to think of this group of saints, as authentic as any other, as "matching" the incontinent or the penitents of pride, envy, and anger — and yet it does, though in different ways. For the purgatorial category is furthest from the summit of the mount as the lower spheres are furthest from the highest heaven; that the incontinent are furthest from lowest hell is a reversal in a hierarchical sense, but morally speaking the sins of the flesh are far removed from malice and by the same token the attraction of the sensual (as illustrated in the

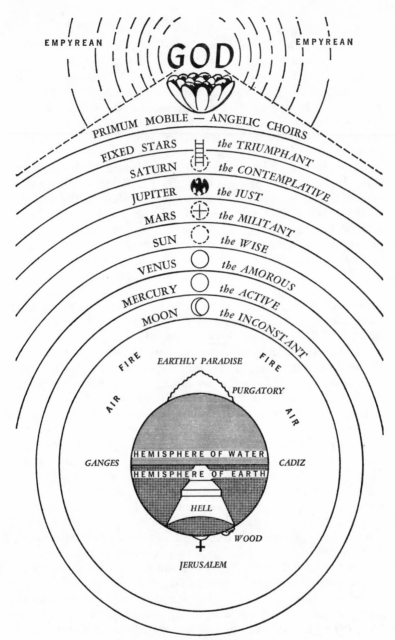

EMPYREAN — EMPYREAN

GOD

PRIMUM MOBILE — ANGELIC CHOIRS
FIXED STARS — the TRIUMPHANT
SATURN — the CONTEMPLATIVE
JUPITER — the JUST
MARS — the MILITANT
SUN — the WISE
VENUS — the AMOROUS
MERCURY — the ACTIVE
MOON — the INCONSTANT

AIR   FIRE   EARTHLY PARADISE   FIRE   AIR

PURGATORY

GANGES   HEMISPHERE OF WATER   CADIZ
HEMISPHERE OF EARTH

HELL

WOOD

JERUSALEM

Dante's Cosmos

sphere of Venus) bars the soul from the highest ecstasy of the spirit. Reverence may be restored if we recall that unlike the first categories of hell and purgatory, these souls are not truly inhabitants of their spheres. Reverence is, I think, in part at least, the reason why Dante does not hear from Beatrice, as he had heard from Virgil, a precise outline of heaven's classifications. The expression of such distinctions would be as invidious as it is, in fact, unnecessary, for the souls we have seen have made their position quite clear, and in the upper heaven we shall find them equally articulate. Yet indirectly Dante does bring out his hierarchical concept. As he prepares to enter the sphere of the sun he bids the reader to reflect on God's providence in the disposition of the planets and the circle of the zodiac which makes human life as we know it possible. God, he says explicitly, has made everything revolving through mind or space and with such order as to arouse our love if we but think of it. This is enough for us or should be: "I've put the food before you, now eat it for yourself," thus his apostrophe concludes.

There is yet another sense in which Dante has been thus far living in the shadow of his own earth, and in which the inhabitants of the lower heavens have had, collectively, something in common with those of hell and purgatory. As in the two lower kingdoms, so here in the lesser heavens Dante has met souls whom he knew in life: Piccarda, Charles Martel, and (probably) Cunizza. Henceforth this will no longer be so. We might even, reverence again permitting, discover some resemblances. Is Piccarda a refined and purified Francesca or is she a corrective to her, illustrating in a kind of mirror way marginal salvation as Francesca illustrates marginal damnation, and all through the use or misuse of the will? Does Cunizza not serve too as a corrective to Sapia? Lustful as she discreetly avows herself to have been and as the scandalized earlier commentators document with horror, she assuredly did not lack in charity, a deficiency of which has blinded the embittered woman of the second terrace. Do we not find in Justinian a glorification of the Ghibelline faith, illustrated in its partisan extremity in Farinata and defended (though in an atmosphere of compassion) in the example of Manfred, saved in spite of the vindictive rituals of his clerical enemies? There is an echo of Brunetto Latini in Charles Martel's affectionate affirmation that he would have done more for Dante had life permitted him; and Folquet, the troubadour priest, reproves the venality of Rome as Sordello, the troubadour courtier, had exposed the flaws of the secular rulers. Such echoes as these, sometimes tenuous, sometimes quite obvious, not only serve the consistent purpose of the pattern in weaving the whole canvas together but also bring the first division of heaven into a kind of kinship with the world that Dante is perhaps not quite so ready to leave after all.

But what has happened to the narrative as narrative? It must be conceded that the pace has slackened. "Drama has disappeared, giving place to the lyric," as Attilio Momigliano remarks.[15] By the time we had gone through nine cantos of the *Inferno*, Dante had met Virgil, passed through the gate, seen no less than seven different groups of sinners, had a rather trying moment at the gates of Dis, and undergone two memorable boat rides. He had, in a similar number of lines in the *Purgatorio*, undergone a considerable variety of experiences and had also been obliged to climb with an expense of effort which he is at some pains to tell us about. But in the *Paradiso* he has been wafted effortlessly and almost imperceptibly from heaven to heaven. The poet too has "participated" very little; curiosity, to be sure, is as alive as ever, and, properly encouraged by Beatrice, he has not hesitated to ask questions. But he has done an extraordinary amount of listening. Out of the 1281 lines of the nine cantos so far covered, Beatrice has spoken for 463. She is in fact even more loquacious than these figures would indicate, for in three of the cantos the poet's strategy gives her no scope for speech, and we must therefore think of her as taking advantage of 463 lines out of the 849 where she has the opportunity. She is also quite capable of sustained discourses, speaking for 88 lines without interruption in canto II, and reaching her height in canto VII, where she holds forth for 130 lines without pausing to draw breath. An elder sister with a Ph.D., to paraphrase Croce.[16] And in the cantos where she is silent, Dante is no less a listener: Justinian speaks for the entire duration of canto VI, and in the heaven of Venus we have uninterrupted discourses of 36, 39, and 60 lines from Charles Martel, Cunizza, and Folquet respectively. Our erstwhile pilgrim participant has become a docile pupil "and not a pupil of the Muses," as Quasimodo says.[17] He is safe at home — or in school. All danger has passed, and with it something of the excitement of the journey. Yet the narrative, tame though it may have become, continues to hold even the reader who is not especially interested in the keeping of vows or in the Roman Empire. It holds him in part, I believe it must be confessed, on the level of pure childish curiosity. From one point of view the *Paradiso* may be considered a science-fiction story, and we cannot but continue the reading — even if (though it be heresy) we skip the doctrinal parts — just to see what Dante will find in the successive heavens. We are encouraged to go on too by some of the most magnificent bits of imaginative description that ever adorned a poem. We know — the poet knows it too — that the depiction of heaven is by definition an impossible task, since it would not be heaven if it could be described in human terms, and hence we are fascinated by the attempt. Dante has told us himself in the *Convivio* that a most potent allure to the reader is the promise of disclosing "new and great things," and it is this promise which is made and fulfilled as we follow Beatrice *"di stella in stella."*

Quick as thought, then, Dante arrives in the heaven of the sun, and finds himself encircled by a ring of splendors. One of them is St. Thomas, who introduces himself and his colleagues, relates the life story of St. Francis, and deplores the degeneration of his own order, the Dominicans (X–XI). Another ring appears; the spokesman of this outer circle is the Franciscan St. Bonaventure; he first tells the story of St. Dominic, then speaks sadly of the shortcomings of the contemporary Franciscans, and concludes by presenting himself and his fellows. St. Thomas answers Dante's unvoiced question on the nature of Solomon's wisdom (XII–XIII), and Solomon himself reassures Dante that after Judgment Day our eyes will be able to support the splendor of our new flesh. A third ring is dimly perceptible beyond the first two; subsequently the atmosphere's change to a ruddy hue informs Dante that they have risen to Mars. Against the ruby-red glow of the heaven Dante sees a great silver cross, on which myriads of sparks are in continual movement (XIV); one of them comes to the foot of the cross to greet Dante. It is his ancestor Cacciaguida, who tells of his death as a crusader, describes the simple Florence of old, and goes on to predict Dante's exile and the fame he will win by his poem, urging him to speak out fearlessly even at the risk of offending the powerful (XV–XVII). He identifies for Dante a number of warrior spirits whose souls sparkle in the cross, among them Joshua, Charlemagne, and Robert Guiscard, who drove the Saracens out of southern Italy. Again the atmosphere changes color — this time to white. Beatrice's beauty increases, and they stand in Jupiter, where the receptive spirits group themselves to form one by one the letters *DILIGITE JUSTITIAM,* the final M taking on the shape of an eagle (XVIII). This bird of collective human justice answers the question which has long tormented Dante: why virtuous souls who have had no opportunity to know of Christ must be denied the supreme vision. God's justice is of necessity beyond understanding, the eagle answers; even so, many who know not Christ will stand nearer him on Judgment Day than some Christian monarchs whom it names with scorn (XIX). It goes on to point out that the souls whose coruscant sparks make the pattern of its eyebrow include the spirit of Trajan, given opportunity to return from limbo and embrace Christianity, and the Trojan Ripheus, who had received baptism of desire even before the coming of Christ. None may fathom God's predestination, not even the elect (XX).

The heavens of the sun, Mars, and Jupiter contain the second heavenly group, usually known as the Saints of the Active Life. Such they are indeed: scholars, warriors, and lawgivers — and it is interesting to note Dante's hierarchical arrangements. Within the pattern would we be justified in thinking of them, collectively, as somehow set off against the violent of the *Inferno,* active too in their misguided way? Is it fanciful to see in the emphasis placed on the pagan figures in the eagle's eye a link with the centaurs who preside, with classical severity and a kind of justice, over the murderers in the river of blood? It is not quite so far-fetched perhaps to equate in a way the two teachers, however different their destiny, both important to our poet — Brunetto Latini and St. Thomas. And was not Pier delle Vigne, like Cacciaguida, a loyal servant to his emperor? (If Cacciaguida has in his paternal aspect something of Brunetto, and recalls in his conservative assurance the attitude of Farinata, this need not surprise us; the rugged old crusader is a celestial synthesis both of Dante's Florentinism and his Ghibellinism. It is he who finally answers Farinata's question: "Who were your forebears?") Such correspondences stir our memories and tease our interest as we follow the new and strange things that the narrative continues to disclose. The principal novelty in these heavens is in the replacement of the representational by the symbolic; no longer do the souls appear as individuals — though they may speak as such — but as part of great symbols: the garland, the cross, the eagle. This is part of the steady dehumanizing process that goes on in the *Paradiso,* a process which enables Dante to illustrate his doc-

trine (the primary concern of this *cantica*) possibly at some expense to what we might call the human interest. But happily he is not consistent. There is no more human, moving, and purely personal episode in the whole *Commedia* than the encounter with Cacciaguida, which contains the author's defense of his work and a certain amount of self-analysis as well. Here he avows his didactic purpose; here he shows himself aware of the risks his historical-realistic method must signify for him; here he explains, and quite reasonably, why the *Commedia* has an aristocratic — some have said a "snobbish" — tinge; here, in all honesty, the exile, the patriot, and the conservative speak out in a moving blend of melancholy, resignation, pride, and purpose.

To resume the narrative: in the seventh heaven of the contemplative, in whose austere air Beatrice refrains from smiling and no song is heard, Dante is welcomed by souls, mere points of light, coming down a ladder to meet him. One, Peter Damian, tells of his life and assails the corruption of the contemporary clergy; the souls give an outraged shout of assent which almost stuns Dante (XXI). St. Benedict approaches, and from him Dante learns that while the souls appear in the spheres as symbolic splendors, in the empyrean he will be privileged to see their faces. To that heaven, the saint says, the mystic ladder leads, but none now climb it, and his own rule has become as so much paper. He does not despair of a God-inspired change, however. The company of saints then rises up like a whirlwind; Dante and Beatrice follow up the ladder and find themselves in the heaven of the fixed stars, entering under Gemini. Thanking his natal sign for this favor, Dante looks down through the spheres and smiles at the "meanness" of our mortal "threshing floor" (XXII).

Overcome by the combined radiance of the Court of Christ and the renewed smile of Beatrice, Dante apologizes to the reader for his inability to reproduce what he saw; his is "not a voyage for a little bark." Special grace enables him to sustain the vision of the heavenly court when he beholds Gabriel circling the glory of Mary. Then Son, Mother, and Archangel ascend, followed by the throng of saints; Dante remains behind to undergo his qualifying examination (XXIII). He is examined by St. Peter on faith (XXIV), St. James on hope (XXV), and St. John on love, "passing" successfully, to the satisfaction of Beatrice and the attendant saints. He also has converse with the soul of Adam, who tells him of the duration of his life in Eden and on earth, and states that the language he spoke had died before the Tower of Babel was built (a revision of the theory set forth in *De Vulgari Eloquentia*) (XXVI). St. Peter delivers yet another invective against the papacy, denouncing Boniface and two of his successors yet to come; he exhorts Dante to carry his message back to earth, and then he too sweeps upward with all the glittering saints, like a snowstorm "falling" in reverse.

Glancing down for a second time at the remote earth, the celestial travelers move into the *primum mobile*, the sphere that initiates all lesser movements, having its own existence in the mind of God. Explaining this to Dante, Beatrice deplores the perversion of humanity in following earthly cupidity instead of raising its eyes to the heavens; she too foresees a change to come (XXVII). In this heaven Dante has a symbolic vision of God, a mere point of light encircled by brilliant spinning gyres of splendor — the choir of angels, which Beatrice enumerates for him (XXVIII). She goes on to discuss the nature and history of the angels (XXIX). Warning us that he is bringing his "arduous theme" to a close, Dante now tells of his entrance into the empyrean — the heaven of pure intellectual light, replete with joyous love. Here, Beatrice assures him, he will see the heavenly court of angels and saints as it will appear on Judgment Day. At her bidding he bends to drink of the river of grace and finds it suddenly changed to the aspect of a great white rose, large as a vast amphitheatre. Dante, standing on the "floor," can yet see all the tiers above him very clearly, for we are beyond the laws of nature. Beatrice points out the seat "reserved" for Henry VII (XXX); as Dante in ecstatic wonder surveys the rows of the blessed and the ministering angels flying ceaselessly between them and the Godhead, she slips away and Dante, turning, finds in her stead St. Bernard standing by his side. The venerable mystic first reassures him, pointing out that Beatrice has resumed her assigned place in the rose. Then, at the saint's bidding, he looks up to see the Virgin Mary appear at the top of the amphitheatre, glorious as a sunrise (XXXI). Bernard indicates the "seating plan," mentioning some of the saints by name (XXXII). They join in St. Bernard's prayer that Dante may be granted the supreme vision. In spite of a memory numbed by the very glory of that vision, he tries to recall what he saw, first the "substances and accidents" of the universe bound together with love, then three circles within a great light, the second seeming to have our human semblance,

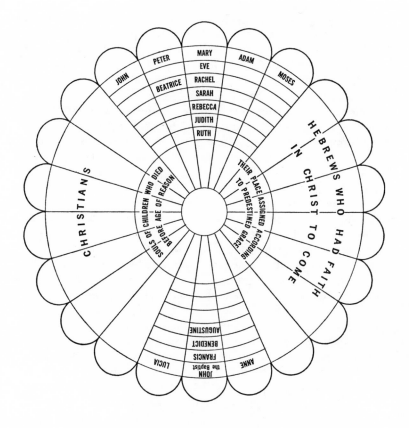

The Heavenly Rose

finally a flash of transcendent understanding; desire and will wheeling harmoniously under the impulse of the Love "which turns the sun and all the stars" (XXXIII).

"Strange and new things" indeed. No poet before or since has ever given us their like. But in terms of the pattern, new though they be, the events and appearances in these last cantos have their earlier correspondences, their *figurae,* in what has gone before. In *Inferno* I there was a sunrise over the mountain, unattainable at the time, but seen nevertheless and longed for with a hopelessness that has here changed to ecstasy. There was also a venerable sage who interceded for Dante as St. Bernard intercedes for him here — and now that we let our memory play over the richness that has gone before, there was a similar sage — surely true *figurae* are Virgil and Cato — to give him his first instructions on the shores of purgatory. And it is the Virgin Mary who obtains for him, moved in her turn by her faithful follower, the privilege of the ultimate vision even as it was she who first became aware of his plight and initiated her own chain of rescuers. It is not inappropriate to recall too that just as the great saints in their hierarchical disposition are enumerated here by Bernard, so under Virgil's sponsorship the great champions of the virtuous life of antiquity were shown us in limbo, and thanks to Sordello a not dissimilar gallery of the great of this world was set before our eyes in the valley of the princes. The cantos of the empyrean are set apart by a tone of ecstasy verging on the mystic — there is nothing quite like them in the rest of the poem. Yet they recall what has gone before, as they must if we are to have the harmony, the unity — perhaps the best word is the integrity — that Dante is impelled to give his poem and would like to see in his world. It is all here — very specifically, all the substances and accidents which we have seen before in the course of the journey, but here "bound with love." "The time has passed that holds you slumber bound," says Bernard. How long has this slumber gone on? The verbal echo is with the *"sonno"* of line 11 of *Inferno* I. Has the poem been all a vision? If so, it is a vision which begins in effort and ends in triumph, begins in terror and ends in glory, begins on the brink of despair and ends in salvation. Though not strictly appropriate to the narrative, we may note too the recurrence of "stars" as the last word of each *cantica.* Of them Momigliano has well said that they carry us from aspiration ("so we came forth once more to see the stars") to faith ("pure and prepared to mount up to the stars") and ultimately to the affirmation of a divine law — "the love that moves the sun and all the stars").[18] It is interesting too and this has some bearing on the narrative — that the final lines of the first two *cantiche* have as subjects the poet and a companion (respectively Virgil and Beatrice), but in the last line of the third the subject is no longer personal; it is love which has taken over, and in the course of finding himself (no *cantica* is more full of the personal than the *Paradiso*) the poet has lost himself. As in the last cantos of the *Purgatorio,* but on a still higher level narrative, allegory and doctrine here fuse: this is journey's end, the ultimate symbol and the supreme indoctrination. It is at the same time also the basic one and hence the first. For as the pilgrim's journey ends the prophet's mission begins.

❧ 13 ❧

The *Commedia*: Allegory

A GENERATION ago it was usually held necessary in discussions of the *Commedia* to interpolate a word of explanation, if not actual apology, for the embarrassing element of allegory in the work. Grandgent's excellent summary of the allegory of the poem contains, for example, the following faintly defensive sentence: "The habit of allegorical interpretation and composition, the search for hidden meanings in literature and life, and the consequent development of symbolic art, not only in words but in stone as well, lent to the Middle Ages a character quite different from that of the periods which preceded and followed."[1] Fortunately for our purposes defense of allegory is no longer required. A generation familiar with Kafka, Faulkner, and Camus, to say nothing of the popular esoteric ambiguities of Graham Greene, needs no such indoctrination. In this area the cultivated taste of our day is probably closer to that of Dante's time than that of any generation since the seventeenth century. There are, of course, differences between the medieval and contemporary treatment and uses of allegory, but one may argue that Dante, taking full advantage of the symbolic devices made familiar to him by his own tradition, also anticipated some of the modern refinements in subtlety and ambiguity.

In fact, instead of thinking simply of *the* allegory of the *Commedia*, we must, after the most cursory of glances at the work,

250

conclude that it is a question of various allegories, sometimes sharply different in genesis and purpose, frequently interweaving, and not always easy to distinguish. We shall in this chapter merely allude to the principal members of the vast family of hidden senses; to deal fully with any one of them would require a book-length study — and some have had shelves of erudition already dedicated to them.

It will be helpful if we begin with some definitions of the commonly used terms. Dorothy Sayers in her *Introductory Papers on Dante* supplies a few useful, crisply phrased definitions: "An allegory," she writes, "is a dramatised metaphor. A metaphor is a compressed simile. A simile is the perception of likeness in unlike things, presented in such a way that the understanding of the one helps to understand the other."[2] To illustrate by example, let us look at Dante's picture of the souls on the bank of Acheron answering Charon's summons in *Inferno* III, 112–20:

> And just as leaves swayed by the autumn winds
> Drop from the tree, each falling in its turn
> Until the branch is all despoiled and bare,
> So here did Adam's evil seed descend,
> And one by one they stepped off from the shore,
> Like hawk to hunter's call, at Charon's sign.
> Thus speed they on their way o'er the dark wave
> And scarcely have they left the bank behind
> When yet another throng takes up its stand.

We have never seen the souls fall to Charon's command, but we have seen leaves drop from the tree in autumn and we can now visualize the scene — this is the basic simile. If we see in Charon's call an illustration of a doctrinal and moral law by which the sinner is drawn to recognize his guilt and accept his punishment, we have an allegory, composed of the metaphorical elements of sin and conscience.

In a sustained allegory there is also much symbolism. This will come out especially in the characters who take part in the play, as it were. In straightforward allegories, the characters tend to be named after qualities; the classical example of this for the Dante student is the *Roman de la Rose,* in which there are such characters as Jealousy, Danger, Fair Greeting, and the like. Dante sometimes uses this kind of allegory, though only, I would say, incidentally; the richness and originality of his symbols lies in the fact that he works just the other way around. (It is for this reason that Siro Chimenz strenuously denies that the fundamental conception of the *Commedia* is allegorical.[3]) To quote Miss Sayers again: "We may see the difference at once if we compare Dante with Spenser. In the *Faerie Queene*, we find a personified Chastity called Belphoebe, who allegorically represents (among other things) Queen Elizabeth; if Dante had written the poem, we should have met, wandering about that enchanted woodland, Queen Elizabeth herself, allegorically representing chastity."[4] Dante's method, as many critics have observed, has the great advantage of richness and multiplicity of dimensions in the symbol: Virgil does not always have to be Human Reason (to give him the traditional interpretation) or even Classical Learning or Philosophy; he can sometimes be the poet Dante revered or simply the good companion on a long journey. Beatrice does not have to be Revelation whenever she speaks — or whenever Dante thinks of her (for the thought of her is an essential motif of the pilgrimage); she may be too the beloved of his youth or, alas, the offended woman not inclined to forgive his straying. It should be said that from a strictly didactic point of view Dante's method has its dangers: the disciple of the poet, eager for instruction, may be a little uneasy not knowing whether he is listening to Revelation or merely to a character in the narrative. But perhaps this is the place to affirm that Dante, for all his purpose in inculcating doctrine, for all his insistence that the allegory is the "true" meaning, was at least as much concerned with giving his fiction and characters depth and verisimilitude as he was in his pedagogical mission. The existence of the *Commedia* is in itself evidence enough for that; otherwise the *Convivio,* perhaps expanded or revised, would have suited his purpose. I do not know, incidentally, whether it has ever been remarked that in the Dantesque canon the *Commedia* is the only work of creative fiction in the strict sense of the word. We may assume that when the poet turned to that approach he was concerned to make it as effective as possible.

We have spoken of symbols, but some of our examples might also be classified as images, since the terms are used somewhat loosely by many critics. Father Herbert Musurillo has summed up the differences as well as anyone: symbols, he says, are "objects or events which are considered to have, in addition to their original, objective function, another deeper reference or relationship, whereas 'image' usually stresses the aspect of sensuous picture . . . again, symbols tend to be more explicit, whereas imagery may be 'sunken' and barely suggested."[5] So we may think of Dante's images as the visual elements of his poem; used traditionally and with intent to communicate they may be symbols as well.

Virgil is (among other things) a symbol of reason; the evidence is not in what he looks like but in what he says. The Mount of Purgatory is an image-symbol of ascent from sin through contrition and penance to absolution, the ice of Cocytus is an image symbolic of the cold heart of treason, and the mystic rose a visual image-symbol of the joys of paradise. Images of the purer sort may be seen in many casual metaphors and in such recurrent elements as the wood or the river. The wood where Dante lost his way in *Inferno* I reappears in intensified horror in the thicket of the suicides in *Inferno* XIII, and turns up again with a suggestion of wilful perversion as the giant drags off the harlot into its recesses in *Purgatorio* XXXII: these are its evil aspects. Clean and sweet-smelling, however, it can afford a proper background for Matilda, and a setting for the earthly paradise itself. Similarly, the dreadful rivers of hell are recalled in Dante's description of the Arno in *Purgatorio* XIV, counterbalanced by Lethe and Eunoë in the earthly paradise, and canceled forever by the wonderful river of grace from which the poet drinks in the empyrean. Such images are multivalent, and a part of the poet's esthetic rather than strictly didactic equipment.

Remembering that all such categories are, by their very nature, related and often interchangeable, we may turn to a consideration of Dante's use of allegory and its affiliates.

We have alluded to the scriptural tradition of the four meanings in our discussion of the *Convivio*. We must note here that Dante, not dealing with the Bible, cannot undertake to give us consistently four meanings in his "beautiful fiction," and indeed in his rather indirect way he admits it. In the *Convivio* he puts the three nonliteral meanings on the same plane, distinguishing between the allegorical, moral, and anagogical. In the letter to Can Grande he uses "allegorical" in a general sense, and makes subcategories of the moral and anagogical. In the *Convivio* he states frankly that in his odes he will disclose the allegorical meaning in detail but will merely touch on the others. When he defines the subject of his poem in the letter to Can Grande as "man, liable to the reward or punishment of Justice, in accordance with the use he has made of his free will," he gives no moral

or anagogical clue, but distinguishes only between the literal and
allegorical (a fact which has not stopped critics from supplying
the necessary quartets: Charles Williams, for instance, sees Virgil
as Virgil, poetry, philosophy, and "the Institution or City"[6]). He
has given us both less and more than seems at first reading to
be implied in the four meanings, for if two of them are often
missing or undetectable, there are other allegories which the poet
silently presses upon us, and still others generously supplied by
critics which Dante might or might not accept. The prime allegory, the message that Dante most of all wished to convey
through the great metaphor of the world of the dead, the basis for
the doctrinal function of his work (which must have been his
prime conscious motivation in the writing of the *Commedia*), is
the depiction of the state of the souls in this world, under the
aspect of their eligibility for reward or their liability to punishment, as he himself says. In the letter to Can Grande, Dante says
that the *Paradiso* depicts "man according as by his merits he is
deserving of reward by justice": good men, but something more
than that, since the medieval ethics are rigorous, and to be truly
"deserving" has lofty implications; hence, saintly men. The *Inferno* shows us bad men who are impenitent in their badness, the
Purgatorio shows us men who have made the right choice but still
have not overcome certain evil tendencies. The *Commedia* portrays our world with all its morally diversified citizenry. So the
"true" meaning is essentially what all great literature — and most
inferior literature — is about: the revelation of the human heart,
the continuous struggle between good and evil. But Dante's allegory is more realistic and self-conscious than a detective story,
for instance, or the myth of Atreus, and is put to the service of
a very elaborate ethical code. It is also very carefully worked
out. Sweet, seductive lust, tormented by restless, forever unsatisfied desire, is exemplified by Francesca da Rimini; snake and man
blend in the *bolgia* of the thieves, because there is in the sneak
thief, betrayer of our common bond of brotherhood, an element
of the serpentine; the heart of the traitor is indeed icy; the face
of the hypocrite is gilded without but base metal underneath; and
so on. Symbols reinforce the allegory and narrative. The very
shapes of the kingdoms are symbols: a funnel-shaped hell with
a gravitational pull to the bottom, a terraced mountain, the vast
universe of stars. Symbolic figures abound: Minos, the agent of
God's justice and our own consciences; the centaurs, half beast,

that dominate the violent; the sly, mocking demons that both punish and symbolize the slippery grafter; Cato exemplifying the stern demands of free will; Matilda; and, of course, above all, the figures of Virgil and Beatrice.

The peculiar texture of the poem derives in large part from the fusing of this essentially Dantesque allegory with the story he has to tell. Generally speaking, the two currents do not so much blend as run parallel, occasionally intertwining. The allegory may be understood and accepted while the literal narrative may stand on its own feet for its human values. Brunetto Latini is in the circle of the violent because, in terms of the allegory, he is a type of man, intellectual and honorable, betrayed by his passion, which has led him to violate the laws of nature. But his paternal interest in Dante, his touching and unselfish pride in his pupil, give him his flesh and blood and his humanity. So in the case of Mark the Lombard: in penance for his wrathful excesses he wanders in the dark and sullen cloud of intemperate anger on the third terrace of purgatory; but as we learn this, even from his own lips, our interest focuses rather on his discussion of mankind's responsibility in its choice of goals and the decadence of the two great guiding powers which should lead the medieval world aright but have failed in their mission. Perhaps the best example of this happy ambivalence is the case of Cacciaguida. So far as concerns man "deserving reward by his actions in this world," Cacciaguida typifies the saintly warrior; we might extend this and call him the man of action whose deeds are in the service of virtue. But the literal here all but submerges the allegory; in simple fact Cacciaguida is a fine old conservative, full of family pride and a yearning for things as they used to be, with all the vigorous virtues and stubborn prejudices that one associates with the type. The great sea of the *Commedia* carries both meanings effortlessly; and more too, as we shall see.

Once in a while Dante seems to feel the need of establishing a nexus — usually going out of his way to point out the allegory. Virgil reminds Capaneus that not the fiery flakes that scorch his skin but his own stubborn resistance to the Divinity is his true punishment — hardly an appropriate suggestion for the narrative but applicable to the self-willed blasphemer "in this life." So too the poet's first apostrophe to the reader, as Dante and Virgil stand outside the gates of Dis, while the Furies line the walls, seems calculated to remind us that we are reading something more than an adventure story. Perhaps the "truth" is pushed rather too purposefully through the veil when, on the hillside of purgatory, the penitents utter the Lord's Prayer, including "lead us not into temptation." This is justified on the level of the narrative by the comment that it is said on behalf of the living but it seems clear that we are to be reminded here that these souls are "in truth" still in this life and winning their way to "the reward of their just actions."

Yet such collisions are rare — at least in terms of the truly Dantesque allegory. This portrayal of the world of man through a narrative that is also convincingly realistic and full of its own significance, with all the attendant diversities and fecund ambiguities that we have remarked, is Dante's own and essentially original allegory. He is nevertheless a child of his age, and his poem is studded with the conventional or traditional allegories, made of stock figures and images that would be readily familiar to his contemporaries. With such he avoids the risk of doctrinal ambiguity — though at some cost to the vigor of his "fair fiction." This kind of allegory indeed is meant not so much to assist or embellish the narrative as to aid in the exposition of the doctrine. The Old Man of Crete (*Inferno* XIV) exemplifies very well what I am saying here. Fashioned of material gathered from the Book of Daniel and Ovid's *Metamorphoses,* he is brought on stage with the pretext of supplying further information about hell's rivers and their sources, and he serves the purpose well enough and quite poetically. On the allegorical level, the picture of mankind, originally sound, but split and becoming increasingly degenerate with the centuries, stands clearly before us, and the Old Man's clay foot enables Dante to introduce his political belief in the two feet (empire and church) which should support mankind. But it is, for all that, an artificial thing; the Old Man isn't even there, as Minos and the centaurs and Geryon are there, but is merely a subject of Virgil's conversation. The allegory does nothing to advance the tale; indeed it slows it up. I believe, though I am aware opinions sharply differ on this, that the figure of Lucifer is of the same stuff. It is all carefully worked out; the three symbolic heads, the mouths chewing the appropriate traitors (to church and state, of course), the tears of chagrin, the icy blast stirred by the batlike wings, the ugliness. As doctrine who could take exception to it? But it is too formalized to add anything to the conviction of the narrative; the abundant realistic details are, as Natalino Sapegno remarks, more the product of intellect than imagination.[7] In this kind of allegory doctrine comes first; this is in truth a theological devil. Even in terms of Dante's own human allegory something is missing; if we are seeing here the souls in this life as helpless captives of sin, we are certainly not seeing any of the superficial seductiveness that temptation, one would think, must carry somewhere in its arsenal.

Overt doctrinal allegory is much more evident in the *Purgatorio* than in the other *cantiche.* Dante's three dreams are of this nature, though it must be said that the first of them is very successfully used to advance the action. The guardian angels of the terraces too are conventional allegorical figures. And there are two sustained allegories of the truly medieval sort in the entrance to purgatory and the great procession at the top of the mount. In the first, objects become unambiguous symbols: the three steps signifying the three stages of the confessional, the two keys clearly indicating authority and discernment, the grey of the porter's robe symbolizing the humble patience of the confessor. The allegory had more immediate doctrinal point in Dante's time than it would nowadays perhaps, only at the Lateran Council in 1215 was it laid down as an obligation for the good Catholic to confess to a priest.

The symbolic procession in the earthly paradise merits a summary. As Dante follows Matilda up the stream, he is aware first of the forest becoming illuminated; then he catches sight of the seven candelabra (the sevenfold spirit of God) trailing streamers of light behind them (the gifts of the Holy Spirit); under this brightness march twenty-four elders clad in white (the books of the Old Testament). On their heels come four animals (the gospels), all with six many-eyed wings. Then comes the great triumphal chariot (the church) drawn by a gryphon (Christ), that is, a creature half golden eagle (indicating the purity of the divine nature), half lion colored white and red like human flesh. Three "nymphs," red, green, and snow-white (the theological virtues), dance on the right of the chariot; on the left wheel four others (the cardinal virtues) likewise dance, all dressed in purple and one of them (prudence) having three eyes. Seven ancients, white-clad and crowned with red roses (the seven books of the New Testament, other than the gospels,) close the procession. Beatrice (revelation), riding on the car, in due course makes her appearance to Dante, at which point the allegory takes on a somewhat different meaning. This medieval artifact has been called a kind of *auto sacramental;* it may owe something to the Corpus Christi processions which Grandgent[8] reminds us were coming into vogue in the years of the *Commedia.* Dante introduces it with a special invocation and surrounds it with much embellishing detail, and doctrinally it is all quite clear (at least until Beatrice comes to merge the personal with the institutional). But this doctrinal clarity is supplied at the expense of the richness of the more truly Dantesque allegory, and indeed even of the realism normally so characteristic of Dante. Taylor rather harshly characterized the procession as "formal and lifeless,"[9] and it is certainly, in one sense, un-Dantesque. A female who is green all over may be an excellent symbol of hope, but she is hardly attractive to look upon; the three eyes of prudence, whatever they may do to intensify her allegorical impact, seem rather an unpleasant abnormality on the purely visual plane; nor is a hybrid beast a very appealing picture of the Savior.

After the Beatrician interlude, conventional allegory takes over again: we see the chariot of the church drawn to the tree of law, shattered and later feathered by the eagle (the persecutions and the Donation of Constantine), raided by a vixen (heresy) which Beatrice chases away, half dismembered by a dragon (the Great Schism?), covered by lush growth (clerical corruption), and finally serving as a vehicle for a harlot (the Roman Curia) wantoning with a giant (the House of France) who later beats her and drags the chariot off into the forest (the "Babylonian captivity" of Avignon.) This part of the allegory, more historical than doctrinal, is presented with vivid vigor, but is cut from essentially the same formalized cloth. A vixen as heresy, whose evil deeds and defeat by true doctrine we witness, is not as moving a picture as that of the heretic Farinata in the *Inferno,* though no doubt safer doctrinally, for Farinata is more appealing than heresy should be.

Another meaning that the poem intentionally bears, although Dante does not mention it in his letter to Can Grande, is what one might call the personal allegory. While Dante is the privileged witness and faithful reporter of the events of the *Commedia,* he is also the central figure of the drama. In a sense, he is the drama. The *Commedia* is a very subjective poem, a confession and an autobiography, perhaps the first true autobiography of the middle ages, even though it is, in Curtius' term, "stylized."[10] A good deal of what Dante says about himself is straightforward: he tells of his exile, his friends, his masters, and his literary models from Virgil to Arnaut Daniel; but much is offered as allegory, usually but not always transparent.

The first canto of the poem is a good example. No sinners or penitents have appeared, so what goes on in the dark wood can have no bearing on "rewards or punishments" in this life. It is Dante's story; he tells us that at the age of thirty-five *("nel mezzo del cammin")* he had strayed from virtue, was confused in mind and soul, knew where to look for succor but could not find the way by himself. The high hill represents the difficult path of reform, and the beasts he encounters symbolize his own evil impulses (the conventional interpretation identifies the beautiful leopard with lust, the lion with pride, and the wolf with avarice, but the exact identification does not matter greatly) that stand in the way of his salvation. Neither reason nor philosophy nor classical learning (for Virgil represents all three indifferently) is enough to save him, though they do slow his downward flight. Only Christianity, represented by Beatrice, who also specifically represents revelation and theology, can do it, and before he can be saved, someone (here the Virgin Mary) must spontaneously confer the needed grace. And here the allegory merges into the theological. There are other flashes of personal allegory in the *Inferno:* Dante's sympathy with Francesca; his terror before the walls of Dis when the Furies stand before him and only Virgil's warning saves him from being turned to stone by Medusa; his self-caution as he prepares to study the false counselors, who have a mental keenness that he knows is his birthright too; his vulnerability to Virgil's rebuke as he seems to take too much pleasure in the exchange of abuse between Sinon and Adam of Brescia.

But the personal allegory, like the other kinds of allegory, is most evident in the *Purgatorio*. Dante's reactions to the sins he encounters in the terraces of purgatory amount to a catalogue of his own sinful propensities and an examination of his own conscience. The only sin that frightens him significantly is lust, and he can be brought through its fires only by an appeal to Beatrice, the pure, unsensual love of his youth. As for the rest, he bows with the proud, makes the point that he does not expect to spend much time among the envious (in whose terrace he is the only one who can see), and is not really concerned with the avaricious and the gluttonous. He does, however, suffer the obscurity of the wrathful. There are subtler evidences of the personal allegory also. Casella's singing Dante's song and so bringing on the reproach of Cato for postponing the beginning of his penance is an allegory of general and "moral" nature but it contains something of the personal. The three steps of the gate mentioned above may be seen as having a personal, as well as a general, point of reference, and the great purgatorial procession is of the same mixed nature until the dialogue with Beatrice begins, at which point it becomes purely (or at least primarily) personal. It becomes cryptic as well, since we do not know whether the *"pargoletta"* (the error or straying for which Dante is so mercilessly chided here) is a real "other woman," or sensual attraction, or merely a philosophical-spiritual deviation. Probably it is one and all. Charles Williams remarks: "The guilt which every lover must sooner or later feel towards the vision . . . may here be named according as every lover must in his own case name it,"[11] which is an excellent statement of the human allegory.

The purely personal allegory is not much in evidence in the *Paradiso*. Dante tells us more about himself in this *cantica* than he does in either of the others, but mainly in open, "unveiled" language, although the outburst on the joys of contemplation in canto XI is an outstanding exception. This is a symbolic expression of a kind of Augustinian rapture, couched in easily translated narrative terms. Magnificent similes are found in the attempt to describe the ultimate vision in the last canto, but from Dante's point of view there is nothing allegorical about his state; he is simply groping for ways to describe a mystic vision.

The personal allegory can also be extended to include the rest of mankind. In the first *terzina* of the *Commedia,* Dante has lost his way in "the middle of *our* life's journey," so that we are involved in his sinfulness, and Dante is a kind of Everyman. Thus the subject includes the second person as well as the first; we may think of the "souls in this world properly rewarded or punished" as the third person. Even as Dante is a spectator of his own openly advertised allegory, but also a participant, the subject, indeed, of the more intimate one, so too is the reader. His hell-probings, his glance into the potential horrors of his own soul, his eagerness to strive once the freedom of choice is made clear to him — these are the reader's also. And so too may be the ecstasy of the vision, after due instruction and preparation, provided he has eaten of the bread of the angels and is not attempting to follow the mighty ship in too small a bark. Certain aspects of the "moral allegory" come into play here: turning left in hell and right in purgatory, the arduous path up from the center of

evil to the stars of a hopeful dawn, the dark, uncertain change
of direction in the last canto of the *Inferno* (in which reason and
the dead weight of sin have their part), the triumphant winning
of spiritual innocence and serene self-assurance, are ours as much
as Dante's.

This aspect of Dante's allegorical variety has come in for much
study in recent years, and under the aspect of the fourth level
of meaning, or supersense, has been given a mystical interpretation by many contemporary scholars. Charles Singleton's *Journey
to Beatrice* is a subtle and eloquent study of the "prodigious
apocalyptic epiphany" (as Northrop Frye calls it[12]) of the meeting on the mount. He develops in great detail the anagogical
meaning of the soul's return to God. A necessary part of this
kind of exploration is the medieval "figural" allegory. As in the
traditional scriptural exegesis, for example, Joshua, historically
true himself, prefigures Jesus, so Beatrice, while remaining the
Florentine girl and not necessarily surrendering her role as revelation, is a figure of Christ. The richness of the figural method in
the *Commedia* has been stressed by Auerbach, who sees in it
Dante's main allegorical strategy and ultimately, if paradoxically,
the source of his realism.[13] Critics such as Singleton and Charles
Williams would make Dante a true mystic. For the latter, Dante
is a mystic of a very special kind, a follower of the Way of
Affirmation.[14] Even if it does not make mystics of us all, even
if we have some doubts about Dante's own mysticism, yet the
personal allegory, closely woven into the fragment of the narrative, gives the poem its dynamism. It involves the reader in the
pilgrim's journey, and in the poet's epic. By the time we have
reached paradise the poet is our intimate, sharing with us his
hopes and his difficulties when he says in canto XXIII:

> Wherefore in symbolizing paradise,
> The sacred poem, as it were, must leap
> As one who finds obstruction in his path.
> Yet one considering the weighty theme,
> And the mortal shoulders that are charged therewith,
> Will blame them not if under it they quake.
> It is no voyage for a little bark,
> The course my daring prow cuts through the waves,
> Nor for a helmsman sparing of himself.

Subtle-minded exegetes have found other hidden meanings in
the *Commedia,* including various political and quasi-political in-

terpretations. Gabriele Rossetti in the early nineteenth century propounded the theory that the work was a vast anti-papal Ghibelline tract, an anticipatory gospel of the Reformation, couched in cryptic language because of the author's fear of persecution.[15] For Rossetti the narrative was a mere shallow pretext, and he elicited political meanings even from the embellishing metaphors. Such a theory was perhaps a natural product of the Risorgimento, eager to find in its somewhat romantic concept of the middle ages support for its own contingent anti-clericalism. After all, could not the savior Veltro (greyhound) be read as an anagram of Lutero (Luther)? And many an ardent Fascist of recent memory saw in the Dux of *Purgatorio* XXXIII a prophecy of his own Duce. Another reading of the poem sees it as a defense of the Templars, which would explain Dante's hostility to Philip the Fair though almost none of the rest of his political opinions. This theory has considerable vitality and was revived not long ago by R. L. John.[16]

Other esoteric interpretations, stressing less the political than the cultural, may be mentioned. The exposition of the poem by the poet Giovanni Pascoli is based on a mixture of Virgilian and Augustinian associations. It is often fanciful and inconsistent, but rich in fruitful observations which have found their way into many editions of the *Commedia*. Valli's studies, which owe much to Pascoli, find in Dante and his fellow poets a secret beauty cult, a sort of unorthodox Platonism. It must be said that if some of these readings of hidden meanings seem rather farfetched, Dante is not entirely free from blame. His numerology, his apocalyptic monsters, and his occasional sybilline pronouncements have encouraged the cabalistic-minded. A poet who would find a secure niche in heaven for Joachim da Fiore reveals a certain respect for mystification and may be expected to indulge in it himself when the humor takes him.

Another kind of allegory, related to the personal, is what we might call the literary. There are many passages in the poem clearly intended to tell us something about Dante the artist. When he makes himself sixth of the group of poets in *Inferno* IV, he is deliberately putting himself on a level with them — at least in aspiration. If we find him presumptuous, we may excuse him by seeing in his statement a kind of professional assertion. He is a spokesman for the new vernacular poetry and is simply affirming the dignity of that poetry. Stambler, commenting on *Purgatorio* XXIV, says: "When Forese, his youthful companion in one kind of poetry, strides off on the path he must take, Dante follows —

or by this time, walks beside — the two marshals of another concept of poetry."[17] Louis Rossi, in an interesting unpublished dissertation,[18] recalls that one of the earlier commentators, Benvenuto da Imola, pressed this kind of interpretation very far, making Dante's composition of his book all but synonymous with his mission. According to Benvenuto, Dante's hesitation in following Virgil in *Inferno* II is not that of a pilgrim frightened by the journey but that of a poet alarmed at the task he has set himself. The heavenly messenger who comes to his aid outside the walls of Dis is a personified eloquence, sent to enable him to deal with the difficult task of describing the lower hell. Rossi, who has collected and summarized a number of such interpretations, calls them examples of "a professional and technical allegory." In our time, Gertrude Leigh finds that the souls in limbo allude to Dante's early childhood readings in the classics.[19] Recently the French critic André Pézard has suggested that Brunetto Latini is in hell not for sodomy but for the "sin" of writing his great work in French rather than in his native Tuscan.[20] The interpretation is worked out through a theological approach, but in its conclusions it is an example of "literary" allegory.

The character-symbols of the poem are rich in provocative possibilities of interpretation. On the central trio of Virgil, Beatrice, and Dante the pilgrim much has been written. We have noted Charles Williams' four meanings of Virgil; Beatrice too is susceptible of multiple interpretations, ranging from the traditional theology or revelation to the analogue of Christ in her appearance to Dante at the summit of the Mount of Purgatory. Dante himself is a character-symbol of many facets: he is Everyman, he is the Christian on the way of redemption.[21] Helen Flanders Dunbar calls him a "type of Christ . . . in his destined and foretold sufferings and in the fruits of his victory . . . his mission undertaken at last in knowledge and love."[22]

Deeper than these rather specialized interpretations lie the hidden meanings of image, symbol, and suggestion which, if less easily definable, are even more fundamental in giving the *Commedia* its enduring strength and appeal. The poem contains many elements which have their origins in prehistory and their correspondences in folklore and which appeal to us, whether or not we stop to analyze their nature, on a subconscious, almost instinctive, level. August Rüegg relates the journey to the world of the dead not only to Virgil and through him to Homer, but to roots lying far below these obvious literary sources. He stresses the aspect of solemn obligation in this ritualistic exploration: "Necessity, not sport, leads him on," says Virgil of his pupil in *Inferno* XII, even as Odysseus, obeying an ancient law, was compelled to carry out the inexorable commands of Circe.[23] We have already mentioned the affinity of the narrative scheme to the age-old quest motif. At the beginning and the end of the *Paradiso* Dante refers to Jason's voyage, and his vision is his own golden fleece. Northrop Frye says: "Of all fictions, the marvellous journey is the one formula that is never exhausted, and it is this fiction that is employed as a parable in the definitive encyclopedic poem of the mode, Dante's *Commedia*."[24] He elsewhere remarks on certain archetypal figures which make their appearance as Dantesque symbol-images: "the prison or dungeon . . . like the city of Dis" (hell itself is in fact "the cave"); the "labyrinth or maze, the image of lost direction," which "can also be a sinister forest"; "the refining fire"; and the like.[25] The "light metaphysics" too, particularly evident in the *Paradiso,* may have its immediate intellectual origins in Neoplatonism but surely is rooted in the sun-worship of our forgotten ancestors. The recurrent ritual of immersion or token immersion of the protagonist at significant moments in his pilgrimage — in Acheron, on the shores of purgatory, in the rivers of the earthly paradise, and in the lucent stream of grace — suggests not only Christian baptism but ancient rituals of lustration, practised before Jordan was named. Although I am not acquainted with any thorough Freudian exegesis, it would not be hard to see Freudian symbols in many of the monsters, and indeed the forms of the three realms are very suggestive. For Gertrude Leigh the vestibule of the indifferent is a figure of the stillborn; the crossing of the Acheron, the process of birth; and Dante's fainting, a clear allusion to the birth shock.[26] Father Musurillo sees the descent to hell as "a return to the womb of humanity";[27] several contemporary critics have seen the mother and father images patently set forth in Virgil and Beatrice.

How much of the compelling imagery of the *Commedia* is self-consciously doctrinal and how much has its roots in the barbarous sublimity so much admired by Vico would be hard to say. It seems likely that at least most of it was Christian and didactic, but the sophisticated allegories are built on ancient and firm foundations of which the architect must have been instinctively aware. The four — or more — meanings intellectualize and channel but never dissipate the intuitional vitality of the poem.

❧ 14 ❧

The *Commedia*: Doctrine

THE didactic motivation which characterizes all of Dante's work is patent in the *Commedia;* one need not look either to allegory or to indirect suggestion to find it. In *Inferno* XVII the poet expresses the hope that his poem will be full of spiritual profit for the reader; in the *Purgatorio* he accepts Beatrice's charge to bring back report of what he has seen for the good of mankind; in the *Paradiso* we hear Cacciaguida encourage him to publish his work not only for the sake of his own immortal fame but because, in spite of its bitter savor to some, it will be beneficial to the world.

Instruction is of course inherent in the allegory of the poem; and as the narrative is designed to support the "true" sense, so is the latter intended to teach. The whole journey is instructional, primarily but by no means exclusively in Christian doctrine. But aside from the pedagogical aspects of allegory, whether inherent or incidental, there is also a good deal of overt, "unveiled" instruction in the *Commedia,* increasing in proportion as Dante moves from realm to realm — one is tempted to say, from class to advanced class.

Inferno XI, essential to an understanding of the journey through hell, where Virgil describes its doctrinal plan, is an instructional passage unadorned by allegory. Virgil's description begins with a general statement that malice, the end of which is injury, is offensive to heaven, and that this end can be achieved by

265

either violence or fraud. Violence can be directed against neighbor, self, or God (in ascending order of heinousness), and each of these three kinds of violence can be subdivided. Violence against neighbor comprehends murder and assault; against self, suicide and wanton waste of property (since property is in a way part of oneself); violence against God directly is blasphemy, but disdaining nature, which is God's creature, is also violence against Him, so that sodomy and usury (which is violence against human industry) are included here. The violent are punished in the seventh circle.

Fraud is divided into two categories. Sinners guilty of deceiving their fellow men are confined in the *malebolge* of the eighth circle, and those guilty of the more vicious fraud of betraying a particular trust are in the ninth circle. The worst of this last group are Judas, as betrayer of the church, and Brutus and Cassius, as betrayers of the state.

Virgil adds that the sinners in the first five circles are guilty of incontinence only, which is less offensive, according to Aristotle, than violence and fraud.

We may note in passing that the doctrine as here expounded also strengthens the narrative interest; the reader, like the pilgrim Dante, feels a shudder of curiosity as to just who is to be found in the categories yet to come, and what kind of punishment is to be dealt out to them. Noteworthy too is the very rigorous schematization: not only do the three successive descending main divisions signify the increasing gravity of the sin, but within these large groupings the same hierarchical principle is at work. Violence against God is lower, i.e., worse, than hostility towards one's neighbor. We may assume that in the *malebolge* Dante, for reasons not always clear and often purely subjective, considers flattery worse than seduction, simony graver than either, and so on down. Broadly speaking (but, happily for the narrative, not consistently), the reactions of Dante the pilgrim reinforce the concept. Francesca's story moves him to compassion, while on the ice of Cocytus he casually and cruelly kicks one sinner in the face and does not hesitate himself to betray a traitor.

The reasoning back of Dante's design has attracted the attention of commentators for years. One would normally expect a medieval poet dealing with moral error to follow the accepted canon of the seven deadly sins, which is indeed what our poet does in the *Purgatorio*. For his hell Dante was seeking a philosophical rather than a purely religious base. It is to be open to all; Christian, pagan, and unbeliever. His scheme, by no means unorthodox, must be truly nonsectarian. His sinners, says Father Kenelm Foster, "would be sinners in any world that is human at all," and he remarks that only the heretics and simonists "are Christian sinners, in the sense that their sins presuppose a Christian world."[1] It may be added that all the heretics we hear of are Epicureans, deniers of the soul's immortality, whom Dante would consider sinners under any religion, as he indicates in the *Convivio.* Limbo might be thought of as another exception, perhaps, but the souls there are not truly sinners and undergo no torment. It is interesting to note that in his exposition Virgil does not mention either limbo or the heretics.

Dante finds his principle in Aristotle, but an Aristotle perhaps misunderstood, modified, and filtered through St. Thomas Aquinas. In *Ethics* VII three kinds of wrongdoing are mentioned; which, in the Latin translation available to St. Thomas, come out as *malitia, incontinentia,* and *bestialitas.* But neither in Aristotle nor in St. Thomas do the terms have quite the meaning that Dante gives them. He did, however, find in Cicero's *De Officiis* the distinction between *vis* and *fraus* which he adapted to the Aristotelian trio, coming out with an arrangement essentially his own. Francesco Flamini, whom I have followed in this discussion, justifies the presence of pagans and heretics in hell, remarking that

Dante has reserved for them a kind of moral weakness that Aristotle, who lived "before Christianity," could not know: infidelity. And he has placed that infidelity which proceeds from lack of faith in the first circle of the entire abyss (as a negative sin less grave than the others); and that which proceeds from opposition to faith . . . , which is called heresy (*haeresis*) inasmuch as it implies choice, in the sixth circle, which is the first of those comprised within the city of Dis, the abode of "moral evil from choice."[2]

We may add that the attitude of Dante the pilgrim is very sympathetic to the first group — he rejoices in the opportunity granted him to see the great pagans of antiquity — and not without respect for the second, so heroically symbolized by Farinata. He looks upon both categories with a very different glance from that cast contemptuously upon the indifferent, a class not even worthy of a place in hell.

It will be useful here to look beyond the *Inferno* to the doctrinal disposition of the *Purgatorio*. The pattern of exposition is quite similar. As the poets pause on the terrace of the slothful (again well after the beginning of the ascent), Virgil, at Dante's urging (as before), embarks upon his lecture. He begins with the axiom that all creatures are endowed with two kinds of love: the natural sort that cannot err and the love *"d'animo"* (where free will comes into play) that can — and in three different ways. Love can be misdirected, i.e., it can choose evil; it can be insufficient; and it can be excessive. Virgil clarifies his meaning yet further: the misdirected love must be in effect hatred of one's neighbor, for one cannot hate oneself nor, since we all exist in God, the Godhead. The sins of pride, envy, and anger are all seen as aspects of hatred of one's fellow man. Insufficient love must be understood as meaning insufficient love of the true Good, i.e., of God. Excessive love, on the other hand, means excessive love of secondary goods (food or possessions, for example), which are not evil in themselves but are not "the true essence." Such error is subdivided according to its object and is spelled out as avarice, gluttony, and lust.

Certain similarities to the scheme of the *Inferno* are immediately apparent. In both cases the subdivisions reveal Dante's moral hierarchy. The order of gravity in the *Inferno* is incontinence, violence, and fraud; on the Mount of Purgatory the categories of misdirected love are lowest (i.e., worst) while incontinence appears at the highest level and is clearly regarded as less pernicious than the trio of hate. The total parade of sinners and penitents begins and ends with lust. As it is exemplified by characters for whom Dante professes respect and sympathy, it would not be unreasonable to assume that he had a certain tolerance for this weakness, either professionally in his capacity of love poet or (as Boccaccio openly affirms) temperamentally. Another similarity may be seen in the abundance of subcategories; this is richer in the *Inferno*, with its six classes of violence and the ten ditches of the *malebolge*, but purgatory is not lacking in such distinctions. Three kinds of pride and two kinds of lust are exemplified on the appropriate terraces. The Ante-Purgatory (which is Dante's own invention) is quite subtly divided into four areas, and it serves a double purpose. It reinforces the doctrinal point that the sufferings of purgatory are, in spite of their severity, a privilege; the souls are impatient to begin their penance, and those who have for one reason or another put off making their peace with God are actually envious (if such a word may be used of embryonic saints) of those already undergoing the various torments. But the Ante-Purgatory is also, as Wilkins has pointed out,[3] an esthetic necessity. If we were to go straight from *Inferno* XXXIV to *Purgatorio* X we should have one series of cruel and painful scenes superimposed on another. Some surcease is needed and it is given us as we tread the shore and lower slopes of purgatory in the company of Casella, Manfred, Belacqua, and the rest, whom we can see in approachable humanity, not yet blinded, choked, or groaning under massive burdens.

As we compare the two doctrinal patterns of hell and purgatory we are struck by the discrepancies in the treatment of the sins of incontinence. Anger in the *Inferno* follows directly on avarice; in the *Purgatorio* it belongs to the trio of misdirected love, and is not a sin of incontinence at all. Sloth is not clearly defined in the *Inferno;* a kind of sullen indolence is apparent in the souls sunk in the Stygian slime in canto VII but it is hard to dismiss the notion that the real slothful are to be found among the indifferent in the vestibule, and so are not classified as a part of hell. But — most puzzling absence of all — where are pride and envy, those mighty champions without whose vigorous collaboration the Adversary would be all but helpless against the children of Eve?

Essential to the understanding of this apparent lacuna in Dante's adaptation of his own system to the conventional one of his day is an appreciation of the distinction between the souls of the *Inferno* and those of the *Purgatorio.* It is strange, looking back over the long history of Dante exegesis, to find so many commentators either silent or uncertain on this point. It was not until the nineteenth century that critics saw the problem clearly — or at least gave it clear exposition. Witte was among the first, and he is worth quoting. In his *Essays on Dante* he says:

In juridical language the punishment of the damned is exclusively penal, the penance of the souls seeking purification remedial. . . . The penal codes of earth and hell are . . . analogous in taking note of deeds only, and not of guilty thoughts which have resulted in no overt acts. . . . It is the act then which is punished, not the sinful motives that prompted it. Cain was impelled to fratricide by envy, but it is for fratricide, not for envy, that he is banished to the deepest chasm of Hell.[4]

In short it is the act (if unrepented) which is punished in hell. But in purgatory all sinful acts have been repented of, otherwise the souls would not have found the way there; what has to be purged (not punished) is what Witte calls "sinful propensities." This is indicated clearly enough in Dante's language in *Purgatorio* XVII: love *"si torce"* ("is twisted") or *"corre"* ("runs," "turns") toward good with insufficient or excessive zeal. In Dante's view, so far as the sins of incontinence are concerned, act and tendency may be of the same stock, as it were. Francesca is in hell for an act of lust, but presumably had she repented she would be purging herself on the uppermost terrace of the mount. But the act of violence of the highwayman Rinier Pazzo in *Inferno* XII, for example, may have been rooted in avarice, the deceit of Ulysses in pride, and the treachery of Bocca degli Abati in envy. Envy and pride are therefore by no means absent from the *Inferno,* for the unrepented acts of which they were the source are punished in the various categories Dante has set up for deeds of wickedness. As a corollary (if one may borrow Dante's own phrase), an understanding of this distinction is helpful also in explaining another seeming inconsistency. For Dante says — or makes Virgil say — in the *Purgatorio* that it is impossible for the human soul to hate itself, and, since all souls dwell in God, impossible also for the soul to hate God. Yet most readers at this point will pause and ask, "What then of the suicides and the blasphemers?" To which the same answer can be made: the *act* of Pier delle Vigne was against himself; the motivation, as his story makes clear, was pride.

There is a curious anomaly in Dante's scheme, both in the *Inferno* and the *Purgatorio:* his stress on the identity of prodigality and avarice. In *Inferno* VII both the spendthrifts and the avaricious endure the same punishment, "because they made no expenditure in moderation," and in *Purgatorio* XXII Statius explains that he is atoning for his spendthrift years in the terrace of the avaricious. It is difficult to make sense of this in a Christian context; the examples of Christ and St. Francis should have induced, one would think, a certain contempt for material goods in Dante. Further, in neither of Virgil's expositions of sins does he mention prodigality. Grandgent suggests that Dante has in mind "the Aristotelian arrangement of vices in pairs of extremes,"[5] and Statius' statement that the opposites of sins purged in purgatory are also "withered away" seems to confirm this, although how a Christian can think of too much mildness or too much chastity as a sin is difficult to imagine. The classical idea of "nothing in excess" is a kind of marketplace morality which has always had its appeal, both in the ancient authors Dante was so fond of and in Bertran de Born and Sordello, to name only two of his contemporaries that he was probably familiar with. Still, the notion is puzzling, and it has been ignored by most commentators. Grandgent does suggest that Dante was warning his readers of a sin that he was guilty of,[6] but there is no evidence that he was a spendthrift.

With the exception of canto XI, there is not a great deal of doctrinal instruction in the *Inferno* — at least by comparison with the other two *cantiche.* The major lesson of dogma, illustrated by the case of Guido da Montefeltro and voiced by the suave demon who bears him off, is the crucial Christian tenet that the fate of the soul depends on its state at the moment of death. Another area recurrently touched on is the condition of the damned after Judgment Day, but such matters are dealt with briefly.

The didactic content of the *Inferno* is not limited to the purely theological. Dante tells us what he thinks of Florence, how "new people and easy money" have created an arrogant and pretentious society, and Brunetto Latini enlarges upon the jealousies rampant in the wicked city; we get a good deal of historical information, such as the story of the founding of Mantua; while the invectives against the papal court, Pistoia, Genoa, Pisa, and Florence, and reports such as the one made to Guido da Montefeltro, are statements of the poet's opinions on the nature of various Italian cities and institutions.

Francesca's speech is a summary of the code of courtly love and its compulsions; and the passage on Fortune, though slightly allegorized, may be regarded as Dante's findings on the question, fascinating and puzzling to the middle ages, of the movement of worldly goods from family to family and state to state.

In the *Purgatorio* there is more direct instruction than in the *Inferno.* Cato lays down the law of the realm in no uncertain terms in canto I, Manfred adds his word on the limitations of the clergy in the matter of absolution in canto III, and the doctrine of the prayers of the living as helpful to the souls in purgatory is clearly set forth by Belacqua and annotated by Virgil in canto VI. The remarks of Guido del Duca in canto XIV on earthly and spiritual goods are the beginning of an almost unbroken straight-forward exposition of dogma which ends with the lengthy disquisition of Virgil in canto XVII on the nature of the Mount of Purgatory and the evil tendencies purged on its terraces. Theological definitions of love, instinct, and free will dominate canto XVIII, and the addition of Statius to the company leads to further and longer informational passages, of which the most notable is the discussion of human generation and the relation of the soul to the body. Most of what Statius has to say is not only orthodox but Thomistic, but the picture of a kind of aerial frame forming around the potential of the soul is Dante's own invention and is vital to his narrative. Much more doctrine is presented by Matilda and Beatrice, even though in the last cantos it is the allegory that predominates.

Aside from the allegory of the history of the church to which we have referred, there are several long passages of historical information or commentary in which Dante speaks directly or through a character without benefit of the poetic veil. After his encounter with Sordello he steps directly into the story, to tell about the miserable state of Italy, suffering from the venal usurpation of imperial authority by the papacy and the neglect of the emperor, divided into warring factions and finding no peace. Immediately after that passage a survey of recent rulers in the valley of the princes enables Dante to inform — or indoctrinate — the reader about contemporary political conditions throughout Europe.

Canto XX contains a capsule history of France, with particular reference to the events of Dante's own generation and a rather partisan exclusion of St. Louis, whose presence might have blunted the diatribe on the consistent depravity of the Capetian line. Guido del Duca in canto XIV, aside from the doctrinal content of his remarks, portrays the varying degrees of wickedness of the cities of the Valdarno (the allegory of the beasts is so patent as to be mere name-calling) and proceeds with more outspoken comments on the decadent nobility of Romagna. With like clarity Sapia tells of the foolish attempt of the Sienese to build a harbor and to tap their underground water supply, Marco Lombardo reports on the unhappy state of civic morality in the March of Treviso, and Forese Donati speaks with feeling of the wanton style of dress of the women of Florence. Scientific information is given here and there, notably in the discussion of the sun's path in canto IV, where Dante almost indicates that he finds Virgil a little unnecessarily informative. Statius' exposition on the nature of the soul begins with a straightforward passage that is more biological than doctrinal, although the ornamental metaphors are unusually beautiful.

Of particular interest is Dante's avowal of his poetic inheritance and his theories. He tells Guido Guinizelli openly of his indebtedness to Guido's work, and he indicates, by allowing him to introduce Arnaut Daniel, his admiration for that rather enigmatic troubadour. He speaks disparagingly of Guittone, and in canto XXIV openly proclaims his own credo:

> . . . Io mi son un che quando
> Amor mi spira, noto, e a quel modo
> ch' e' ditta dentro, vo significando.

I am one who, when/love inspires me, takes note, and according/as he dictates within me, so I signify.

This statement has been much discussed by critics and remains still somewhat obscure. It sounds as though Dante meant that he thought of himself as a kind of spontaneous "nature's child," which could not be further from the truth. Perhaps he means that he did not, as his predecessors had done, "substitute convention for introspection," in Grandgent's phrase;[7] perhaps he merely felt, as all "new" poets feel when they come of age, that the older school simply did not have the right understanding of poetry; perhaps "love" means a complex of intellectual-emotional attitudes which Dante thought to be original with him and his fellow writers of the *dolce stil nuovo*. The word *"amor"* here "takes on a sense of intimate and almost religious experience," says Sapegno.[8] In any event, the tercet is on the surface a clear-cut expression of poetic theory, and it may be considered another aspect of the "informational" Dante.

In speaking of the transitory nature of worldly fame in canto XI, he tells us through the mouth of Oderisi da Gubbio that Cimabue has been replaced by Giotto in popular esteem, and

> "così ha tolto l'un all'altro Guido
> la gloria della lingua; e forse è nato
> chi l'uno e l'altro caccerà del nido."

"likewise one Guido has taken from the other/the glory of our tongue; and perhaps one is (already) born/ who will chase both from the nest."

The passage shows us, to quote Sapegno once more, that Dante "had a true awareness of his own worth and his position in history."[9]

For Dante, paradise was clearly the place where one learned things, so that there is more overt didactic matter in the *Paradiso* than in the other *cantiche*. It is not entirely fanciful to find significance in the fact that the word *"dottrina"* occurs twice in the *Inferno*, four times in the *Purgatorio*, and six times in the *Paradiso*; nor to note that the *Inferno* begins with a straight-forward narrative statement, the *Purgatorio* with a metaphor, and the *Paradiso* with a statement of dogma. And with dogma, clearly and forcefully put, the *Paradiso* is replete. To enumerate all the informational items would be to repeat a good deal of our summary in Chapter 12, for even the "action" of the *Paradiso* is instructional. In canto I Beatrice's explanation of the "great sea of being" is pure dogma, as is her affirmation of the soul's natural tendency to rise. Her discussion on the origin of souls in canto V is followed by a discourse on the nature of vows, as we have noted. These are outright lectures — and there are many more. This is the *cantica* in which Dante is talked to (as again our summary has made statistically clear): his role throughout is that of the patient and attentive listener. The figure of the opening chapters of the *Convivio* comes to mind here; Dante does scarcely anything else but pick up the crumbs falling from the saintly tables of the *Paradiso* and share them — almost too zealously — with those not so privileged as he.

To follow yet a little further the stout thread of doctrine: in the heaven of Mercury, Beatrice outlines the dogma of the incarnation and redemption; in Venus Dante learns, by the examples shown him, of God's mysterious ways of bringing a soul to salvation; St. Thomas, in the sun, cautions him on how to read the Bible; we have Solomon's reassurance on the state of our resurrected flesh in the same sphere. We have alluded to the dogma involved in the salvation of Ripheus the Trojan; the great souls in the eagle of Jupiter spell out divine justice for us; we learn that for all the evil effects of his famous Donation, Constantine is saved because of the purity of his intention. St. Benedict in the heaven of Saturn touches on God's predestination. In the starry sphere, after a symbolic vision of the heavenly court and its Queen, Dante undergoes his climactic examination on faith, hope and charity. Benedetto Croce finds this scene very human and slightly comic, as though great scholars, Peter and his colleagues, were good-naturedly examining a youngster on elementary subjects.[10] In fact Dante compares himself to a candidate for a degree. His orthodox answers come forth almost too complacently, one feels, and they are in essence simple dogma, plainly phrased, though adorned by beautiful rhetoric. In the *primum mobile* Beatrice takes advantage of another symbolic vision to expatiate on the nature of the angels.

A magnificent allegorical passage brings us into the presence of the Rose, in the empyrean heaven beyond time and space, and here the symbolic embellishment all but carries us away, yet there is plenty of overt dogma. St. Bernard points out to Dante that the Mystic Rose is very carefully compartmentalized. Half the places will be filled after Judgment Day with those who had faith in Christ to come, half with those who followed Him after His advent. The lower half of the great amphitheatre — for such is the function of the Rose — will be filled with the souls of children saved by the forethought of their parents in attending to their baptism (or circumcision in the case of the Jews); each individual place is assigned in accordance with the child's potential, known only to God. Even Dante's ultimate ecstasy ends with a dogmatic symbol of the three Persons of the Trinity in which, in a way not to be explained, the human semblance is blended.

Dante expounds too a good deal of medieval science. Perhaps the most celebrated passage of this sort is Beatrice's discussion of the spots on the moon, which has interested many commentators because of her use of the experimental method in making her point. A description of the Ptolemaic cosmography, the nature of years and seasons, and minor points such as the length of the Earth's shadow and the epicycle of Venus are mentioned sometimes with allegorical purposes, but always as scientific truths. Dante does not forget his linguistic interest either; and we have noted in the summary of the *Paradiso* Adam's remarks on languages in canto XXVI.

The longest sustained passage of historical information is the story of the Roman eagle in canto VI, which is in effect an outline history of the empire. It is a matching piece to the embittered chronicle of the House of France in canto XX of the *Purgatorio,* and may be regarded as a kind of corollary to the story of the church in canto XXXII, where the empire is symbolized by an eagle. As in the *De Monarchia*, Dante seems to accept without question the long gap between Titus and Charlemagne.

He turns his historical survey to political purpose, advising his contemporary Ghibellines not to use the imperial standard as a partisan symbol, and the Guelphs to beware of "the claws/ Which have reft the pelt from mightier lions" than they may claim to be. Charles Martel critizes the bad government of his brother. Cunizza deplores the sad state of Treviso in terms reminiscent of Guido da Montefeltro's Romagna, or of Mark the Lombard's decadent province. St. Peter inveighs against his successors of Dante's day. The eagle, after its pronouncement on the nature of divine justice, makes a scathing survey of contemporary rulers, who, it contends, will shame all Christendom. History and biting commentary are also artfully combined in the "biographies" of St. Francis and St. Dominic.

But perhaps the most interesting information in the *Paradiso* is the purely autobiographical. Probably for most readers the Cacciaguida cantos are the most absorbing, and these are cantos of open confession. Through Cacciaguida we learn something of the history of old Florence, interesting as much because it represents Dante's ideal as for its historical authenticity. We learn also of Dante's own feeling about his exile, his bitterness, his sense of injustice and misunderstanding even by those who share his banishment. Most important of all, we learn his purpose in writing the *Commedia:* to assure that immortality which alone could right the wrong done him by his contemporaries, and to serve a high moral purpose. In canto XXII he gives us the only real information we have about the date of his birth, and in canto V he tells of his nature, describing himself as *trasmutabile* (impressionable) in all ways. Poet's pride and exile's hope are both openly voiced in the unforgettable opening lines of canto XXV:

> If ever it may be the sacred poem —
> Whereto both heaven and earth have so set hand
> That it has made me lean year after year —
> May overcome the harshness barring me
> From the fair fold where I slept as a lamb,
> Foe to the wolves that war upon it now;

Then, with another voice, with altered fleece,
I shall return a poet, and at the font
Of my baptizing shall receive the wreath. . . .

Further testimony of what the poem has come to mean to its creator is to be found in canto XXIII where he speaks of the "weighty theme" borne by a "mortal shoulder," and in canto XXX with its reference to the "arduous substance." Arduous in truth it is and much of it medieval too; the *Paradiso* is the most medieval of the *cantiche.* Yet paradoxically it remains the most personal of the three; if doctrine is not poetry, yet as it is set forth in the *Paradiso* we can see it as essential to our knowledge of the poet — a poet who would as gladly learn and teach as compose a fair fiction.

❧ 15 ❧

The *Commedia*: Tools and Tactics

To say that Dante's greatest asset is the quality of his language is not as obvious as it may seem. There are poets whose basic language is something to be fought through and mastered before the substance of their poems can be understood, but Dante's language is nearly always clear and easy to understand, even when his thought is subtle and his implication obscure. T. S. Eliot says that his style is "the perfection of a common language."[1] Auerbach lists its "hallmarks" as "reality, adjuration, unity,"[2] and to them I would venture to add "intimacy" because, though Dante is both preacher and teacher, his tone suggests that he is eager to come down from the podium and talk directly to the reader.

He had achieved both language and style by way of a long and varied apprenticeship. In the *Commedia* it is not hard to find echoes of the delicacy of the *Vita Nuova*, the sturdy prose of the *Convivio*, and the various stages of study and training represented in the *Rime*. Dante remembered also — and, remembering, turned to his purpose — all he had heard and read, from the marketplace exchanges of his fellow citizens to the liturgical Latin of the church. Auerbach says: "The noble style in which the poem is written is a harmony of all the voices that had ever struck his ear."[3] He called on all such resources in the casting of the work that "made him lean," and his is not a triumph easily

278

won: we can all but see him struggling for it in the very simplicity which we admire, for the simple style is a very difficult one for the writer.

That he chose to write his great work in the language he had so painfully worked out for himself is a tribute to his assurance and to his belief in its future. Italians who like to build up the figure of Dante the patriot are right in seeing in this poem an act of faith in his country, a country which in a sense comes into being only with the *De Vulgari Eloquentia.* Readers who must approach Dante through another language may well be impressed by how much comes through even in translation. Although no poem can be translated without loss, the substance of the *Commedia* is so meaty that style, manner, and adornment, however beautiful, are of minor importance, as Dante meant them to be. Keats and Shelley, among others, came to know Dante first in Cary's translation and were sufficiently impressed to seek him in the original.

For Dante the beginning was in the word. The *De Vulgari Eloquentia* is proof of the careful attention that the poet gave to the proper selection of words, and though the prescriptions laid down in that work are not those followed in the great poem, the concern for the meaning and appropriateness of words is greater than ever. The range of his vocabulary is vast, from the "tongue calling 'mamma' and 'daddy' " and the scatological terms of the second *bolgia* of the *Inferno* to the high-sounding "umbriferous prefaces" and "flying plentitude" of the *Paradiso.* Most of his words are simple, however: he has nothing of the richness of Shakespeare or of the ornate verbalism characteristic of later Italian poets. There are occasional Latinisms and coined or unusual words, and a few technical terms, from the shop and the farm as well as from the world of scholarship, but, considering vocabulary alone, Dante is the easiest major Italian author to read. This is true in spite of the archaic nature of some grammatical forms, for in some matters of vocabulary and morphology today's Tuscan language is not the same as that of the fourteenth century, although of course Italian has suffered much less variation than English or French. We may add that Dante has rather infrequent recourse to diminutive endings and superlatives in *-issimo.* His use of these beguiling half-tones is the more effective as it is sparing. We cannot forget the *"timidette"* ("timid little") sheep, of which Manfred is one, in the *Purgatorio,* or the *"lagrimetta"* ("little tear") which saved Bonconte's soul, and how luminous is the *"chiarissima ancella"* ("brightest handmaiden") of the sun, an epithet that occurs nowhere else in the poem!

Although Dante is skilled in the arts of word-play and word-coloring, the impression one gets is that he is picking his words simply for their meaning rather than for connotation or rhetorical effect. He is not afraid, as any well-schooled Italian is nowadays, of repetition. There are many cases of a word repeated often within the same canto, and the poet does not try to find alternatives for the frequent "So he began," "He replied," "I turned," and the like.

Many cases of repetition are in fact deliberate, and may be classified under the heading of *annominatio,* a favorite figure of late antiquity and the middle ages. Curtius has counted two hundred examples (increasing in number with each *cantica*) of such pairs as *"selva selvaggia"* ("wild wood") and *"più volte volto"* ("turned several times"), and he remarks that not all commentators have seen the figure in such passages.[4] More obvious are the passages of epideictic (many-membered) *annominatio.* Curtius cites the words of Pier delle Vigne:

> "Infiammò contra me li animi tutti,
>   e li 'nfiammati infiammar si Augusto. . . ."

"(She) inflamed against me all spirits/and those inflamed so inflamed Augustus. . . . ,"

and the somewhat more subtle manipulation of "honor" and its derivatives in lines 72–78 of *Inferno* IV: *"orrevol"* ("honorable") *"onori"* ("honorest"), *"onranza"* ("honor"), *"onrata"* ("honored"), *"onorate"* ("do honor"). Another good example is the celebrated *"Amor ch'a nullo amato amar perdona"* ("Love which exempts no beloved from loving").

The figure is more successful in Italian than in English, since stress in English remains on the stem of the word, and a certain phonetic monotony is inevitable, whereas in the Italian, though the semantic affinity is clear, the stressed syllable is pleasantly varied. There are also many examples of word-play, or *bisticci,* as the Italians call them, not quite so easily definable: for example, the rather baroque phraseology of *Paradiso* XIV, 136–37, ". . . *escusar puommi di quel ch'io m'accuso/per escusarmi* . . ."

("[he] . . . may excuse me for that whereof I accuse myself/ in order to excuse myself . . ."); the pure and pointed puns: *"Savia non fui, avvegna che Sapía/fossi chiamata"* ("Not sapient I, although Sapía named"), *". . . perché fuor negletti/li nostri vóti, e vòti in alcun canto"* ("because neglected and in some sense void our vows"), or the rich double *annominatio* (if we may call it that) in the *Paradiso: "e moto a moto e canto a canto colse"* ("and measured move to move and song with song"). Highly functional is the celebrated *"Cred'io ch'ei credette ch'io credesse . . ."* ("I think he thought that I was thinking . . ."), which prepares us linguistically and conceptually for the courtier suicide; suggestive too is the seemingly casual juxtaposition of *"vero"* ("truth") and *"velo"* ("veil") in *Purgatorio* VIII.

Of the related device of alliteration, Dante is also a master, using it very frequently. *"E caddi come corpo morto cadde"* ("and I fell as a dead body falls"), is a little like the line from the *Paradiso* quoted above, with its admixture of *annominatio;* more authentic cases of simple alliteration may be seen in *"la colpa che là giù cotanto costa"* ("the crime that costs so cruelly below"), *"piangendo parea dicer: 'Più non posso'"* ("in tears seemed to be saying, 'I can bear no more'"), *"come per acqua cupa cosa grave"* ("as in dark water sinks a weighty thing").

Simple denotation is made to serve a high poetic purpose; all but unobtrusive, it yet colors all the realms. It has long been remarked that *Cristo* and *Maria* are never mentioned in hell, but this is a small item in the general area of denotational suggestion. For instance, there are fifty-four examples of the family *"dolore," "dolente," "doloroso"* in the *Inferno* as against eighteen in the *Purgatorio* and four in the *Paradiso.* Conversely, the family of "light" words (*"luce," "lucente," "lucere,"* etc.) is represented only nine times in the *Inferno* as against twenty-seven times in the *Purgatory* and eighty-nine times in the *Paradiso.* This includes all references, whether used for what the poet is describing or figuratively or tangentially. All cases of *"ridente"* ("laughing," "smiling") occur in the *Paradiso;* conversely the *Inferno* contains no form of the verb *"ridere"* ("to smile, laugh") and only one *"riso"* ("laughter"). *"Paura"* ("fear") is, on the other hand, an infernal word, occuring in the *Inferno* eighteen times as against nine in the other two *cantiche* combined; *Inferno* I very suggestively contains five examples of the word, a concealed but effective *annominatio.*

Typically Dantesque too, and a recurrent delight to the reader, is the poet's technique of association. I mean cases where the word is not so much straw in thematic brick, as it were, as a kind of conceptual cement used opportunely and skilfully to recall an image, to link concepts, or to suggest emotional or doctrinal parallels. For instance, the forest of *Inferno* I is *"aspra"*; this word is used five times in the *Inferno,* three times in the *Purgatorio,* and naturally is banished from heaven. Its use in the canto of the suicides again in connection with a wood is a subtle signal with both esthetic and doctrinal overtones; later, when towards the end of the first *cantica* the poet longs for *"aspre e chiocce"* rhymes to describe the bottom of the universe, the echo of both unholy woods comes back to us. Or again, in the love axioms of the successive realms, although something more than the word is involved here, yet *"amore"* ("love") is the key. *"Amor ch'a nullo amato amar perdona"* is enough for Francesca and the romantic code she has died for; in the *Purgatorio* Virgil echoes the phrase but with an all-important minor premise: *"Amore,/acceso di virtù, sempre altro accese"* ("Love,/kindled by virtue, never failed to kindle another"); and in heaven we find at last *"amor di vero ben, pien di letizia"* ("love of true good, replete with happiness"). The repetition of the word, in all cases in a position of syntactical and rhythmic stress, is rich and suggestive. The three instances of the Latinism *"cive,"* two of them pronounced by Beatrice, are all given the prominence of rhyme, and provide a verbal clue to our poet's political conviction — or, better, faith. Erich von Richthofen, from whom I have borrowed a few of the items above, well speaks of the *"Leitmotive"* of the *Commedia.*[5] Before leaving the consideration of pure vocabulary, we may remark how effectively Dante uses his word arm to give the *Paradiso* its special character; the great majority of words of his own coinage, sixty-two out of ninety-three, according to E. A. Fay's *Concordance of the Divine Comedy* (pp. v–vi), are found in that *cantica,* which abounds also in Latinisms and scholastic terms.

The examples cited also show evidence of Dante's awareness of tonal qualities, vocalic chords, and harmonies (the terms are not out of place). If he is a poet who makes you see what he sees, his poem is one that makes you hear a very special kind of music. There are examples of simple onomatopoeia, including the celebrated *"Che gir non sa ma qua e là saltella"* ("No longer walks but random leaps and bounds") and *"leccando come bestia che si liscia"* ("licking like a beast that smooths itself"), but Dante's artistry transcends such devices; his sound composition is a subtle and persistent delight. *"Lo giorno se n' andava e l'aere bruno"* ("The day was dying and the darkling sky") has in its notes all the melancholy of twilight and leave-taking; *"conobbi il tremolar de la marina"* ("I saw the scene of sea-crests by the shore") sparkles with the morning sea-spray; *"Quale nei plenilunii sereni"* ("Even as, in plenilunes serene") is a night of calm yet evocative moonlight even if one doesn't understand a syllable. Von Richthofen says that the poem was meant to be recited as the Romance epics were[6] and in fact much of the beauty is missed if one does not read the lines aloud. Let us stress that in this sound-painting the word is all: for its vocalic quantity and quality, for its suggestion, for its harmony with the pattern and color scheme.

A discussion of Dante's syntax would take us prematurely into a consideration of his metrics (for his syntax is rhythmical as well as grammatical), but we may risk the statement that here too the keyword is simplicity. As for most medieval poetry, Dante's mode is essentially paratactical: more often than not a grammatical element synchronizes with a line of verse; often a thought is complete in a line, very often in a *terzina* (of which more presently). But Dante's parataxis is rarely naive, being usually masked by various stratagems, rhetorical, grammatical, or rhythmical. Here example will serve us better than exposition. A passage from the journey of Ulysses, literally translated, may serve to illustrate his narrative style:

> "When
> I took leave of Circe who detained
> me more than a year yonder near Gaeta —
> before Aeneas so named it —
> Neither tenderness for my son, nor the filial piety
> for my old father, nor the due love
> which should have made Penelope happy,
> could overcome within me the ardor
> that I had to become expert of the world,
> and of human vices and valor;
> But I set forth on the high open sea
> alone with one ship and with that company
> small, by which I was not deserted.
> One shore and the other I saw as far as Spain,
> as far as Morocco and the isle of the Sards
> and the others that that sea washes around."

It will be seen at once that although there are examples of enjambment (here rather more frequent than is normal), yet the syntax
breaks up easily enough into definable elements. Very effective
(and quite unusual) is the enjambment of the *terzina* with which
the passage begins.

Here is an allegorical passage from the *Purgatorio*:

> As light follows light in heaven
> there came after them four animals,
> encrowned each one with green leaves.
> Each one was pinioned with six wings,
> the feathers full of eyes, and the eyes of Argus,
> if they were alive, would be of that kind.
> To describe their forms I do not squander
> rhymes, reader; for another expense binds me
> so that I cannot be generous with this one.
> But read Ezekiel, who depicts them
> as I saw them from the colder part
> coming with rain and cloud and fire;
> And as you will find them in his pages
> so were they here, except that for the pinions
> John is with me, and turns aside from him.

In eight out of the fifteen lines quoted, the punctuation mark indicates the end of the grammatical unit as well as the end of the
line. There is only one true enjambment. All the *terzine* are
separated by strong punctuation barriers; the last two, composing
a kind of built-in footnote, do indeed belong together as far as
the sense is concerned, but grammatically each has its own
autonomy.

As we might expect, the doctrinal passages are somewhat more
elaborate. Perhaps Beatrice on the creation of angels offers as
good an example of the "high" or at least theological style as we
could find:

> "Not to win a gain of good for Itself
> (for that cannot be) but in order that Its splendor
> could, in its answering shining, say, 'I subsist,'
> in Its eternity outside of time,
> beyond all other understanding, as It pleased,
> the Eternal Love opened Itself into new loves.
> Nor before that did It lie as one senseless [*torpente*],
> for neither 'before' nor 'after' preceded
> the passage of God upon these waters.

Form and matter, both united and unmixed,
came forth into being that had no flaw,
like three arrows from a three-stringed bow;
And as in glass, in amber, or in crystal
a beam so shines that between its coming
and its full being there is no interval,
so the three-form effect of its Lord
in its being shone all at once
with no distinction in origin."

This is all one piece of rather subtle exposition and in that sense the *terzine* are linked, but as syntactical units they are easily isolated, as the punctuation indicates. We may note in passing that although this may be considered a difficult passage to construe, depending, as it does, on our knowledge of certain scholastic terms, yet the vocabulary, even in Italian, is not difficult.

A discussion, even an enumeration with appropriate examples, of Dante's rhetorical figures and devices would enlarge this chapter out of proper proportion. We must, however, comment on his similes, of which the *Commedia* offers an enormous range, a recent census giving a total of 676. Their genesis is partly in the allegorical mode of his time, partly in his own taste; their source is in his reading, both of classical and Romance authors (and though many of them can be found in previous writers, that detracts nothing from the poet's skill in adapting them and placing them opportunely), and in his observation and experience (these are the most enthusiastically admired by proponents of Dante's realism). For Olschki "Dante's poetical reality rests on the abundance and precision of the similes that substantiate his imaginary world."[7]

T. S. Eliot says that the nature of the Dantesque simile is to make you "see what he saw," and, following Matthew Arnold, he cites the figure of the tailor squinting to thread his needle as effective in portraying Brunetto's group peering through the gloom in order to recognize Dante.[8] There are many such figures. Describing the merging of man and snake in the seventh *bolgia*, the poet writes that: "neither was what it had been before:/just as a moving barrier of brown,/not yet charred black and yet no longer white,/foreruns the fire on a burning page" — admirable for the depiction of the metamorphosis itself and the sense of dynamism in the process. And among others: the itching alchemists scratching so vigorously that "ne'er did ostler ply his currycomb,/under his master's eye or 'gainst his will/kept from his bed, with speedier stroke"; the proud in the *Purgatorio* bent down under their burdens giving the appearance of caryatids; the souls of the blessed eagerly and noiselessly approaching the poet "as fish within a pure and tranquil pool/will rise if from outside they see approach/a shape they fancy may be food for them." These and hundreds like them do in fact make us see what the poet saw.

They cover all kinds of human activities, giving us such a richness of objective correlatives as to bring into the great "hall of the *Comedy*" all forms and features of the medieval world. "Everything is there," says Erich Auerbach,

croaking frogs in the evening, a lizard darting across the path, sheep crowding out of their enclosure, a wasp withdrawing its sting, a dog scratching; fishes, falcons, doves, storks; a cyclone snapping off trees at the trunk; a morning countryside in spring, covered with hoarfrost; night falling on the first day of an ocean voyage; a monk receiving the confession of a murderer; a mother saving a child from fire; a lone knight galloping forth; a bewildered peasant in Rome; sometimes very brief, half a line — *attento si fermò com'uom che ascolta* (he stopped attentive like a man who listens) — sometimes rolling on at length, so that a landscape, an incident, a legend unfolds in all its breadth, always in order to serve the movement of the poem.[9]

Some figures are recurrent — those drawn from archery or birdlore, for example, or the ship figure, three times applied by Dante to his own poem (let us note that his "little bark" of *Purgatorio* I becomes a "bold prow" too mighty for easy steering in the *Paradiso*). Indeed, the *Paradiso* has another distinction: it contains some very oddly, one might say unnaturally, phrased similes — the poet's arrival in the moon as fast as a dart "hits the target, flies and is sped from the notch," his entrance into the eighth heaven "as fast as you would have pulled your finger from the fire and thrust it in," the snowstorm falling *up* in *Paradiso* XXVII.

Many similes that "roll on at length" serve the purpose of adornment or decoration of the poem as well as the purely functional role of the figure. Mario Fubini suggests that some of them — for example the picture of the shepherd dismayed by the hoarfrost in *Inferno* XXXIV, a vignette lovingly developed by the poet — seem to call for an illustrative miniature in the manuscript.[10]

But Irma Brandeis is right in seeing a somewhat unnecessary limitation in Eliot's definition.[11] Many of Dante's similes do not so much make us see what he sees as feel as he feels. He compares his state of mind when checked by the she-wolf to that of a man who has won much and then loses all; this depicts rather a state of mind than a visual image. There are many comparisons of this nature beginning "as one who," often with no very strong visual element. Consider the magnificent simile in the *Purgatorio:*

> And as the snow amid the living beams
> Of Italy's backbone is frozen hard,
> Beset and blasted by Sclavonian gales,
> And later, flowing, trickles through its crust
> (Seeming like wax that melts before the flame)
> Under the breath of lands whence shadows flee,
> Even so stood I, yielding no sigh or tear,
> And heard the song of those who choir always
> Following the notes of the eternal gyres.
> But when through their sweet chords I heard them voice
> Compassion for me, more than had they said,
> "Why do you so dismay him, Lady?" — ah then
> The ice which clutched so tight around my heart
> Was changed to breath and water and poured forth
> Through mouth and eyes in anguish from my breast.

Here, to be sure, the poet "makes us see" the snows melting on the Apennines, but obviously he does not himself see any such grandiose spectacle; he makes us rather feel, by the scope of the simile, the dimension of his emotional release.

We may glance briefly at two of Dante's tactical operations — one cannot quite call them figures — of which he makes use in the deployment of his poem. The first is digression. Digressions are a common feature — one might almost say the habitual vice — of medieval narrative. The *Commedia* is no exception; disciplined and ultimately unified as it is, it yet contains many digressions. Some of the similes alluded to above are of a digressive nature, as are the catalogues of virtuous pagans in the *Inferno,* penitent princes in the *Purgatorio,* and the like. The expositions of Virgil in the *Inferno* and the *Purgatorio* and the homilies of Beatrice in the *Paradiso* are digressions — at least insofar as we consider the poem a narrative. But Dante's digressions are in the main discreet and, as compared with those of other medieval writers, brief. We have but to compare even the longest Beatrician lecture with any of the interminable monologues of the

Roman de la Rose, for example, to see how well Dante preserves his sense of proportion and keeps his doctrinal interest in bounds. Further, as we have by now noticed, the poem is not merely a narrative; it is encyclopedic, and in the nature of things bound to be digressive. Rarely does the reader feel that the digression is nonfunctional. One cannot quite say "never" — some readers have felt that the detailed account of Manto's vicissitudes in *Inferno* XX could have been omitted, and it may be argued that there is rather too much about spots on the moon in the early cantos of the *Paradiso.* To those who object to the doctrinal material in the *Paradiso,* it can be answered that however arid it may be for the nontheological-minded, it is a part of the author's plan, and as such must be admitted to be artfully distributed and effectively and economically set forth.

Periphrasis is another medieval device of which Dante makes considerable use. Curtius has counted a hundred and fifty examples in the *Commedia,* one of which (*Purgatorio* XXXIII) he cites as an example of "tasteless mannerism."[12] An even more annoying example is Folquet de Marselha's long introduction of himself in the *Paradiso,* in which he takes up twelve lines simply to say, "I was born in Marseilles."

But again it must be said that many cases of periphrasis are very effective as ornament, medieval in taste though they may be. The astronomical circumlocutions of the *Purgatorio* and the *Paradiso* do not lack in appeal (even though we may have to look in the footnotes to understand exactly what the poet is trying to tell us — or to conceal from us). Let one example suffice:

> As much as of that circle may appear
> That ever like a child disports itself
> Between the third hour's end and break of day,
> Just so much of his course toward eventide
> It seemed the sun had left to him to run;
> It was vespers yonder and full midnight here.

Here "that circle" is the ecliptic, which, as it were, skips from one side of the equator to the other; it is worth noting that after having his fun with his riddle, Dante breaks down and tells us what he means. In *Paradiso* XI, speaking through St. Thomas, Dante shows that he is aware of the danger of speaking "too obscurely." And to conclude these hasty remarks on his style, for all the rhetorical ornaments his purpose is to be understood and clarity is his high achievement.

A few remarks on poetic techniques may be useful. In his choice of the hendecasyllable, Dante was faithful at least to one of his dicta in the *De Vulgari Eloquentia;* as we have noted in the discussion of that work, the choice was not as inevitable as it would seem nowadays. Nor do we need here to enlarge upon the advantages of such a syllabic span for a sustained narrative work. In Italian the hendecasyllable has advantages similar to those we are familiar with in our own pentameter; it has even certain advantages over it. The rules of Italian prosody are more flexible, based on the number of syllables rather than the number of accents in the line — at least in theory, although perhaps the languages are closer in practice than the rules suggest. But Italian has another weapon in that the synalepha which is the normal practice in syllable count may at the author's discretion give way to hiatus; Dante can and does make "Beatrice" either a three-syllable or a four-syllable word as suits his purpose. Syntactical inversions (available to the Italian in greater degree than to the English poet), together with considerable freedom in the placing of the caesura, offer a vast range of metrical possibilities. Dante's earlier sonnets and *canzoni* had given him a mastery of the hendecasyllable; it can be truly appreciated only in the original, of course, but here again I think we may say that a sympathetic translator (Laurence Binyon, for example) can reproduce much of the metrical effect in English.

The rhyme-scheme, original with Dante at least so far as consistent self-conscious use is concerned, is based on linked *terzine,* the central rhyme of each group carrying over to the next, i.e., aba bcb cdc, etc. Each *terzina* is a self-contained unit, a little individual brick, perfectly square — or shall we say triangular? — that can be taken out and examined for its own beauty and perfection. It is in itself formally perfect and may be made the vehicle of a surprising amount of substance, e.g., in *Inferno* V:

> "Amor ch'al cor gentil ratto s'apprende
> Prese costui de la bella persona
> Che mi fu tolta e'l modo ancor m'offende."

"Love that takes swift hold on gentle heart/seized him for the fair person/that was taken from me and the way still grieves me."

The unit contains not only a summary of the narrative that is to follow, the passion of Paolo and its end in the death of his beloved, but also a doctrinal pronouncement (not religious this time but amatory, yet doctrine for all that). An axiom is published and a story told. Formally the rhyme binds the lines together; we are given a prosodic assurance of integrity. This is the lapidary aspect. But the unrhymed middle line, while not in itself suggesting incompleteness, does prepare our ear for the next *terzina,* providing the mortar, as it were, for the next brick. So we have a verse system at once lapidary and cursive; combining, as Curtius says, "the principle of continuous progressive concatenation with ineluctable discipline,"[13] lending itself alike to aphorism (or doctrine) and narrative, to reflection and motion.

One more example:

> La gloria di colui che tutto muove
> per l'universo penetra e risplende
> in una parte più e meno altrove.

> The glory of the mover of all things/perfusing the whole universe, yet glows/more brightly in one part and less elsewhere.

This is a statement of dogma to which the *terzina* lends solemnity, beauty, and impact. It will do as an affirmation to be pondered, and indeed — with an assist from the grave melody of the rhyming vowels of the original — it is impossible not to memorize it. Yet there is in the middle line a suggestion of more to come. The suggestion does not have to be taken up, but when it is we are aurally and so psychologically prepared for it.

There has been much investigation of the possible sources of the Dantesque *terzina.* Provençal origins have been proposed, and the tercets of some forms of the early Italian sonnet have not been overlooked. Fubini argues very persuasively that Dante may have created the pattern by adapting the rhyme scheme of certain old Italian *sirventesi.* Appealing to the definition of De Lollis, who saw in the *Commedia* a kind of vast *sirventese,* Fubini remarks that the Italian practitioners of this form were much given to catalogues and enumerations; he quite rightly finds many such in the *Commedia:* the virtuous ancients, the Christian kings and princes, the rings of teachers and mystics, the great warriors, even the roll call of the saints in the Mystic Rose. And we may add that the satirical side of the truly Provençal *sirventes* is more than adequately represented in our poet's frequent invectives. So, Fubini argues, from a study of such works, where triple rhyme is indeed found (though not in Dante's pattern), the poet may well have fashioned his *terzina.* But the Italian scholar detects as well what he calls a "cultural" genesis: he holds that the *terzina* is syllogistic in form (containing three lines even as the syllogism has the three elements of major and minor premise and conclusion), and that the syllogism was — or had become — for Dante a natural method of expression. Fubini then illustrates how many of Dante's *terzine,* taken individually or in groups, do reveal a truly syllogistic construction.[14] This is very convincing, and does not necessarily exclude Vossler's suggestion that the form is a gesture of the poet's devotion to the Trinity.[15] On a more utilitarian level, J. S. P. Tatlock shrewdly argued that the pattern appealed to Dante because a canto of *terza rima,* closed with the stopping rhyme, is practically secure against interpolation or addition — and to Dante the integrity of his *sacro poema* was a matter of concern.[16]

The next larger unit in the metrical plan of the *Commedia* is the canto. It is notable that the canto, unlike the *terzina,* is sealed off: the *terzina* (save for the first in a canto) looks back to its predecessor and forward to its successor; the canto is regularly closed with a rhyme to match the middle rhyme of the last *terzina;* one could say that it ends with a quatrain. Every canto of the poem thus consists of lines numbering some multiple of 3 + 1, even as the cantos themselves add up to 33 + 1. The cantos are remarkably uniform in length; on the average they grow a little in size in the successive *cantiche,* the *Inferno* averaging a little less than 139 lines, the *Purgatorio* and the *Paradiso* a little more than 144. An average, of course, is an artificial concept; we can get a better idea of the dimensions of the cantos from *cantica* to *cantica* if we look at the typical length of the cantos in each division. In the *Inferno* the favorite number of lines is 136, seven cantos being of that length; twenty cantos have less than 140 lines, and only five have more than 150. The three shortest cantos of the *Comedy* are all in the *Inferno* (two of 115 lines and one of 124); of the seven cantos in the poem of 130 lines or less, six are in the *Inferno.* The range is great — from 115 to 157 lines — but in general the cantos run small. In the *Purgatorio* the favorite number is 145 lines; nine cantos, or more than a quarter of the total number, are of that length. There are twelve cantos under 140 lines and eight over 150; *Purgatorio* XXXII is the longest canto, running to 160 lines. Thus the cantos of the *Purgatorio* are somewhat more spacious, and bear out the evidence of the line average cited above. The range between extremes of 133 and 160 is less than in the *Inferno*. What seems to me interesting about the cantos of the *Paradiso* is that with respect to length they are somewhat bunched together. There are only eight cantos with fewer than 140 lines and only four with more than 150; there are nine each of 142 and 148 lines. If we take into consideration the three of 145, we shall see that two thirds of the cantos are very much of a size; the extremes overall are not great either: 130 lines to 154. It would seem to me that as he went on with the poem, Dante learned to manage his canto divisions with increasing facility, and his notion of the ideal canto length became not only clearer, but easier for him to realize. If, as Fubini suspects,[17] the *Fiore* (whether or not Dante was the author) had given our poet some notion of the form of his narrative poem, it was very likely that he aimed at uniform length for his divisions. Allan Gilbert has remarked that Dante did not learn this uniformity from the *Aeneid* and the *Thebaid*.[18] The *Fiore* is a sonnet sequence, and it seems not unlikely that Dante thought of his work as a *canzone* sequence. It is true that in *Inferno* XX he applies the term *"canzone"* to the whole *Inferno,* but by the end of the *Purgatorio* he has chosen the word *"cantica"* (perhaps as more Latin or elegant-sounding) for his main divisions. But this does not necessarily mean that the individual cantos may not have originally been thought of as *canzoni.* The canto is certainly closer to the *canzone* in form and substance than to any other medieval form with which Dante was familiar, save of course the *sirventese,* which, for the Provençal, had the same form as the *canso.*

Dante, like all medieval poets writing in a time when rhyme was the formal essence of verse, must have devoted the most scrupulous attention to his rhymes, which may be said to compose a kind of musical and verbal veneer applied to the whole edifice of the poem. And I believe that in no other area of his strategy does the poet's *temperateness* come forth so clearly as in this highly technical department. A glance at a *rimario* will illustrate what I mean.

The total number of lines in the *Commedia* is 14,233. The

number of rhyming groups runs to some 750. We would then come out with an average frequency of approximately nineteen for any one group. Here too the average is somewhat misleading, since certain rhymes appear a good deal more often. I find the most frequent to be the group in *-ura* (153 times), closely followed by *-io* (140) and *-etto* (133). Even these are hardly excessively used in a poem of such length. At the other extreme there are single occurrences of 207 groups of three and twenty-eight pairs, the latter possible of course only in the first terzina or in the last three lines of a canto. Again, the variety is noteworthy. Perhaps an even more striking discovery emerges from the count of words used in rhyme. Among the most frequent are *parte* (thirty-five times, but five cases are from the verb and many cases are in adverbial combinations), *era* (the verb, thirty-one times), and (significant perhaps for the psychoanalyst and certainly indicative of the subjective aspect of the *Commedia*) *io* (twenty-eight times), which are hardly so numerous as to give any impression of undue repetition. These statistics reinforce, I think, the impression that we have in reading the poem of enormous variety in the range of rhymes. More than that, the same vastness of range and use of very common Italian phonemic groups (other quite common combinations are *-ando, -ella, -ente, -ia,* and *-ore*) with infrequent repetition combine to make the rhyming unobtrusive; it strikes the ear pleasantly but without forcing itself upon us. Dante does not overdo the easy grammatical rhymes afforded him by the inflection of the language (of the very common verb ending *-ava* there are only some eighty cases in the poem, rhyming very often with syllables which are not verbal endings). But he has taken full advantage of the character of his language and of his pattern. Speaking of the *Commedia* as a whole, we may, I think, say that rhyme is an effective but discreet ornament.

However, it can be used as a powerful weapon for emphasis, for suggestion, for a kind of emotional punctuation, and, let us admit freely, more than once for a display of virtuosity. For example, most of the rhymes are what the Italian calls *piani*, i.e., paroxytonic. To give a dramatic staccato or accelerated movement to his rhythm Dante occasionally employs *versi tronchi* (oxytonic) or *sdruccioli* (proparoxytonic). Of the former there are thirty-seven examples in the *Commedia* (not counting the six Provençal words and the rhymes in *-ai, ei,* etc. which run to nearly two hundred but which, according to the rules of the Italian prosody, do not count as *tronchi*). The *sdruccioli* are used even more sparingly, numbering only seventeen. Other examples of virtuosity include such rhymes as *urli* with *pur lì, per li* with *merli, sol tre* with *poltre, ne lo* with *candelo,* and a few *rimes riches,* e.g., *volto,* "face" and "turned," *saggi,* "essays" and "sages," and *palma* with the different meanings of "palm." True repetition is rare. *Cristo* appears in four *terzine* of the *Paradiso,* rhyming always with itself, a gesture of atonement, it has been suggested, for the casual rhyme of the name in the sonnet exchange with Forese Donati, though no such hypothesis is really necessary to justify the implicit reverence. There is also the very ironic repetition *per ammenda* in the recital of the wicked deeds of the House of France in *Purgatory* XX, and, perhaps most effective of all, that of *vidi* in *Paradiso* XXX, calculated to emphasize the truth of Dante's ultimate vision.

Even from this rather arid survey of Dante's technical resources we can get, I think, a glimpse of his hidden power, and the source of his enduring fascination for us. Choice of word, variation in rhythm, use of figures, artful manipulation of rhyme, rhetorical tactics, combine in different proportion and degree to give a sense of novelty and excitement to the poem. It is not too much to say that every *terzina* has its own impact, dramatic, rhetorical, evocative — often all at once. It is no wonder that the writing made the poet lean; no wonder either that readers, once captivated by Dante, return to him again and again, certain that there will be always new discoveries and new delights. The *Comedy* welcomes you on first reading, as Eliot has observed, and with each successive reading it rewards you more richly.

Beauty of ornament and rhetorical polish — these are the poet's lures to capture the reader. But, now that we have come to the end of our study, to what purpose? What was Dante's purpose in writing his poem, what *is* the poem, and how shall we assess his achievement?

The purpose is in part social and didactic, in part personal and confessional. And here we may profitably stand off a little and see how our "grand marshal" (to borrow his own phrase), deploying his tactical resources to good use, also disposes his great divisions to the achievement of his strategic purpose.

As we have noted in the discussion of the narrative pattern, the chief weapons are correspondences and contrasts. In each of the realms a pilgrim, guided by a faithful and wise companion, proceeds through successive regions; each province has its guardians (or receptionist); each journey ends in a climactic and apocalyptic vision. Yet with what differences! Hell is black and bleak, heaven suffused with splendor, purgatory rich in the fruitful sunlight of penitential effort alternating with the consoling shadow of meditation. Demons and monsters in hell, angels in purgatory, and in heaven the very saints come forth to greet the traveler. Perhaps the most meaningful distinction is in the nature of the transitions or check-points. The circles of hell are entered with anguish and stress, the successive grades of the Mount of Purgatory are made accessible by the warm welcome of the wardens and the reassurance of the beatitudes, the spheres of heaven are all but indistinguishable, revealed only by a change in hue or by the increasing beauty of Beatrice. The nature of these divisions suggests a difference of rhythm, even of time, in the successive kingdoms. The levels of time, discontinuous in hell, continuous in purgatory, and simultaneous in heaven, remind us of St. Thomas' remark that "some hold that eternity has neither beginning nor end, eviternity a beginning but no end, and time both beginning and end."[19] These are distinctions applicable to heaven, hell, and purgatory respectively, illustrated by the nature of the transitions within each realm, and underlined too, I think we may say, by the condition of the various wardens. In hell, as Dante happily notes while fleeing the *Malebranche,* the jailers, like their prisoners, are confined to their own circle; in purgatory the pardoning angel stands between the terraces, both welcoming and dismissing, linking rather than dividing; and heaven, beyond space as it is, must also be beyond all laws of let or hindrance.

Yet when all is said, as we reflect on the sacred poem, it is the similarities of the great divisions that we are likely to remember; formal, conceptual, and thematic as they are, they bind the work together and also help us, I think, to grasp its meaning. For as we study their correspondences the veil lifts from before our eyes and we see not the three realms of the *fabula* but three aspects of mankind, in its ethical, spiritual, and existential embodiment. Our world too contains its recalcitrant and embittered citizens, its hopeful and striving aspirants, and, few though they be, its secure souls, serene in their inner faith and peace. Yet this too is but halfway to the truth: the social aspect is itself an allegory; ultimately what we contemplate is a picture of the human heart in its various and varying attitudes toward its destiny. Each one of us is to some extent sinner, penitent, and potential saint.

So too the genesis (to use a word critics are fond of) of the *Commedia* lies in the poet's experience and his burning desire to share his learning (of both the bookish and the experiential kind) with the reader. It is easy to say and indeed has been said, that Dante's point of departure is in the sixth book of the *Aeneid,* in his reading of philosophers or theologians, in his self-conscious sense of mission concerning his role as a new poet and the inheritor of the lyric tradition of his predecessors. Some have found his motivation in the search for justice, the defense of the tradition of Rome, the justification of the empire. The true genesis of the work is somewhat broader and deeper; it lies in Dante's idealized love for Beatrice, in the bitterness of exile, in meditations on the course of human affairs as he was obliged to see them, in his effort to understand and to discipline his own heart.

What then is the *Commedia?* One is tempted to say that the answer does not matter; it is a work meant to be savored and studied, not to be catalogued. But Dante, a lover of categories himself, would not be displeased at the well-intentioned efforts of his admirers to find the proper definition of his work. It has been called a *sirventese,* as we have seen, an encyclopedia, and a lyric. Vossler speaks of it as a Danteid, thus giving it the classification of an epic, in which general category it is often placed; others have called it a lay *summa.* All these terms are true enough, but none is quite adequate. Some of them would limit its range (if it is a *sirventese* it certainly transcends the medieval implications of that term), some its character (of course it is a lyric but charged with intellectualism), some its color (if it is an encyclopedia, then it is disposed according to a unique and poetic scheme). It can be studied historically; it is interesting that Vossler's book on Dante has been given in its English form the title *Medieval Culture,* and years ago Henry Osborn Taylor called his chapter on our poet "The Medieval Synthesis." There is in truth no better single book for the study of the medieval world. It is indeed a part of the poet's purpose to depict that world, which he does with graphic accuracy and subjective participation. It is true too that Dante's cultural objective is to bring into harmony the two legacies that have come down to western man. We take it for granted now that we have an equal right to Solomon and Pythagoras, Moses and Aeneas, the Book of Kings and the Oresteiad. This was not always so, and I feel that Dante scholars have insufficiently stressed this aspect of his poem. Who before Dante would have compared Mary's visitation with Caesar's Spanish campaign, or would have spoken of "Jove crucified on earth"? He is doing on a cultural level and for laymen a work similar to the great accomplishment of St. Thomas, which was in effect a Christianization of Aristotle. So I think the *Commedia* is something more than a medieval synthesis; it summarizes the past and the poet's present, to be sure, but it looks also to the future.

It looks to eternity too. The world of Dante, to paraphrase and perhaps somewhat distort a familiar thesis, is a world of reality, but a reality destroyed, remade, and placed forever on a plane of the enduring and the significant. Dante sought desperately for meaning and order in life, but the hunger for order (which comes out in the arrangement as well as the substance of the *Commedia*) would have been artistically fruitless if the poet had not been at the same time a man of deep and fervent emotion.

Because he is afflicted by lust he will idealize love, because he is troubled by doubt he will seek and find justice, because the iniquities of the world bite into him he will find order and purpose in them. Father Kenelm Foster has given to an article of his a title which I think is a perfect summary of Dante's psyche and the key to his accomplishment: *The Mind in Love.* Dante's is an eager and voracious intellect, prepared not only for philosophical contemplation but for penetrating study of his fellow man with all his pathetic vicissitudes and noble strivings; his is an ardent heart, disposed not only to the rapture of the mystic but to a deep concern for the contingencies of humanity, for his language, his city, his teachers, and his art. The *Commedia,* rationally conceived, realized with intuition, written with passion, and adorned with a kind of tender virtuosity, is both the creation and the depiction of a mind in love.

BIBLIOGRAPHICAL NOTE

The *Vita Nuova*

The *Vita Nuova*, written in Italian, contains 31 poems (25 sonnets, 5 *canzoni*, and one *ballata*) and approximately 14,000 words of prose. It was composed in 1292 or a little later. Some forty manuscripts are extant, many fragmentary. The first printed edition is that of B. Sermartelli (Florence, 1576), a copy of which is in the Fiske Collection of the Cornell University Library. The authoritative edition is Michele Barbi's (Florence, 1932), which is reproduced in the *Opere di Dante* published by the Società dantesca (2d edition, Florence, 1960). Kenneth McKenzie's edition (Boston, 1922) contains introductory material and notes in English and also an Italian-English glossary. Available English translations include those of D. G. Rossetti in *The Early Italian Poets* (London, 1861, and frequently republished), Thomas Okey in the Temple Classics (first published London, 1906), and Mark Musa (New Brunswick, N. J., 1957; slightly revised, Bloomington, Ind., 1962).

The *Rime*

Modern editors definitely attribute 54 "rhymes" to Dante (aside from those in the *Vita Nuova* and the *Convivio*), with an additional 26 in the "dubious" category. The poems, varying in form, tone, and content, were composed at different times during the poet's life, and for most of them dating has proved an insoluble problem. A few may have preceded the *Vita Nuova*, and it seems likely that few if any were written after the *Convivio*. The manuscript tradition defies easy summary; each poem has its own history. Some are found in only one manuscript, others only in copies. Perhaps the Giunta edition of 1527 (Florence) may be thought of as the *editio princeps*, although 14 of the poems had been published with the Venetian edition of the *Commedia* in 1491, and 11 in a Milanese edition of 1518. Michele Barbi prepared the texts of the poems for the *Opere di Dante* of the Società dantesca (2d edition, Florence, 1960), and also published (with F. Maggini) the text, with commentary, of the

Rime della "Vita Nuova" e della giovinezza (Florence, 1956). The editions of D. Mattalia (Turin, 1943) and G. Contini (Turin, 1946) follow Barbi's texts and attributions and have a complete critical apparatus. Translations of most of the *Rime* may be found in the Temple Classics edition (published with the *Vita Nuova*, London, 1906); there are also the versions in verse of Lorna de' Lucchi (Oxford, 1926) and H. S. Vere-Hodge (Oxford, 1963).

The *Convivio*

The *Convivio* (styled *Convito* by some earlier scholars) is a work of some 70,000 words in Italian prose, having the form of a commentary on three *canzoni*. It is divided into four treatises of respectively 10,000, 13,000, 16,000, and 31,000 words. Some thirty manuscripts exist, many fragmentary and all somewhat corrupt. The work was first printed by Francesco Bonaccorsi (Florence, 1490); a copy of this book is in the Fiske Collection of the Cornell University Library, and another is in the Yale Library. The standard edition is that of G. Busnelli and G. Vandelli (Florence, 1934). The *Opere di Dante* of the Società dantesca (2d edition, Florence, 1960) contains the edition of E. G. Parodi and F. Pellegrini, text only. In English the translation by Philip Wicksteed in the Temple Classics (London, 1903), with useful notes, is available.

De Vulgari Eloquentia

The *De Vulgari Eloquentia* (sometimes called *De Vulgari Eloquio*) is a prose work of approximately 12,000 words, written in Latin. It is divided into two books, of which the first is slightly longer than the (unfinished) second. It was composed in 1303–4 and was probably never "published" (i.e., circulated by the author). The first edition is that of Jacopo Corbinelli (Paris, 1577), although G. G. Trissino's Italian translation had been printed at Vicenza in 1529. The standard edition today is that of A. Marigo (Florence, 1938). The *Opere di Dante* of the Società dantesca reproduces the text of Pio Rajna. A. G. Ferrers Howell's English translation may be found in the Temple Classics edition of *The Latin Works of Dante Alighieri* (London, 1904). See remarks at the end of Chapter 9.

De Monarchia

The *De Monarchia* is written in Latin prose, approximately 18,000 words long. It is divided into three books, the first containing some 5,000 words, the second a little more than 6,000, and the third nearly 7,000. It was written probably in 1313. Eight manuscripts are extant, four of the fourteenth century. It was first printed in Basel, 1559, "per Joannem Oporinum." Enrico Rostagno edited the text printed in the *Opere* of the Società dantesca (2d edition, Florence, 1960). The most recent authoritative and annotated edition is that of Gustavo Vinay (Florence, 1950), using essentially Rostagno's text. Among the English translations are those of Dean Church (London, 1879), Philip Wicksteed, in the Temple Classics edition of Dante's *Latin Works* (London, 1904), and Donald Nicholl (New York, 1954).

Letters

The generally accepted canon of Dante's epistolae consists of the ten letters discussed in Chapter 11. In addition there are three letters which Dante is said to have written on behalf of the Countess of Battifolle; they do not reflect his own thought. Toynbee prints them following letter VII of his edition. Latham includes the letter (numbered 8 in his edition) supposedly written by Dante to Guido da Polenta; if it were authentic, it would be the only extant letter written by Dante in Italian, but it is now generally considered to be the invention of a sixteenth-century editor. The manuscripts of the letters are very few. Letters I, II, III, and VI are found in only one manuscript, now in the Vatican. A manuscript in Boccaccio's handwriting in the Laurentian Library in Florence is likewise our sole source for letters IV, VIII, and IX. Letter V is found in the above-mentioned Vatican manuscript and in another now in the possession of the Victor Emmanuel Library in Rome. Letter VII is also found in those two manuscripts and in a fifteenth-century codex now in the Biblioteca Marciana in Venice. For letter X there are six manuscripts, only three of which (all of the sixteenth century) contain the entire letter. The first printed edition of any of the letters is that of Anton Francesco Doni, editor and publisher (Florence, 1547), in a volume entitled *Prose antiche di Dante, Petrarcha et Boccaccio,* etc.; he printed an Italian translation of Dante's letter to Henry VII and the letter (now considered spurious) to Guido da Polenta. Various fragmentary editions appeared in the seventeenth and eighteenth centuries; the first edition of all the letters (including the Battifolle letters and the one to Guido da Polenta) was brought out by Alessandro Torri (Leghorn, 1842). The standard edition today is that of Paget Toynbee (Oxford, 1920), with introduction, copious notes, and English translations of the letters. English versions may also be found in the Temple Classics edition of Dante's *Latin Works* (London, 1904) and in C. S. Latham's *Dante's Eleven Letters* (Boston, 1891). The *Opere* of the Società dantesca prints the edition of Ermenegildo Pistelli (text only).

Lesser Works

The *Questio* is a "lecture" of some 4500 words written in Latin. Dante's *Eclogues* consist respectively of 68 and 97 hendecasyllabic lines. Ermenegildo Pistelli has supplied the text of both works for the edition of the *Opere* by the Società dantesca. The Temple Classics edition of Dante's *Latin Works* (London, 1904) contains Wicksteed's English version of both items; Wilmon Brewer has supplied a metrical translation of the *Eclogues* (Boston, 1927). Five manuscripts of the poem are known; the first edition of the verses may be found in *Carmina Illustrium Poetarum Italorum* (Florence, 1719), I, 115–19. (See Wicksteed-Gardner, *Dante and Giovanni del Virgilio*, for critical edition and full comment.) Further bibliographical information on the lesser works will be found in Chapter 11.

The *Commedia*

The *Divine Comedy* (called simply *"Commedia"* by its author) is a poem of 14,233 lines in hendecasyllabic triple rhyme. It is divided into a hundred cantos, of which 34 are assigned to the first *cantica*, the *Inferno*, and 33 each to the second and third *cantiche*, the *Purgatorio* and the *Paradiso*. The *cantiche* are almost equal in length, being respectively of 4720, 4755, and 4758 lines. The cantos average 142⅓ lines each; the median length may be considered as shared between those of 139 lines and those of 142 lines (there are 16 of each). The extremes are 115 lines (*Inferno* VI and XI) and 160 lines (*Purgatorio* XXXII). (See Chapter 15.)

Dante did not finish the *Commedia* until very nearly the end of his life; when he began work on it is more difficult to say. Barbi suggests about 1307; some critics have argued, however, that the entire work must have been written after the death of Henry VII (1313); at the other extreme Chimenz is disposed to see some plausibility in Boccaccio's statement that the first seven cantos were composed before the poet went into exile and speculates that "the work that was to become the Comedy" may have been begun shortly after the *Vita Nuova*. (See Aldo Vallone, "Per la datazione della *Divina Commedia*" in his *Studi*, etc., Florence, 1955, pp. 1–18.)

There are nearly six hundred manuscripts of the poem extant, of which over a hundred are of the fourteenth century. They have never been collated, although Moore examined 256 in the course of preparing his edition. No autograph manuscript exists, nor any written during Dante's lifetime; among the oldest and most respected we may mention the Landiano (1336), the Trivulziano (1337), the Laurenziano (1391), and the Vatican MS 3191 which served as a basis for the Aldine editions (beginning 1502) and so, as Scartazzini says, "practically fixed the text for three centuries." The standard editions nowadays are Moore's (Oxford, 1894) and G. Vandelli's for the Società dantesca (Florence, 1921; 2d edition, very slightly revised, 1960). Many editors make their own changes in spelling, punctuation, and occasionally readings, but the text of the Società is commonly accepted today as the text of reference. A new and possibly definitive text is now in preparation by Giorgio Petrocchi, again under the aegis of the Società dantesca. S. Chimenz, in the foreword to his edition of the *Commedia* (Turin, 1962, pp. 96–108), gives an excellent summary of bibliographical data.

The first printed edition is that of Johannes Numeister (Foligno, 1472). It is reprinted, along with the texts of the editions of Jesi, Mantua, and Naples, by Lord Vernon: *Le prime quattro edizioni della Divina Commedia* (London, 1878); a copy is in the possession of the Fiske Collection of the Cornell University Library. Of the many excellent editions of the *Commedia* now available, we may mention those of A. Momigliano (Florence, 1948) and N. Sapegno (Florence, 1955–57) as of particular interest for their contemporary approach; the editions of Casini-Barbi (Florence, 1926) and Scartazzini-Vandelli (Milan, 1938) are standard and informative. C. H. Grandgent's edition (revised edition, Boston, 1933) with Italian text and English commentary is of great value to the English-speaking reader. There are many English translations of the poem in print; we may mention the prose versions of the Temple Classics (London, 1899–1901 and frequently reprinted) and John D. Sinclair (London, 1939–46), and the *terza rima* versions of Laurence Binyon (London, 1933–46; reprinted in *The Portable Dante*, New York, 1949) and Dorothy Sayers and Barbara Reynolds (Penguin Classics, 1949–62).

* * * * *

Essential bibliographical information for the works I have cited will be found in the appropriate place in the notes. For some of the books quoted there are other editions than the one I have had at hand. Wherever possible — and especially for critical and inter-pretative material — I have made use of books either written in English or available in translation.

For orientation in Dante study the following titles are particularly valuable: Barbi's *Life of Dante* (translated by Paul Ruggiers), Vossler's two-volume *Mediaeval Culture*, and the useful manual of Umberto Cosmo. I have quoted from the Italian of Cosmo, but the work is available in an English translation: *A Handbook to Dante Studies* (Oxford, 1950). All of these books have excellent selective bibliographies.

I am of course indebted to many good and useful works which I have not had occasion to cite. Perhaps it would not be out of place to mention that the essays of such great critics as Coleridge, Carlyle, Lowell, and Santayana, though in varying degrees "dated," will always be valuable.

NOTES

✻

1. Dante's Europe

1. *The Poet and the Politician,* etc. (Carbondale, Ill., 1964), p. 79.
2. *The Holy Roman Empire* (4th edition, New York, 1904), p. 101.
3. *Selections from the First Nine Books of the Croniche Fiorentine of Giovanni Villani,* translated by Rose E. Selfe, edited by Philip H. Wicksteed (Westminster, 1897), p. 113.
4. G. G. Coulton, *From St. Francis to Dante* (London, 1906), p. 241.
5. *Selections,* p. 393.
6. LVIII, 79–80; *Laudi,* etc., edited by Franca Ageno (Florence, 1953), p. 232.
7. II, 774.
8. *Decline and Fall of the Roman Empire,* chap. 69.
9. *Naissance de l'Europe* (Paris, 1962), p. 381.

2. Dante's Florence

1. *Selections,* p. 30.
2. Ibid., pp. 59–61.
3. *Ventisette secoli di storia d'Italia* (Florence, 1956), p. 78.
4. *Selections,* pp. 121–23.
5. Dino Compagni, *Chronicle,* translated by Else C. M. Benecke and A. G. Ferrers Howell (London, 1906), p. 213.
6. *Firenze ai tempi di Dante,* translated by E. D. Theseider (Florence, 1929), p. 452. I have drawn largely on chapter 6 for architectural information.
7. Libro XI, cap. xciv.
8. Translation by Thomas Caldecott Chubb, *The Months of the Year. Twelve Sonnets by Folgore da San Gimignano* (Sanbornville, N. H., 1960), no. 7. Reprinted by permission.
9. Loc. cit.
10. Ibid. For other details about the city see G. Salvemini, "Florence in the Time of Dante," *Speculum* XI (1936), 317–26.
11. G. A. Borgese, *Goliath* (New York, 1937), p. 10.

3. Dante's Life

1. *The Early Lives of Dante*, translated by Philip H. Wicksteed (London, 1904), pp. 10–11.
2. See Nicola Zingarelli, *La vita, i tempi e le opere di Dante* (Milan, 1931), chapter IV, for further details.
3. Siro Chimenz in *Dizionario biografico degli italiani* (Rome, 1961), s.v. "Alighieri, Dante," summarizes the facts about Dante's family and life now generally accepted.
4. *Early Lives*, p. 117.
5. Ibid., pp. 15–17.
6. *Selected Essays* (new edition, New York, 1932), p. 233.
7. *Life of Dante*, translated and edited by Paul G. Ruggiers (Berkeley and Los Angeles, 1954), p. 6.
8. *European Literature and the Latin Middle Ages*, translated from the German by Willard R. Trask (New York, 1953), pp. 372–78.
9. Chimenz, art. cit.
10. *Life of Dante*, p. 71.
11. Chimenz, art. cit.
12. In *Dizionario Bompiani degli autori* (Milan, 1956), I, 53.
13. *Chronicle*, p. 123.
14. Ibid., p. 136.
15. Umberto Cosmo in his *Guida a Dante* (Turin, 1947), p. 84, accepts the statements of Villani and Boccaccio, and Curtius (*European Literature*, p. 352) says boldly: "Dante studied at Paris." If he did, it seems strange that the *Commedia* is so lacking in specific allusions to the city; most modern critics are skeptical.
16. *Early Lives*, p. 128.
17. *Frederick the Second* (New York, 1957), pp. 255–56.
18. *Henry VII in Italy* (Lincoln, Neb., 1960), p. 211.

4. Dante's Reading

1. Maurice Valency, *In Praise of Love* (New York, 1958), p. 26.
2. *The Allegory of Love* (London, 1936), p. 11.
3. *Jaufre Rudel e Bernardo di Ventadorn; Canzoni* (Naples, 1949), p. 82.
4. Translation by Thomas G. Bergin, *The Poems of William of Poitou* (New Haven, 1955), pp. 33–35. Text in Alfred Jeanroy, *Les chansons de Guillaume X* (Paris, 1927), pp. 22–24.
5. Joseph Anglade, *Les poésies de Peire Vidal* (Paris, 1923), p. 124. (Translation mine.)

6. Jules Coulet, *Le troubadour Guilhem Montanhagol* (Toulouse, 1898), p. 70. (Translation mine.)

7. Text in Albert Stimming, *Bertran von Born* (2d edition, Halle, 1913), pp. 139–40. (Translation mine.)

8. Text in Stimming, p. 107. (Translation mine.)

9. In his debate with Guiraut de Bornelh; see Walter T. Pattison, *The Life and Works of the Troubadour Raimbaut d'Orange* (Minneapolis, 1952), pp. 173–74.

10. For the lines quoted see Gianluigi Toja's edition of Arnaut's *Canzoni* (Florence, 1960), p. 274.

11. *Translations* (Norfolk, Conn., 1963), p. 173. Quoted by permission of the publisher, New Directions.

12. *Dante: Poet of the Secular World*, translated by Ralph Manheim (Chicago, 1961), p. 22.

13. *Storia della letteratura italiana* (Milan, 1947), I, 37.

14. *A History of Italian Literature* (Cambridge, Mass., 1954), p. 18. Later, in *The Invention of the Sonnet and Other Studies in Italian Literature* (Rome, 1959), Wilkins accepts the attribution of the creation of the sonnet to Giacomo da Lentini.

15. Text in Kenneth McKenzie's edition of *La Vita Nuova* (Boston, 1922), pp. 104–5. (Translation mine.)

16. *Dante* (New York, 1921), p. 266.

17. *The Symbolic Rose* (New York, 1960), p. 3.

18. Text in Ernesto Monaci, *Crestomazia italiana* (new edition, Rome, 1955), p. 273. (Translation mine.)

19. *Sordello, Le poesie* (Bologna, 1954), pp. clxxxii–clxxxv.

20. *European Literature*, p. 360.

21. *Islam and the Divine Comedy*, translated and abridged by Harold Sunderland (New York, 1926), pp. 246–54.

22. *A Companion to Dante*, translated from the German by Arthur John Butler (London, 1893), p. 385.

23. *The Mediaeval Mind* (4th edition, London, 1938), II, 571.

24. *Studies in Dante*, First Series (Oxford, 1896). All references to Moore in this chapter may be found in that volume, under the author indicated.

25. *Dante and Virgil* (Oxford, 1949), p. 73.

26. *La Divina Commedia* (revised edition, Boston, 1933), p. 510. See also the article of C. S. Lewis in *Medium Aevum* XXV, 3 (1957), 133–39.

27. *Studies in Dante*, First Series, p. 6.

28. *A Companion to Dante*, pp. 58–59.

29. *Dante and the Idea of Rome* (Oxford, 1957), pp. 18–19.

30. *A Companion to Dante*, p. 248.

31. *A Dictionary of Proper Names and Notable Matters in the Works of Dante* (Oxford, 1898), p. 531.

32. *Dante the Philosopher*, translated by David Moore (New York, 1949), p. 307.
33. *European Literature*, p. 372.
34. See *The Fragile Leaves of the Sybil* (Westminster, Md., 1962).
35. *The Mediaeval Mind*, II, 577.
36. *Dante the Philosopher*, p. 306.
37. *The Mediaeval Mind*, II, 464.
38. *Dante the Philosopher*, p. 275.
39. *Studi preparatori illustrativi* with his edition of the *Commedia* (Padua, 1881). The English-speaking reader may consult E. G. Gardner, *Dante and the Mystics* (London, 1913), pp. 44–76.

5. The *Vita Nuova*

1. *European Literature*, p. 353.
2. *History of Italian Literature*, translated by Joan Redfern (New York, 1931), I, 64.
3. *Lettura del "De Vulgari Eloquentia" di Dante* (Rome, [1959?]), pp. 226–27.
4. See McKenzie's edition of *La Vita Nuova*, p. xi.
5. *Dante*, p. 61.
6. Louis Gillet, *Dante* (Paris, 1941), p. 31.
7. *The Ladies of Dante's Lyrics* (Cambridge, 1917), pp. 107–8.
8. *Mediaeval Culture* (New York, 1958), I, 315.
9. *The Figure of Beatrice* (London, 1943), pp. 7–8.
10. *An Essay on the Vita Nuova* (Cambridge, Mass., 1949), p. 112.
11. *History of Italian Literature*, I, 62–63.
12. *Rossetti, Dante and Ourselves* (London, 1947), p. 31.
13. *Mediaeval Culture*, I, 316.
14. *La Vita Nuova*, pp. xiv–xvi.

6. The *Rime*

1. In *Le Opere di Dante* (2d edition, Florence, 1960), pp. 53–142.
2. *Rime* (2d edition, Turin, 1946), p. 64.
3. Ibid., p. 91.
4. Barbi, *Rime della "Vita Nuova" e della giovinezza* (Florence, 1956), p. 292, is "convinced they were jesting"; Daniele Mattalia in his edition of the *Rime* (Turin, 1943), pp. 70–71, is not so sure. See also M. Marti, "Sulla genesi del realismo dan-

tesco" in *Giornale storico della letteratura italiana* CXXXVII, 4 (1960), 497–532.

5. See Contini, ed. cit., p. 119.
6. See Alfred Jeanroy, "La 'sestina doppia' de Dante et les origines de la sextine," *Romania* XLII (1913), 481–89. The poem of Peire Vidal may be found in Anglade's edition, pp. 51 ff.
7. Ed. cit., p. 148; see also Mattalia, pp. 124–25.
8. *Storia della letteratura italiana*, I, 140.
9. *The Poet and the Politician*, p. 73.
10. See Umberto Cosmo, "Se io ebbi colpa," *Cultura* N. S. XII (1933), 652–57. Not all commentators agree; see Mattalia, pp. 169–71, and Contini, pp. 168–69, and also Michele Barbi, *Problemi della critica dantesca*, Second Series (Florence, 1941). K. Foster has an illuminating study of the poem in *God's Tree* (London, 1957), pp. 15–32.
11. *Dante*, p. 74. On the *"montanina"* see also Colin Hardie (for whom the cruel lady is Beatrice) in *Modern Language Review* LV (1960), 359–70.
12. At least he seems the most likely candidate; see Contini, p. 176.

7. The *Convivio* (I)

1. In his introduction to G. Busnelli and G. Vandelli's edition of the *Convivio* (Florence, 1934), I, xix.
2. *Life of Dante*, p. 44.
3. *Mediaeval Culture*, I, 153.
4. I, 96. See also C. S. Singleton, "Dante's Allegory," *Speculum* XXV (1950), 78–86.
5. *Dante the Philosopher*, pp. 140–41.
6. See Paget Toynbee, *Dante Studies and Researches* (London, 1902), pp. 56–77.
7. *Dante the Philosopher*, p. 100.
8. Art. cit. (see above, Chapter 3, note 3).
9. *Mediaeval Culture*, I, 155.
10. Busnelli-Vandelli, I, 188. See also H. Wieruszowski, "An early anticipation of Dante's 'cieli e scienze,'" *Modern Language Notes* LXI (1946), 217–28.
11. *Dante* (Milan, 1903), p. 397.
12. *The Mind in Love* (London, 1956), p. 10.
13. Busnelli-Vandelli, I, 301 n.
14. *Studies in Dante*, Third Series (Oxford, 1903), p. 46.
15. Busnelli-Vandelli, I, 471–72.

8. The *Convivio* (II)

1. Busnelli-Vandelli, II, 11.
2. *Convivio* (Temple Classics, London, 1903), pp. 231–32.
3. *European Literature*, pp. 85–86.
4. *Dante as a Political Thinker* (Oxford, 1952), p. 35.
5. Pp. 45–46.
6. *Mediaeval Culture*, I, 156–57.
7. Pp. 138–39.
8. See Busnelli-Vandelli, II, 284.
9. See Toynbee, *Dante Studies and Researches*, pp. 285–86.
10. In *Dizionario letterario delle opere* (Bompiani, Milan, 1947), II, 434.
11. *Dante, disciple et juge du monde Gréco-Latin* (Paris, 1954), p. 64.
12. *Guida a Dante*, p. 95.
13. *Le "Convivio" de Dante* (Paris, 1940), pp. 121–29.
14. "Dante's Allegory," *Speculum* XXV (1950), 82.
15. *Storia della poesia di Dante* (Naples, 1962), pp. 260–61.

9. *De Vulgari Eloquentia*

1. See his edition (Florence, 1938), pp. xxx–xl.
2. *A History of Criticism and Literary Taste in Europe* (New York, 1900), I, 418.
3. *The Romance Languages* (London, 1960), p. 457.
4. Ibid., p. 474.
5. *Saggi critici* (Naples, 1878), p. 407.
6. Ibid., pp. 383–90.
7. *Lettura del "De Vulgari Eloquentia,"* pp. 145–46.
8. *Dante*, p. 416.
9. *Mediaeval Culture*, I, 164.
10. Art. cit. (see above, Chapter 3, note 3).
11. *History of Criticism*, I, 429.
12. *Dante*, p. 50.
13. *De Vulgari Eloquentia* (in Temple Classics *Latin Works of Dante*, London, 1904), p. 89.
14. Ibid., p. 90; see also C. T. Davis, *Dante and the Idea of Rome*, chap. 1, pt. 1.
15. Ed. cit., p. cxxix.
16. *History of Criticism*, I, 430.
17. *Saggi critici*, p. 413.

18. Ibid.
19. Ed. cit., p. 226.
20. Ibid., pp. 249–50.
21. See Temple Classics *Convivio*, p. 388. The text may be found in *Opere di Dante* (2d edition, 1960), p. 92.
22. *A Short History of Literary Criticism* (New York, 1963), p. 25.
23. *The Philosophy of Literary Form* (New York, 1957), p. 13.
24. Ed. cit., pp. xvi–xix.
25. Ibid., p. xli.
26. Ibid., pp. xxii–xxiii.
27. *Guida a Dante*, p. 103.
28. *Life of Dante*, p. 52.
29. *European Literature*, p. 355.
30. Ed. cit., pp. clv–clvi.
31. Art. cit., p. 409.
32. Temple Classics *Latin Works*, pp. 119–20.

10. *De Monarchia*

1. *De Monarchia* (Florence, 1950), pp. xxix–xxxviii.
2. See C. T. Davis, *Dante and the Idea of Rome*, pp. 263–69, and Colin Hardie's note to D. Nicholl's *Dante: Monarchy and Three Political Letters* (New York, 1954), pp. 117–21.
3. *Life of Dante*, p. 57.
4. *Dante as a Political Thinker*, pp. 49–50. For further comment on this "odor of heterodoxy" see E. Kantorowicz, *The King's Two Bodies* (Princeton, 1957), pp. 451–95.
5. Ed. cit., p. 83.
6. Ibid., p. 90.
7. *De Monarchia* (in Temple Classics *Latin Works*), pp. 175–76.
8. *Dante and the Legend of Rome* (London, 1952), p. 89.
9. Ed. cit., p. 186.
10. Actually it was Leo III who crowned Charlemagne.
11. Ed. cit., p. 281.

11. Letters and Lesser Works

1. Wicksteed, *Early Lives of Dante*, p. 89.
2. *A Handbook to Dante*, translated by Thomas Davidson (Boston, 1893), pp. 261–62.
3. *Dantis Alagherii Epistolae. The Letters of Dante* (Oxford 1920), p. 12.
4. Ibid., p. 32.

5. Temple Classics *Latin Works*, p. 307. See also Toynbee, p. 21.
6. C. Hardie's note in Nicholl's *Monarchy*, p. 118, suggests that this discrepancy may indicate a real shift in Dante's attitude.
7. *Henry VII in Italy*, p. 111.
8. *Selection* (see above, Chapter 1, note 3), pp. 369–75.
9. Temple Classics *Latin Works*, p. 337. Toynbee concurs, p. 131, n. 7.
10. *A Translation of Dante's Eleven Letters* (Boston and New York, 1891), pp. 184–86.
11. *Life of Dante*, pp. 55–56. Essential references on this debatable attribution may be found in Chimenz, art. cit., pp. 446–47.
12. *Life*, p. 56.
13. *European Literature*, p. 467.
14. *Dante*, p. 324.
15. *Studies in Dante*, Second Series (Oxford, 1889), pp. 303–56.
16. *Latin Works*, p. 424. See also F. Mazzoni in *Studi danteschi* XXXIV (1960), 163–204.
17. Wicksteed's translation, *Latin Works*, p. 419.
18. "Egloghe di Dante," *Dizionario letterario delle opere* (Bompiani, Milan, 1947), III, 36–37.
19. In his edition of the *Rime*, p. 450. See also Erich Köhler, "Das *Fiore*-Problem und Dantes Entwicklungsgang," *Germanisch-Romanische Monatsschrift* XXXVIII (1957), 273–86.

12. The *Commedia:* Narrative

1. *Selected Essays*, p. 225.
2. *Scienza nuova prima*, capov. 314.
3. See *Discussions of the Divine Comedy*, edited by Irma Brandeis (Boston, 1961), p. 44.
4. *The Invention of the Sonnet*, pp. 103–11.
5. *Selected Essays*, p. 211.
6. *The Genius of Italy*, pp. 136–37.
7. *The Poet and the Politician*, p. 77.
8. *Dante's Divina Commedia*, edited by Henry Sebastian Bowden (2d edition revised, London, 1894), p. 101.
9. *Dante's Drama of the Mind* (Princeton, 1953), p. 62.
10. *Selected Essays*, p. 222.
11. *The Fragile Leaves of the Sybil*, pp. 64–65.
12. *Mediaeval Culture*, II, 304.
13. *Dante's Other World*, p. 111.
14. *The Figure of Beatrice*, p. 102.
15. *Storia della letteratura italiana* (Milan, 1936), p. 53.
16. See *La poesia di Dante* (Bari, 1931), p. 135.

17. *The Poet and the Politician*, p. 78.
18. *La Divina Commedia: Paradiso* (Florence, 1948), pp. 856–57.

13. The *Commedia:* Allegory

1. *Dante*, p. 246.
2. (New York, 1954), p. 5.
3. Art. cit., p. 439.
4. *Introductory Papers*, p. 7.
5. *Symbol and Myth in Ancient Poetry* (New York, 1961), p. 2.
6. *The Figure of Beatrice*, p. 70.
7. *La Divina Commedia: Vol. I, Inferno* (Florence, 1955), p. 380.
8. *La Divina Commedia*, p. 591.
9. *The Mediaeval Mind*, I, 584.
10. *European Literature*, p. 360.
11. *The Figure of Beatrice*, p. 186.
12. *Anatomy of Criticism*, p. 204.
13. See "Farinata and Cavalcante" in *Mimesis*, translated by Willard Trask (Princeton, 1953; Doubleday Anchor Edition, pp. 151–77), and also "Figurative Texts Illustrating Certain Passages of Dante's *Commedia*," *Speculum* XXI (1946), 474–89.
14. *The Figure of Beatrice*, pp. 7–16.
15. *Comento analitico della Divina Commedia* (London, 1826–27). See Aldo Vallone, *La critica dantesca nell'ottocento* (Florence, 1958), for further titles and critical comment.
16. *Dante* (Vienna, 1946). For comment on this and other contemporary interpretations see H. Hatzfeld, "Modern Literary Scholarship as Reflected in Dante Criticism," *Comparative Literature* III (1951), 289–309. On the Veltro-Dux there is a whole library; see L. Olschki, *The Myth of Felt* (Berkeley and Los Angeles, 1949).
17. *Dante's Other World*, p. 211.
18. "The Commentary of Benvenuto da Imola," Yale, 1958.
19. *New Light on the Youth of Dante* (London, 1929), pp. 80–95.
20. *Dante sous la pluie de feu* (Paris, 1950).
21. See C. S. Singleton, "The Pattern at the Center," in *Commedia: Elements of Structure*, Dante Studies I (Cambridge, Mass., 1954), pp. 45–59.
22. *Symbolism in Mediaeval Thought and Its Consummation in the Divine Comedy* (New Haven, 1929), pp. 67–69.
23. *Die Jenseitsvorstellungen vor Dante* (Cologne, 1945), I, 13–22.
24. *Anatomy of Criticism*, p. 57.
25. Ibid., pp. 147–62.
26. *New Light on the Youth of Dante*, pp. 61–62.
27. *Symbol and Myth in Ancient Poetry*, p. 123.

14. The *Commedia:* Doctrine

1. *God's Tree,* p. 54.
2. *Introduction to the Study of the Divine Comedy* (Boston, 1910), pp. 43–44.
3. *A History of Italian Literature,* p. 65.
4. (Cambridge, 1898; translated by Laurence and Wicksteed), pp. 129–30.
5. *La Divina Commedia,* p. 520.
6. Ibid., p. 519.
7. Ibid., p. 539.
8. *La Divina Commedia: Vol. II, Purgatorio* (Florence, 1956), p. 273.
9. Ibid., p. 127.
10. *La poesia di Dante,* p. 153.

15. The *Commedia:* Tools and Tactics

1. *Selected Essays,* p. 213.
2. *Dante,* p. 59.
3. Ibid., p. 127.
4. *European Literature,* p. 280.
5. *Veltro und Diana* (Tübingen, 1956), p. 93. For other studies of Dante's words and rhymes see E. G. Parodi, *Lingua e Letteratura* (Venice, 1957), II, 203–300 (an essay first published in 1921), and E. P. Vincent, "Dante's Choice of Words," *Italian Studies* X (1955), 1–18.
6. *Veltro und Diana,* p. 102.
7. *The Genius of Italy,* p. 136.
8. *Selected Essays,* p. 205.
9. *Dante,* p. 153.
10. *Metrica e poesia* (Milan, 1962), p. 206.
11. *The Ladder of Vision* (Garden City, 1961), p. 131.
12. *European Literature,* pp. 277–78.
13. Ibid., p. 379.
14. *Metrica e poesia,* pp. 185–221.
15. *Mediaeval Culture,* II, 57.
16. "Dante's Terza Rima," *PMLA* LI (1936), 895–903.
17. *Metrica e poesia,* p. 188.
18. "Dante's Hundred Cantos," *Italica* XL (1963), 99.
19. *Summa theologiae,* Q. 10, art. 5.

INDEX

315